_Edited Book_

# INTERDISCIPLINARY RESEARCH AND INNOVATION

## Editors

**Dr. Kirti Verma**
_Associate Professor, Department of Engineering Mathematics, Lakshmi Narain College of Technology, Bhopal, Madhya Pradesh, India_

**Dr. Suyash Yashwantrao Mullemwar**
_Assistant Professor & Head, Department of Physics, D. D. Bhoyar College of Arts and Science  Mouda, Nagpur, (M.S.), India_

**Prof. Ganga Singh**
_HOD (CSE) & Assistant Professor, Bagula Mukhi College of Technology, Bhopal, India_

**_Mr. Lalit Malik_**
_Assistant Professor Department of Computer Science, Ganga Technical Campus, Village Soldha, Bahadurgarh, Jhajjar, Haryana, India_

**Mr. Tarakant**
_Managing Director, Eduguide Consultancy Private Limited, Bhopal, India_

**_Published by_**

# JPS Scientific Publications
# India

*Published by*

JPS Scientific Publications, Tamil Nadu, India.
E.mail: jpsscientificpublications@gmail.com
Website: www.jpsscientificpublications.com

Published in India.

**First Edition: 2021**

**International Standard Book Number (ISBN): 978-81-947154-6-7**



JPS Scientific Publications also publishes its books in a variety of Electronic formats. Some content that appears in print may not be available in Electronic formats. For more information visit our publication website **www.jpsscientificpublications.com**

ISBN: 978-81-947154-6-7

businesses must be aware of the market at all times as customers need keeps changing. A good knowledge of the market means that an entrepreneur can establish its services among competing brands in the market; identifies consumer decision-making and purchase behavior, know the ideal means for collaborating with key decision-makers and the basic insight into the configuration of the market by knowing the major market user characteristics

## Market Connection

The Private Equity Network is a web enabled meeting place for entrepreneurs, investors, advisors even consumers to consummate business exchanges. It is a level playing ground where those who have ideas, need or have services to offer, can enhance their personal networks. Networks and market connections are interchangeably used in this section. Market connection is a customer communication and campaign management technique. Market networks are genuinely personal, intertwining business concerns and social commitments in individual ties (Johannisson, 1998: 299). By way of personal networking, the entrepreneur makes a venturing career by prominently projecting its business. There are many dimensions that characterize a network; the space (local vs. international network), the length of the relationship (long-term/stable vs. short-term/unstable network), the degree of homogeneity (homogeneous/industry-based vs. heterogeneous/cross-industry network, or the nature of sponsorship (public/open vs. private/tight network). Not with standing these different aspects, there are important success factors in connecting the market. Huggins (2000) observed that formal groups are the most potent for networking activities, although, through an initially informal structure, they are best facilitated. Market communications use technology products and services including Google Analytic, Vimeo, and Apach web server to network of which its employees are showing high interest in paid time off, application security, and network congestion. It uses different marketing channels and tools in combination. The channels focus on ways business communicates a message to its preferred market or the entire market. Market connection or integration has great importance in developing economies due to its potential application (Heman & Faten, 2005 in Tiku, Inyang, Ovat, & Igbodor, 2015). The extent of integration gives the government a direction of how to formulate policies of providing infrastructure and regulating service to avoid market exploitation. An analysis of market integration is useful for studying the degree of co-movement of price in spatially separated market (Tiku, Inyang & Igbodor, 2015).

## Dealer Linkage

Dealer linkage could be seen as sets of individuals or organizations that facilitate end to end integration of the entire supply chain-mobilization, train, provide necessary infrastructure and capacity, supply inputs and buy-back the finished product. The concept of dealer linkages portends cordial connections, developed by different organizations or dealers with the aim of pursing commonly shared objectives for desired outcomes. The market linkage model of social enterprise is advanced on the facilitation of trade relationship between the target markets; small producers, local firms, cooperation and the external markets. Entrepreneurs can as well use these linkages to nurture a chain, develop, create and explore other resources (Johannisson, 1998). Though some organizations' have successfully created market linkage and achieved scale, the service industry must create more robust market linkages which if successful, hold tremendous potential for large scale impact. As no organization can operate in isolation, so also many big corporations in reality and in principle are desirous of establishing connections with other organizations on areas of value chains (Beth, Anna, Brad and Amanda, 2007). Consequently, Creating dealers' linkages are usually expensive to develop, maintain and are not so easily created or ran; hence, it falls within the top management business expansion decision. Similarly, the inclination of dealers to form linkages is determined by organizations' and industry specific risks, costs and benefits; it can also be based on dealers' level of perception and strategies, which could find its relevance in the domestic export market philosophy, government incentives and requirements, etc. (Beth et al., 2007). According to UNIDO Harvard research outlines, dealers linkage opportunities may exist in procurement, agricultural out-grower schemes, manufacturing sub-contracting, outsourcing of non-core functions and services, distribution, retail, franchising & leasing, sales of financial services, information & communication technologies, as well as other tools and inputs for production (Nelson, 2006). Within the contest of service, it is advised to develop long-term relationships among retailers and other service agents for the purpose of patronage and provision of extended third-party services. Accordingly, the most essential aspect of dealers' linkage is made up of the support system; the suppliers and markets (Oladele et al., 2006), coordinated for the overall benefits of all the stakeholders. Organizations, entrepreneurs or groups pursuing the course of dealers' linkages must contribute to the creation, diffusion and application of increased knowledge, technologies, that influences the processes of different areas of change, creating helplines to save costs of operations and improving of the overall profits (Christopher and Ryals, 2014). This corporation and coordination of dealers is perceived to result to the creation of new knowledge, products or services (Khurram, Qadeer, Muhammad, Syed and Iram, 2017). By this, linking dealers up to a strong community of similar dealership, providing guidance on a one-on-one basis for market expansion can as well be done by the entrepreneur, allowing them understand what information is important, what service goal is pursued and the likely benefit that every committed dealer gets. It is believed that an ideal interaction using dealer linkages would help to accelerate information, skills and knowledge transfer. Many have also assumed that poor services are associated with weak linkages whereas positive outcomes were based on the strength of linkages between stakeholders (Oladele et al., 2006). In a related view, it was suggested that due to the increasing rate of competition among organizations and individuals in the present day business operations, dealers are devising best means through which they can be successful in hostile markets by joining forces strategically (Engadget, 2014). in order to overcome some of the challenges that would arise from the micro level (market) unit, an entrepreneur should go beyond their value chains architecture that relies solely on their own resources and collaborate other resources with many other value chains (Wisner et al., 2015).

**Conclusion**

Entrepreneurial outfits are structured perhaps in two braces of scissors whose two ends stand for task and the holistic assessment of proficiencies of the person behind the business. These edges of the scissors could cut the hitches into a much smaller area that is possible to measure material and in a shape that describes the designer's intent. The intent of any designer is in what is desired to be achieved which comes in the tablets of objectives. Basically, the traditional entrepreneurs feel inept, nascent and often believe they possess not enough skills in business. Those personal deficiencies as felt are further worsened by a lack of information and some fundamental resources. Personal resources ought to be mobilized to enact new endeavors that are perhaps uncommon but viable. The speed and density required, the scope of knowledge essential in new venture creation tend to increase workable prospects while allocating resources and developing capabilities entails that management deal with internal and external factors that favors or resist implementing the adopted business strategy. These activities are however heralded with high-tech entrepreneurial features as is the case with entrepreneurial service development; their capability to strategically direct business resources on a continuous basis is even more critical as it forms the nucleus of the discussed theme.

**References**

1) Aaker, D. A. and Joachimsthaler, F. (2000). Brand Leadership: Building Assets in the Information Society. Free Press, New York.
2) Alan, H. & Yeloglu, O. (2013). Markalasma ve yenilikçil. *Siirt Universitesi Iktisadi ve Idari Bilimler Fakultesi Iktisadi Yenilik Dergisi*, 1 (1), 13-26
3) Bass, B.M. (1985). Leadership and Performance beyond expectations. New York: Free Press.
4) Bass, B.M. (1990). Bass & Stogdill's Handbook of leadership: Theory, research, and managerial applications. New York: The Free Press.
5) Bass, B. M., Waldman, D. A., Avolio, B. J., & Bebb, M. (1987). Transformational Leadership and the falling dominoes effect. *Group and Organization Studies*, 12, 73-87.
6) Beth, J., Anna, A., Brad, R. & Amanda, G. (2007). *Business Linkages: Lessons, Opportunities, and Challenges.* IFC, International Business Leaders Forum, and the Kennedy School of Government, Harvard University.
7) Calof, J. I. & Wright, S. (2008). Competitive Intelligence. *European Journal Marketing*, 42 (7/8), 717-730
8) Christopher, M. & Ryals, L. J. (2014) The Supply Chain becomes the Demand Chain. *Journal of Business Logistics*, 35, 1, 29-35.
9) Engadget, (2014). *Bigger and better, but with Stiffer Competition* [Online]. Retrieved from: http://www.engadget.com/products/apple/iphone/6/ [Accessed 2 August 2015].
10) Erenkol, H.D & Oztas, Y.B.B (2015). Entrepreneurial branding. *Procedia - Social and Behavioral Sciences* 195, 1138 – 1145
11) Fletcher, D (2003). Framing organizational emergence: discourse, identity and relationship, in Steyaert, C. and Hjort, D. (eds) New Movements in Entrepreneurship (Cheltenham: Edward Elgar Publishing) 125-144.
12) Guido, G (2014). Marketing intelligence, Wiley Encyclopedia of Management. John Wiley & Sons Ltd.
13) Harrison, D & Kjellberg, H (2010). Segmenting a market in the making: Industrial market segmentation as construction. *Industrial Marketing Management*, 39(5), 784-792.
14) Huggins, R. (2000). The success and failure of policy-implemented inter-® rm network initiatives: motivations, processes and structure. *Entrepreneurship & Regional Development, 12: 111-135.*
15) Jaworski, B., Kohli, A. K., & Sahay, A. (2000). Market-driven versus driving markets. *Academy of Marketing Science Journal*, 28(1), 45-54
16) Johannisson, B. (1998) Personal networks in emerging knowledge-based firms: spatial and functional patterns. *Entrepreneurship & Regional Development*, 10: 297-312.
17) Kavanaugh, R. R. and Ninemeier, J. D. (2001). Supervision in the Hospitality Industry. (3rd ed.). Michigan: The Educational Institute of the American Hotel & Lodging Association
18) Keller, K, L. (2008). Strategic Brand Management: Building, Measuring, and Managing Brand Equity. Pearson/Prentice Hall
19) Kelly, E. M. (1968). The Profitability of growth through mergers. *The Journal of the American Finance Association*. 23, 3, 546-54
20) Khurram, A., Qadeer, R., Muhammad, A., Syed, S. H. & Iram, S. (2017). Suppliers' Integration: Associated Challenges and Future Direction. *IJSSHE-International Journal of Social Sciences, Humanities and Education*. 1, 4, 2-11.
21) Lamb, C.W., Hair, J. F & McDaniel, C (2009). Marketing, 12.ed., Southwestern Cengage Learning.
22) Lee, J. K., Ro, K. K., (1996). Environment and technology strategy of firms in government R&D programs in Korea. *Technovation*. 16 (10), 553–560.

23) Lilien, G.L & Rangaswamy, A. (2006). Marketing Engineering. Trafford Publishing, Victoria, Canada.

24) Lybaert, N. (1998). The association between information gathering and success in industrial SMEs: the case of Belgium. *Entrepreneurship & Regional Development*, 10, 335-351.

25) McGuire, L. (2005). Assessment using new technology. *Innovations in Education and Teaching International*. 42, 265–276

26) Medal, A. (2018). 6 Innovative ways to increase brand awareness.

27) Nelson, J. (2006). *Building Linkages for Competitive and Responsible Entrepreneurship: Innovative Partnerships to Foster Small Enterprise, Promote Economic Growth, and Reduce Poverty in Developing Countries*. Geneva and Boston, MA: United Nations Industrial Development Organization (UNIDO) and the Fellows of Harvard College.

28) Okon, F. I. & Ekaette, U. I. (2016). Management Styles and Employees' Performance in Small Scale Business Enterprises in Akwa Ibom state, Nigeria. *International Journal of Small Business and Entrepreneurship Research*. 4, 1, 51-61,

29) Oladele, O. I., Sakagami, J. & Toriyama, K. (2006). Research-Extension-Farmer Linkage System in Southwestern Nigeria. *Journal of Food, Agriculture & Environment*, 4, 1, 197-200. Pascale, R. T. & Athos, A. (1981), *The Art of Japanese Management*, New York: Simon and Schuster

30) Robbins, D. W., Young, W. B., Behm, D. G., & Payne, W. R. (2010). Agonist-Antagonist paired set resistance training: A brief review. *Journal of Strength and Conditioning Research*. 24, 10, 2873-2882.

31) Robbins, S.P. (2003). Organisational behaviour (10th ed). San Diego: Prentice Hall.

32) Rowe, A. J., & Boulgarides, J. D. (1992). Managerial decision making: A guide to successful business decisions. New York: Macmillan.

33) Sadiq, M.S., Singh, I.P., Grema, I.J., Umar, S.M., & Isah, M.A (2017). Generating Market Information and Market Outlook of Major Cassava Markets in Africa: A Direction for Nigeria Trade Investment and Policy. *Acta Scientific Agriculture*, 1 (2), 25-35

34) Schwaninger, M. (1987). A Practical Approach to Strategy Development. *Long Range Planning*, 20 (5), 74-85

35) Slatter, S., (1992). Gambling on Growth: How to Manage the Small High-Tech Firm. Wiley, New York.

36) Steyaert, C (2003). The prosaics of entrepreneurship; narration, drama and conversation, paper presented at EURAM, Milan, April.

37) Tiku, N. E., Inyang, J.O., Ovat, K.E. & Igbodor, F. O. (2015). The Estimation of Market Integration of Yam Marketing in Cross River State, Nigeria. *Gashua Journal of Irrigation and Desertification studies*. 1, (1&2), 10-19

# CHAPTER – 2

## TANZANIA ONLINE EDUCATION CHALLENGES DURING CORONAVIRUS PANDEMIC
### BY

**Muraina Kamilu Olanrewaju & Josephine Donald Mremi**


**Abstract**

Coronavirus (COVID-19) pandemic caught the many countries in the world into surprise. To respond to the pandemic different measures were taken by different countries including closure of schools from pre-school, primary, secondary schools and the universities. More than one billion students are impacted worldwide. The closure aimed at minimizing the spread of the coronavirus and ensuring a critical measure precaution through social distancing. Like many other countries Tanzania switched from classroom learning to online learning. Most of the digital technologies used to provide education include radio and TV programs, social media groups using both text and visual clips. Some of the learning materials were available in the websites of the Ministry of Education and the National Examination Council. Also in some places where there is no internet network hindered students access to the materials in websites. It was suggested that parents or guardians should embrace the online learning which come as unplanned activity with less preparation may also end up with ineffective implementation.

**Keywords: Coronavirus, COVID-19 pandemic, online learning and Tanzania.**


**Introduction**

Coronavirus which cause Coronavirus Disease (COVID-19) come on the earth at first time when it was reported from Wuhan China in December 2019. This coronavirus started to spread to other countries all over the world. For less than three months the coronavirus was already in all seven continents in the world. However, many countries are affected at different extent in the infection rates and the impacts. The spread of Coronavirus has caused different effects to each country including many people losing their employment, many human deaths, business closure and also the closure of schools worldwide. Coronavirus has alerted everybody and become a global pandemic. COVID -19 has no cure and also has no vaccine at this juncture. According to Li & Lalani 2020; Conservation; 2020; Onyema, Nwafor, Fath, Sen, Atonye, Sharma, & Alsayed, 2020), over 1.2 billion children are not in the classroom globally due the coronavirus pandemic. The healthy personnel advised that social distancing one of the way of preventing the coronavirus (Murphy, 2020). In response to the physical or social interaction among students' schools were closed. In line to this, provision of education has changed melodramatically with distinctive rise in online learning where teaching is conducted on digital stages. In some countries with high digital technologies teaching has become easier and took less time, thus learning has now become more effective. Digital technologies use the adaptive and interactive software that allows student to learn. Through digital learning students are able to learn in their own pace, making learning personal and appealing.While some countries have done a lot and shift away from classroom routine in many places in the world, some has done little to help the students to use online learning programs. The countries that have done little are also possessing low digital technologies. Many children do not have computer, book, internet connection or proper support from parents at home (Saavedra, 2020). Tanzania like many other developing countries is facing challenges to reach all students through online learning. In Tanzania many different ways have been undertaken to help the students especially those which are finalizing their courses by

November 2020. In middle-income countries like Tanzania, there are limited appropriate and inadequate infrastructures to facilitate online learning on the side of teachers who are not oriented to it. In Tanzania the Ministry of Education, Science and Technology has intensified some it's educational TV and radio programs for different levels of education including pre-primary, primary and secondary schools. Also individual schools have started some social media groups to assist their respective students. In those groups, subject teachers share some learning materials with parents and guardians through their digital device who are responsibility to deliver the activities to their children. The author of this article spoke with about 50 secondary school teachers via social media so as to be able to some information on the challenges these teachers were facing in working through online learning. During conversations with these secondary school teachers the author of this article realised that teachers have been sending assignments to their students through social media groups such as WhatsApp, Instagram, etc during this time of coronavirus pandemic. Moreover, the teachers revealed that there have been poor responses from the parents/guardian on the work sent to them for their children, and about 30% of the sent work provided feedback to the teachers. Also the teachers were sending activities to parents and guardians but were not sure of how the students were doing on such activities. The teachers were sure that only parents or guardian possessed smart phones and computers and therefore belief that it has becoming difficult to connect to all students directly. These teachers explained that most of the students were based in places where network was a challenge. However, during these conversations all teachers involved said that on the school closure the students were given a one month home package assignment as they used to be given during the normal school holidays. The online-leaning started when the closure was extended after one month of the closure. This shows that the online learning in Tanzania is essential during this COVID-19 pandemic. The teachers called for the schools and the education sector to improve online learning so that they can cope with and improve the teaching through online system. In the process of conversations with the teachers, it was revealed that the change from planned classroom learning to unplanned online learning took long time for the learners and educators to adapt the activities and come up with productive results. This was also reported by Allo (2020), in the done in Toraja – Indonesia. Teachers, parents, guardian and the students involved on the online learning lack enough experience of online learning. The conversations also revealed that online learning requires a lot of seriousness in student side since the teachers are not directly and controlling the learning process. Sutton (2020) revealed that students can still be able to get to understand science experiment though teacher's creativity but not as clear as when it is in a classroom setting. Also for practical lessons the teaching was difficult especially when using radio during teaching. Although, radio and TV are reported as strong and powerful tools in learning, the use of mixed media devices is effective in online learning when used with the aim of reaching as many students as possible (Saavedra, 2020).

**Discussion on the Online Challenges**

The spread of coronavirus that cause COVID-19 has become a global learning crisis that might have negative impacts on children. Some impacts include loses in learning, in studying, increase of school dropout rates and students' lives interruption (Saavedra, 2020). The way coronavirus was spreading and the effects caused are what was not expected, although in many countries it arrived in March 2020, three months after it started in Wuhan – China in December 2019. Most countries were caught unprepared especially in the process of providing education during the school closure. The emergence of COVID-19 poses some concern to global education systems, including unscheduled school closure in more than 100 countries in the world (Onyema, et al. 2020; Allo, 2020). Some countries switch to online learning as a means of lessening the time lost in continuing classroom education services. These countries moved up to unplanned online learning programs that are done with little preparation and with no training that may end up with poor results. The online learning is hindered by the poor infrastructures including power inaccessibility, network and poor skills in digital technologies (Saavedra, 2020). The problem affects mostly primary and secondary schools in Tanzania. However, for the case of the universities training suffer a little bit different with less challenges. The main challenges faced online training include unreliable internet access in some places in the country, some families lacking facilities or devices such as radio, TV, smart phone and computers. There is also a big gap between privileged and disadvantaged families. Thus, based on the above challenges the move to online learning is evident that online learning suffers effectiveness in many ways. The objectives of continue with learning in primary and secondary schools through online learning may not be effectively met, if all the students or children are not reached. In Tanzania it has been difficult to reach all the students due to aforementioned challenges. This is the concomitant result of this teaching and learning approach. Parents and guardians who were involved to assist in the process are either unaware on how to help their children or they were busy with other commitments that their roles in the process online learning is insignificant. The children /student themselves commitment is also doubted in this particular process due poor supervision by the close family members including parents who are not teachers. Moreover, the students' perceptive and consider the closure of schools due to coronavirus as a school holiday. Thus, even the motivation behind studying might be very low. This was evidently observed by the author from clips in the social media where the students were celebrating the closer of the school. It is also unclear whether the disabled students were able to cope with the changes from classroom to online learning in Tanzania. Access to connectivity and different type of devices and for ensuring accessibility for students and children with disabilities vary widely across different income levels and this a key challenge that is creating further inequalities among them (World Bank, 2020). Some countries decided to simply putting educational resources on their website, and making available more products for students to access, but they are not necessarily online learning classes (World Bank, 2020).

**Lessons from Coronavirus Pandemic on Provision of Online Learning**

Many countries have turned to online learning as a mitigation to time lost during the school closure as a response to the coronavirus pandemic so as to continue learning (Allo, 2020). Therefore, coronavirus pandemic is whistle blow to many governments and educational systems in many developing countries like Tanzania to consider online learning as an important technique of learning. For the education sector to be able to continue running smoothly, there is need to intensify the digital learning technological systems and setup user friendly online learning programs for use in the future even after coronavirus pandemic. Also all of the educational institutions, teachers and students have to adopt the digital techniques and improve their skills in line with the emerging global trends in education. Teachers are also alerted through COVID-19 pandemic to be prepared and be oriented for online learning. It is important to also orient children on how to learn using these digital technologies so that during some event like the coronavirus pandemic they can be able to cope with and keep learning normally (Allo, 2020). It is the task to the Ministry of education, curriculum developers, Tanzania Institute of Education in collaboration with school management and the teachers. There is a need to put more efforts in future on the subject to ensure that online learning is intensified and worked on to generate some appealing outcomes (Swan, 2019). Online learning instruction should be given through voice note to easy the understanding by the students (Allo, 2020). The Ministry of Education, Science and Technology has the task to ensure that education industry is equipped with the facilities and the program software to continue with improvements of online learning for use even after the disappearance of the coronavirus pandemic.

## Conclusion

While there might be plenty of digital open source content available in the internet, a key challenge is the preparation of pedagogical material to be available in a structured in such way that could be captured all students. Since not all the students are able to connect to internet, online learning is not effective at this juncture. However, in most developing countries like Tanzania, students have access to mobile devices, TV and radio programs and optimizing accessible solutions to those challenges. In future education sector have to consider emphasis on training online learning program teachers and students even post COVID-19 pandemic. Moreover, in addition to infrastructure and connectivity, teachers' and administrators' familiarity with the tools and processes are also key factors in providing distance learning. Also the school management and other private sectors such as telephone companies should join hand to work together in assuring that online learning is well improved.

## Suggestions

- There is a need for in depth research on how COVID-19 has affected learning in secondary schools in Tanzania.
- This paper did not only find the challenges of online learning but also sport light on the availability and internet access and online learning implementation.
- There is a need to find out how to integrate online learning with classroom instructions in a structure, planned and valuable pedagogical fashion.
- Since this article stated only the existing knowledge without through research, there is a need to identify variables and quantify them for future generalizable research findings.

## References


1) Allo, M.D.G. (2020). *Is the online learning good in the midst of Covid-19 Pandemic? The case of EFL learners.*
2) Li C., & Lalani, F. (2020). The COVID-*19 pandemic has changed education forever. This is how.*
3) Murphy, M.P.A. (2020). *COVID-19 and emergency eLearning: Consequences of the securitization of higher education for post-pandemic pedagogy. Contemporary Security Polic*y.
4) Onyema, E.M., Nwafor, C., Fath, A., Sen, S., Atonye, F.G., Sharma, A. & Alsayed, A.O. (2020). Impact of Coronavirus Pandemic on education. *Journal of Education and Practice, 11(13)*, 108-121.
5) Saavedra, J. (2020). *Educational challenges and opportunities of the Coronavirus (COVID-19) pandemic.* Sutton, S. (2020). *Adapting Science Lessons for distance Learning.*

# CHAPTER - 3

# OPTIMUM SOLUTION OF ELECTRICAL POWER SYSTEM OBTAINED BY EVOLUTIONARY TECHNIQUES

## BY
## Nagendra Singh & Yogendra Kumar


**Abstract:**

Electrical power sector is very large and complicated system. Generation, transmission and distribution of power are the main task of power system with maintaining the stability limits. When power is distributed among the consumers, due to inductive nature of load used by the consumer, large power loss arises in the system. Overall efficiency of the system is nearly about 35 percent. Which shows that the system need to improve its performance using compact and efficient operation of the electrical power system. By using economic load dispatch power can be distributed to the consumers in such a way so that all consumer should be fulfill their load demand without overloading of the generating units. The selection of generating unit at different load duration required on the effective and efficient optimization techniques, which optimize the data of power transmission and generation system very quickly. This optimize data will help to operate the power system in efficient way and provide high efficiency and reduce the losses. So many optimization techniques are available which can optimize the linear as well nonlinear data effectively. In this chapter discussed evolutionary techniques which are currently used for optimization of the power system data and give better results than classical methods. Further discuss the application of various optimization techniques in electrical engineering. And at last included the result oriented data and compare the performance of the optimization techniques.

**Keywords**: Electrical power system, Evolutionary techniques, optimization, objective functions.


**Introduction**

Electricity is very important in our life. We cannot imagine the word without electricity. Requirement of electricity is very high where as generation is limited. Due to high demand of electricity required to optimize the schedule of distribution of electricity, so fulfill the demand of all consumer without overloading [1]. Since the electrical transmission and distribution network is very big and complicated, many factors affect the transmitted power on the network. Even due to these factors high losses arises on the transmission network. Such losses creates high voltage drop on the electrical network. Losses and voltage drop also depends on the types of consumers, and load operated by the consumers. Generally large consumers operated high inductive load and hence increase the reactive power, decrease the power factor and hence increases the line losses and voltage drop [2]. In India thermal power plant is the largest power generating plant.

Second largest power generated by hydro power plant. Solar and wind power generation contribution is very less as compare to the load demand [3].

Distribution of the power among the different consumers at different time of the 24 hour, Distribution Companies first prepared the load duration curve. This load duration curve helps to understand how much demand is required at whole day. It also helps to kwon when peak demand required and what is the base load at the whole day required [4]. So for the systematic power distribution and managing the load demand applying economic load dispatch (ELD) system. Economic load distribution system is simple concept; it is used to maintain the load demand according to available generated power at any instant. ELD also maintain the all constraints during the power supply to the various consumers. ELD optimize the power system operation for allocating generation among the committed units so that demand of the consumer will be fulfill and the total generation cost will be minimized [5,6]. Thermal power plant efficiency is about 37 percent. Means system is not efficient, but required system should be economical. Means when operating the power plant its operating cost should be minimum. Generation cost of the thermal power plant shown in Figure 1.

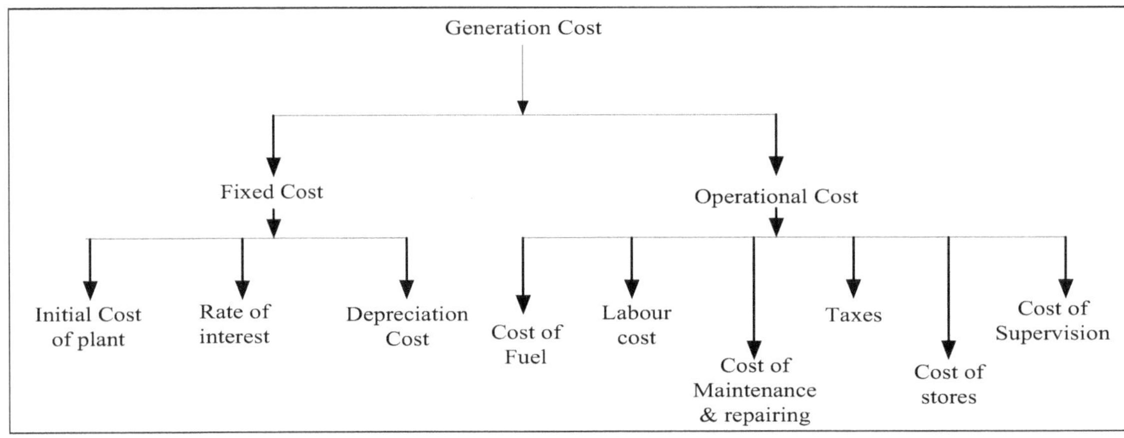


**Figure 1: Operating cost of the Electrical power plant**

ELD techniques required optimization techniques which helps to find out the most suitable generating limits for fulfill the demand at any instant of time. Evolutionary optimization techniques are able to search for the solution of problems using a simplified model of the evolutionary process found in nature. These algorithms provide an alternative for obtaining global optimal solutions of the problems have discontinuous, no-convex, and highly nonlinear in nature [7]. The economic dispatch problem has been solved via many traditional optimization methods such as the economic dispatch problem has been solved via many traditional and new optimization methods shown in Table 1.

**Table 1: Optimization techniques used for solution of ELD problem**

| S. no. | Classical Methods | New Optimization techniques |
|--------|-------------------|------------------------------|
| 1 | Nonlinear Programming[1 | Fuzzy Logic[7] |
| 2 | Pattern Search[2] | Genetic Algorithm [8] |
| 3 | Harmony Search[3] | Simulated Annealing [9] |
| 4 | Lagrangian Relaxation[4] | ANN [10] |
| 5 | Dynamic Programming[5] | Tabu Search [11] |
| 6 | Quadratic Programming[6] | Particle Swarm Optimization[12],[17] |
| 7 | Linear Programming[6] | Ant Colony [13] |
| 8 | Interior Point Method[7] | Differential Algorithm [14] |
| | | JAYA Optimization Algorithm[15] |
| | | Dragonfly Algorithm[16] |
| | | Ant Lion Optimization (ALO) [18] |

## Objective function

For obtaining the optimum solution of the any quantity required an objective function. ELD problem can be formulated in single objective as well as multi-objective. Single objective is formulated for the fulfillment of one objective with constraints. Multi-objectives are formulated for more than one objective, also included constraint. Multiobjective problem are more complex as compare to single objective function [8].

$$Objective\ function\ of\ ELD = minimize(Generation\ cost) \qquad (1)$$

$$F_i(\ P_i) = Minimum(a_i P_i^2 + b_i P_i + c_i\ ) \qquad (2)$$

Subject to constraints

Load balance $\quad \sum_{i=1}^{n} P_i = P_D + P_L \qquad (3)$

Generation limits $\ P_i^{min} \leq P_i \leq P_i^{max} \qquad (4)$

where, $P_i$ is the generated power of the $i^{th}$ generating units between the prescribed limit; $a_i$, $b_i$, and $c_i$ are the fuel cost coefficients of the $i^{th}$ generating unit.

## Optimization techniques

Evolutionary techniques are the robust optimization techniques which are suitable for finding the optimum solution of discontinuous, nonlinear and multi-objective problems. Optimization is a task in a problem to find the most or the best suitable solution of the problem. Optimization process starts randomly in the search space and find the solution of the problem by using the objective function and constraints of such problems to drive its search towards the feasible region and finally find the solution of problems which is near optimum solution by exploring as small as a set of solutions as possible [9]. An evolutionary technique has emerged as a useful optimization tool for handling nonlinear programming problems. In the real world problems, it can implement algorithms without complex procedures and don't require lots of modification in software to handle additional constraints. In evolutionary techniques search process is parallel, that's why it has a high probability of finding the optimal solution of the problems [10]. Another important area of evolutionary technique in which approximate models can play an important role is interactive evolutionary computation. In interactive evolutionary computation, there is no explicit fitness function, and the fitness evaluation is performed directly by a human expert. Interactive evolutionary computation has found a wide range of applications [11].

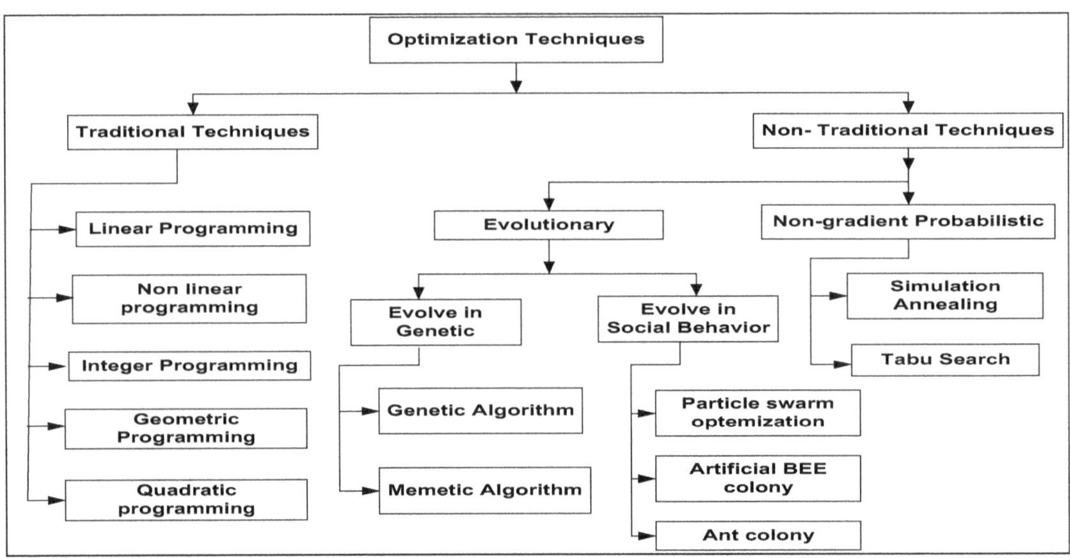


**Figure – 2: Optimization techniques**

Global solution of engineering problems can be obtained by using evolutionary optimization techniques starting from multiple points, which placed weight on the behavioral linkage between the parents and their off spring's, rather than seeking to imitate specific operators as observed in nature to find a solution [12]. Figure 2 shows the various optimization techniques used for the solution of nonlinear engineering problems. Evolutionary techniques are near global search, stochastic optimization methods. It seeks the optimal solution of an optimization problem by evolving a population of candidate solutions over a number of generations or iterations [13]. A new population is formed from an existing population through the use of a mutation operator. This operator perturbs each component of every solution in the population by a random amount to produce new solutions of the problem. The scale of optimality of each of the solutions or individuals is measured by its fitness which can be defined as an objective function of the problem [14].

Following procedure is used for the optimum solution of the nonlinear practical problem.

**Optimal Design**

An optimization technique is used to find an optimal design which will minimize or maximize a design goal. Variable of the proposed problems are designed in such a way so that when they apply in the optimization techniques, it helps to obtain the optimal solution of the problem. The decision variables for any problem can be dimensioned, shapes, materials, etc., which describe a design and objective function, can be the cost of production, energy consumption, drag, lift, reliability, stability margin, etc. In case of proposed economic load dispatch problem the main objective is to minimize the total fuel cost in such a way to handle all constraints [15]. Hence, for the optimal solution of ELD problem, it requires a suitable design of the objective function.

**Optimal Control:**

Optimal solutions of nonlinear problems depend on some parameter and hence it is necessary to control these parameters. Proper adjustment of variables can give an efficient, optimum solution of the problem with less effort and on minimum time.

**Modeling:**

To understand the system better and to improve the system, it is necessary to find the relationships between input and output parameters in a process known as modeling. Such an optimization task involves minimizing the error between the predicted output obtained by the developed mathematical model and actual output. To compute the predicted output, a mathematical parameterized model can be assumed based on some information about the system.

**Scheduling:**

For the optimum solution of the problem, proper sequencing of operations is required. For example, in a machining sequencing problem, it is important to know in what order a job will flow from one machine to the next, instead of knowing when exactly a job has to be done on a particular machine. In such types of optimization task proper timetabling, planning, resource allocation problem is required [16].

**Prediction and Forecasting:**

Many time varying real-world problems are often periodic and predictable. Past data for such problems can be analyzed for finding the nature of periodicity so that a better understanding of the problem can be achieved.

**Data Mining:**

Data mining is a process to analyze multidimensional data and discover the hidden useful information they carry. This is by no means is an easy task, simply because it is not known what kind of information they would carry and in most problems it is not even known what kind of information one should look for. A major task in such problems is to group functionally similar data together and functionally dissimilar data in separate clusters [17].

**Machine Learning:**

In the age of automation, many real-world systems are equipped with automated and intelligent subsystems which can make decisions and adjust the system optimally. In the design of such intelligent subsystems, often machine learning techniques, involving different soft computing techniques and artificial intelligence techniques, are combined. To make such a system operate with a minimum change or with minimum energy requirement, an optimization procedure is needed. Since such subsystems are to be used on-line and the on-line optimization is a difficult proposition due to time restrictions, such problems are often posed as an online optimization problem and solved by trying them on a number of synthetic scenarios.

**Application of Optimization techniques in Electrical Engineering:**

Optimization techniques are used in various applications in electrical engineering; table 2 shows some of them.

### Table - 2: Application of optimization techniques

| Name of techniques | Application in Electrical Engineering |
|---|---|
| Fuzzy Logic[7] | Control of Electrical machine, Electric Transformer Protection System, transmission line protection |
| Genetic Algorithm [8] | Stability analysis of power system Design of Structure of electrical network |
| Simulated Annealing [9] | Generation and transmission expansion planning Generator maintenance scheduling |
| ANN [10] | Combinatorial optimization problems Load forecasting problems |
| Tabu Search [11] | Unit commitment, Reactive power planning |
| Particle Swarm Optimization[12],[17] | Load forecasting and Economic dispatch Distribution systems planning and operation, |
| Ant Colony [13] | Designing power system damping controllers |
| Differential Algorithm [14] | Analog Electronic Circuits Sizing Synthesis of Time-Modulated Antenna Arrays Color Quantization |
| JAYA Optimization Algorithm[15] | Load forecasting problems Optimal Coordination of Over current Relays |
| Dragonfly Algorithm[16] | Optimization of Solar Cell |
| Ant Lion Optimization (ALO) [18] | Optimal reactive power dispatch |

## Results of Optimization Techniques:

This section taking one example to show the effectiveness of optimization techniques for the optimization of ELD problem. Data of IEEE 30 bus system is considered as shown in table 3. Results obtained by different techniques is shown in table 4.

**Table 3: Capacity and cost coefficients for IEEE-30 bus system for the demand of 700MW [11]**

| Unit | $a_i$ | $b_i$ | $c_i$ | $P_i^{min}$ | $P_i^{max}$ |
|---|---|---|---|---|---|
| 1 | 0.0033870 | 0.856440 | 16.817750 | 10 | 125 |
| 2 | 0.0023500 | 1.025760 | 10.029450 | 10 | 150 |
| 3 | 0.0006230 | 0.897700 | 23.333280 | 35 | 225 |
| 4 | 0.0007880 | 0.851234 | 27.634000 | 35 | 210 |
| 5 | 0.0004690 | 0.807285 | 36.856880 | 130 | 325 |
| 6 | 0.0003998 | 0.850454 | 30.147980 | 125 | 315 |

**Table 4: Results of IEEE 30 bus system for the demand of 700 MW**

| Unit Power Output | GA | Ant Colony | DE | PSO | NPSO |
|---|---|---|---|---|---|
| P1(MW) | 27.30096 | 10 | 20.1558 | 92.2921 | 61.428 |
| P2(MW) | 15.61244 | 72.508 | 63.7506 | 15.0865 | 36.9216 |
| P3(MW) | 120.31087 | 35 | 139.7835 | 52.76 | 129.131 |
| P4(MW) | 116.77546 | 116.20 | 128.9605 | 76.888 | 122.39 |
| P5(MW) | 226.8376 | 260.17 | 215.8114 | 262.794 | 176.045 |
| P6(MW) | 212.4505 | 206.1138 | 131.5384 | 200.1733 | 174.03 |
| Power Output (MW) | 700 | 700 | 700 | 700 | 700 |
| Total Cost($/h) | 820.42 | 816.2498 | 813.788 | 811.384 | 810.3483 |
| Computation time (sec) | 1.7800 | 1.6106 | 1.5720 | 1.041 | 0.5324 |

As seen in table 4 the total generation cost evaluated by using the optimum generating data using various methods. All programs are run in Matlab software and obtain the optimum generating point for the load of 700MW. And the using the equation (2) calculated the total generation cost of the plant. All methods are very effective and able to give the global solution of the nonlinear ELD problem. Time taken in optimization is also very less for small data as well as large data.

## Conclusions

Electrical power sector is running in crisis phase in terms of unremitting gap between demand and supply. Looking at present strength of India, and to achieve target in field of electrical power it is necessary to adopt change in form of efficient operation methodology for thermal power plant generation. Optimization techniques recently used for optimum operation of the power plant. Classical methods found so many issues and are unable to give global solutions of the large data, and also taken very long computation time. In this era almost using only new optimization techniques, which are very effective and easy in programming in matlab. These techniques help to operate the power distribution system economically, which is the essential requirement of the generation plants.

**References**

1) Rabih A. Jabr, Alun H. Coonick, and Brian J. Cory, "A homogeneous linear programming algorithm for the security constrained economic dispatch problem", IEEE transactions on power systems, vol. 15, no.3, pp. 930- 936, August 2000.

2) Al-Sumait J.S., Al-Othman A.K. and . Sykulski J.K, " Application of pattern search method to power system valve point economic load dispatch," Electrical power energy system, vol.29, no.10, pp. 720-730, 2007.

3) Arul R., G. Ravi and Velusami S., "Non-convex economic dispatch with heuristic load patterns using harmony search algorithm", International Journal of computer applications, vol. 16, no.1, pp. 26-34, February 2011.

4) Tkayuki S and Kamu W., " Lagrangian relaxation  method for price based unit commitment problem", Engineering optimization taylor Francis  pp. 36-41, 2004.

5) Travers Dean L. and Kaye R. John, "Dynamic dispatch by constructive dynamic programming", IEEE Transactions on power systems, vol.13, no. 1, pp. 72-78, February 1998.

6) Ahmed Farag, Samir Al-Baiyat and Cheng T.C., "Economic load dispatch multiobjective optimization procedures using linear programming  techniques", IEEE transactions on power systems, vol. 10, no. 2, pp. 731-739, May 1995.

7) Momoh J. A. and Zhu J.Z., "Improved interior point method for OPF problems", IEEE transactions on power systems, vol.14, no.3, pp. 1114-1120, August 1999.

8) Amjady Nima and Hadi Nasiri-Rad, "Nonconvex Economic dispatch with ac constraints by a new real coded genetic algorithm", IEEE transactions on power systems, vol. 24, no. 3, pp. 1489- 1502, August 2009.

9) Mantawy A. H., Abdel-Magid Youssef L. and Seliin Shokri, "A simulated annealing algorithm for unit commitment", IEEE transactions on power systems, vol. 13, no.1, pp. 197-204, February 1998.

10) Meshram Miss Sweeka and Sahu Omprakash, "Application of ANN in economic generation scheduling in IEEE 6-bus system", International journal of engineering science and technology, vol. 3, no. 3, pp. 2461-2466, March 2011.

11) Senthil K.  and Manikandan K., "Improved Tabu search algorithm to economic emission dispatch with transmission line constraint", International journal of computer science & communication vol. 1, no. 2, pp. 145-149, July-December 2010.

12) Arul R., G. Ravi and Velusami S., "Non-convex economic dispatch with heuristic load patterns using harmony search algorithm", International Journal of computer applications, vol. 16, no.1, pp. 26-34, February 2011.

13) Rabih A. Jabr, Alun H. Coonick, and Brian J. Cory, "A homogeneous linear programming algorithm for the security constrained economic dispatch problem", IEEE transactions on power systems, vol. 15, no.3, pp. 930- 936, August 2000.

14) Saber Ahmed Yousuf & Dewan Md Fayzur Rahman, "Economic load dispatch using particle swarm differential evolution optimization", IEEE conference, pp. 1-8, 2011.

15) Balamurugan K., Umamaheswari K., Prabhu Raj M., Nivetha S., Giriprasad K., Ravirahul M., Guhaneeswaran V. and Arun R.M., "Solving Economic Load

Dispatch Using JAYA Optimization Algorithm" Research Journal of Chemistry and Environment, Vol. 24, Issue I, 2020.

16) Diptanu Das, Aniruddha Bhattacharya & Rup Narayan Ray, Dragonfly Algorithm for solving probabilistic Economic Load Dispatch problems", Neural Computing and Applications volume 32, pages 3029–3045, 2020.

17) Nikitha M, Pratheksha Jerline L, Aishwarya T, Karthikaikannan D, "Solution of Economic Load Dispatch problem using Conventional methods and Particle Swarm Optimization", International Journal of Innovative Technology and Exploring Engineering (IJITEE), Volume-9 Issue-10, pages 243-247, August 2020.

18) Leena Daniel, Krishna Teerth Chaturvedi, "Economic Load Dispatch Using Ant Lion Optimization", International Journal of Engineering Trends and Technol.

# CHAPTER – 4

# COVID-19 IMPACT ON HIGHER EDUCATION

**BY**
**Iqra Asif**

## Abstract

The global COVID-19-pandemic explosion has adversely affected the education sector. Using publicly accessible data and information on the COVID-19 government dashboard, we analyzed the present status of the COVID-19 outbreak and Pakistan's preparedness. All the educational institutions in Pakistan have been shut down and are transitioning to online teaching. The primary purpose of the proposed manuscript is to address the overall impact of the COVID-19 pandemic on the higher education system. This study provides some suggestions or strategies for educational decision-makers in order to reinforce the university education situation. This study also provides a theoretical analysis of the online teaching experience of some universities. Although government agencies have taken several steps since the onset of the pandemic to encounter the many consequences on the education system whereas students or teachers have also encountered numerous obstacles or difficulties during online learning such as social and privacy issues; lack of qualified teachers, students who are not virtually trained, lack of access to computers, etc. In addition to management, monitoring, and accreditation of educational institutions, HEC Pakistan has also worked with organizations to minimize the influence of lockdowns on academic activities.

**Keywords:** COVID-19 pandemic, higher education, online teaching, preparedness, virtual.

## Introduction

### Coronavirus:

The historical basis of the term coronavirus shows that it derives from the word 'corona' in Latin, meaning a halo crown. Coronaviruses are the groups of related viruses that cause infections ranging only from the frequent cold to more extreme diseases such as Middle East Respiratory Syndrome (MERS-CoV) and the severe acute Respiratory Syndrome (SARS-CoV). These viruses are transmitted within humans by animals i.e. in humans; SARS-Cov is transferred via civet cats whereas the MERS-Cov is transmitted via camel. The novel coronavirus is a new virus that is known as a type of mysterious viral flow and was not previously diagnosed in humans, according to WHO(2020). Although direct transmission of coronavirus from person-to-person is confirmed, yet there is no appropriate medical treatment or vaccine to cure this virus up till now. That is why the transmission of the virus has become impossible to manage because it has become a lethal epidemic, and the coronavirus induced fatality is not a joke, although there are several recoveries. Since coronavirus is detected in Wuhan, China at the end of

December 2019, the number of infected individuals is rising day by day and hourly deaths are being reported globally. For these factors, the coronavirus outbreak has been declared a pandemic by the WHO (2020). The novel virus has been named by Chinese researchers as the novel COVID-19 coronavirus. Despite the Chinese government's precautionary action and locking down the city of Wuhan on 23 January 2020, COVID-19 spread to the other counties and ultimately to the world as a whole. Coronavirus has spread to more than 209countries, according to the data provided by WHO until April 17, while it has infected 3,118, 871 individuals worldwide, resulting in approximately 216, 221 deaths. Sahu (2020) has asserted that many countries, including China, have imposed travel restrictions in order to reduce the risk of COVID-19. Multiple steps, including improved health services, advising people to work from home, age-appropriate mask use, hygiene policies, self-isolation, or quarantine; and social distancing are being taken by Public health workers or government leaders in order to manage the disease. Many countries have declared the closure of gyms, libraries, movie theatres, swimming pools, and large meeting areas, including educational institutions, in order to fight

This invisible enemy. Schools, hospitals, universities, and many other educational/non-educational institutions are also shut down worldwide to mitigate the spread of coronavirus among younger and adult individuals.

**Higher Education:**

Higher education encompasses all forms of secondary education and study offered by universities or other educational institutions after secondary school. These universities are recognized by the state authorities as higher education institutions. Education is the method of bringing about desirable changes in human beings' beliefs and actions. It plays an important part in sustaining, nurturing, and disseminating cultural heritage from generation to generation. Learning is the knowledge of the full use of one's abilities to help an individual to consider and make informed judgments and choices. It is the process that is directly related to the socio-economic and political growth of any developed country in the world. Both the economic sectors and the higher education system around the world are adversely impacted by this novel coronavirus. UNESCO estimates that the shutdown of schools, colleges, and universities has seriously affected 1.4 billion students worldwide. 1.8 million Students are generally enrolled in the higher education system; Pakistan generates around 445,000 university graduates and 80,000 computer science graduates per year. Recent reforms have created many obstacles for students to cancel classes and exams in empty dorms to reduce the quality of the study, with growing uncertainty facing universities in Pakistan. In addition, the reopening of these institutions is not established as COVID-19's global situation is deteriorating day by day. The Higher Education Commission (HEC) in Pakistan is concerned that the loss of students during this lockdown should be reduced. In addition to management, monitoring, and accreditation of educational institutions, HEC Pakistan has also worked with organizations to minimize the influence of lockdowns on academic activities.

**Advantages and Disadvantages of Conventional vs. Online teaching system:**

Pakistan's universities are based on the traditional teaching (T-Learning) system of education, where the teacher is only responsible for running the class based on his teachings, expertise, and experiences, while the students who listen and take notes are at the end of the receiver (passive). This learning is aligned to the classrooms where the meetings with both participants are predefined. It is based on the teaching session of chalk/talk, supplemented by textbooks or teaching notes, and uses seatwork, evaluation, and listening as the strategies of delivery. Traditional learning does not provide students any authority to decide their learning strategies, and they are confined to the materials, text, and documents provided by the teacher. Moreover, universities in Pakistan are implementing the LMS, which has altered distance learning as well. Alternatively, some of Pakistan's tertiary education institutions have used another kind of model called the Virtual teaching system (V-Learning) which is based on a web or software application learning system. It facilitates teachers to educate students through virtual classrooms regardless of their place. It encourages students to learn from various devices from anywhere in any era. This method places students and teachers at a similar level. Students can quickly access the content of the course in this model, get guidance from their professors, share the papers, and use the forums for discussion. It is commonly used by the education industry since it has become an integral part of tertiary education around the world. The interactive method of learning has created an accessible method of learning for learners who choose to take online courses. Unfortunately, Pakistan, like other developed countries, has closed its educational activities during the ongoing coronavirus pandemic, as it is one of those facing the same problem. It encourages the university to continue teaching by incorporating the various systems such as Zoom, Team, Webex Blackboard, and Google Classroom which will further enhance worldwide e-learning. As a result, western and developing countries such as Australia, UK, and the United States, etc have also followed the online teaching method, generally known as virtual or distance learning to continue their educational activities. Although they face similar difficulties during online education like in Pakistan. They still do much better than us because they are more or less equipped with online teaching facilities and have highly trained IT professionals or teachers/students who are virtually trained.

Since taking their courses online, many students encountered significant interruptions in the form of slower internet speeds. Approximately 36.8 percent of the population of Pakistan has internet access, and bringing higher education online has reduced the number of students who can participate. The Economist Intelligence Unit ranked Pakistan 76th out of 100 nations in its annual report in terms of accessibility, affordability, and people's desire to use the Internet. According to students, the online education system has flopped, and because of persistent internet issues, it is almost impossible to finish their tasks or quizzes and attend lectures. They agree that instead of switching to the online education system, universities will recognize this time as a semester break because their grades and practical lessons are negatively impacted.Although educational institutions are depleted of pupils, the expense of institutional growth is increasing. It has two-pronged consequences as students are hesitant to pay their fees because their education is almost at a halt, while universities are under enormous pressure to handle faculty and staff with low or almost no prospects for new investments both in the form of new student recruitment and net tuition income and even in the form of financial assistance or almost no prospects for new investments. Students working as regular wagers from rural areas or from a nominal financial situation have also lost their employment and there are still no new opportunities for them to do part-time jobs to finance their studies. Many of these students are at risk of losing their semester because their finances are drying up.As it is difficult for students trained in traditional classroom settings to learn from a computer screen, the quality of studies has often dropped too much lower levels. For example, natural and mathematical science students need laboratory research and data analysis instruments, such as the Statistical Kit for Social Sciences (SPSS), which can only be obtained by them in universities. The University provides a suitable platform for students from different disciplines to conduct a functional study. Entry to libraries and print materials is one of the main aspects of the education system as students pursue research access libraries. Furthermore, Pakistani universities have also provided their students with access to electronic libraries and secure data sources that are not accessible from home. When searching for information in both print and mobile formats, students have suffered from closed university campuses. Thus, the study's quality is compromised. University is a multi-purpose forum that gives you the requisite practical learning that is very important for students for their career development, apart from educating you about your subject area. COVID-19 has forced many students to let go of their practical learning, which influences their career progress in return.

It is difficult to teach all of the degree courses online, and some lessons should not be held online. It has been shown that when seated in the classroom, most university students in Pakistan are often not even able to concentrate and keep track of the lesson due to lack of attention. Physical school closure and the adoption of online learning may negatively affect students' learning through four main channels: less time spent in learning, stress symptoms, a change in the way students interact, and lack of learning motivation. In spite of this, however, online learning is important to ensure the continuity of learning in situations where in-person lessons are canceled. The student has also encountered numerous obstacles or difficulties during online learning such as social and privacy issues; lack of qualified teachers, students who are not virtually trained, lack of access to computers, Difficulties with the English language, Poor computer knowledge, lack of financial costs to afford online education; technological problems(plagiarism problems, late submission of online assignments, insufficient finances to get online devices, no Wi-Fi or weak internet service, and no Smartphone or laptops), poor family support, lack of administrative assistance, and uncomplicated online laboratory work. During the lockdown, the measures opted by developed countries and Pakistan for online university education do not seem to be effective due to several reasons such as remote areas for the students (most of whom live in the periphery where they do not even have adequate access to electricity and timely internet access), the teachers are not well qualified for online teaching and a suitable online teaching module/ syllabus is not yet accessible (with the exception of some universities that have planned a few inappropriate modules), and lack of IT facilitates or well-equipped labs. In these conditions, it is difficult for universities to resolve online educational problems that should meet the six distance learning requirements listed on the official website of the Pakistan HEC (2020):

a) University Maintenance (an effective operational learning management system (LMS) along with a qualified supervisory authority responsible for certification of courses)
b) Faculty Maintenance (online teaching instruction is provided to faculty members before they are permitted to teach those courses)
c) Library Maintenance (all course assignments or reading contents are accessible by online means)
d) Course Formulation (all key details is available on the LMS regarding a course)
e) Technology Maintenance (the technology used to offer online courses is ready for deployment)
f) Student Preparation (students are helped to overcome any barriers they may have in obtaining the online classes or reading materials).

The above-mentioned requirements for online education rarely seem feasible for all universities in Pakistan, in particular for less-assisted universities such as Balochistan and Interior Sindh. It is still more difficult for students in rural areas to have access to the internet in a timely manner and to have access to electricity in a timely manner, even though university management and IT administration do their best. The main aim of online teaching is only to complete the syllabus or semester. Probably, such online education does not deliver high-quality learning and would further destroy higher education by entirely depleting it from studies or scholarships, whereas face to face interaction produced an intellectual or healthy discussion that gives way to real-world paralogy rather than the completion of online courses. Thus, with the increase of coronavirus pandemic, it appears that the solution to our difficulties is not blindly pursuing western or developed countries. Globally, most teachers and students are happy with the transition to online schooling when universities are closed. The faculty members of entire word institutions have started to get online teacher certifications to offer their students online classes. They have also learned the use of different online teaching tools in order to improve the quality of education. As a result, the majority of postgraduate students are enrolled as part-time students since they serve in firms. Online learning has a greater influence on all types of pupils at a higher education such as part-time, full-time, and distance learning students. For example, Massive open online courses help the students to strengthen his/her existing skills and also enhance various future career opportunities for them.

**Government policies in the coronavirus pandemic:**

Government agencies have taken several steps since the onset of the pandemic to counter the many consequences on the education system. National governments used a range of tools, including instructional kits (textbooks, worksheets, and printouts), radio teaching, and online instructional resources, to promote the education of students when they were unable to come to university. For example, Member States have endorsed the development of teachers' and students' technical capabilities, adequate access devices, and alternate means of connection (educational television, digital platforms), as well as teaching and learning materials. Students would have to pay for the learning loss they suffered, particularly those of less-advantaged families or with disabilities, those who academically struggled long before the COVID-19 crisis, and those who failed after the lockout. This could begin in the summer and last until the start of the next school year. In any case, it would be important to recognize those students who were mildly influenced by the lockdown and established catch-up plans for them. Small group teaching would be a sensible way of supporting the student's low socio-economic status or increasing the academic scores of students. Since certain children from poor backgrounds may be forced to drop out of school if one or both of their parents lose their jobs due to the COVID-19 crisis, in an attempt to prevent this, financial incentives such as scholarships, cash transfers, vouchers, may be offered to these families. Research institutions and universities need to carefully prepare and implement research management standards that meet with social distance guidelines and preserve low campus student density while driving research operations into normalcy. Analysis areas including physical laboratories may need to re-think their operating models and carefully plan and prioritize their studies. Universities will have to invest more in health and safety services and amenities on their campuses to ensure the well-being of students and staff, which may add to the financial pressure on universities. The government may assist and partially fund the safety measures of educational institutions to avoid understanding the educational and research needs of students. In order to keep students and their teacher's safe and secure, institutions for each discipline may be introducing a multi-day rotation schedule in order to minimize physical interactions. Students will get to learn at home online on the days they aren't at university. However, this mixed/rotating learning method (with online and offline elements) poses some difficulties. It is important to upgrade the curriculum and to clearly identify the types of teaching or learning activities that need to be carried out at university and those that can be completed at home. Higher education organizations will need to develop a different value system that reassesses the quality of learning and delivery strategies in the classroom and addresses the demands of an international student

Population that may be less willing to cross borders with the sole purpose of the study. For older students, returning to universities may also cause other forms of challenges, such as difficulties preserving social distance, as the architecture of existing buildings could be insufficient. In this situation, consideration should also be required to prevent the clustering of students during work-based group tasks, classes, laboratory-based research, computer rooms and accommodations such as hostels/dormitories. Governments may lower internet access rates for poorer families and provide computers, laptops or tablets free of charge to disabled students. In the entire process, teachers can be the most critical factor, particularly in relation to the vulnerable students, for whom the family may sometimes only provide modest assistance (in fact, in many cases teachers have a mediating role between students and their family). In order to prevent each teacher or university from selecting its own solution, the general plan for online education, along with teaching and learning resources, should be established through a systematic mechanism that will actually minimize duplication without having greater effectiveness. The broadcasting of educational content by mass Television or radio may be a beneficial complement to internet broadcasting because it gives guidance to those who do not have access to the internet and equalizes the teaching methods and services of schools in a nation or region. It is necessary to recognize students with special needs and to endorse assistive technology in order to effectively incorporate learning strategies for disabled students. Moreover, University leadership's appraisal policy development shall be based on the following principles: a) students shall not be promoted without some sort of evaluation based solely on their previous results. Examinations and tests are an important aspect of the educational process, and efforts to remove evaluations would have a negative effect on the quality of instruction and the success of pupils. b) As a general matter, an attempt should be made during or immediately after the originally stipulated time period to complete the semester influenced by Corona. This concept is appropriate in the case of realistic teaching and planning offered to students during the semester. In cases where the training has been erratic and, overall, incomplete, the course credit shall not be awarded purely on the basis of a final examination. c) If a university administration believes that it is impossible to conduct a sophisticated appraisal of the results of students due to the current circumstance, it should give the students the option to apply for a pass/fail score instead of a letter grade. The GPA of a graduating student would not be impaired in this situation. This is, of course, a less sophisticated metric, more fitting for measurement under minimal data constraints. Students who wish to obtain a letter grade should not be compelled to opt for a pass/fail grade (presumably in order to boost their overall GPA); rather they should be expected to undergo further testing to gather the details required to assign a letter grade. d) Plagiarism and prevention of cheating are the concerns under normal circumstances, but in the modern setting, where students are tested without a meaningful opportunity for supervision or proctoring, they can pose particular obstacles. The plan announced should be sensitive to this in two situations. First, an attempt should be made to forcefully strengthen the importance of learners' academic dignity and the costs inherent with engaging in unethical actions. Second, university administration and instructors must promise that the appraisal methodologies used are those that do not promote unethical actions. e) Using the same form of assessment for all scholars in a course to ensure equal expectations. f) In the publicly announced assessment scheme, a solution protocol for students who encounter unique challenges will be included. While a focus person can be selected, it is important to choose at least three participants to consider the grievances (consisting of at least one faculty member and one senior administration member). The policy shall specifically set out the procedure for lodging a complaint with the committee and shall specify a timeframe (no longer than one week for responding to such complaints. An appeal mechanism can also be set up by the HEC to follow up on complaints from students whose cases remain unanswered. The most popular approach used before the outbreak of the coronavirus is the closed-book test, which is no longer permissible under these terms and conditions. Universities must then develop and implement other evaluation approaches quickly depending on their strengths and the category of course. For example, in the coronavirus epidemic, open-book assessments are globally used by numerous universities. In open-book assessments, students must have to submit online tasks or assignments within a specific duration provided to complete the project. The principle of open-book assessments is that the answer to the questions requires the application of knowledge. An alternative approach is the Oral assessments that can be done over the telephone for certain students without an internet connection. An initiative on the part of university students is also required. They must be registered in globally acclaimed courses that are available at a minimal cost or free of charge. It will allow them to improve their talents and, according to international norms, will enhance their educational skills. Pakistan must strive to create a forum such as MIT Open Course Ware (MIT OCW)-a project of the Massachusetts Institute of Technology (MIT) to publish all its educational materials online that are cost-free and available to everyone, anywhere. Universities in Pakistan have to extend their assistance in this respect. At the University of Karachi, HEC has developed an expanded version of Massive Open Online Courses (MOOCs) aimed at providing students with related resources that most students do not realize and are frequently inaccessible. Therefore, in order to get benefits from them, there is a need to guide students to those sites. In the above introduction, this study outlined some thought-provoking queries and questions.Although we do not guarantee a full eradication of the above-mentioned higher education queries and problems, these suggestions can also include prompt and beneficial solutions for the problem.

## Conclusion

Both the economic sectors and the higher education system around the world are adversely impacted by this novel coronavirus. All the educational institutions in Pakistan have been shut down due to the global COVID-19 crisis. During this time, in order to continue studying electronically via the Internet, television or radio, family and students had to rely more on their own resources, while the educational institutions made concerted efforts to maintain continuity of learning. While higher education institutions were quick to substitute online teaching for face-to-face classes, these closures affected the security and legal status of international students in their host country, as well as learning and exams. The potential obstacles and consequences to online learning systems need to be assessed and effective steps should be taken to deal with them. The crisis will particularly, raise concerns about the quality of university education, which involves networking, social activities, and educational services. Although, for universities and higher education institutions, there are no best practices to follow and no established standards to follow whereas post-pandemic educational institutions will need to consider the difficulties they will face in the coming months and prepare to take tough decisions. University communities will continue to reflect on their educational vision and mission in order to ensure that student learning outcomes and aspirations of educational success are not compromised. Universities will continue to engage and include all their stakeholders in the dynamic balancing of financial uncertainties and public health relevant to the missions of research, knowledge-building, and social service. Higher education institutions need to be prepared for a daunting post-pandemic path ahead, where their decisions will influence the future of their students and steer them.

## References


1) Zaidi S, Salah S. Impact of Coronavirus on Higher Education in Pakistan2020.
2) Akram W, Adeel S, Tabassum M, Jiang Y, Chandio A, Yasmin I. Scenario Analysis and Proposed Plan for Pakistan Universities–COVID–19: Application of Design Thinking Model. 2020.
3) Shahzad A, Hassan R, Aremu AY, Hussain A, Lodhi RNJQ, quantity. Effects of COVID-19 in E-learning on higher education institution students: the group comparison between male and female. 2020:1-22.

4) Di Pietro G, Biagi F, Costa P, Karpinski Z, Mazza JJJR, Ed. The likely impact of COVID-19 on education: Reflections based on the existing literature and recent international datasets. 2020.

5) Rashid S, Yadav SS. Impact of Covid-19 pandemic on higher education and research. Indian Journal of Human Development. 2020 Aug;14(2):340-3.

6) Zahra F, Gul A, Iqbal A, Ghafoor T, Ambreen A. The Impact of Covid-19 on Rural Areas Students of Pakistan: Moderating Role of HEC Policy and Internet Service. Asian Journal of Contemporary Education. 2020;4(2):69-79.

7) Marinoni G, Van't Land H, Jensen T. The impact of Covid-19 on higher education around the world. IAU Global Survey Report. 2020 May.

# CHAPTER – 5

# TECHNOLOGICAL ADVANCEMENT IN GARMENT MANUFACTURING

## BY
### Bikas Agrawal, A. K. Shaw, Rahul Kar


**Abstract:**

Started as a customised slow process, the garment manufacturing has come of age during the past two centuries. Mass production of garments was started around the First World War. The journey was slow, the sector was unorganised and involvement of the manual labour was very intensive. Even at the present time, the involvement of manual labour in the garment manufacturing in mass scale is very high in comparison to the other industries.  The nature and variations in raw material, changes in style, fluctuation in order volume etc. are the chief factors that create high demand for manual labour. But the interesting fact is that this particular industry has also made a remarkable progress in terms of technological advancement and automation. This paper is an effort to underline the areas of garment manufacturing where technology has become a vital intervention.

**Key words:**  Technology, Garment manufacturing, Internet of things, Robotics, Computer aided manufacturing.


## Introduction

Apparel sector is the eighth largest employment provider as per "IBISWorld" report for the month of December 2020. Indian Brand Equity Federation mentioned in their report published on the 4th of December 2020, that Indian Textile and Apparel industry contributed 2.3 % to the GDP of India, 13% to industrial production and 12% to export earnings. According to the published report of the Ministry of textiles 18.09% of the total organized manufacturing sector employees are from Textile and wearable apparel industries (Source: Annual survey of Industries up to 2016-2018, texmin.nic.in) The reports are the indicators of the fact that the apparel sector in India is an important one and is one of the key employment providers. Apparel retail business is more organized now and online apparel business is growing in a fast pace along with the offline organized retail. The apparel business which is apparently one of the largest sectors in India and even in the whole world, still depends on manual workers to a large extent but started as the Tailor-made customised clothing business, it now employs modern technology like Robotics also, though that is in its nascent stage.  Mass manufacturing of garments started for the Military and other organized forces in the 18th Century. During the First World War, the need for mass manufacturing of clothing items increased significantly. In the year 1846, Elias Howe got the first US patent for sewing machine. (Source: National Inventors hall of fame, U.S.) This sewing machine was a refinement of the earlier sewing machines that were invented before. Invention of a sewing machine facilitated a higher amount of production. Later the technological advancements took place in not only the sewing operations but also in the allied mandatory operations that are done pre- and post-sewing of the product. The Apparel manufacturing sector in the present time exists in both organised and unorganised sector. The fact remains that the business can still be started with a low capital due to the factors like variations in designs, low order volumes and even in customer's preference for customised manufacturing. But the changes that can now be seen are overwhelming. Use of modern technology is increasing in an impressive speed. Mentioned below are the different sections or department of the apparel manufacturing where significant technological intervention is seen. As the discussion of Industry 4.0 in apparel manufacturing is growing more and more, further developments are expected to be seen.

**Main areas of technological developments in the Apparel Industry:**

**Cutting room solutions**: In a mass production factory of apparels, the cutting room or cutting department is a very important part. This is the department where the design ideas are turned into the first form of tangible products. Objectives of this department are optimum fabric consumption, that is, minimum wastage of fabric without compromising on the quality and final appearance of the product. Variations in fabrics properties like shrinkage, strength, colour fastness, construction method etc. pose challenges in this department. Perfect size charts are also necessary for producing garments in a mass scale. So, the cutting room needs solutions in terms of perfect sizing or body measurements along with perfect pattern making, spreading and cutting of the garment parts.In the developmental stages of the apparel Industry, perfect size charts have always been a vital requirement. Huge amount of data has always been required in order to create size charts for various groups of people, depending on factors like region, nutrition, gender, height etc. Measuring the human body in a large sample size is quite difficult. So, when we talk about the sizing factor and the accuracy and productivity factor in the cutting room, we can see the following technological developments:

In collecting the human body measurement **3-D body scanners** have provided a lot of ease these days. 3D body scanners create a 3D image virtually using light sensors, real body measurements can be taken digitally without contacting the subjects physically. Using a 3-D body scanner for collecting data is much easier than taking the body measurements with the help of different types of measurement tapes and other hand-held measuring aids. The subjects feel comfortable in giving the body measurements with complete privacy.The body scanners are also being used in case of mass customization. Mass customization is the category of garment production where customised products are produced in big factories using the same state of the art machinery and equipment that are used in mass production. With the growing demand for customised fitting, use of 3D scanners is expected to rise.

**Computer aided design software**, specially designed for the apparel industry are being used commonly now a days and the market leaders in the field like Gerber technology, Lectra, Tukatech, Richpiece, Morgan Tecnica, Optitex etc. keep introducing latest innovation in their solutions. There are multiple modules in the total Apparel CAD solutions, which can be bought by the apparel manufacturer as the full package or as a part of it. Almost all solution providers of Apparel CAD offer similar types of solutions to remain competitive and relevant. The various parts of the Apparel CAD systems are the following:

**Developing new patterns for garments:** CAD software provides the required tool and working area on the computer screen to develop new patterns with a lot of ease of working. Utmost care is taken in developing perfect patterns as per the design. Not only the measurements are taken perfectly but also the variables like surface design of material, stretch factors, construction of fabric etc. are handled perfectly. A huge surface design library helps the user in creating the patterns as per the designs. Matching of the checks, stripes, motifs etc. become very easy with the help of just a few clicks. Learning the software is easy and the tutorials or help menu are there to provide help in each and every step. Productivity in case of the apparel CAD is very high if compared with the tedious process of manual pattern making.

**Digitizing the existing patterns:** The manually made patterns can be easily digitized and kept in the memory of the computer for further adaption, if required. The digitization process has become very fast due to the use of scanners. The earlier digitizers used digitizing board or digitizing tables and point to point clicks were required to scan the patterns which needed well trained people and also the process was time consuming.

**Grading the patterns:**  After a pattern in a particular size is developed in the CAD system multiple sizes are developed from that pattern with the help of simple algorithm. Graded sizes are used in the next step of manufacturing. All the files of various sizes are kept in the memory of computer and can be retrieved quickly whenever required. Pattern Grading requires perfect increments per size while increasing or decreasing the size. It is a very tedious process if done manually. Developing multiple sizes in apparel CAD is very fast and accurate.

**Marker making**: This is the process of placing all the patterns for one size or multiple sizes of the garment, depending on the size mix demanded by the customer, on the fabric of the required width or the available width. The CAD systems provide the options for all possible fabric widths. In this process also, the factors like checks, stripes or other fabric surface designs are taken care of perfectly. The system generates alarms if faults like wrong placement of fabric grain lines or overlap of patterns take place. Marker making can be done by the operator as well as by the in-built command in the system.

**3 D model**: The 3-D models provide the facility of checking the virtual fit on 3-D models. The fit and hang of the garment can be seen virtually with a 360-degree view. Correction in fit and hang of garments can be done easily; the effect of correction in pattern can be seen virtually while doing the correction. This facility reduces a lot of effort in checking the fit by trial-and-error method physically.

Benefits of the apparel CAD systems are many as the advent and use of the system has brought a paradigm shift in the cutting room. Pattern making process has developed from being a slow and time-consuming process to a quick and smart one. Wastage of time and material both are stopped to a great extent. Requirement for highly skilled pattern masters has also reduced. Uniformity in recreating the patterns & elimination of the need to store the patterns for different styles are the other mentionable advantages of apparel CAD systems.

**Computer aided manufacturing in the cutting room:**

The CAD solution providers often provide the hardware solutions like spreading tables and the cutting facilities that are numerically controlled and are very fast and accurate. Computer aided physical cutting blades are the main type of cutter in the system and they can cut a lot of fabric layers together with lot of precision. Tukatech, one of the leading brands in the field of Apparel CAD and machinery solutions provide cutters which can cut as high as 8 cm compressed height of fabric layers with ease. The same company also provides Laser cutting system which is very fast and extremely precise and is suitable for cutting single layer and low height fabric spread. Various companies provide similar solutions. This chapter does not try to vouch for any particular solution provider.

**CNC Cutter (Serkon Makina)**

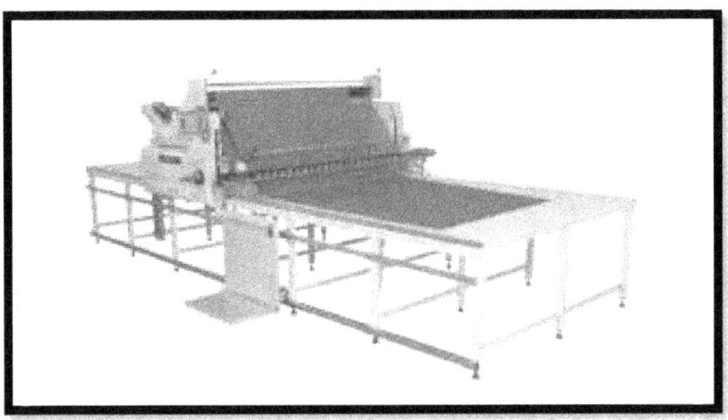

**Fully automatic Fabric Spreader (Serkon Makina)**

When we talk about the highly sophisticated and highly productive computerised cutting machines, it is important to mention about the manually operated cutting machines and equipment. Manually operated cutting machines/ equipment cost much less and are very suitable for the apparel factories having a low investment capacity and that cater to smaller order volumes. Following is a list of operator's controlled cutting equipment:

**Reciprocating straight knife machine**: This is the most popular among the operator controlled cutting equipment and gradual development in this is also done by the manufacturer of the equipment. Various types of cutting blades are used for cutting varieties of materials without creating any distortion. The equipment is mounted on a base plate along with the motor. Small issues like worker's safety and excessive heat generation are taken care by the blade guard and cooling systems attached to the machine.

**Circular blade cutting machine**: Similar to the straight knife machine, circular knife machine is also having similar kind of structure with a circular shape of the blade. This type is more suitable for low height of fabric lay and is particularly suitable for cutting leather that is cut in single layer. Weight of the circular knife machine is comparatively less than the straight knife machine. Both straight knife and circular knife are portable and are easy to handle with an initial training. Both of them have in built knife sharpening devices. Changing of the worn-out knife is an easy process.

**Straight Knife Machine (Eastman Cutters UK)**

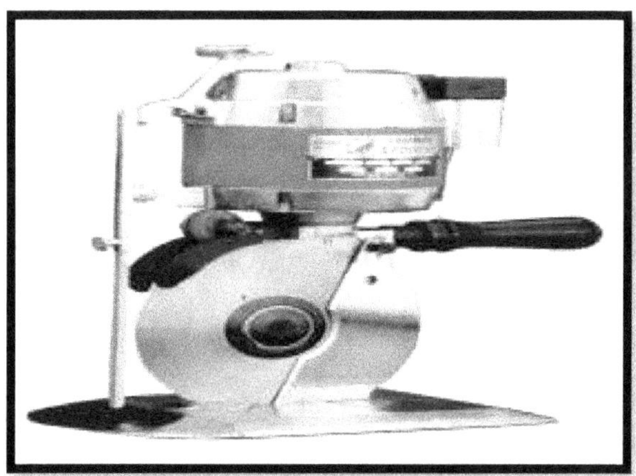

**Circular Knife Machine (Eastman Cutters UK)**

**Band knife**: Band knife is a stationery cutting machine and the fabric lay has to be transported under the blade. This has a much finer blade and the cutting is done very precisely. Usually, small parts are cut in it or precise re cutting is done with this.

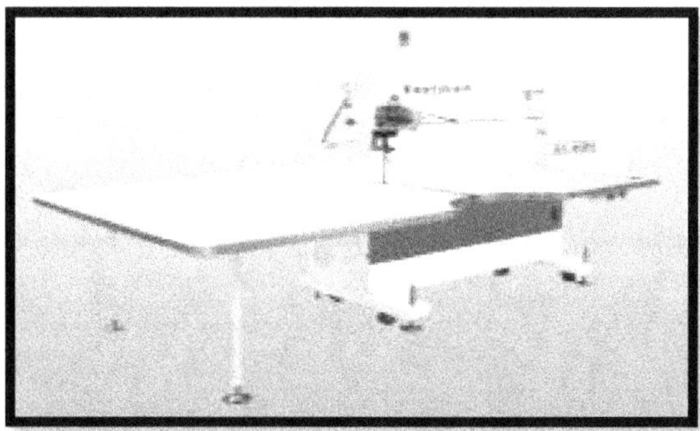

**Band knife (Eastman Cutters UK)**

**Die cutting**: this is another stationery type where the equipment is fixed and the fabric has to be brought under the dies of the desired shape. The cutting takes place by a heavy vertical load and is very precise. But in the flip side, it creates a lot of unnecessary inventory of dices that are not re used.Between the cutting and sewing processes, comes the fusing of interlining. Interlinings are used to reinforce particular parts of the structured garments like formal shirts, jackets, formal trousers etc. The fusing machines are highly advanced in technology now a day and can be semi automatic or fully automatic. Temperature and time controls are automated with the help of sensors. Conveyors are used for loading, fusing and unloading.

**Sewing Department developments**: As mentioned earlier, sewing machine was invented and patented around the mid 19$^{th}$ Century; this was revolutionary in the whole business of clothing. Started as a manually operated machine, sewing machine has seen a lot of improvements in its shape, appearance, productivity, variety, technology etc. Sewing machines are being manufactured for different types of stitches and seams and come loaded with various work aids which have facilitated de-skilling of the operations which were earlier supposed to be high skill operations. Computerised machines provide further ease of operations like selection of stitch length and width, fixed speed of machine, fixed pattern of stoppage and start and can also do stitching in complete pre programmed pattern for achieving a particular type of appearance and other properties of stitch like density, strength etc.

**Following details will give a fair idea of the developments in sewing machines:**

**Variety of machine beds**: To facilitate an easy manipulation of the material under the needle, while being sewn, different shapes of machine beds have been designed by the Engineers. Easy and right movement of the sewn material increases the productivity and quality to a great extent and reduces worker's fatigue. Machine beds come in flat with the machine table, raised above the machine table, cylindrical in shape, tower like shape, situated at the edge of the body of the machine etc. There are further variations among the basic shapes. Each of the bed type has logics behind the particular shape. For example: sewing the side panel of a bag, the tower like shape of the machine bed that is known as the "post bed" in the trade, is used. This shape facilitates easy and quick movement of the shape of the side panels of bags. Similarly, the other bed types, be it flat with the table or raised above the table or any other type, have logics behind that shape.

**Post Bed (Durkopp Adler)**

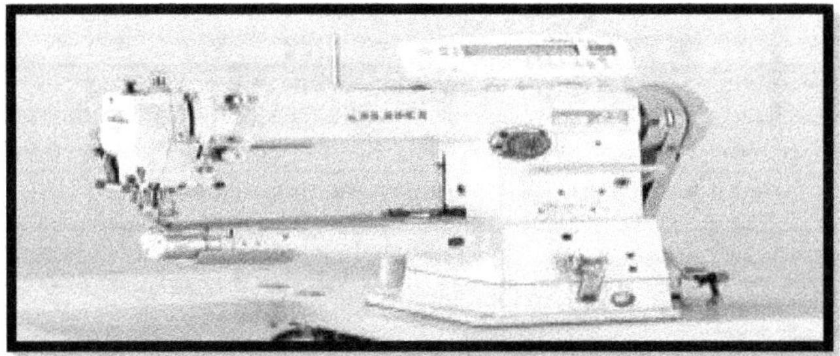

**Cylindrical Bed (Juki)**

**Use of work aids**: Along with the sewing machines, variety of work aids are used in the sewing industry, these work aids are both tactile and sensory. Even the light beams work as work aids. These work aids are also known as the de skilling devices. Presser foot of different shapes, seam guides, pre shaped templates, seam folders, fabric gathering rollers etc. are some common types which contribute to the enhancement of productivity. Pneumatically controlled automatic thread cutters provides very clean sewn edges and have become the choice of quality manufacturers of knitted garments. Different types of sensors are also used for thread cutting and other handling operations during the sewing operations.

**Dry head and direct drive sewing machines**: Dry head sewing machines are gaining popularity as they do not need to be oiled frequently, thus saving the time and effort. Also the fear of spotted clothing is less with these machines. Direct drive machines have the motors attached to the machine arms and prevents wastage of power.

**Computerised machines and work stations**: Workstations in case of the sewing industry are combinations of machine head and various work heads. They are generally semi automatic or fully automatic computerised facilities. All the leading sewing machine manufacturers have been making computerised machines for a few decades now. Length and width of stitches, speed of the machine, cutting of the thread end, handling of cut parts etc. have become automatic and numerically controlled, saving a lot of problems in handling the cut parts and sewn products. Robotics has also come into the scene of sewing machines and will be mentioned in a later chapter.Selection of particular type of developed computerised machines has to be done keeping the return on investment in mind. They are highly productive and are expensive. If the productivity is fully exploited by the manufacturer they are more viable options. But the non computerised sewing machines are still being used as they might be making more business sense and small developments like reduction of noise and equipping   them with useful work aids are still being done by the machine companies.

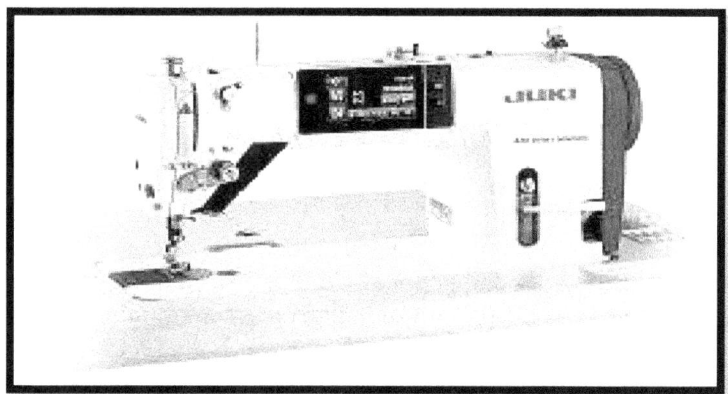

**Computerised SNLS machine (Durkopp Adler)**

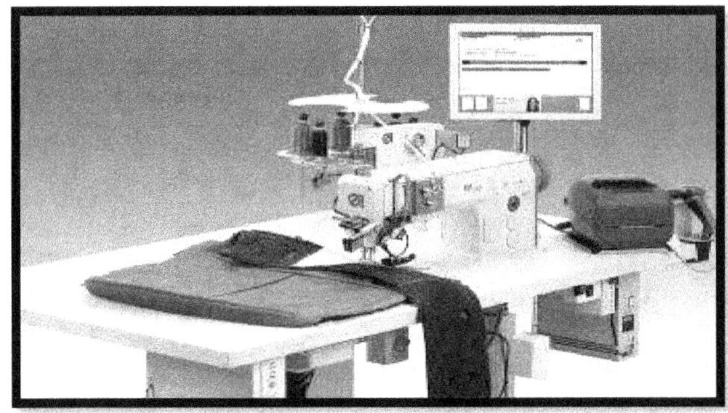

**Computerised sewing workstations (JUKI)**

Apart from the developed of sewing machines, the **automated material handling systems** are also a vital development in the sewing department. The fully computerised overhead transport systems (Cut part handling systems) are capable of giving real time data for the movement of cut parts, thus reducing the chance for missing of parts. These material transportation systems have reduced the need for manual workers and have facilitated a cleaner work place.

**Eton Material Handling**

**Finishing department developments:**

In the finishing department also, computer-controlled machines are used now a days and provide solutions to finish each and every type of garment without distorting the final appearance of them. Operator controlled hand press is still a very popular pressing equipment. Lot of developments can be seen in this equipment, too. They are more energy efficient and highly productive. Apart from this popular category some more technological advancement can be seen in the following pressing equipment:

**Press and buck:** This type of pressing/finishing equipment is a stationery platform where the garment to be pressed is spread flat. A lid or platen is closed over the platform that is also known as the "bed buck" . One or both the surfaces (Top and bottom) is/have heated elements which along with steam pressure remove the unwanted crease from the garment. This type of particularly useful for the types of garments where the hand press movements is not very desired. Productivity of these machines is higher in comparison to that of the hand pressing equipment.

**Carousel Press:** Multiple heads of machines are combined together in order to use the operator efficiency to the fullest. This is a semi automatic machine where loading and unloading operations are done manually by an operator. The movement and time taken to finish one garment is synchronized in each of the head. Each head is subjected to heat and pressure for a particular time. Once the piece is finished that particular head comes in front of the operator while the other heads are still under the operation.

. **Carousel Press (Veit)**

**Form finishers**: Form finisher is the machines for finishing where loading and unloading are done manually.  Garments are draped over the form finisher that is a flat dress form, when the form finisher is activated, steam and pressure are released. The garment is left for the required time and again the dress form is collapsed. Work cycle in this type is very easy and productivity of such equipment is very high. This type is particularly suitable for the garments which cannot be subjected under a heavy pressure from top due to the material composition or surface of the fabric.

**Steam tunnel**: Steam tunnel is a machine where multiple garments are fed through a conveyor system from one end and come out from the other end. Inside the tunnel (chamber), the garments are pressed with the help of steam and pressure. Productivity is very high in this machine. This type of machine is particularly suitable for the garments where heavily structured shape is not desired. Hand pressing is combined along with the steam tunnel if particular parts of the garments are supposed to be given a structured shape.

**Form finisher (Veit)**

**Steam tunnel (Veit)**

**Fusing equipment**: Fusing a stiff material for well structured garments in parts like collar, cuff, front placket of shirt, waist band of trousers, front of jackets and coats is very common desired feature. Fusing the stiff material that is known as inter lining in the trade requires a great amount of precision and technological intervention. The fusible material (base fabric and the glue), the fabric composition of the garment, the time, temperature, cooling time etc. have to be very technically decided. Properties of all the materials have to be studied before the selection of a particular type of fusing material and fusing equipment also. The desired efficiency and investment capacity are other important aspects to be kept in mind while selecting the type of fusing machine/ equipment. In customised tailoring that is done in a tailoring shop, hand iron is used for imparting pressure and heat and that results in inadequate fusing thus damaging the whole appearance of the part. Sewing industry takes a lot of care in selecting the right kind of fusing machine.One small mention of the advancement in packaging is also necessary to understand the kind of technology being used by the apparel manufacturer these days. The packaging section has become very fast due to a lot of automation in the process. Conveyor based packaging systems integrate the operations of folding, packing and unloading in a single workstation with a very fast pace. Multiple options are available to the manufacturer in this category where the systems are partially or fully automatic. The manufacturers can choose based upon their requirement of production and investment capacities.

**ERP solutions**: Communication among the different stake holders and parts of any organization is a very vital thing. With internet the wastage of time in communication has sorted out to a great extent. Various ERP solutions specially customised for the apparel industry are present in the market and have made the life much easier for the apparel manufacturers. From receiving of order from the customers to dispatch of the completed goods require multiple operations in between and due to the variations in lot size, season, style, size set etc. error in communication is very likely to happen. Tracking a particular order or a piece becomes very challenging particularly if the integrated ERP systems are not used. Readers can easily find the name of the solution providers in the web. The author does not intend to recommend any particular name of ERP solution or any other manufacturing or marketing related solution through this chapter.

**Concept of industry 4.0 in apparel industry:**

In its journey from hand sewing to computerised workstations and ERP solutions, the apparel Industry has seen many phases. Even in the present scenario, different stages of developments can be seen in this sector due to the facts like small order quantity and high variations in styles which gives a space to very small manufacturers who do not necessarily look for high productivity and bulk uniform products. Simultaneously the industry is constantly looking beyond the existing modern technology. The concept of Industry 4.0 has come into this field also and lot of brainstorming is going on about the use of the main concepts of this modern Industrial revolution in the apparel sector, too. Klaus Schwab, executive chairman of the World Economic Forum introduced the phrase "Fourth Industrial Revolution" through his published article by "Foreign Affairs" in the year 2015. The fourth industrial revolution envisages the use of computer-based technologies like Artificial Intelligence, Internet of things, 3-D printing, Augmented reality, Cloud computing, Blockchain technology, machine learning, nanotechnology etc. to be more and more in use for a faster pace of the Industrial development. Current use of Industry 4.0 concepts in Apparel Industry: In an article published on "Online Clothing" by Saumyadeep Saha, in the month of November 2018 talks about the current scenario of the new solutions and the solution providers. **Cognex,** an American manufacturer of machine vision system, sensors and software provides a solution that can learn the surface design and construction methods of the fabric and can sense the defects after a training, thus saving the tedious job of manually inspecting the fabric '**Datacolor,** an American company, offers colour management instrument and software in various categories. The artificial intelligence enabled software provides solution for the users to objectively measure and communicate the colours of trims, yarn, prints, laces etc. The company offers colour measuring solutions for multiple fields, textile is one of the fields they cater to. "Advanced hyper spectral spectrophotometer is used along with the industry proven quality control software to measure, analyze, report, communicate and visualize accurate colour results." **Soft Wear Automation**, an American company, has developed sew bots (Robots) for providing fully automatic sewing operations. The other sections like spreading & cutting of apparels have been using fully automatic computerized solutions but in the field of sewing, manual work is still predominant. With the sew bots, the company has started a disruptive technology in the area of sewing also. The sewbots move over the product, instead of the product moving beneath the sewing machine needle. Soft wear Automation sew bots can sew multiple products like apparel, bags, shoes, pillow cover and many more.

## Conclusion:

Industry automation has taken place in different sectors in different pace. Since the apparel industry involves a lot of manual work automation, use of computers and robots are comparatively less. In India the apparel manufacturing sector was not open for large sectors till very recent past. This type of restrictions on investment deters the use of modern technology, which are costly and requires a lot of capital. Although in the long run the modern technology gives an economic advantage, the initial investments are high. At the same time the World is moving towards the 4th Industrial revolution where AI, Blockchain, Augmented reality, robotics, cloud computing and other advanced tools are being used successfully. To be in tune with the industrial advancement as a whole, the apparel Industry is also trying to shape up itself in a new form. More advancement in the industry is expected quicker than anticipated. The 4th Industrial revolution tools are disruptive and can change things in a very high speed.

## Further scope of the study

This chapter discusses about the current apparel industry and the use of modern technology in the sector currently. Effect of industry 4.0 has started showing and will keep increasing in the near future. So the study provides a lot of scope to further investigate about how the new entrants are entering into the market and what solutions are being provided by them. It has to be analyzed if the upcoming technological solutions are economical viable, environment friendly and sustainable or not.

## References:


1) Godley, A. (1997), 'The development of the clothing industry; technology and fashion', Textile history, 28 (1) 3-10
2) Aldrich, W. (2000), 'Tailor's cutting manuals and the growing provision of popular clothing 1770-1870', Textile History , 31, (2), 144
3) Kunick, P. (1984), Modern sizing and pattern making for Women's and Children's garments, Philip Kunick, London, pp. 1-11.
4) Cooklin G. (1990), Pattern Grading for Women's clothes: the technology og sizing, BSP Professional books, London.
5) Gray S.N. (1998) CAD in Clothing & Textiles, Gower, London.
6) Carr and Latham, The technology of clothing manufacture, Blackwell Publishing, U.K.
7) Tyler D.J. (1991) Materials Management in clothing production, Blackwell Scientific Publications, Oxford.
8) BS 3870:1991: Stitches and seams. Part 1: Classification and terminology of stitch types and part 2 : Classification and terminology of seam types.

9)  Cooklin G. (1990) Fusing technology. The Textile Institute, Manchester.

10) Glock & Kunz, 2015, 'Apparel manufacturing, sewn product analysis', fourth edition, Pearson.

11) Abernathy, F. H. Dunlop, J.T. Hammond, J.H. & Weil, D. (1999). A stitch in Time. New York: Oxford University Press.

12) Gray S. (1998, February). Virtual reality in fashion. IEEE Spectrum. 18-25.

13) Heyn, U. & Jung, R. (1987 March). Choosing a mechanized cutting system. Bobbin, 28 (7) 82-83.

14) American Society for testing and materials. 1998. Standards related to stitches and seams. West Conshohocken, PA: Author.

15) American Apparel Manufacturers Association: (1992), Technical Advisory Committee Report. The impact of technology on apparel. Part II. Arlington, VA: Author.

16) Saha Soumyadeep (November, 2018) Online clothing study. Retrieved from www.onlineclothingstudy.com

# CHAPTER – 6

# SYNTHESIS OF CROWN ETHER BY MICROWAVE-ASSISTED ROUTE: A REVIEW

## BY
## Dattatraya B. Bharti

**Abstract:**

This short review summarizes the synthesis of crown ether and different techniques used for synthesis and how to improve yield and reduced the time of synthesis. Recently, microwave-assisted reactions have received much attention due to the higher conversions and shorter reaction times possible under microwave irradiation compared to those of conventional heating. As a result, microwave irradiation as a chemical reaction means has been widely applied in various synthetic fields of chemistry such as organic and polymer synthesis.

**Key words -** Microwave irradiation, methods of synthesis, crown ether synthesis, yield, time factor

**Introduction:**

Since the pioneering work of Pederson on the preparation and properties of macrocyclic polyethers (crown ethers), [1-3] there have been waves of interest concerning the synthesis of a wide variety of oxygen, sulfur and nitrogen-containing crowns.[4] The crown ethers have proved to be enormously popular and extremely useful ligands (host) for a startling range of metal ions and neutral or ionic organic species.[5] In the early days of microwave synthesis, experiments were typically carried out in sealed Teflon or glass vessels in a domestic household microwave oven without any temperature or pressure measurements [6]. Kitchen microwave ovens are not designed for the rigors of laboratory usage: acids and solvents corrode the interiors quickly and there are no safety controls. The results were often violent explosions due to the rapid uncontrolled heating of organic solvents under closed vessel conditions. In the 1990s several groups started to experiment with solvent-free microwave chemistry (so-called dry-media reactions), which eliminated the danger of explosions [7].Microwave (MW) activation as a non-conventional energy source has become a very popular and useful technology in organic chemistry. The number of annual publications on microwave assisted organic chemistry is growing rapidly with almost one thousand publications in print since the pioneering work of Gedye [7] in 1986 (Fig.1)

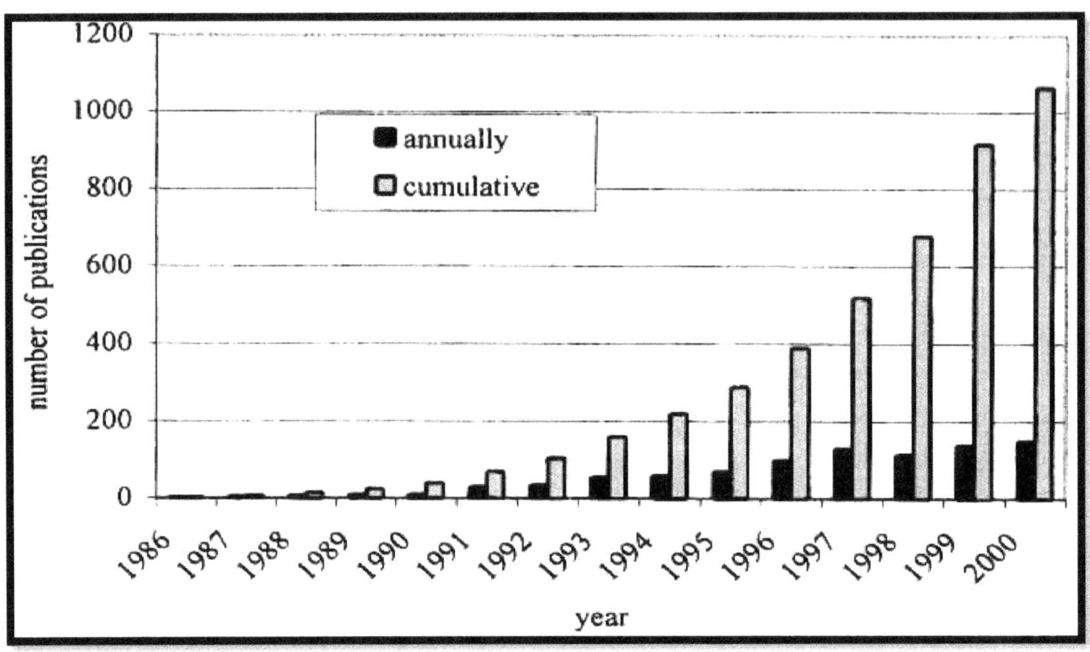


**Figure 1.Number of publications dealing with microwave irradiation in organic synthesis for the period (1986 – 2000)**

The combination of solvent-free reactions conditions and microwave irradiation leads to large reductions in reaction times, enhancements in conversions and, sometimes [8, 9] in selectivity with several advantages of the eco-friendly approach, termed green chemistry. Probably the greatest impetus was given to these studies by Pedersen who in 1967 reported the synthesis and metal ion complexation properties of a large number of polyether type macrocycles which he named crown ethers [10]. Within two decades the research which started by crown ethers developed to the field of host-guest chemistry [12] and then that of supramolecular chemistry [13]. The achievements reached in these fields were awarded by the 1987 Nobel Prize in Chemistry to three prominent pioneer scientists C. J. Pedersen [12], D. J. Cram [14] and J. M. Lehn [15]. From the point of view of our recent studies, the earlier research on chiral pyridino-18-crown-6 ether type macrocycles carried out in Bradshaw's laboratory should be mentioned [16].A convenient nomenclature for crown ethers was proposed by Pedersen [17] in which macrocyclic ring 1 and 2 are designated 18- crown-6 and dibenzo-18-crown 6, respectively. The specific 1 designation "crown" is preceded by the kind and number of substituent's on the polyether ring and the total number of atoms which constitute the polyether ring and is followed by the number of heteroatoms in the ring. The term dibenzo refers to the two benzene rings connected on the ring.The stability of a crown ether complex is measured by the stability constant Kg which is defined by the law of mass equilibrium.[18]

**Table 1. Cation Diameters and Cavity Sizes of Crown Ethers.**

| Cation | Cation Diameter [A°][19,20] | Crown Ether | Cavity Diameter [A°] |
| --- | --- | --- | --- |
| Li | 1.36 | 14-crown-4 | 1.2a. 1.5b |
| Na | 1.90 | 15-crown-5 | 1.7 - 2.2 |
| K | 2.66 | 18-crown-6 | 2.6 - 3.2 |
| Rb | 2.98 | 19-crown-6 | 3.0 - 3.5 |
| Cs | 3.38 | 21-crown-7 | 3.4 - 4.3 |

The synthesis of macrocyclic ring compound usually gave low yields and oligomers. These problems can be avoided by use of high dilution condition [21] which facilitates the cyclization reaction by use of very low concentrations of reactants. The presence of one or more rigid groups also enhances of cyclization yields by reducing the conformational possibilities of the reactants.[22] The most widely used approaches for cyclization are shown in Figure 3.[23] Approaches 2 and 3 provide the most efficient one-pot.

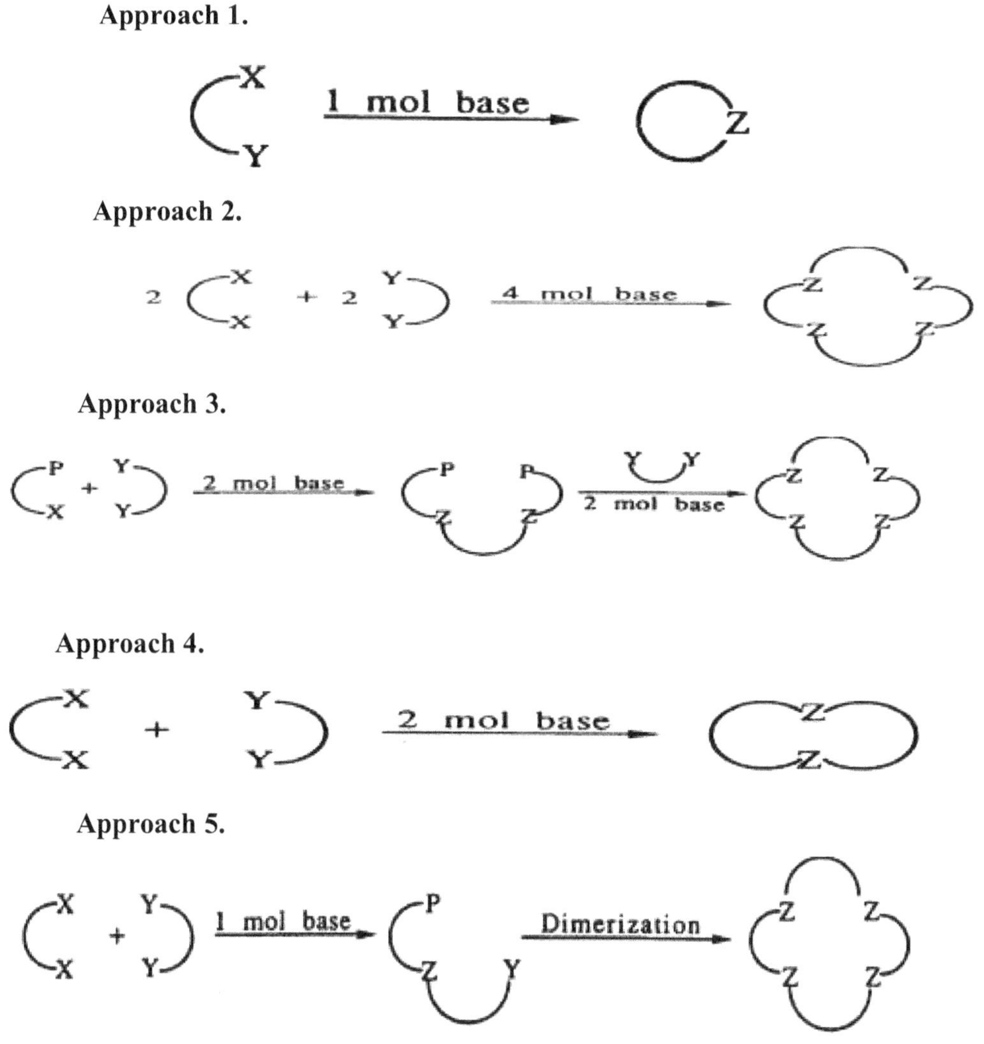

**Approach 1.**

**Approach 2.**

**Approach 3.**

**Approach 4.**

**Approach 5.**

**Figure 2. Synthetic Approaches for Cyclization Reactions.**

The interest in the microwave assisted organic synthesis has been growing during the recent years. Drug companies are exploiting microwaves in the area of organic/pharmaceutical synthesis for drug screening and discovery [24-29]. Scientists have demonstrated the potential of microwave -assisted organic synthesis using ionic liquids as solvent, co-solvent, additives and/or catalyst [30]. The development of cleaner technologies is a major emphasis in green chemistry. Among the several aspects of green chemistry, using efficient and less hazardous energy sources such as microwave energy is recommended. Drug companies and research institutions are exploiting microwaves in the area of organic synthesis for drug screening and discovery. Microwave-assisted organic synthesis has several advantages over conventional reactions in that the microwave allows for an increase in reaction rate, rapid reaction optimization, and rapid analogue synthesis. It also uses both less energy and solvent, and it enables difficult compound synthesis [31].Some related to synthesis of diaryl ether under micro wave assisted synthesis are given below Table .Synthesis of diaryl ethers under microwave irradiation.

**Table2. Shows yield for diaryl ether synthesis by microwave method**

| Entry | R | Ar | Yield (%)[a] |
|---|---|---|---|
| 1 | H | $4\text{-}NO_2\text{-}C_6H_4$ | 92 |
| 2 | $2\text{-}CH_3$ | $4\text{-}NO_2\text{-}C_6H_4$ | 92 |
| 3 | $2\text{-}CH_3$ | $4\text{-}NO_2\text{-}C_6H_4$ | 90 |
| 4 | $4\text{-}CH_3O$ | $4\text{-}NO_2\text{-}C_6H_4$ | 92 |
| 5 | 2-*tert*-butyl | $4\text{-}NO_2\text{-}C_6H_4$ | 90 |
| 6 | 2-*tert*-butyl | $4\text{-}NO_2\text{-}C_6H_4$ | 91 |
| 7 | 4-Cl | $4\text{-}NO_2\text{-}C_6H_4$ | 87 |
| 8 | $4\text{-}NO_2$ | $4\text{-}NO_2\text{-}C_6H_4$ | 76 |
| 9 | H | $2\text{-}NO_2\text{-}C_6H_4$ | 91 |
| 10 | $2\text{-}CH_3$ | $2\text{-}NO_2\text{-}C_6H_4$ | 90 |
| 11 | $3\text{-}CH_3$ | $2\text{-}NO_2\text{-}C_6H_4$ | 91 |
| 12 | $4\text{-}CH_3O$ | $2\text{-}NO_2\text{-}C_6H_4$ | 88 |
| 13 | 2-*tert*-butyl | $2\text{-}NO_2\text{-}C_6H_4$ | 88 |
| 14 | 4-*tert*-butyl | $2\text{-}NO_2\text{-}C_6H_4$ | 87 |
| 15 | 4-Cl | $2\text{-}NO_2\text{-}C_6H_4$ | 80 |
| 16 | $4\text{-}NO_2$ | $2\text{-}NO_2\text{-}C_6H_4$ | 72 |

[a]Isolated yield.

In the above Table Synthesis of diaryl ethers under microwave irradiation, all of the reactions are completed in 10 min with very high yields. Noteworthy among these are very rapid and efficient reactions of bulky 2-*tert*-butylphenol with 2-fluoronitrobenzene and 4-fluoronitrobenzene, which required 68 h and 84 h of reaction times respectively in previous conventional method in solvents (entries **5** and **13**).[32] Electron deficient phenols such as 4-chlorophenol and 4-nitrophenol were reacted smoothly with aryl fluoride to give the corresponding diaryl ethers (entries **7-8** and **15-16**), which would not proceeded effectively under classical Ullmann type diaryl ether synthesis.Micro wave assisted synthesis is done under specific condition and have specification other information regarding the use of micro wave oven as domestic as well as instrument in industries and in laboratories for research and production purpose.

• Specification with frequency and its application year.

- microwave 2.45 GHz

- WWII – radar (magnetron)

- 1950s food industry

- 1984 first application in chemical synthesis

Microwave Ovens: domestic use

• Chemical Reactions – usually requires activation energy

      - Conductive energy transfer

      - Microwaves (dielectric heating)

First instrument - Hull

• Reliable magnetron – Randall and Both (WVII)

• USA, 1950s food industry

• 1970s-1980s reliable domestic instruments

• First application 1969

-Aqueous emulsion polymerization (acrylic acid, butyl acrylate, methacrylic acid)

• Biological geological samples

• Water treatment

• "Real" synthetic applications

    -Gedye

    -Giguerr

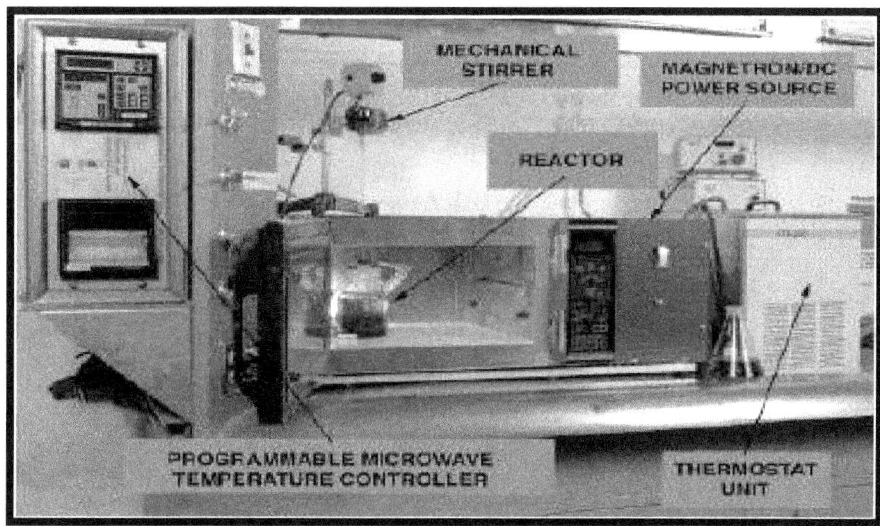


**Figure - 3. Micro wave oven for organic synthesis**

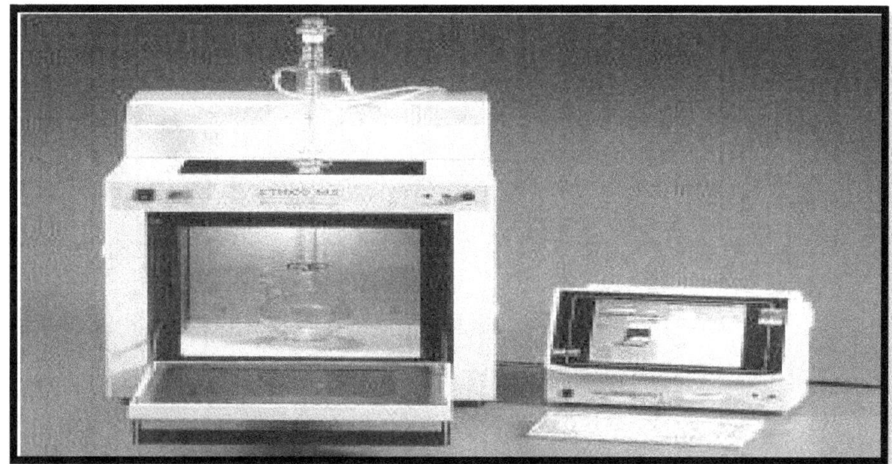

**Figure 4. Synthetic instruments MilestonProlabo, Berghof, CEM**

**Table 3: In short brief information about its historical overview of Microwave Irradiation**

| Frequency (GHz) | Tolerance (% & MHz) | Area permitted |
|---|---|---|
| 0.434 | 0.2% | Austria, Netherlands, Portugal, Germany, Switzerland |
| 0.896 | 10MHz | United Kingdom |
| 0.915 | 13MHz | North and South America |
| 2.375 | 50MHz | Albania, Bulgaria, CIS, Hungary, Romania, Czech /Slovak Republics, |
| 2.450 | 50MHz | World-wide, except where 2.375 is used |
| 3.390 | 0.6% | Netherlands |
| 5.800 | 5MHz | World-wide |
| 6.780 | 0.6% | Netherlands |
| 24.150 | 25MHz | World-wide |
| 40.680 | 25MHz | United Kingdom |

As micro wave work on heating effect and only rotates the molecule and no any bond cleavage but it is temperature  dependence   of Ea of different  reaction could be significantly different due to this change in selectivity also. Hence microwave only increases the internal very fast heating of reaction mixture and help to proceed the reaction soon with effective high yield with less side product .Some solvent  and their temperature change under micro wave irritation are give below. Now in micro wave assisted synthesis we are getting product with good yield and purity. For synthesis of organic compound used various methods called as conventional methods of synthesis now a day's micro wave assisted Synthesis play a major role because of improved yield with decrease in time of reaction and have purity too. Now in next part we are discuss the micro wave synthesis with other methods and their advantage over conventional and other method with some chemical reaction as follows.

**Table 4. Temperature change of materials after 2.45 GHz frequency microwave irradiation (RT samples, 50 cm3 liquid, or 25 g (1000 W) or 5-6 g (500 W) solids).**

| $T$ (°C) | $P$ (W) | $t$ (min) | Sample |
|---|---|---|---|
| 81 | 560 | 1 | Water |
| 56 | 560 | 1 | Methanol |
| 78 | 560 | 1 | Ethanol |
| 110 | 560 | 1 | Acetic acid |
| 49 | 560 | 1 | CHCl3 |
| 28 | 560 | 1 | CCl4 |
| 56 | 560 | 1 | Acetone |
| 131 | 560 | 1 | DMF |
| 25 | 560 | 1 | Hexane |
| 577 | 1000 | 6 | Al |
| 1283 | 1000 | 1 | C |
| 1290 | 1000 | 3 | Co2O3 |
| 41 | 1000 | 4 | FeCl3 |
| 1305 | 1000 | 6.2 | NiO |
| 83 | 500 | 30 | CaO |
| 701 | 500 | 0.5 | CuO |
| 532 | 500 | 0.5 | WO3 |
| 701 | 500 | 9 | V2O5 |

## Methods And Material

## Microwave Technique for Synthesis Of Crown Ether Compound

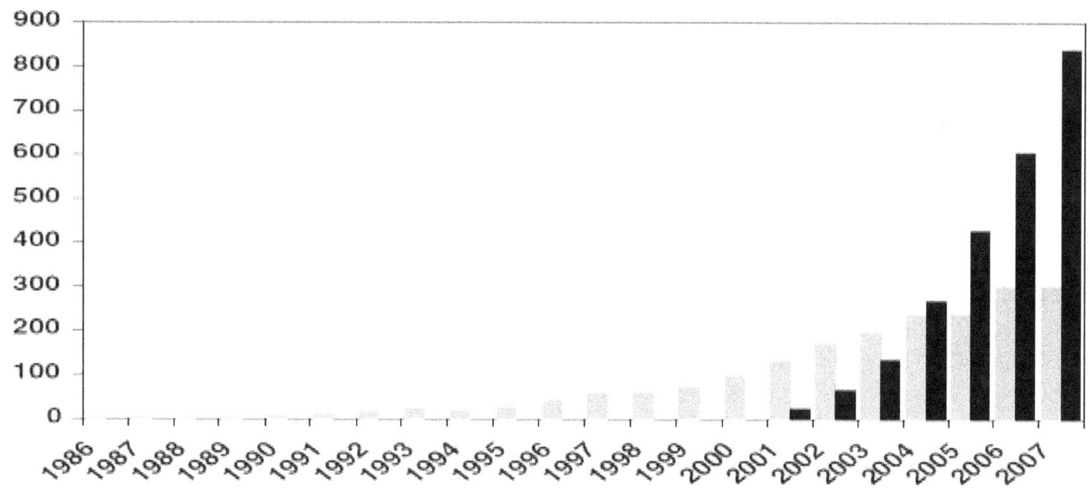

**Figure 5. Publications on microwave-assisted organic synthesis (1986–2007).**

**Gray bars:** Number of articles involving MAOS for seven selected synthetic organic chemistry journals (J. Org. Chem., Org. Lett., Tetrahedron, Tetrahedron Lett., Synth. Commun. Synthesis, Synlett. SciFinder Scholar keyword search on microwave.). The black bars represent the number of publications (2001–2007) reporting MAOS experiments in dedicated reactors with adequate process control (about 50 journals, full text search: microwave). Only those articles dealing with synthetic organic chemistry were selected. Recent innovations in microwave reactor technology now allow controlled parallel and automated sequential processing under sealed vessel conditions, and the use of continuous or stop-flow reactors for scale-up purposes. In addition, dedicated vessels for solid-phase synthesis, for performing transformations using pre pressurized conditions and for a variety of other special applications, have been developed. Today there are four major instrument vendors that produce microwave instrumentation dedicated to organic synthesis. All these instruments offer temperature and pressure sensors, built-in magnetic stirring, power control, software operation and sophisticated safety controls. The number of users of dedicated microwave reactors is therefore growing at a rapid rate and it appears only to be a question of time until most laboratories will be equipped with suitable microwave instrumentation.Recently, microwave-assisted organic synthesis in various solvents as well as under solvent-free conditions have received tremendous investigation.[33,34] By applying microwave irradiation to certain organic reactions, it is often possible to reduce reaction times from many hours to a few minutes. In addition, recent large demand for environmentally-friendly and less hazardous chemical reaction processes have stimulated the development of clean reactions that avoid use of excess amount of toxic and volatile organic reaction solvents. In particular, microwave-assisted reactions coupled with solvent-free conditions that involve the exposure of neat reactants to microwaves received great attention. [35] This eco friendlier technique has many practical advantages over conventional methods in terms of rapid reaction, operational simplicity, cleaner reaction, and increased yield.

A recent survey has, however, found that as many as 30% of all published MAOS papers still employ kitchen microwave ovens [36], a practice banned by most of the respected scientific journals today. For example, the American Chemical Society (ACS) organic chemistry journals will typically not consider manuscripts describing the use of kitchen microwave ovens or the absence of a reaction temperature, as specified in the relevant publication guidelines [37].Microwaves do not change chemical reactions, but they can greatly increase the energy efficiency of the process. Green chemistry has been one of the keywords when microwaves have been introduced. It is hard to immediately see where microwaves are located in the field of green chemistry. The value of microwaves is that they usually reduce reaction time by efficient heating and ease the path to high temperature reactions. The synthesis of such amounts of molecules takes considerable amount of time and by reducing the reaction time from 1 hour to 10 minutes libraries are synthesized much faster. This saves on labor costs significantly and at the same time less energy is used in synthesis. Cost savings are actually one of the key points in green chemistry, since if synthesis is not economically feasible it is not green even if it produces less waste and uses microwaves. Microwaves are electromagnetic radiation with a frequency range from 300 to 300 000 MHz, with free space wavelengths of 1 m to 1 mm. The energy of microwaves is so low that only molecular rotation could be induced. Microwaves have no effect on molecular bonds or electron clouds such as infrared (IR) or the visible region of electromagnetic radiation has. The frequency used in heating applications is usually 2 450 MHz (wavelength 12.2 cm) and for industrial heating applications 915 MHz (wavelength 32.8 cm) can also be used. The development of microwave technology was initiated by the invention of radar. Radar applications needed single frequency microwaves and this demand lead to the development of the magnetron. The heating effect of microwaves was discovered by accident. Percy Spencer from Raytheon Company was the first to realize the potential of microwaves as an everyday life application. Spencer's invention lead to the first commercial microwave oven in 1954. [38-40] Microwave heating has been intensively used in analytical applications since the early days. [41]After microwave reactors were developed specially for organic chemistry (pressure, temperature and power can be precisely measured and adjusted) microwave heating has reached ever-growing popularity, especially in pharmaceutical industry. It is well known that microwaves enhance reaction rates, increase selectivities and yields. Every time when discussing with people with little or no experience in microwave heating at some point of the discussion a question about the "microwave effect" comes up. Microwave effect(s) can be seen in rare cases when the reactant acts as a solvent and no additional solvents are added. Reaction coordinates play an even more important role in this case, since reactants absorbs the microwave energy. This increases the probability of meeting of the activated complexes. There is a proposal that "hot spots" are generated in the reaction mixture and the reaction would take place mostly in the "hot spots". The existence of "hot spots" has been proved in solid and highly viscous materials, but the existence of "hot spots" in liquids is still under debate. [42, 43].

**General process of synthesis of Crown Ether by Microwave Synthesis**

**A.** (1 mL). The mixture was placed in an unmodified microwave oven for the indicated time. Progress of the reaction was monitored by TLC. After completion of the reaction, the resulting thick, brown slurry was diluted with dichloromethane (10 mL) and filtered. The filtrate was dried over MgSO4 and evaporated to dryness to afford the corresponding crown ether. The final product was purified by vacuum distillation.

**B.** A finely mixed diol (10 mmol), alkyl dichloride (10 mmol), and sodium hydroxide (0.8 g, 20 mmol) in DMSO (2 mL) was irradiated in a microwave oven at 700 W for 8 min. The reaction temperature was raised to $95^0$C in the course of the reaction. After the reaction was completed (TLC), the reaction mixture was cooled, treated with concentrated HCl (5 mL), and extracted with dichloromethane (2x20 mL). The organic layer was washed with water (10 mL), dried over anhydrous MgSO4 and evaporated. The final crude product was purified by vacuum distillation or recrystallization from n-heptane.

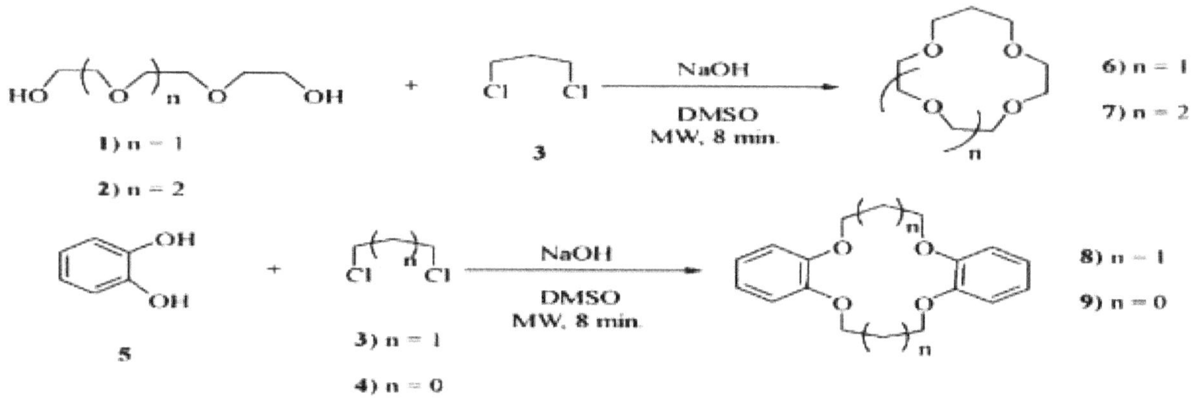

## c) Ionic liquid for synthesis of Crown Ether Compounds

The history of ionic liquids (ILs) starts from 1914 when the synthesis of ethyl ammonium nitrate was carried out. [44] The first ILs with chloroaluminate anion was published in 1948. [45, 46] Spectroscopy and electrochemical studies were carried out in the 1970s [47-49], and solvent properties were studied in the 1980s. [50-56] In 1967 liquid salt based on tetrahexyl ammonium benzoate was reported. [57] It was not until 1980 that interest toward ionic liquids was really awoken. The focus on the etherification part of the literature survey is on recent research on the classical Williamson ether synthesis (see Fig. 63) and on the reaction of epoxides with oxygen nucleophiles.

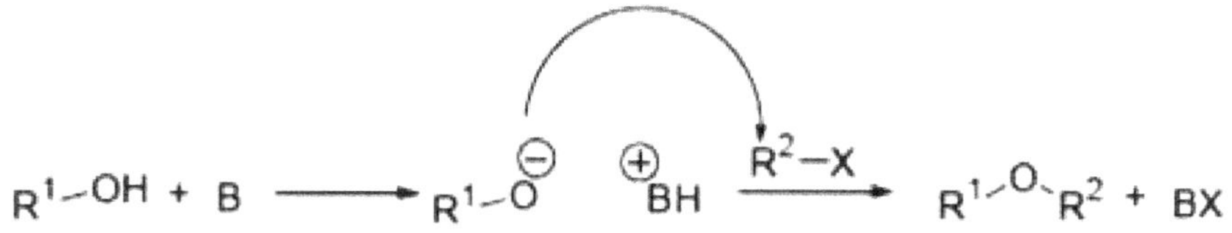

**Figure 6. Reaction mechanism for Williamson ether synthesis (R1 = R2 = Alkyl or aryl, B = base)**

The etherification of alcohols was challenging for ionic liquids because basic reaction conditions were required. Only little was known about using ionic liquids under basic conditions when project was started. Developing ionic liquids for basic conditions was one of the key issues in succeeding in etherification reactions. The ultimate goal would be to manufacture basic ionic liquids. The etherification reaction is usually carried out under basic conditions. Basic conditions were not used extensively with ionic liquids when this study was started. The carboxy methyl and quaternary ammonium groups attached to starch have been used in the paper industry for increasing fiber wet strength. Since a new process for acetylation was realized, etherification could be improved with ionic liquids as well. The experience gained so far had shown that [BMIM][Cl] was the only choice to use in carbohydrate chemistry. It was published that [BMIM]-salts were successfully used with bases such as KOH and NaOH. [58] These pieces of information provided the starting point for studying etherification's in ionic liquid.

**d) General methods for synthesis of Crown ether compounds**

The first synthesis of crowns was achieved in an attempt to prepare an alkyl phenolic ether. An unexpected product was obtained instead, due to the presence of contaminating catechol in the reaction mixture. The product was isolated to be dibenzo- 18-Crown-6. Many other crowns were subsequently prepared in Pederson's laboratory. The general methods for the synthesis of crown ethers are given below.

**General Method**

Compound **1** (1 mmol) and an appropriate dihydroxy compound were mixed with polyethylene p-toulenesulphonate in presence of methyl cyanide and heating upto $80^0C$. Although these methods showed high efficiency for benzocrown ether synthesis, they also have certain disadvantages. The latter method which was developed by Bartsch and coworkers also gave high yields for the synthesis of crown ethers with benzo group substituents. Benzo-12-crown-4 30 was obtained 29% yield by this method. Now days in conventional methods some cesium cations are use to enhanced the yield of reaction Bartsch's approach used CsF which is more expensive than $CS_2CO_3$. Also fluoride anion can act as a nucleophilie and produce competitive displacement reactions on polyethylene glycol ditosylates. [59] Therefore, optimization of reaction conditions becomes very important.

In the current research, a new combination of reagents for the cesium-assisted cyclization was discovered and evaluated for the preparation of monobenzo or dibenzocrown ethers with varying ring sizes. Cesium carbonate was chosen as the base due to its cheaper price than cesium fluoride, availability and a proven effectiveness for macrocyclization. Mesylate was selected as the leaving group because of its higher reactivity than tosylate. Acetonitrile was used as the reaction solvent because its appropriate boiling point as well as high dielectric constant and polar aprotic nature which should provide good solubility for the reactants and possible rate enhancement of reaction. But still we are working for hrs so reduced this span we have to think for advanced technique and yes it is micro wave assisted synthesis now below information about synthesis in different medium and its yield are give this will prepared by conventional methods only [60]

**Table 5: Showing % Yield of ether**

| Reactants and Solvent | Yield (%) |
| --- | --- |
| catechol, ditosylate, CsF, CH3CN | 29 |
| catechol, dimesylate, CS2CO3, CH3CN | 45 |
| catechol, dichloride, NaOH, 1-BuOH | 4 |

Ts= p-Toluenesulfonate

29%

**e) Yield and time of synthesis of Crown ether compound**

Yield and time of synthesis of crown ether compounds varied according to the techniques are used for the synthesis. As microwave technique is so liable it take less time for completion than other methods and also improve the yield of the reaction.

**For example**

"SYNTHESIS OF DIBENZO-14-CROWN-4" by conventional method as well as micro wave method. This will change the trend of synthesis by traditional method means by simple heating. 1, 2-dihydroxybenzene (1.21 g, 0.011 mol), sodium hydroxide (0.8 g, 0.02 mol), and 1, 3-dichloropropane (1.12, 0.01 mol) were mixed in DMSO (1 mL). The mixture was placed in a household microwave oven for 8 min. The crude product was taken up in conc. HCl (2 mL) and filtered. The filtrate was extracted with $CHCl_3$, dried, and evaporated to afford a crude residue, which was crystallized from n-heptane to afford the title compound. Yield 72%, m.p. 150, 150–152 lit. [61] This compound when synthesized bye general methods of crown ether synthesis gives 92%yield. Here after work up and purification chromatography dibenzo-14-crown-4 was obtained in 92% yield. This is a dramatic yield improvement from the 27% reported by Pedersen. [62] No 2 + 2 adduct was detected by TLC. In view of the smaller ring size, the absence of 2 + 2 adduct is remarkable. but the process is as follows Under nitrogen, the diol or bisphenol (2.09 g, 19.0 mmol) was dissolved in 100 mL of MeCN and powdered $CS_2CO_3$ (15.48 g, 47.50 mmol) was added. The resulting mixture was refluxed for 3 h. To the mixture, the appropriate dimesylate (6.48 g, 19.0 mmol) in 50 mL of MeCN was added during an 8-h period with a syringe pump. After an additional 24 h at reflux, the reaction mixture was cooled to room temperature and filtered through a pad of Celite on a sintered glass funnel. The collected solid was washed with $CH_2Cl_2$ (20 mL). The combined filtrate and washing were evaporated in vacuo and the residue was dissolved in $CH_2Cl_2$ (100 mL). The solution was washed with water (50 mL) and dried over $MgSO_4$. After evaporation of solvent in vacuo, the residue was chromatographed on alumina with EtOAc as eluent this process is time consuming and that's why we are not use this method for industrial purpose. {The crude product was chromatographed on alumina with EtOAc-hexane (1:3) as eluent to give a white solid with mp 149-151 $^0$C (lit) mp 150-152 $^0$C in 92% yield. IR (deposit from chloroform on a NaCl plate): 1126 (C-0) cm-l. 1H NMR ($CDCl_3$): 5 2.28 (m, 4H), 4.25 **(t,** 8H), 6.92 (m, 8H).}

Synthesis of dibenzo-14-crown-4 by microwave assisted technique (1a) and general heating with reagents are(1b) as follows

1a.

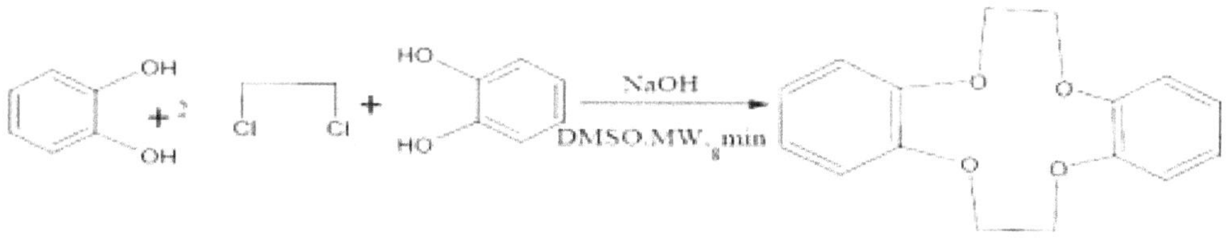

1b.

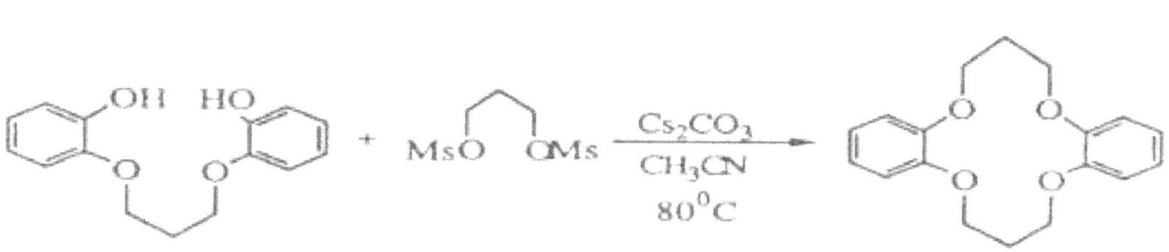

**Table 6. Comparison of Cyclization Yields for Reaction at different conditions**

| Compound | Ring Size | Yield (%) for synthesis with | | | Reference |
|---|---|---|---|---|---|
| | | $CS_2CO_3$/ dimesvlate | MOH/ dihalide | MW | |
| dibenzo-14-crown-4 | 14C4 | 92 (37 hrs) | 27 (more than 48 hrs) | 72(8 to 15 min) | 61-62 |

## Conclusion and Recommendation

Microwave assisted organic chemistry is a relatively new technology that has been shown to significantly improve productivity in the rapid generation of complex molecules. Crown ether synthesis is done by simple chemical reaction with reflux heating and using different reagents and yield also increases in some synthesis. But microwave assisted technique important because by this process synthesis of crown ether is done within minutes rather go for reflux heating for hours with good yield and purity as less side product. In ionic liquid synthesis yield is so good but because of more time consumption and cost of ionic liquid makes matter. Hence synthesis done in minutes increases the production and yield of crown ether. Before assessment of this microwave technique synthesis of crown ether is tedious job but now we get easily crown ether for research purpose, as industrial reagents because of its versatility, now today crown ether are used for different purpose. Micro wave assisted synthesis called as one time investment and low manual work with beneficial yield.

## References


1) Xing, R.G.; Liu, S.; Yu, H.H.; Guo, Z.Y.; Wang, P.B.; Li, C.P.; Li, Z.; Li, P.C.. Salt-assisted acid hydrolysis of chitosan to oligomers under microwave irradiation. Carbohydr. *Res.*, 2005, 340 : 2150-2153.
2) Sha, Y.W.; Wang, Y.; Ge, J.; Wang, X.. Application of microwave irradiation in the synthesis of heterocyclic compounds. *Chin. J. Org. Chem.*, 2001, 21: 102-115.
3) a) C. J. Pederson,. The discovery of crown ethers (Noble Lecture). *J. Am. Chem. Soc.* 1967, 89: 7017.
4) For reviews on Crown Ether Chemistry, see a) C. J. Pedersen and H. K. Frensdorff,. Angew. Chem. *Int. Ed. Engl.*, 1972, 11: 16; b) J. J. Christensen, D. T. Eatough, and R. M. Izatt,. *Chem. Rev.*, 1974, 74: 351; c) G.W. Gokel and D. J. Cram,. *J. Org. Chem.*, 1974, 39: 2445.
5) G. Gokel, Crown Ethers and Cryptands. *Royal Society of Chemistry, Cambridge* (1991).
6) Gedye, R., Smith, F.,Westaway, K., Ali, H., Baldisera, L., Laberge, L. and Rousell, J.. The Use of Microwave Ovens for Rapid Organic Synthesis. *Tetrahedron Letters,* 1986, 27: 279–282.
7) F. L. Cook, T. C. Caruso, M. P. Byrne, C. W. Bowers, D. H. Speck, C. L. Liotta,. Preparation of derivatives and analogs of the macrocyclic oligomers of ethylene oxide (crown compounds).*Tetrahedron Lett.*, 1974, 46: 4029.
8) Gedye, R.N.;Smith F.; Westaway, K.; Ali. H.: Baldisera. L.; Laberge. L.; Rousell. *J.Tetrahedron Lett.* 1986, 27,279-282.
9) Loupy,A,;Petit.A.;Hamelin, J.;Texier-Boullet. F.;Jacquault.P.;Mathe,D.. New solvent-free organic synthesis using focused microwaves.. *Synthesis* 1998, 1213-1234.

10) Verma,R.S.. Solvent-free organic syntheses. using supported reagents and microwave irradiation. *Green Chem..* 1999, 43-55.

11) Pedersen CJ,. Cyclic Poliethers and Their Complexes with Metal Salts, *J. Am. Chem. Soc* 1967, 89: 7017-7036.

12) Vögtle F, Weber E, Host-Guest Complex Chemistry: Macrocycles, *Spinger Verlag, Heidelberg,* 1985.

13) Steed JW, Atwood JL, Supramolecular Chemistry, *JohnWiley & Sons Ltd, New York,* 2000.

14) Pedersen CJ,. Die Entdeckung der Kronenether (Nobel-Vortrag), *Angew. Chem.* 1988, 100: 1053-1059.

15) Cram DJ,. Von molekularen Wirten und Gästen sowie ihren Komplexen (Nobel-Vortrag). *Angew. Chem.* 1988, 100 : 1041-1052.

16) Lehn J-M.. Supramolekulare Chemie-Moleküle, Übermoleküle und molekulare Funktionseinheiten (Nobel-Vortrag), *Angew. Chem.* 1988, 100: 91-116.

17) Izatt RM, Wang TM, Hathaway JK, Zhang XX, Curtis JC, Bradshaw JS, Zhu CY, Huszthy P,. Factors Influencing Enantiomeric Recognition of Primary Alkylammonium Salts by Pyridino-18-crown-6 Type Ligands, *J. Incl. Phenom. Mol. Recogn. Chem.* 1994, 17: 157-175.

18) Pedersen, C. J.. Cyclic polyethers and their complexes with metal salts. *J. Am. Chem. Soc.* 1980, 80: 2495.

19) Izatt, R. M.; Bradshaw, J. S.; Nielsen, S. A.; Lam, J. D.; Christensen,J. J.: Thermodynamic and kinetic data for cation-macrocycle interaction. *Chem. Rev.* 1985, 85: 271.

20) Shannon, R. D.; Prewitt, C. T.. Effective Ionic Radii in Oxides and Fluorides. *Acta Crvst..* 1969, B25: 925.

21) Shannon, R. D.. Revised Effective Ionic Radii and Systematic Studies of Interatomie Distances in Halides and Chaleogenides. *Acta Crvst.* 1976, A32: 751.

22) Story, P. R.; Bush, P.. Advances in Organic Chemistry. *Wiley-Interscience*, New York, 1972, 8: 67-95.

23) Pedersen, C. J.. Cyclic polyethers and their complexes with metal salts. *J. Am. Chem. Soc..* 1967, 89: 7017.

24) Lehn, J. M.. Structure and Bonding 1973, 16: 1.

25) Kappe C. O., Dallinger D.. The impact of microwave synthesis on drug discovery. *Nat. Rev. Drug Discovery*, 2006, 5: 51-63.

26) Kappe C. O., Dallinger D., Murphree S. S., Practical microwave synthesis for organic chemists - Strategies, instruments, and protocols. 1st Ed. Wiley- VCH, Verlag GmbH & Co. KGaA, Weinheim, 2009.

27) Tierney J.P., Lidström P., Eds., Microwave assisted organic synthesis. *Blackwell Publishing, Oxford*, 2005.

28) Larhed M., Hallberg A.. Microwave-assisted high speed chemistry: A new technique in drug disvovery. *Drug Discovery Today*, 2001, 6: 406-416.

29) Microwave-assisted synthesis in the pharmaceutical industry -a current perspective and future prospects.2006.

30) Lidstrom P., Tierney J., Wathey B., Westman J.. Microwave assisted organic synthesis-a review. *Tetrahedron.*, 2001, 57: 9225–9283.

31) Martínez-Palou R.. Ionic liquid and microwaveassisted organic synthesis: A "green" and synergic couple. *J. Mex. Chem. Soc.* 2007, 51: 252-264.

32) Algul O., Kaessler A., Apcin Y., Yilmaz A., Jose J.. Comparative studies on conventional and microwave synthesis of some benzimidazole, benzothiazole and indole derivatives and testing on inhibition of hyaluronidase. *Molecules*, 2008, 13: 736-748.

33) Sawyer, J. S.; Schmittling, E. A.; Palkowitz, J. A.; Smith, W. J.. Arene Chemistry: Reaction Mechanisms and Methods for Aromatic Compounds. *J. Org. Chem.* 1998, 63: 6338.

34) Perreux, L.; Loupy, A.. Pyrazole alkylation in basic media. *Tetrahedron* 2001, 57: 9199.

35) Lidström, P.; Tierney, J.; Wathey, B.; Westman, J.. Microwave Assisted Organic Synthesis—A Review. *Tetrahedron* 2001, 57: 9225.

36) Varma, R. S.. "Greener" chemical syntheses using mechanochemical mixing or microwave and ultrasound irradiation. *Green Chemistry* 2007, 1(1): 37-45.

37) C. Oliver Kappe, Doris Dallinger, and S. Shaun Murphree. Practical Microwave Synthesis for Organic Chemists: *Strategies, Instruments, and Protocols.* 2009.

38) M. Antonia Herrero, Jennifer M. Kremsner, and C. Oliver Kappe.. Nonthermal Microwave Effects Revisited: On the Importance of Internal Temperature Monitoring and Agitation in Microwave Chemistry. *J. Org. Chem.* 2008, 73 (1): 36–47.

39) Spencer P. High-frequency apparatus, 1952.

40) Spencer P, L . Method of treating foodstuff. US patent US patent office. 1950, 2605383.

41) Spencer P, L. Means of treating foodstuff, 1952.

42) Kingston HM & Jassie LB.. Introduction to Microwave Sample Preparation Theory and Practice. *ACS publishing*, 1988.

43) Hayes BL.. Microwave Synthesis - Chemistry at the Speed of Light. CEM Publishing, *Matthews*, 2002.

44) Loupy Ae .. Microwaves in organic synthesis. *Wiley-VCH, Weinheim,* 2002.

45) Walden P. Bulletin of Academy Imperial Science: 1914, 1800.

46) Hurley FH.. Electrodeposition of aluminium. US. Patent. U. p. office, 1948, 4: 446,331

47) Wier Jr. TP & Hurley FH.. Electrodeposition of aluminium. US. Patent. U. P. 1948

48) Chum HL, Koch VR, Miller LL & Osteryoung RA.. Electrochemical scrutiny of organometallic iron complexes and hexamethylbenzene in a room temperature molten salt. *Journal of American Chemical Society* 1975, 97(11): 3264.

49) Gale RJ, Gilbert B & Osteryoung RA.. Raman spectra of molten aluminum chloride: 1-butylpyridinium chloride systems at ambient temperatures. *Inorganic Chemistry* 1978, 17(10): 2728.

50) Robinson J & Osteryoung RA.. An electrochemical and spectroscopic study of some aromatic hydrocarbons in the room temperature molten salt system aluminum, 1979.

51) Appleby D, Hussey CL, Seddon KR & Turp JE.. Room-temperature ionic liquids as solvents for electronic absorption spectroscopy of halide complexes. *Nature* 1986, 323(6089): 614.

52) Dent AJ, Seddon KR & Welton T.The structure of halogenometallate complexes dissolved in both basic and acidic room-temperature halogenoaluminate (III) ionic liquids, as determined by EXAFS. *Journal of Chemical*, 1990.

53) Hussey CL.. Room temperature haloaluminate ionic liquids. Novel solvents for transition metal solution chemistry. *Pure and applied Chemistry* 1988, 60(12): 1763.

54) Laher TM & Hussey CL.. Copper(I) and copper(II) chloro complexes in the basic aluminum chloride-1-methyl-3-ethylimidazolium chloride ionic liquid. *Inorganic Chemistry* 1983, 22(22): 3247.

55) Scheffler TB & Hussey CL.. Electrochemical study of tungsten chlorcomplex chemistry in the basic aluminum chloride-1-methyl-3-ethylimidazolium chloride ionic liquid. *Inorganic Chemistry* 1984, 23(13): 1926.

56) Scheffler TB, Hussey CL, Richard SK, Kear CM & Armitage PD.. Molybdenum chloro complexes in room-temperature chloroaluminate ionic liquids: stabilization of hexachloromolybdate(2-) and hexachloromolyb date(3-). *Inorganic Chemistry* 1983, 22(15): 2099.

57) Wilkes JS, Levisky JA, A. WR & Hussey CL. Dialkylimidazolium chloroaluminate melts: a new class of room-temperature ionic liquids for electrochemistry, spectroscopy and synthesis. *Inorganic Chemistry* 1982, 21(3): 1263.

58) Swain CG, Ohno A, Roe DK, Brown R & Maugh T.. Tetrahexylammonium benzoate, a liquid salt at 25.degree., a solvent for kinetics or electrochemistry. *Journal of American Chemical Society* 1967, 89(11): 2648.

59) Wasserscheid P & Welton T.. Ionic Liquids in Synthesis. Wiley-VCH, Weinheim. Auke, G. T.; Vossen, H.V.; Sudholter, E. J. R.; Erden, J. V.; Reinhoudt, D. N.1986. *Synthesis* 2003, 680.

60) Czech, B. P.; Czech, A.; Bartsch, R. A.. Synthesis of hydroxymethyl-functionalized diazacrowns and cryptands *J. Heterocvcl. Chem* 1986, . 1297.

61) Yingdi Li, Yifei Teng, Ziqing Zhang, Yi Feng, Peng Xue, Wenming Tonga and Xiaoyang Liu.. Microwave-assisted synthesis of novel nanostructured Zn3(OH)2V2O7·2H2O and Zn2V2O7 as electrode materials for supercapacitors. *New J. Chem.* 2017, 41: 15298-15304.

62) Sangita Mandal, Swagata Mandal, Sumanta K. Ghosh, Pintu Sar, Aniruddha Ghosh, Rumpa Sahab and Bidyut Saha.. A review on the advancement of ether synthesis from organic solvent to water. *RSC Adv.* 2016, 6: 69

# CHAPTER – 7

# CONDUCTION MECHANISM OF BLEND POLYMER FILM

## BY
## R Y Bakale, Y G Bakale, S V Khangar


**Abstract**

The electrical conduction mechanism of blend film (PVC and PMMA) has been studied at various temperatures in the range 313K to 353K. The results are presented in the form of I-V characteristics. Analysis has been made in the light of Poole-Frenkel, Fowler-Nordheim, Schottky, Ln(J) versus T plots, Richardson and Arrhenius plots. Results analysed suggest that, Schottky-Richardson mechanism is primarily responsible for observed conduction.

**Keywords:** Blend film, Conductivity.


## Introduction

A good amount of work has been reported on conduction mechanism in polymeric materials during past few years. Polymers are not simple covalent crystals of conventional solid state physics.[1] They exist as crystalline materials, as amorphous materials or as a mixture of crystalline and amorphous materials. The electrical conduction in iodine doped polystyrene (PS) and polymethyl methacrylate (PMMA) has already been reported.[2,3] Japanese scientists have been particularly active in early research and development of these devices with work[4] on natural and synthesis polymers. Most of the early polymer electret work in US has been focused on using the polyelectric response for electromagnetic radiation detection.[5,6]Burghate et al.[7] have reported the electrical conduction mechanism of succinic acid doped glycine pellet. The dc-conductivity of glycine was measured by Mishra et al.[8] to study the mechanism of electrical conduction. Belsare et al.[9] have reported the increase in electrical conductivity of polystyrene (PS) and polymethyl methacrylate (PMMA) with the increase in iodine doping concentration. In the case of organic solids, whose conductivity due to electrons excited from valence band to conduction band[10,11] is negligible, a complex conduction behaviour[11,12] has been explained usually in terms of electron emission from cathode i.e. Schottky-Richardson mechanism[13] or by electron liberation from the traps in the bulk of the material i.e. Poole-Frankel mechanism.[14] The possibility of tunneling[15], space charge limited conduction[16] etc. have also been investigated in the literature. In the present chapter, dc-conductivity of blend film (PVC and PMMA) was measured to identify the mechanism of electrical conduction. It is shown how the I-V data of the sample can be used to arrive at possible conclusions. Results have been discussed by plotting different mechanisms, such as Poole-Frenkel, Fowler-Nordheim, log (J) versus T plots, Schottky plots, Richardson plots and Arrhenius plots. In case of Schottky-Richardson mechanism, the current shows strong temperature dependence but not in case of Poole-Frenkel mechanism. The study of temperature dependence of current density is, therefore, of great importance.

## Experimental Details

The polyvinyl chloride (PVC) of commercial grade supplied by Polychem Industries, Mumbai and polymethyl methacrylate (PMMA) supplied by Dental Products of India Ltd., Mumbai, were used for the study.

## Preparation of samples

For the preparation of films, 1.5 gm of PVC and 0.5 gm PMMA were dissolved in 20 ml of tetrahydrofuran (THF) (AR grade) and uniform solution was obtained by subjecting it to 2 hours heating at a constant temperature 313 K. The solution so prepared was gradually and carefully poured over a perfectly plane and clean glass plate, which was kept floating on a pool of mercury, for leveling, thereby ensuring uniform thickness of the film. The whole system was placed inside the constant temperature and dust free chamber, to allow the solvent to evaporate completely. In this way the films were prepared by isothermal evaporation technique.[17-18] The films were subjected to 12 hours heating at constant temperature, to remove the traces of solvent. Both the sides of the sample film were coated with quick drying silver paint (supplied by Elteck Pvt. Ltd., Bangalore) to ensure good electrical contacts. The coated sample film was subjected to uniform heating at a temperature of 353K in furnace.

## Measurements:

For the measurement of current and voltages, the thermostatically controlled furnace supplied by Tempo Industrial Corporation, Mumbai, was used for heating purpose. The mercury thermometer with an accuracy $\pm$ 1°C was used to record the temperatures. The regulated power supply supplied by Nuper India was used as the voltage source, while the current was recorded by using highly sensitive Pico-Ammeter (Model DPA III with accuracy $\pm$0.2% supplied by Scientific Equipments, Roorkee). The sample pellet coated with silver electrodes was sandwiched between two brass-electrodes of the sample holder specially fabricated in the laboratory having electrode diameter of 2.4 cm each. This formed the metal-insulator-metal (M-I-M) system, which was placed in a furnace. The current (I) - voltage (V) measurements have been made at various constant temperatures from 313K to 353K.

## Results and Discussion:

The ln I - ln V plots of sample at various temperatures 313, 323, 333, 343 and 353K are shown in Fig. 1. The current increases non-linearly with the applied voltage and does not follow a power law, $I = kV^m$, where k and m are constant.

The current in the beginning at low values of voltages increases at a faster rate while it increases at a slower rate, at higher values of voltages. Figure 1 indicates that    (i) the current at a constant temperature increases with applied voltage (ii) the current at constant applied voltage increases with temperature. The mechanism operative in present case is discussed in the light of the Poole-Frenkel, Fowler-Nordheim, and Schottky, ln (J) versus T plots, Richardson and Arrhenius plots.

**Fig 1 : Current Voltage Characteristics**

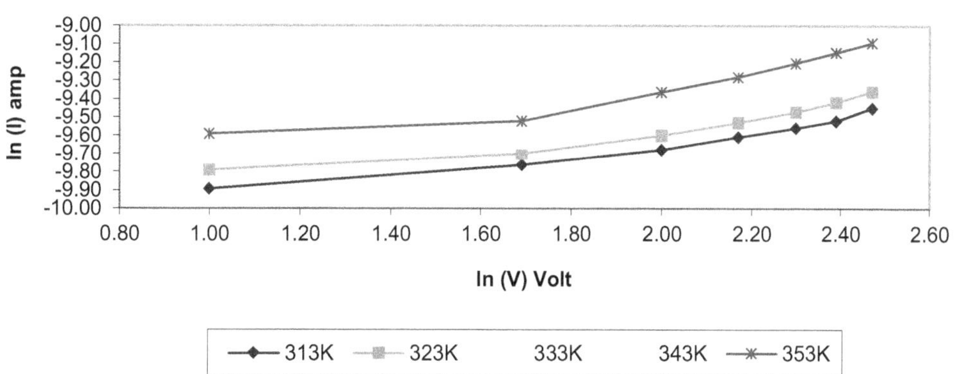

**Poole-Frenkel Mechanism:**

The current-voltage relationship for Poole-Frenkel mechanism[19] is expressed as,

$$J = Be^{\frac{-\phi}{kT} + \beta_{pf} E^{1/2}}$$

$$\text{Where} = \beta_{pf} = \frac{\rho}{kT}\left[\frac{\rho}{\pi \in \in_0 d}\right]^{1/2} = \text{constant} \quad \text{--------------- (1)}$$

and predicts a field dependent conductivity as

$$\sigma = \sigma_0 e^{\frac{\beta_{pf} E^{1/2}}{2kT}} \quad \text{------------------ (2)}$$

or

$$\log \sigma = \sigma_0 + \frac{\beta_{pf}}{2kT} E^{1/2} \quad \text{------------------ (3)}$$

so that the Poole-Frenkel mechanism is characterized by the linearity of $\ln\sigma$ versus $E^{1/2}$ plots i.e. Poole-Frenkel plots predicted by Eq. 3 are linear with a positive slope.In the present case of PVC and PMMA blend film the $\ln \sigma$ versus $E^{1/2}$ plots are linear but with a -ve slope (Fig. 2) indicating the absence of PF mechanism.

**Fig 2 : Poole Frenkel Plots**

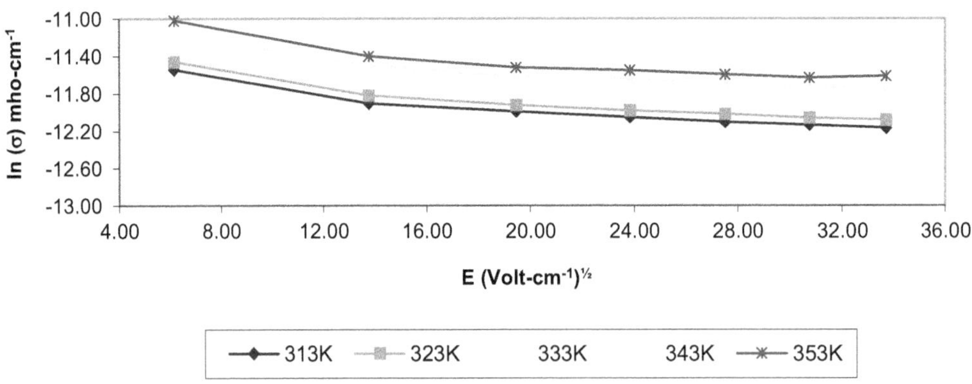


**Fowler-Nordheim Mechanism:**

The Fowler-Nordheim relation[20] for current density is $J = AV^2 e^{\frac{-\phi}{v}}$

$$\text{so that, } \ln \frac{J}{V^2} = \ln A - \left(\frac{-\phi}{V}\right)$$

And the ln (J/V²) versus 1/V plot is expected to be linear relation with a -ve slope. In this case the ln (J/V²) versus 1/V plot for the sample is presented in    Fig. 3 excepting few points which have strayed away, the graphs are nearly straight line with a +ve slope, indicative of the absence of tunneling current as is suggested by F-N relation.

**Fig 3 : Fowler-Nordheim Plots**

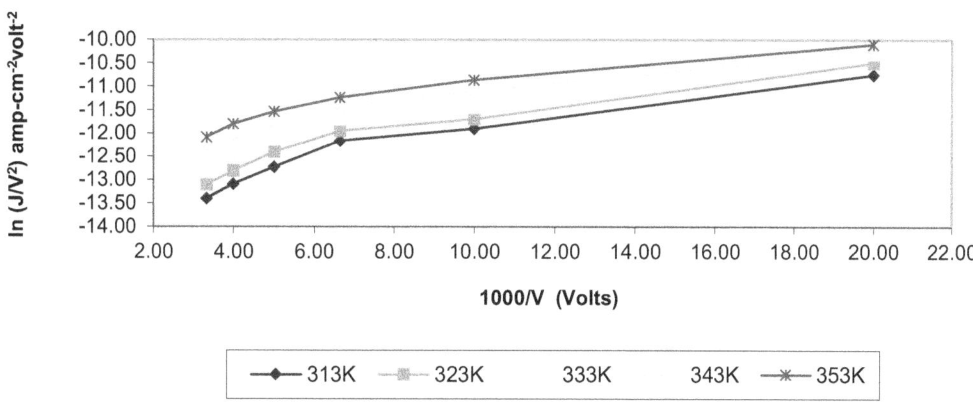



**Schottky plots:**

Thermal activation of electron, may occur over the metal insulator interface barrier, which is further helped by the applied electric field effect, which reduces the height of the barrier. The Schottky-Richardson current voltage relationship is expressed as:

$$J = AT^2 e^{\frac{-\phi_s}{kT} + \beta_{SR} E^{1/2}}$$

$\beta_{SR}$ being the field lowering constant given by

$$\beta_{SR} = \frac{e}{kT} \left( \frac{e}{4\pi \in \in_0 d} \right)^{1/2}$$

and hence $\ln J = \ln AT^2 - \dfrac{-\phi_s}{kT} + \beta_{SR} E^{1/2}$ and that ln J versus $\sqrt{E}$ plot should be a straight line with a +ve slope.

Schottky plots for the present case are shown in Fig. 4. The relation expects a +ve slope, which is observed in the present case, and as such indicates the applicability of the mechanism. Further, in case of Schottky-Richardson mechanism the current shows strong-temperature dependence but not in case of Poole-Frenkel mechanism. The study of temperature dependence of current density is, therefore, of great importance.

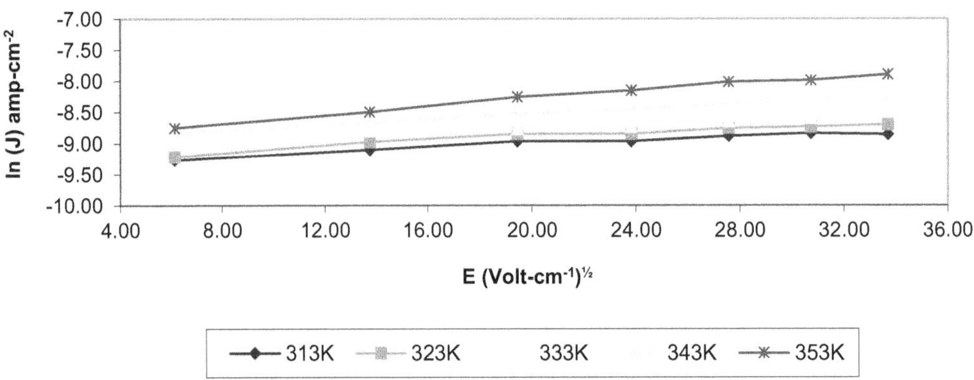



**Current density versus temperature plots:**

The temperature dependence of current density is presented in the form of ln J versus T plots in Fig. 5, which shows that ln J increases non-linearly with temperature. The strong temperature dependence is in agreement with the Schottky-Richardson mechanism.

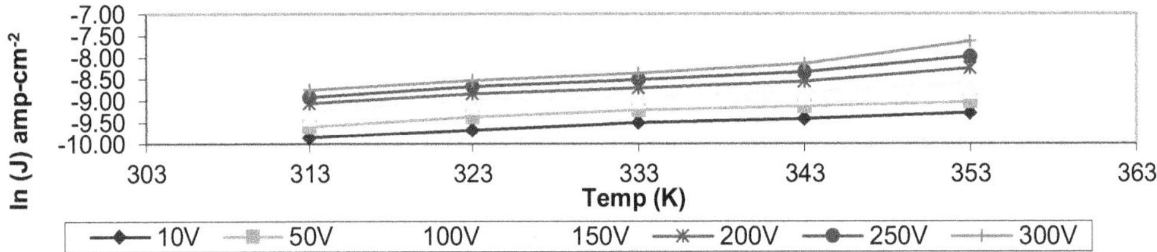



**Richardson mechanism:**

The Richardson current voltage relationship is expressed as,

$$J = AT^2 e^{\frac{-\phi_s}{kT} + \beta_{SR} E^{1/2}}$$

$$\frac{J}{T^2} = A e^{\frac{-\phi_s}{kT} + \beta_{SR} E^{1/2}}$$

$$\log \frac{J}{T^2} = \log A + \left( \frac{-\phi_s}{kT} + \phi_{SR} E^{1/2} \right)$$

$$\log \frac{J}{T^2} = \log A + \beta_{SR} E^{1/2} - \frac{\phi_s}{kT}$$

The graph between $J/T^2$ versus $1/kT$ plots from this relation should be a straight line with a negative slope.

In the present case straight line graphs have been obtained with a -ve slope excepting one or two points. The linearity of the plots support Schottky-Richardson mechanism (Fig. 6).

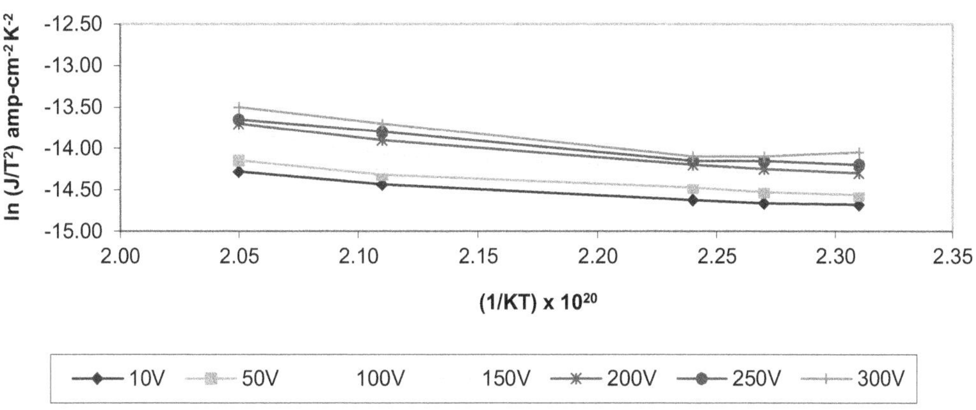

**Fig 6 : Richardson Plots**



**Arrhenius plots:**

The $\ln \sigma$ versus $1/T$ plots (Fig. 7) at all values of applied voltages show parallel straight line with -ve slope. From the slope of straight line, the activation energy is calculated and is found to be in the neighbourhood of 0.13 eV. This is in good agreement with the reported order of magnitudes.

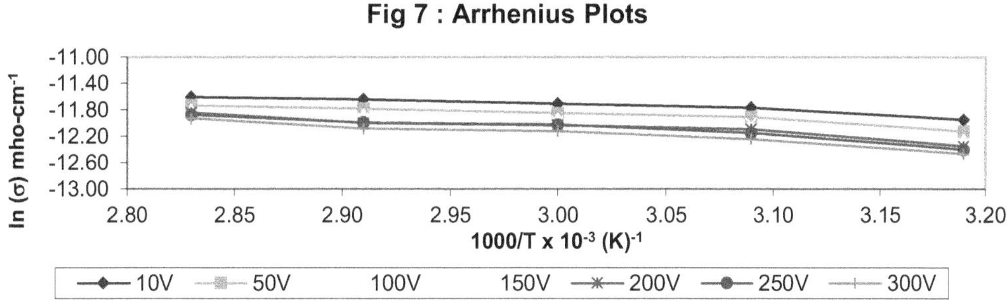

**Fig 7 : Arrhenius Plots**



**Conclusion:**

S-R mechanism of conduction predominates over other mechanisms in the sample. The applied field value seems to be insufficient to liberate electron from traps, showing absence of PF mechanism. Even though the electric field value and the temperature range is lower to activate contribution from other mechanism, yet the activation energy can safely be calculated and is found to be well within range for similar samples.

**References**


1) Seanor D A, *Electrical properties of polymers* (D A Seanor Ed) chapter 1 Academic Press New York London 1982
2) Chakraborty S C, Patil N B, Das S K & Basu S, *Indian J Pure & Appl Phys*, 29(1991) 478
3) Sangwar V S, *PhD Thesis*, Amravati University (1995)

4) Fukada E, *Prog poly sci*, Jan 2 (1971) 329

5) Mefee J H, Borgman T G & Crane G R, *Ferroelectric*, 3 (1972) 305

6) Kepler R G, Greaber E J & Beeson P M, *Bulletin APS* Series 1120 (1975) 350

7) Burghate D K, Deshmukh S H, Akhare V P, Laxmi Joshi and Deogaonkar V S, *Indian J Phys*, 78A(3) (2004) 331-335

8) Mishra V & Nath R, *Indian J Pure & Appl Phys*, 35 (1997) 514

9) Belsare N G & Deogaonkar V S, *Indian J Pure & Appl Phys*, 36 (1998) 280

10) Keton J E (Ed), *Organic semiconducting polymers* (Marcel, Dekker, New York) (1968) 267

11) Pavan Khare & Shrivastav A P, *Indian J Pure & Appl Phys*, 29 (1991) 1410

12) Parak N C & Garg T C, *Indian J Pure & Appl Phys*, 25 (1987) 110

13) Schottky W Z, *Phys*, 15 (1994) 872

14) Frenkel J, *Phys Rev*, 54 (1938) 647

15) Fowler R H & Nordheim L, *Proc Roy Soc London*, 119 (1928) 173

16) Rose A, Phys Rev, 97 (1955) 1538

17) Narayan A and Singh H P, *Indian J Pure & Appl Phys*, 29(1991) 814-816

18) Bhari R and Seth R K, *Indian J Pure & Appl Phys*, 35(1997) 104-108

19) Frenkel J, *Phys Rev*, 54 (1938) 647

20) Fowler R H & Nordheim L, *Proc Roy Soc London*, 119 (1928) 173

# CHAPTER – 8

# A STUDY ON IMPACT OF VIRTUAL LEARNING IN EDUCATION SYSTEM

BY
**Rajesh Gupta**

## Abstract

This study explores the impact of virtual learning classes, it also shows different pros and cons of virtual classes on teachers as well as students. In this study my primary objective is to elicit perception of students about virtual class based on learning experience from virtual classes. Virtual learning is used nowadays as another option to face to face education. As a matter of fact, it rises the trend in a direct proportion with the increase of the number of learners in this pandemic situation.Eradicate the distance constraint, Flexible timing of classes, easily interactive and easy assessment process with the help of technology are the pillar of virtual classes.This study mainly focused on exploratory research design, in this study I used convenience sampling, for this study I conducted collected data from different teachers & students of Rajiv Gandhi Proudyogiki Vishwavidyalaya (state technological university of Madhya Pradesh). In this study I have used questionnaire as sampling tools for collection the data.

**Keywords:** online education, online teaching, virtuallearning, online learning.

## Introduction

Virtual learning is used nowadays as another option to face to face education. As a matter of fact, it rises the trend in a direct proportion with the increase of the number of learners in this pandemic situation. This has made educators brings a lot of effort to help the learners to get interactive material that is beset withaudiovisual aid as it has been verified that it has a substantialupshot on the process of learning. The impression of blogs and wikis has also been examined on learners' teamwork and likeness and it was testified that they both have anoptimistic effect. Virtual learning has been presented as a device in the learning process in the majority of the international universities worldwide. In this 21st century virtual classes and online study material plays a vital role in fulfillment of need of students. In the starting of virtual classes was using for mature learners especially in distance education, but in this year 2020, due to corona pandemic many teachers and mentors using different online platforms for sharing their knowledge.Virtual learning is well-defined as any learning that includes using internet or intranet. Or to make it more effective we can say that it is everything that delivered, enabled, or mediated by electronic technology for explicit purpose of learning.The another name of virtual learning is E- learning, "E" in E-learning should not stand for electronic; it should be an abbreviation for "evolving, enhanced, everywhere, every time and everybody." In fact, the citation of demonstrations most of the benefits of e-learning or virtual learning for learners and mentors. Although the e-learning term and tools do exist for over a decade, the educational research field has not given adequateconsideration to the study of student inspiration under the effect of e-learning. E-learning has grown in significance as an educational tool just like technology has developed and progressed over the years. Remarkably, there have been more determinations at advancing technology than on trying to recognize the needs and learning styles of individual learners and instructional design.Education can become transformative when teachers and students combinematerialthrough subjects and experiences, critically evaluate significantly different standpoints, and incorporate various inquiries. Teachers are able to build such potentials by adopting critical learning spaces, in which students are cheered to grow their abilities of, imagination, analysis, creative expression, intentionality, self-awareness, and critical synthesis.Virtual classroom environment reduce the physical presence of student as well as rote learning practice and repetitive experimental tests in laboratory. In the physical classroom most of the students are not easily mixed with all the students so they cannot ask the questions in classroom. Eradicate the distance constraint, Flexible timing of classes, easily interactive and easy assessment process with the help of technology are the pillar of virtual classes. In tradition classes all students have to reach at the same place on same time, for which they have different constraints while in online classes teachers and receivers or students can teach and learn from their own house, at present different online platforms i.e. zoom, Microsoft team, google meet and MOODLES programme etc. also gives facility for sharing notes takes attendance as well as chatting option for Question & Answer.

**Origins of Online Education:**

Virtual guidance is changing the academic scene as an expanding number of researchers are looking for online training. Schools and colleges are presently touting the efficiencies of Web-based training and are quickly executing on the web classes to fulfill understudy needs around the world. One examination revealed "increments inside the quantity of online courses given by colleges are very emotional in the course of the most recent couple of years" (Lundberg et al., 2008). Research organizations likewise are dispersing insights on Web-based guidance. "In 2010, the Sloan Consortium found a 17% expansion in online understudies from the prior years, beating the 12%increase from the earlier year" (Keramidas, 2012). In opposition to mainstream thinking, online instruction isn't a substitution wonder. The essential correspondence and separation learning instructive projects were started inside the mid-1800s by the University of London. This model of instructive learning was snared in to the mail and hence wasn't found in American until the later Nineteenth century. It had been in 1873 when what's viewed as the essential authority correspondence program was set up in Boston, Massachusetts alluded to as the "General public to Encourage Home Studies." Since at that point, non-conventional examination has developed into what it's today viewed as an increasingly suitable online instructional methodology. Innovative progression apparently improved the speed and openness of separation learning courses; presently understudies worldwide could go to classes from the solace of their own homes.

**Characteristics of online and traditional face to face (f2f) classroom education:**

On the web and conventional instruction share numerous characteristics. Understudies are as yet required to go to class, get familiar with the material, submit assignments, and complete gathering ventures. While instructors, still need to structure educational programs, augment instructional quality, answer class questions, persuade understudies to learn, and grade assignments. Regardless of these essential similitudes, there are numerous contrasts between the two modalities. Generally, study hall guidance is known to be educator focused and requires detached learning by the understudy, while online guidance is frequently student centered what's more, requires dynamic learning. In educator focused, or aloof learning, the teacher typically controls homeroom elements. The instructor addresses and remarks, while understudies tune in, take notes, and pose inquiries. In understudy focused, or dynamic learning, the understudies for the most part decide study hall elements as they autonomously investigate the data, build questions, and approach the educator for explanation. In this situation, the educator, not the understudy, is tuning in, detailing, and reacting (Salcedo, 2010). In training, change accompanies questions. Despite all current reports advocating on the web instruction, scientists are still scrutinizing its viability. Examination is as yet being directed on the viability of PC helped instructing. Money saving advantage investigation, understudy understanding, and understudy execution are presently being painstakingly thought about while deciding if online instruction is a feasible substitute for classroomteaching. This choice procedure will most presumably convey into the future as innovation improves furthermore, as understudies request better learning encounters. Up to this point, "writing on the viability of online courses is sweeping and isolated" (Driscoll et al., 2012). A few investigations favor conventional study hall guidance, expressing "online students will stop all the more effectively" and "internet learning can need input for both understudies and teachers" (Atchley et al., 2013). As a result of these inadequacies, understudy maintenance, fulfillment, and execution can be undermined. Like conventional educating, separation learning additionally has its theological rationalists who assert online training produces understudies who proceed also or better than their conventional study hall partners (Westhuis et al., 2006). The preferences and weaknesses of both instructional modalities should be completely fleshed out and analyzed to genuinely figure out which medium creates better understudy execution. Bothmodalities have been demonstrated to be generally viable, be that as it may, as referenced before, the inquiry to be posed is in the event that one is genuinely better than the other.

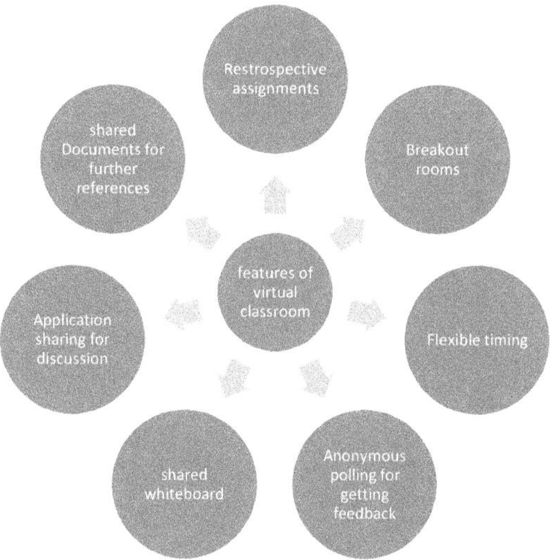


Virtual classroom is not a platform for just sharing the notes it provides the contextual, live and collaborative environment for teaching and learning. Teachers have control on learning, teaching and assessment as traditional learning system. In the technology advancement time online classes are mainly used for distance learning exclusively for mature learners. In same active learners are easily convert in passive learners in the traditional classrooms, while persons who born after 80's they are familiars with technology so they easily adopt new technology for teaching or learning.Virtual classroom is an online learning environment that encompasses all course material we can define the virtual classroom as web based system or environment which gives all opportunities for teaching and learning process beyond the physical limits of the traditional or board and chalk classroom. Before corona pandemic online learning mainly related to PPT presentation based learning or learn from different online platforms i.e. youtube etc. but after COVID situation online learning market increase more than three times in this periods. In online learning most of the material are present in open access network, in open education resources we can easily learn or read different material for class or knowledge. In present time virtual classroom provide the positive meaningful and constructive learning on internet, online classroom is also learner centered as tradition learning with the facilities of flexibility of timing, online help guidance, online quiz and examination and same time assessment facility and easily shares the notes and books on electronic forms with all at same time, chat room, discussion board etc. these features attract the learners to learn with zeal and enthusiasm, more than simply reading the books.

**Data analysis and Interpretation:**

In this survey I have collected data from different respondents by structured questionnaire. This section of survey puts emphasis on the procedure that will be followed by me during the research study. This facilities a reader to understand the research work easily and clearly. The methodologies that will use in the research study as follows.

| Research Design | Descriptive Research |
|---|---|
| **Sampling Design** | |
| Sampling Frame | Students and faculties of university |
| Sampling Size | 100 respondents |
| Sampling Methods | Convenience Sampling |
| **Data Collection Methods** | |
| Primary Data | Survey Methods |
| Secondary data | Data were collected from respondents and journals and from previous study related to the retailing sector. |
| Type of Schedule | Structure Questionnaire with suitable scaling. |

**Demographic Characteristics of respondents**

| Variable | Frequency | Frequency | Valid Percent | Cumulative Percent |
|---|---|---|---|---|
| Gender | Male | 56 | 56 | 56.00 |
| | Female | 44 | 44 | 100.00 |
| Age | Less than 20-30 Years | 42 | 42 | 42.00 |
| | 30-40 Years | 18 | 18 | 60.00 |
| | 40-50 years | 22 | 22 | 82.00 |
| | Above 50 years | 18 | 18 | |
| Educational Qualification | Bachelor Degree | 37 | 37 | 37.00 |
| | Master Degree | 43 | 43 | 80.00 |
| | Doctorate Degree | 15 | 15 | 95.00 |
| | Other | 5 | 5 | 100.00 |

**Interpretation of Likert Scale**

This study used Likert's Scale to evaluate the respondents' level. The scale is highly reliable when it comes to the ordering of people with regard to a particular satisfaction level.
N-1/N
5-1/5= 0.80

**Table of Likert's Scale:**

| Results | Interpretation of weighting level |
|---|---|
| 4.21-5.00 | Strongly Agree |
| 3.41-4.20 | Agree |
| 2.61-3.40 | Neutral |
| 1.81-2.60 | Disagree |
| 1.00-1.80 | Strongly Disagree |

**On the basis of above scale, I have conclude following results**

| FACTOR | MEAN VALUE | STANDARD DEVIATION | RESULT |
|---|---|---|---|
| sharing notes in virtual classroom | 4.40 | 1.05 | Strongly agree |
| Perception about delivering lectures in virtual classroom | 3.91 | 1.03 | Agree |
| Perception about convenient timing for classroom in virtual classroom | 4.59 | 0.82 | Strongly agree |
| Perception about Conduct Exams or Mid semester Exam on MOODLE/virtual classroom | 3.61 | 1.15 | Agree |
| Experience of learning on virtual classroom | 4.20 | 1.05 | Agree |
| Overall, Virtual classroom is useful for learning | 3.72 | 1.32 | Agree |
| Impact of virtual classroom on getting feedback | 4.28 | 0.94 | Strongly Agree |
| Level of understanding of lecture content through virtual classroom | 4.40 | 1.01 | Strongly agree |
| Knowledge increased after virtual classroom study | 3.76 | 1.08 | Agree |
| Possibility for virtual classroom to become recognized as primary learning environment | 3.57 | 0.99 | Agree |

## Discussion and Conclusion

Virtual training is almost certain to remain and develop. The survey of its history plainly shows online instruction has grown quickly, filled by Internet network, progressed technology, and a gigantic market. It has developed from nineteenth century correspondence projects to the 21st century's dynamic and all around planned institutional online contributions. We can well foresee that online training will keep on expanding its quality and impact advanced education through an incredible procedure of reshaping, refining, and rebuilding. It is far-fetched, in any case, to supplant traditional advanced education yet simply to be another option. Be that as it may, attributable to its adaptability, accessibility and reasonableness, online training is picking up in prevalence, particularly for individuals who are otherwise unfit to acquire instruction in light of physical separation, plan clashes, and afford-capable expenses. Above data analysis is clearly shows that at present time teachers as well as students are prepared to adopt virtual class study, some respondents face problems related to internet connectivity and non-availability of computers and other electronics components. All through this examination, the essential center was to talk about how speculations, practices and appraisals apply to the internet learning condition. It began with an essential diagram of online training as contemplated and saw by Garrison et al. (2000), which filled in as the hypothetical structure for this investigation. We at that point analyzed how introduced hypotheses have applied to different parts of online course plan and improvement. We originally inspected the online condition after some time, its evolvement, and the technologic impacts on online training. In internet instructing, we concentrated on the connections among psychological and instructing existences to decide the best and most alluring practices and techniques for online teaching method. Inside the domain of web based learning, we coordinated our consideration on the production of a Web based learning network by methods for advancing social nearness, connections, and joint effort between the educator and understudies and among understudies.

## References:


1) Anderson, T. D. (2003). Modes of interaction in distance education: Recent developments and research questions. In M. G. Moore and W. G. Anderson (Eds.), *Handbook of Distance Education* (pp. 129–144) Mahwah, NJ: Erlbaum.
2) Falloon, G. W. (2011b). Exploring the virtual classroom: What students need to know (and teachers should consider). *Journal of Online Learning and Teaching (MERLOT),*

*7*(4), 439– 451.

3) Hrastinski, S. (2008). Asynchronous and synchronous e-learning: A study of asynchronous and synchronous e-learning methods discovered that each supports different purposes. *EDUCAUSE Quarterly, 31*(4), 51–55.

4) McInnerney, J., & Roberts, T. (2004). Online learning: Social interaction and the creation of a sense of community. *Educational Technology and Society, 7*(3), 73–81.

5) S.R. Hiltz (1986), the virtual classroom: using computer- mediated communication for university teaching, Journal of Communication, vol.36, no.2, pp 95-104.

6) SubramaniamNantha, &Kandasamy (2011), the virtual classroom: A catalyst for institutional transformation, Australasian Journal of Educational Technology, Vol. 27,pp. 1388-1412

7) Xenos M. (2018),"The Future of Virtual Classroom: Using Existing Features to Move Beyond Traditional Classroom Limitations". In: Auer M., Tsiatsos T. (eds) Interactive Mobile Communication Technologies and Learning, pp. 944- 951. IMCL 2017. Advances in Intelligent Systems an

# CHAPTER – 9

# Molecular Interactions of Ultrasonic Parameters in aqueous Polymer solutions

## BY

## S.V.Khangar, O.P.Chimankar, R. Y. Bakale , Y. S. Tamgadge

## Abstract

Molecular interaction study in polymers provides valuable information regarding internal structure, molecular association, etc. Ultrasonic investigations of polar- polar or polar- non polar components are important in understanding the intermolecular interaction between component molecules[1]. The propagation of ultrasonic waves and the measurement of their velocity in solution form an important tool for the evaluation of various acoustical and thermo-dynamical parameters which give an insight into the nature of miscibility/compatibility and molecular interactions in polymer solutions. In order to utilize polymers to create new multi-component polymer systems the fundamental principles related with their microstructures, solubility, phase separation, thermodynamical properties and degradation must be studied. Recently the use of ultrasonic waves has shown a great potential for characterization of polymer solutions. The molecular interactions study using low amplitude ultrasonic waves retain intrinsic state of polymer solution. The polymers under investigation are perturbed by such waves but no permanent changes are induced. Various thermo acoustic parameters such as adiabatic compressibility ($\beta_a$), acoustic impedance (z), relaxation time ($\tau$), free length ($L_f$), volume expansivity($\alpha$) and Moelwyn-Hughes parameter ($C_1$) of aqueous polyacrylamide (PAA) solution were obtained from the measurement of ultrasonic velocity (u), density ($\rho$) and viscosity ($\eta$). All these measurements have been carried out by Pulse Echo technique at concentration range 0.05 to 0.3wt.% and at temperature range 288K-308K at 2MHz frequency. The results have been used to discuss the nature and strength of intermolecular interactions in the Polyacrylamide + water and polyvinyl alcohol + water system. The linear and nonlinear behavior of these parameters are used to deduce information about the system used. Therefore, such studies would yield the knowledge about various interactions among the molecules[2-3]. These variations depend on structural changes due to intermolecular interactions in short region around the molecules. In present system polyacrylamide is a carbon- carbon chain polymer which is highly water-absorbent used for forming a soft gel. It is also used in various applications such as polyacrylamide gel electrophoresis and in manufacturing soft contact lenses when hydrated. In the straight-chain form, it is also used as a thickener and suspending agent. More recently, it has been used as sub dermal filler for aesthetic facial surgery. Aqueous PVA used in medicine as a binder.

**Keywords**: Ultrasonic, acoustic and optical parameters, polyacrylamide, polyvinyl alcohol, molecular interactions, pulse echo technique etc.

## Introduction:

The different acoustical parameters interpret the nature and strength of molecular interaction that exist in the system. The propagation of ultrasonic waves and the measurement of their velocity in solution form an important tool for the evaluation of various acoustical and thermo- dynamical parameters which give an insight into the nature of molecular interactions such as hydrogen bonding, dipole- dipole interactions and charge transfer complexes for homogeneous polymer-solvent mixture. Polyacrylamide is a carbon-carbon chain polymer having molecular formula $(C_3H_5NO)_n$[1]. It is formed from acryl amide subunits. It can be synthesized as a simple linear-chain structure or cross-linked. It is water- soluble and is used as a thickening agent and flocculent. It is highly water-absorbent, forming a soft gel when hydrated, used in such applications as polyacrylamide gel electrophoresis and in manufacturing soft contact lenses. In the straight-chain form, it is also used as a thickener and suspending agent. More recently, it has been used as sub dermal filler for aesthetic facial surgery and as a flocculent in west water treatment industry. Structural analysis of polymer is a subject of considerable interest in polymer science. Polyvinyl Alcohol (PVA) having molecular Formula $[C_2H_4O]_n$[1]. It is an environmental friendly and water-soluble synthetic polymer with excellent film forming property, and emulsifying properties and outstanding resistance to oil, grease, and solvents. It has been extensively used in adhesive, in textile warp sizing and finishing, in paper size and coating, in the manufacturing of PVAc emulsion, in the suspension polymerization of PVC, and as binder for ceramics. It is sometimes supplied as beads or as solutions in water[1]. A review of literatur[2-5] reveals that ultrasonic parameters, such as adiabatic compressibility $(\beta_a)$, relaxation time $(\tau)$, acoustic impedance (z), free length $(L_f)$, volume expansivity $(\alpha)$ and Moelwyn-Hughes parameter $(C_1)$ and optical parameter refractive index have been used to study the molecular interactions in polymer solutions. In present work, the authors have prepared the polyacrylamide and polyvinyl alcohol solutions at different concentrations (wt.%) in water solutions and have measured ultrasonic velocity, density and viscosity using ultrasonic pulse echo technique at temperature range 288K-308K and at three different frequencies 1MHz, 2MHz and 5MHz and optical parameter refractive index $(\mu)$ in order to study the structural changes to the solutions, if any. Ultrasonic pulse-echo systems are widely used to estimate properties of liquids. A common principle is to use a buffer material (buffer-rod) fixed to the ultrasound transducer. Assuming the acoustic properties of the buffer-rod are known, it is then possible to calculate the acoustic impedance of the unknown material from reflections between the buffer-rod and the unknown material. From acoustic impedance and speed of sound it is the possible to calculate density and adiabatic compressibility of the material. This was first introduced by Lynnworth[1] and Papadakis[2], and later further developed by P"uttmer[3] and Deventer[4] for density measurement of liquids. The nature of polymer and polymer-solvent interactions and effect on molecular interactions have been studied.

**Experimental**

Polyacrylamide (AR grade) and polyvinyl alcohol from Otto Chemi was used. Ultrasonic velocity, density, viscosity and refractive index $(\mu)$ values are estimated in the aqueous polyacrylamide and polyvinyl alcohol solutions. The solution was prepared by adding a known weight of polymer (i.e. polyacrylamide and polyvinyl alcohol) to a fixed volume of distilled water and then stirring until clear solution were obtain. The concentration range chosen in the solution are 0.05, 0.1, 0.15, 0.2, 0.25, & 0.3 wt. %. Velocity measurements are carried out using ultrasonic pulse echo technique by using MHF-400 High frequency pulser- receiver supplied by Roop Telsonic Ultrasonic Limited; Mumbai- (India) at different frequencies of 1 MHz, 2MHz & 5MHz and at temperature range 288K-308K with an accuracy of ±0.1m/sec. Density has been measured by pycnometer method. The viscosity of liquid was measured by Oswald's viscometer. And refractive index is measured by Abbes refractometer. Temperature is maintained at a constant range by Plasto Crafts (LBT-10) Thermostat and other related parameters calculated by standard formulae[6].

**Theoretical formulations**

1. Ultrasonic velocity   $u = 2d \,/t$  m/sec
   Where, d – Separation between transducer & reflector, t – Travelling time period of ultrasonic wave

2. Density   $$\rho = \frac{M_l}{M_w}\,\rho_w$$
   Where $M_l$- mass of experimental liquid, $M_w$- mass of water & $\rho_w$- density of water

3. Viscosity   $$\eta = \frac{\rho_l t_l}{\rho_w t_w}\,\eta_w$$
   Where $\rho_l$ – Density of experimental liquid, $\rho_w$ - Density of water, $\eta_w$- Viscosity of water, $t_l$- Time required to experimental liquid to flow from mark A to B in viscometer, $t_w$- Time of flow of water

4. Adiabatic compressibility   $$\beta_a = \frac{1}{u^2 \rho}$$

5. Relaxation Time   $$\tau = \frac{4}{3}\eta.\beta_a$$

6. Acoustic Impedance   $$Z = \rho.u$$

7. Free Length   $$L_f = K_j \beta_a^{1/2}\, Where,\ K_j \text{- Jacobson's constant}$$

8. Volume Expansivity   $$\alpha = -\frac{1}{\rho}\left(\frac{\partial \rho}{\partial T}\right) Where,\ T\text{- temperature}$$

9. Moelwyn-Hughes parameter   $$C_1 = \left[ {}^{13}/_3 + (\alpha T)^{-1} + {}^{4}/_3\,\alpha T \right]$$


**Experimental Results and Discussion**

The variations of ultrasonic velocity (u), density ($\rho$), viscosity ($\eta$), refractive index ($\mu$) and the related parameters such as adiabatic compressibility ($\beta_a$), acoustic impedance (z), relaxation time ($\tau$), free length ($L_f$), volume expansivity($\alpha$) and Molwen Moelwyn-Hughes($C_1$) of the various concentrations (wt.%) at temperature range 288K-308K and at 2MH

**Frequency for PAA in water and aqueous PVA are given below:**
* **Figure 1** represents the linear variation of ultrasonic velocity (u) with the concentration (wt.%) of PAA in water. It is maximum at higher concentration (0.3 wt. %). This behavior is due to strengthening of intermolecular forces with increase in concentration (wt.%) indicating association in the component molecules. This also suggests that disruption of water structure is enhanced further with the addition of PAA in water. The increment in velocity with concentration (wt.%) implies a decrement in the compressibility. As the temperature increases, kinetic energy of molecules in the solution increases. Those molecules present nearer the solute (PAA) trap into the cavity formed by water. Therefore the solution becomes thick which response to increase the ultrasonic velocity[1-2]. In

polyacrylamide, polar amide side groups can interact with water molecules via hydrogen bonding. Such interactions in hydrogels typically occur over a period of the order of microseconds.

- **Figure 2** represents the variations of ultrasonic velocity with concentration (wt%). From the graph It is observed that ultrasonic velocity increases with increase in concentration (wt. %) of polyvinyl alcohol in water indicating association in the component molecules. The increment in velocity with concentration implies a decrement in the compressibility. This behavior suggests the formation of a more rigid structure, possible due to polymer-water hydrogen bonding at sites on the polymer's hydroxyl (OH) group[3]

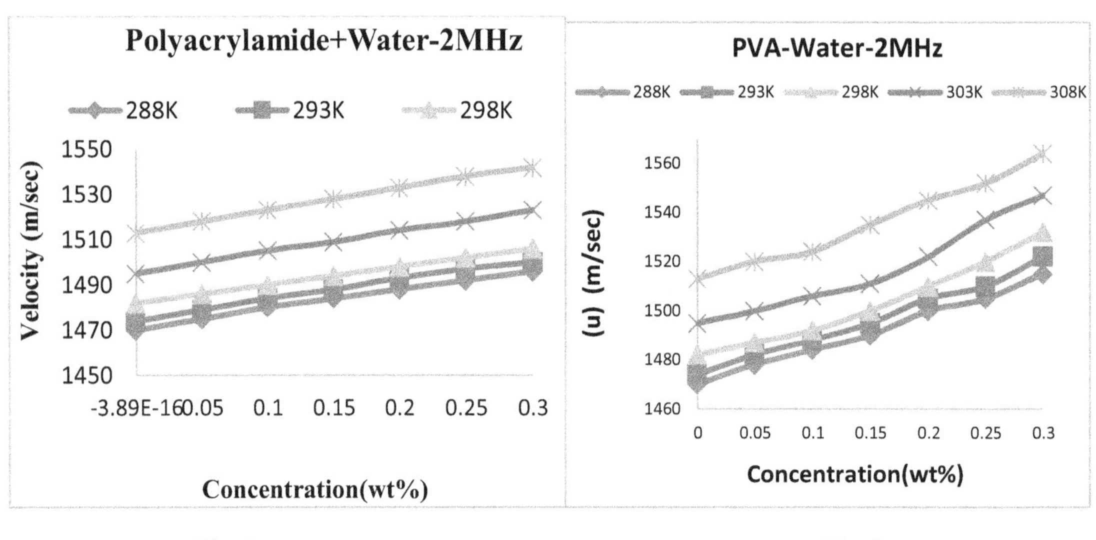


Fig.1       Fig.2

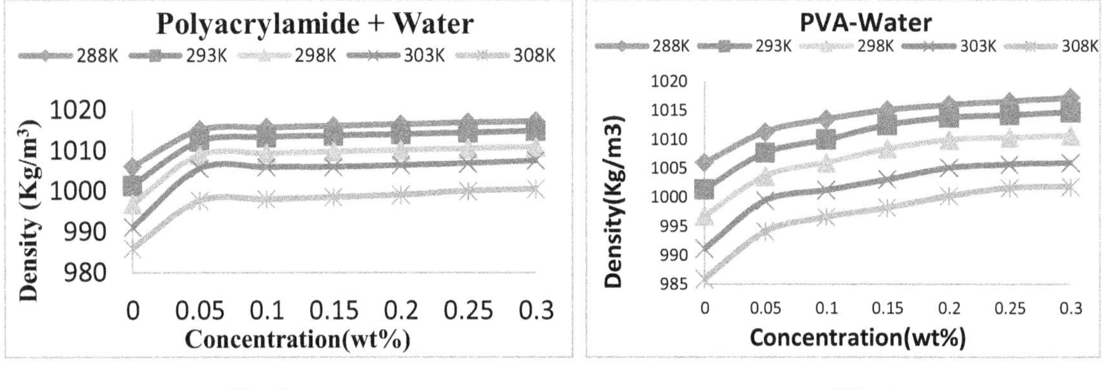


Fig.3       Fig.4

From figure 3, it is observed that density increases with increase in concentration (wt.%) of polyacrylamide (PAA) in water, The increase in density with increase in concentration(wt.%) is due to the fact that the number of polymer chain added to the solution increases with increase in concentration of polymer solution[5]. Figure 4 shows variation of density with concentration (wt.%). From graph It is observed that density increases with increase in concentration of polyvinyl alcohol in water, increase in density decreases the volume indicating association in component molecules

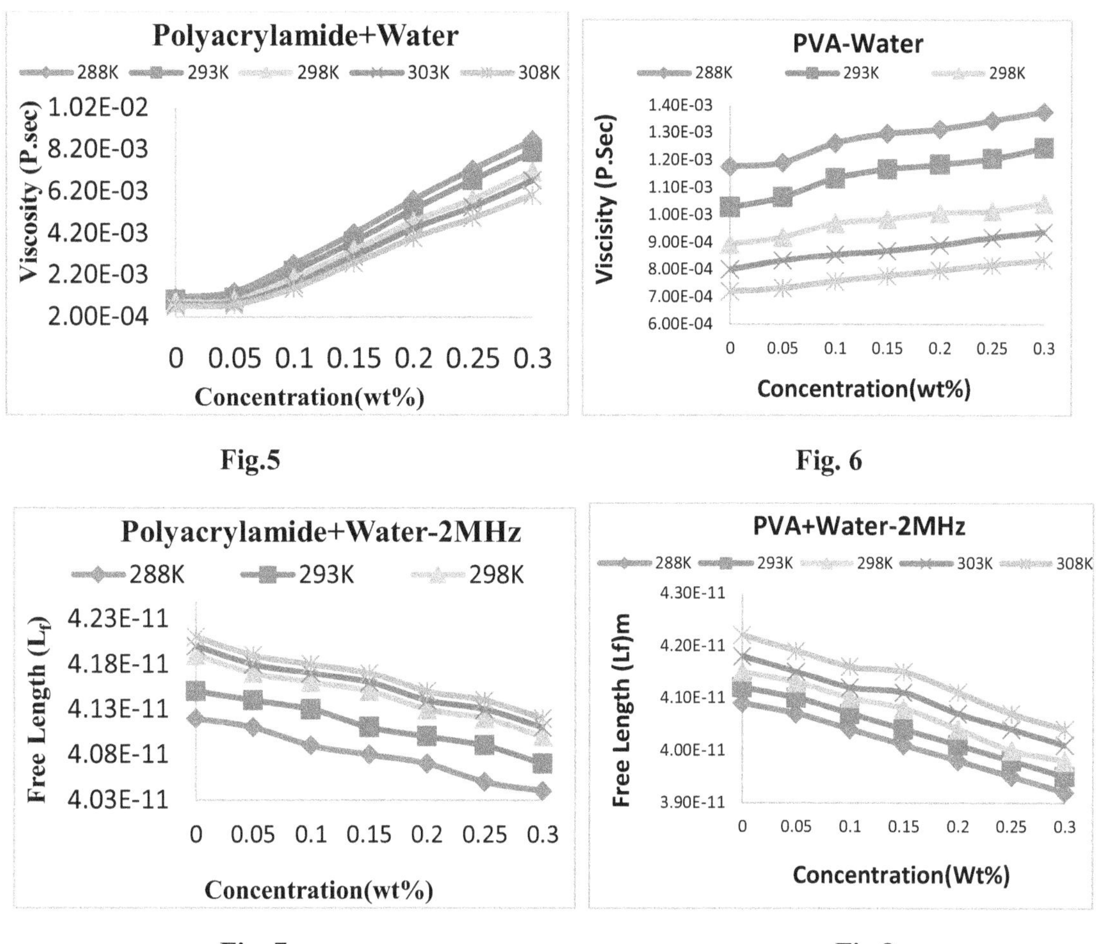


Fig.5     Fig. 6

Fig. 7     Fig.8

**Figure 5 and 7** shows that the viscosity linearly increases and free length decreases linearly with increase in concentration (wt. %) of polyacrylamide (PAA) in water. The viscosity of a mixture strongly depends on the entropy of mixture[3-4], which is related with the liquid structure as well as molecular interactions between the components of the mixtures. Thus, viscosity depends upon the molecular interaction as well as on the shape and size of the molecules. Increase of temperature favors increase of kinetic energy and volume expansion and hence decreases of density ($\rho$) and viscosity ($\eta$), while it increases intermolecular distance (free length)[5].

**Figure 6 and 8** shows the plot of viscosity ($\eta$) and free length versus concentration (wt. %) in aqueous PVA solutions. It is observed that viscosity slightly increases with increase in concentration (wt. %) of polyvinyl alcohol in water while free length decreases. Measurement of viscosity in binary mixture yields some reliable information in the study of molecular interaction. The viscosity gives the strength of molecular interaction between interacting molecules. The dipole-dipole interactions of permanent dipoles in constituent molecules increase the viscosity in the polyvinyl alcohol + water system

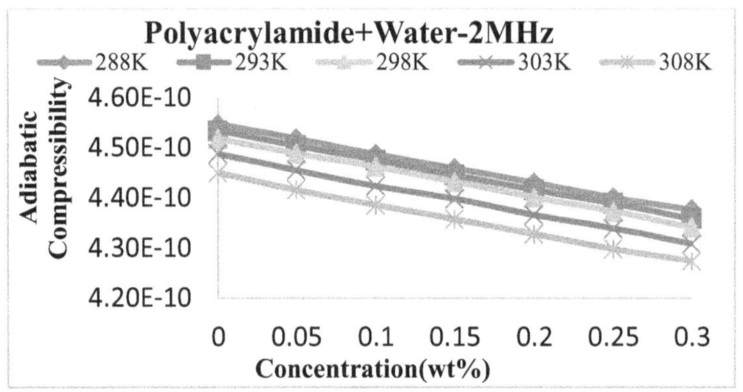



**Figure - 9**

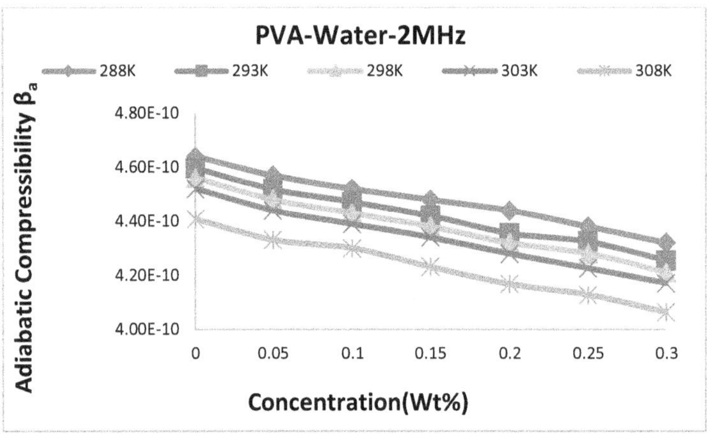



**Figure - 10**

**Fig.9** shows the variation of adiabatic compressibility with concentration (wt.%). Adiabatic and isothermal compressibility shows linear decrease with increase in concentration (wt.%) and temperature, which is due to strengthening of intermolecular forces with the supply of heat energy. While acoustic impedance increases linearly with increase in concentration (wt.%) and temperature which is attributed to increase of ultrasonic velocity with concentration and temperature of PAA in water[5-7].

**From figure 10,** It is also observed that adiabatic compressibility decreases with increase in concentration (wt. %) of polyvinyl alcohol in water indicating strong intermolecular interaction in the component molecules in this system shows associating tendency of the component molecules. The observed decrease of adiabatic compressibility and isothermal compressibility with concentration indicates the enhancement of degree of association in the component molecules. Hence the intermolecular distance decreases with increase in concentration. It is primarily the compressibility that changes with structure which leads to change in ultrasonic velocity[8].

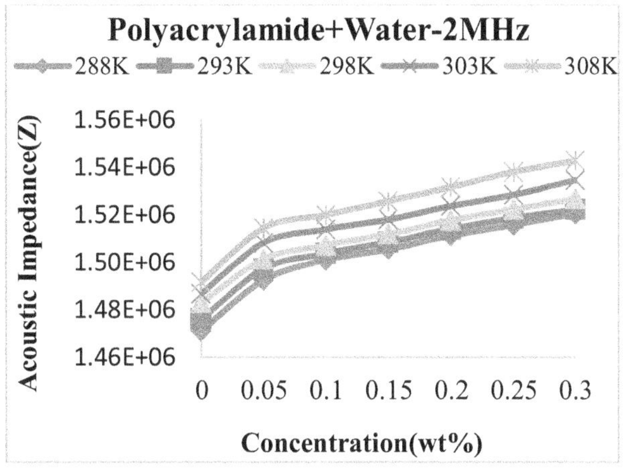

Figure - 11

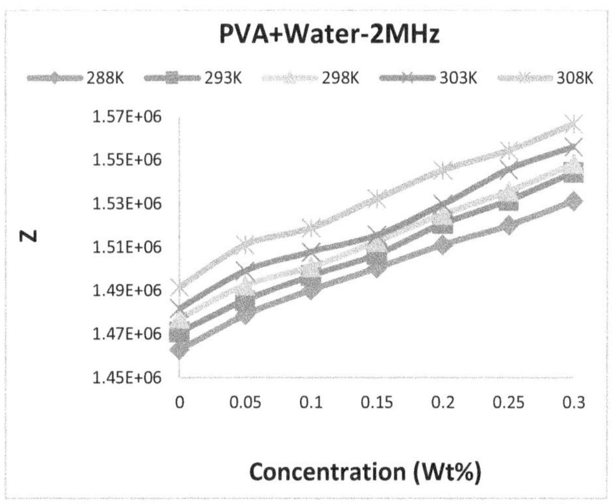

Figure - 12

**Figure 11 and 12** shows the variation of acoustic impedance with concentration (wt.%) in aqueous PAA and aqueous PVA solutions respectively. It is observed that, the values of acoustic impedance increase with increase in concentration. It is in good agreement with the theoretical requirements because ultrasonic velocity increases with increase in concentration. The increase in acoustic impedance (Z) with concentration can be explained on the basis of intermolecular interaction between component molecules, which decreases the intermolecular distance, making relative fewer gaps between the component molecules[9].

**Figure 13** shows that relaxation time slightly increases with increase in the concentration (wt.%) of polyacrylamide in water indicating high stability of polyacrylamide molecules. Motion of amide side groups on the polyacrylamide polymer chain also contribute to relaxation processes. In this case energy exchange can occur between the wave and vibrational and rotational energy associated with motion of the side chain groups[5]. With increase in the concentration of amide side chain groups increases and also the pathways for energy dissipation

**From figure 14,** it is observed that relaxation time increases slightly with increase in concentration of polyvinyl alcohol in water indicating high stability of polyvinyl alcohol molecules. Polyvinyl alcohol is a polymer having compact structure and hence molecules are not

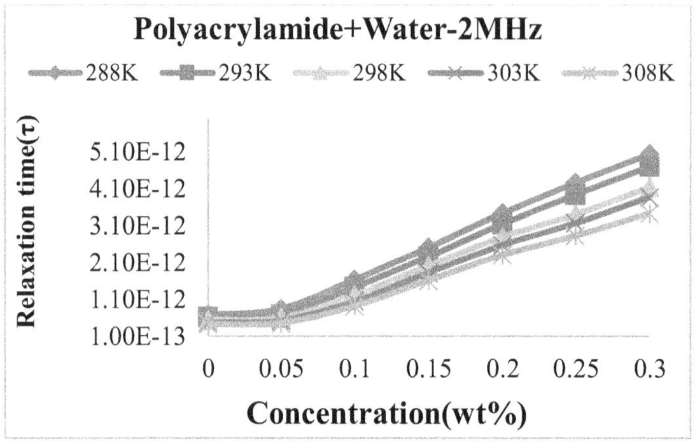

Figure - 13

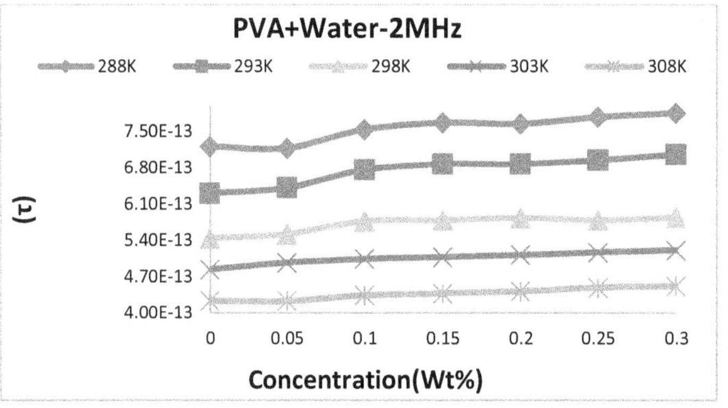

Figure - 14

Stable which increases the relaxation time. The relaxation can be caused by the energy transfer between translational and vibrational degrees of freedom and all these degrees take part in the observed process[9]. Its behavior depends on viscosity and adiabatic compressibility of the liquid solution. In this system viscosity plays very important role for increasing relaxation time with increase in concentration.

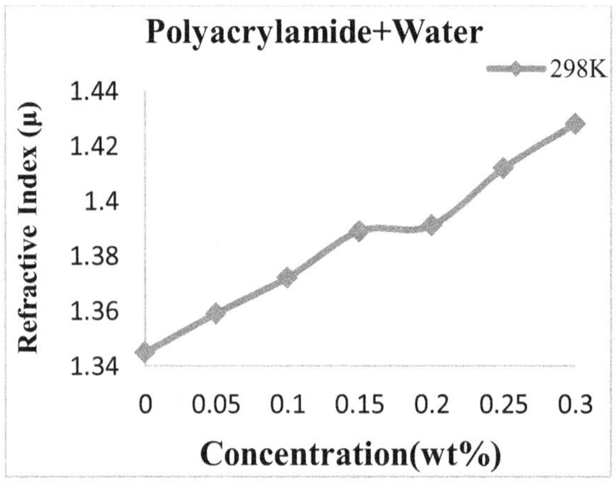

Figure - 15

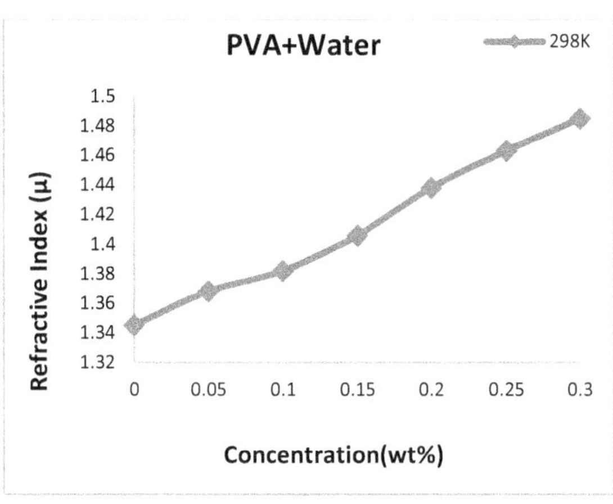

Figure – 16

**Figure 15 and 16** shows the variation of refractive index with concentration in aqueous PAA and aqueous PVA respectively. Refractive index (μ) increases with increase in concentration of polyacrylamide in water. It may be due to possible specific interactions like hydrogen bonding to some extent between the hydroxyl group of water and amide group of polyacrylamide (PAA). Hence the present study indicates the existence of miscibility windows only.

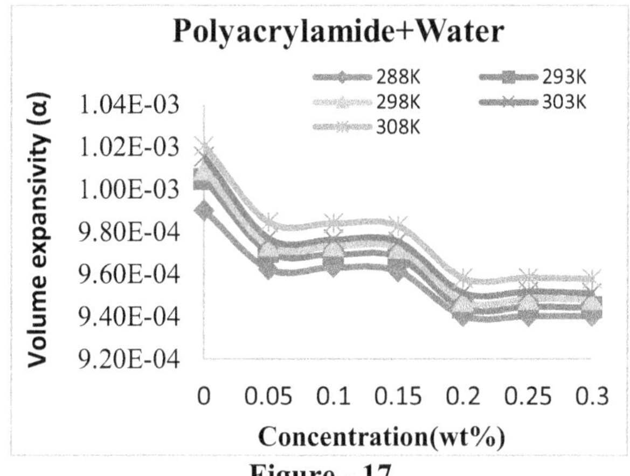

Figure - 17

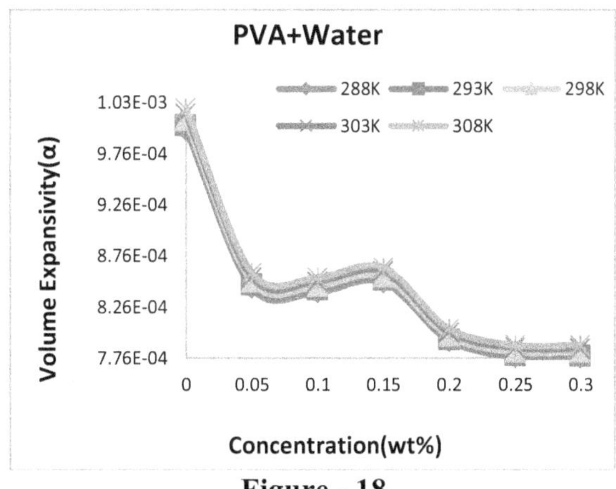

Figure - 18

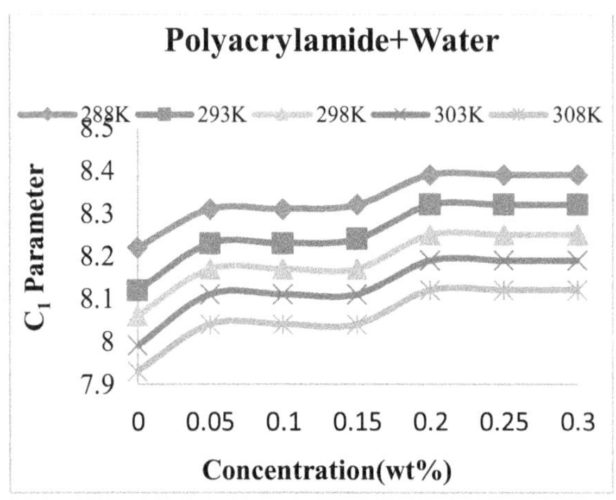


Figure - 19

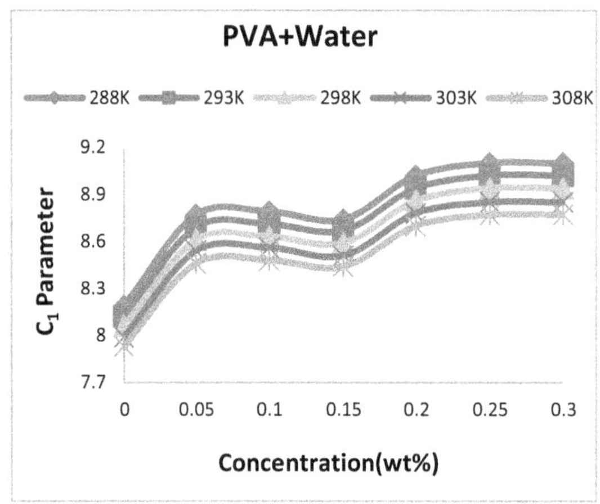


Figure - 20

**Figure 17 and 18** shows variation of volume expansivity with concentration (wt.%) in aqueous PAA and aqueous PVA solutions respectively. Also Plot 19 and 20 shows the variation of $C_1$ parameter with respect to concentration (wt.%) in both the system respectively. The variation of $C_1$ and volume expansivity ($\alpha$) shows the opposite behavior with increase of concentration. If $C_1$ increases then $\alpha$ is found to be decrease with concentration and vice-versa. This may be due to associating tendency of the liquid molecules[6-11].

**Conclusions**

- The linear variation of ultrasonic velocity with concentration gives the evidence to enhance the compatibility among the molecules presence in the PAA solution.
- The linear decrease in adiabatic compressibility and free length with increase in concentration of PAA solution indicates the strong interactions, association and non-dominance of PAA in water.
- The linearity in all the parameters indicates there is a single phase formation. It predicts strong polymer-solvent interaction and strong association in the PAA solution.
- Linear increase in refractive index shows the miscibility present in polyacrylamide + water system.

**Applications**

From the study of molecular interactions in aqueous PAA and aqueous PVA solution, these polymers are used for various industrial as well as medical applications.

- Polyacrylamide (PAA) + water solution use in waste water treatment industry for cleaning water.
- Aqueous Polyvinyl alcohol (PAA) solution use for tablet binder in pharmaceutical industries due to its miscibility property.

**References**


1) Chimankar O P etal, J. Pure Appl. Ultrason.32, 18  (2010).
2) Ravichandran S and K. Ramanathan,; Polymer-Plastics Technology and Engineering, 47: 169-173, 2008
3) Ramanathan, K.; Ravichandran, S. Ultrasonic study of mixed salt solutions of ammonium and ammonium chloride solution. Ind. J. Pure App. Ultrason. 2004, 26, 12.
4) Sugandha V. Khangar and Omprakash P. Chimankar; "Study of Miscibility of aqueous polyacrylamide (PAA) solution" ;International J. of Engineering and innovative technology (IJEIT);  Volume 3, Issue 11, May 2014; pp. 148-150, ISSN: 2277-3754.
5) Khangar S. V. and Chimankar O.P.; "Ultrasonic Investigation of Dipole- Induced dipole interactions in binary solution of cellulose acetate with cyclohexanone and carbon tetrachloride ($CCl_4$) "; International J. of Advanced Information Science and Technology (IJAIST); Vol. 25, No. 25, May 2014; pp. 102-108, ISSN: 2319-2682
6) Schmelzer, C.E.H.; Zwirbla, W.; Rosenfeld, E.; Linde , B.B.J.  Acoustic investigations of pseudo stable structures in aqueous solutions of polyethylene glycols. J. Mol Struc. 2004, 699, 47.
7) Sugandha V. Khangar and Omprakash P. Chimankar; "Ultrasonic Characterization of aqueous Polyvinyl Pyrrolidone (PVP)"; International journal of physical sciences; pp. 1351-1357, ISSN: 2348-0130 ; 4(10) 2014
8) Sugandha V. Khangar and Omprakash P. Chimankar,Ranjeeta S Shriwas and Sushma Patil; "Ultrasonic investigation of dipole- dipole interaction in binary solution of Cellulose acetate + water"; International journal of Science and Research (IJSR); pp. 331-334 ISSN (online): 2319-7064, 2015.
9) Falguni D. Karia; Parsania, P.H. Ultrasonic velocity studies and allied parameters of poly (4-4'- cyclohexylidene- R-R'-diphenylene diphenylmethane-4-4' disulfonate) solutions at 30'.Eur. Polym. J. 2000, 36, 519
10) S.U.Patil, O. P. Chimankar , S. V. Khangar and M.S. Deshpande; "Ultrasonic and spectroscopic investigation of Polychloroprene and Poly Methyl Methacrylate blends"; Acoustical society of America; vol. 38, issue 4; ISSN: 0001-4966, 2020
11) Sugandha V. Khangar, O. P. Chimankar, D. V. Nandanwar, J. N. Ramteke & Swapnil Kale; "Study of highly viscous polyacrylamide and  measurent viscocity and ultrasonic velocity"; Journal of Pure and Applied Ultrasonics (JPAU);Volume 41, pp 94-96;  ISSN: 0256-4637; 2019

# CHAPTER – 10

# SPEED CONTROL STRATEGY OF PMBLDC MOTOR

## BY
## Mukesh Kumar Kumawat & Nagendra Singh

## Abstract

Brushless Motor is likewise drawn out as stepper engine yet the term stepper engines, Brushed Direct current (DC) motor are around since the mid-nineteenth century, however brushless engines range unit a sensibly late entry. In this chapter Describing about the Permanent Magnet Brushless Direct current Motor (PMBLDCM) working, application Advantages & disadvantages of the Motor. How it worked, what is controlling circuit of the PMBLDC motor, what is the application available of this motor. Also describe about design circuit & modelling Equation of the PMBLDC Motor.

**Keywords-** PMBLDC Motor, Controller Circuit, BJT, MOSFET, IGBT, SCR, etc.

## Introduction

Permanent Magnet BLDC Motor Conventional Direct current (DC) Motor zone unit to a great degree temperate then their makings brand them appropriate for custom as servomotors. Be that as it might, their lone disadvantage is that they essential an electronic change and encounters that variety unit topic to attire then need upkeep. In this section examined with the essential structures of PMBLDC Motor drive circuits, crucial working standards and enduring state qualities of PMBLDC Motor and utilizations of the PMBLDC Motor will be quantified Constructions then Determination Routes

## PMBLDC Motor

The expansion of late-night brushless locomotives is importantly almost comparable the air conditioner engine, known as the static magnet electric engine as Figure 1 valuable outline of a three-stage PMBLDC engine.

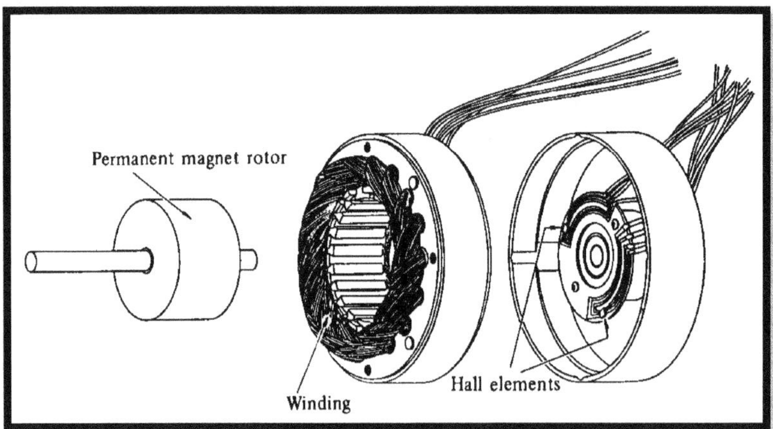


**Figure - 1 Dissembled read of a PMBLDC Motor**

The stator windings zone unit like those in a poly-stage air conditioning engine, and the rotor comprises of 1 or additional unchanging lodestones. Brushless Through existing (DC) machines are selfsame astounding after air habituation synchronous engines in that the past consolidates a few implies that to see the rotor position (attractive shaft) to Diagram out how to give signs of the semiconductor electronic based switches as appeared in figure 2 the most widely recognized position (post locator) [3] gadget is that the Hall component, however a few engines use optical sensors.

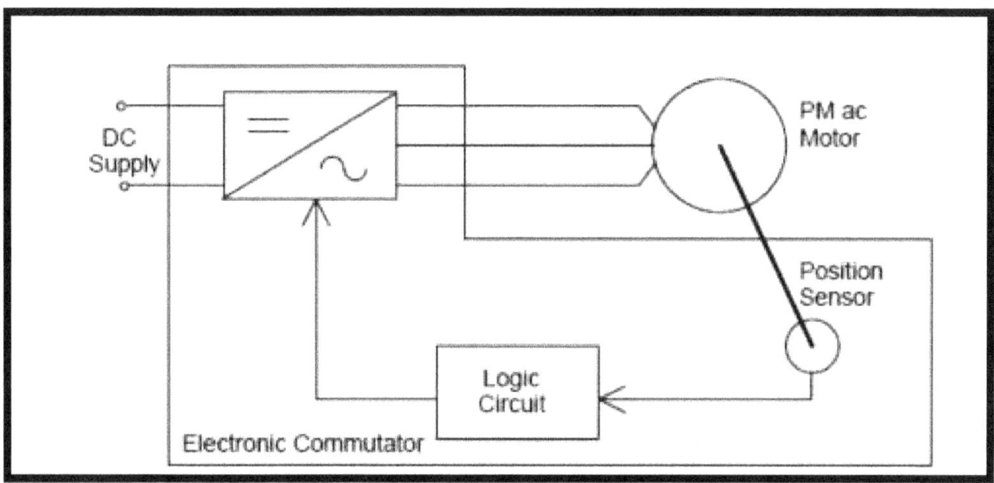


**Figure 2 BLDC motor and PMAC motor**

Electric switch despite the fact that the most customary and prudent engines zone unit three-stage, two-stage brushless Direct current (DC) engines are conjointly horribly ordinarily utilized for the humble expansion and determination trips. Figure 2 validates the irritable sectional standpoint of a two-stage machine partaking helper anticipating shaft.

**Correlation of average and PM brushless Direct current (DC) engines:**

In spite of the fact that it is beforehand supposed that brushless Direct Current (DC) engines and standard Direct current (DC) engines region unit comparative in their static attributes, they really have excellent varieties in a few perspectives. A Two-stage engine having helper remarkable shafts as appeared in underneath Figure 3

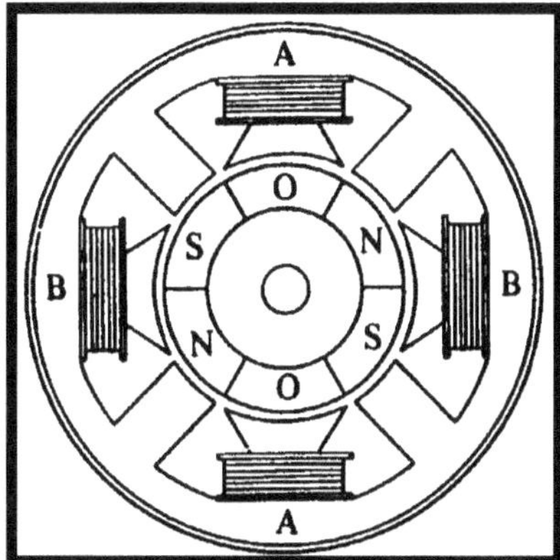


**Figure 3   diagram of motor having auxiliary Projecting poles.**

When we incline to associate both motor-powered in footings of present knowledge, a conversation of their alterations somewhat than their resemblances might be a ration of valuable in sympathetic their precise requests. Table 1 associates the consecrations and problems of these 2 sorts of motors.

**Table 1 Comparison of typical and PMBLDC Motor** [4]

Comparison of conventional and brushless DC motors

|  | Conventional motors | Brushless motors |
| --- | --- | --- |
| Mechanical structure | Field magnets on the stator | Field magnets on the rotor<br>Similar to AC synchronous motor |
| Distinctive features | Quick response and excellent controlability | Long-lasting<br>Easy maintenance (usually no maintenance required) |
| Winding connections | Ring connection<br>The simplest: Δ connection | The highest grade: Δ or Y-connected three-phase connection<br>Normal: Y-connected three-phase winding with grounded neutral point, or four-phase connection<br>The simplest: Two-phase connection |
| Commutation method | Mechanical contact between brushes and commutator | Electronic switching using transistors |
| Detecting method of rotor's position | Automatically detected by brushes | Hall element, optical encoder, etc. |
| Reversing method | By a reverse of terminal voltage | Rearranging logic sequencer |

**Drive circuit (unipolar Drive):**

Figure 4 shows a clear three-stage unipolar-worked engine those utilizations optical sensors (phototransistors) as position discoverers. Three photon based transistors PT1, PT2, and PT3 are determined to the end-plate at 120° between times, and are revealed in course of action through a turning shade coupled to light weight to the motor shaft. As showed up in Figure 4, the north post of the rotor now stands up to the remarkable shaft P2 of the stator circle, and the phototransistor PT1 perceives the sunshine and turns transistor Tr1 on.. Starting now, the screen shades PT2, and the phototransistor PT3 is introduced to the sunshine.By repeating in sequence such a switching action given in Figure 5.The  PMR (rotor) revolves  continuously in Figure 4 Three-phase unipolar driven PMBLDC motor shown in Figure 5 shift revolution and arrangement of stator attractive arena.

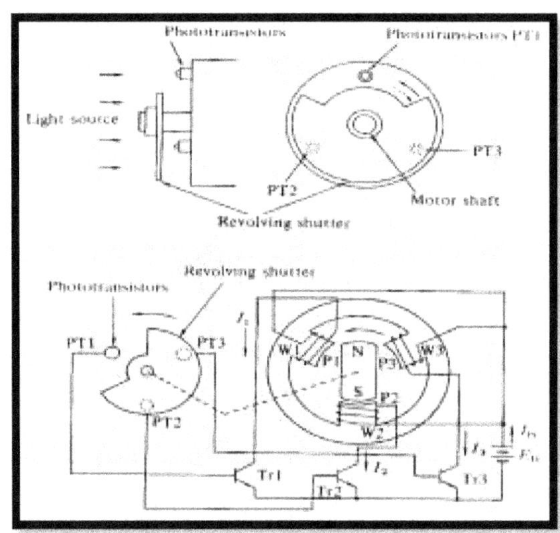


**Figure 4 Three-phase unipolar-driven brushless Direct current (DC) motor**

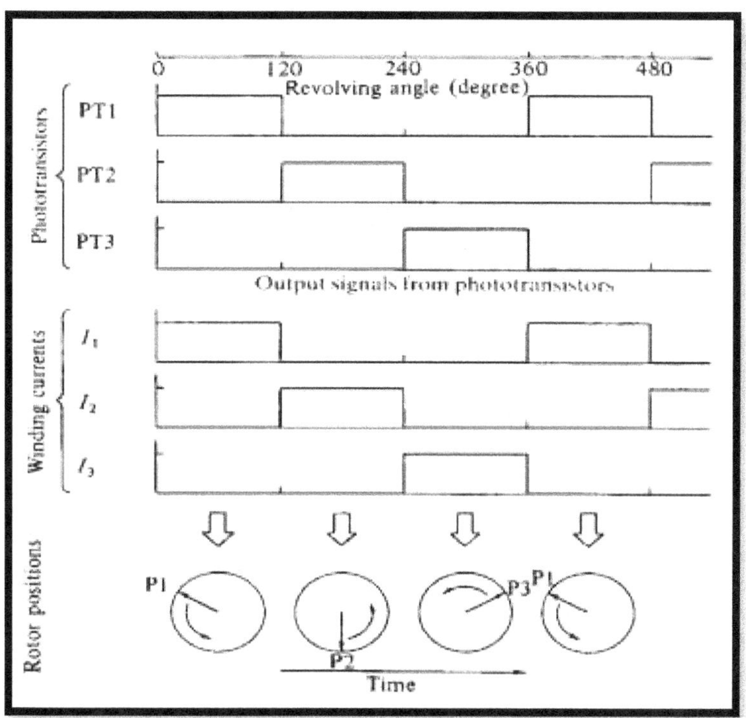


**Figure 5 switch rotation and sequence of stator's magnetic field Bipolar Drive System**

Determination when a three-stage PMBLDC (brushless) train is ambitious through a three-stage span controlled converter circuit, the productivity, which is the quantitative connection of the pole yield power (mechanical yield force) to the electrical information power, Here, "bipolar" implies that a twisting is as an option stimulated inside the south and north shafts. I will presently review the standard of the three-stage controlled converter span circuit of Figure 6. Here too I utilize the optical strategy for constabularies exertion the rotor location; six phototransistors terrain component customary on the end-plate at corresponding interludes. Meanwhile a winding diagram shows to the extreme, these photograph parts range unit presented in grouping to the lightweight transmitted from a light put inside the left of the Diagram. Quickly the downside is that the association between the ON/OFF state of the transistors and accordingly the lightweight police work phototransistors. The clearest association is close about once the honest to goodness progression is created in such the fundamental of the way that when a phototransistor checking with an express range is displayed to lightweight, the transistor of the same degree starts. Outline 6 shows that electrical streams course through Tr1, Tr4, and Tr5, and terminals U and W have the battery voltage, while terminal V has zero potential.[5] In this express, a present will spill out of terminal U to V, and another current from W to V as spoke to in Figure 7. We could acknowledge that the solid jolts in this Figure show the headings of the alluring fields created by the streams in every part. The centre is that of the fat arrow within is resultant magnetic flux in the stator of the machine.

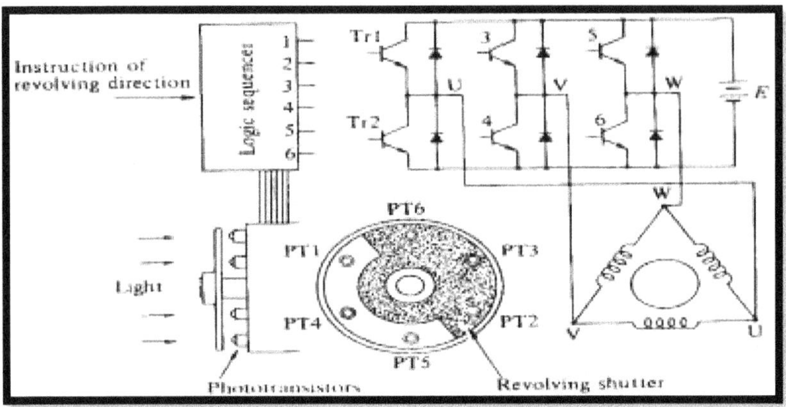

**Figure 6 Three part bipolar-driven   PMBLDC Motor**

The rotor is set in such a position, to the point that the ring fluidity will have a 90° advantage with orientation to the stator's attractive fluidity as seemed in Figure 7. In such a State a right-handed twisting container be complete on the blade. Lengthways these outlines when the blade's South Pole draws nearby to, the stator's south shaft greeneries additional toward frame interminable upheaval. The ON-OFF grouping and the turn of the transistor region unit appeared in Figure 8.

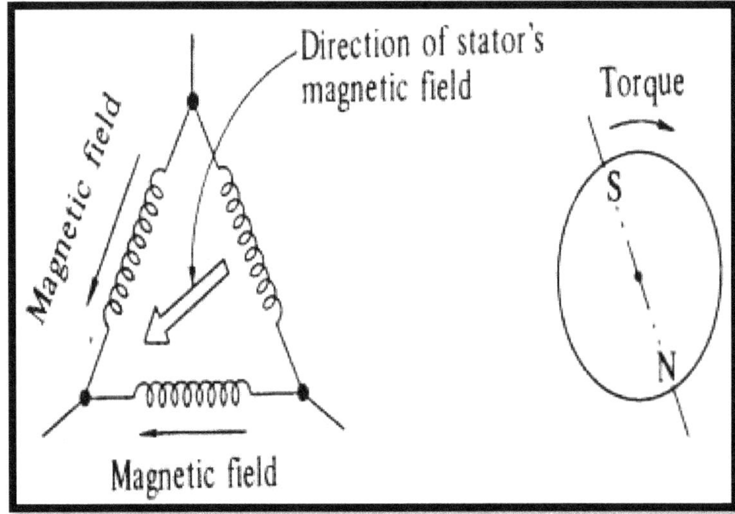


**Figure 7 Stator's magnetic field within the shutter state of field and rotor**

| Tr 1 | 1 | 1 | 1 | 0 | 0 | 0 |
|---|---|---|---|---|---|---|
| 2 | 0 | 0 | 0 | 1 | 1 | 1 |
| 3 | 0 | 0 | 1 | 1 | 1 | 0 |
| 4 | 1 | 1 | 0 | 0 | 0 | 1 |
| 5 | 1 | 0 | 0 | 0 | 1 | 1 |
| 6 | 0 | 1 | 1 | 1 | 0 | 0 |

**Figure 8 clockwise revolutions of the stator's magnetic**

The rotational bearing could be switched by forming the rationale sequencer in such the easiest way that once an introduction finder set apart with a beyond any doubt extent is presented to lightweight, the transistor of the same reach is killed. Then once more, when a phototransistor is not exhibited to lightweight, the transistor of the same degree is turned ON. In the positional state of Diagram 6 , Tr2, 3, and 6 region units ON, and the battery voltage E appears at terminal V, while U and W have zero electrical potential. By then, as showed up in Diagram 9. As the rotor makes another counter-clockwise torque, the counter-clockwise development continues and the field gets the chance to be as showed up in (c) This action is supplanted in the progression of (a) (b) (c) (d) to convey unending counter-clockwise development.

| ON-OFF sequence | 1 | 2 | 3 | 4 | 5 | 6 |
|---|---|---|---|---|---|---|
| Tr 1 | 0 | 1 | 1 | 1 | 0 | 0 |
| 2 | 1 | 0 | 0 | 0 | 1 | 1 |
| 3 | 1 | 1 | 0 | 0 | 0 | 1 |
| 4 | 0 | 0 | 1 | 1 | 1 | 0 |
| 5 | 0 | 0 | 0 | 1 | 1 | 1 |
| 6 | 1 | 1 | 1 | 0 | 0 | 0 |

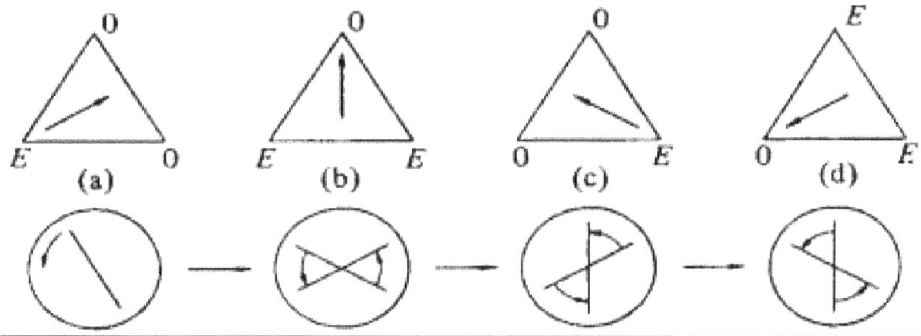

**Figure 9 Counter-clockwise revolutions of the stator's magnetic field and rotor**

The engine examined higher than has - associated windings, however it could conjointly have Y-associated windings. Figure 10 demonstrates a non perfect circuit that is utilized as a part of and tremendously LB imprinter or a hard-plate determination. As seemed in Figure 11, three Hall portions range unit set at interims of 60° for location of the rotor's attractive shafts. Since this engine has four attractive posts, an electrical edge of 120°  a compares to mechanical edge of 60 D.

**Proportional Circuit and General Equations:**

The per stage corresponding circuit is showed up in Figure 11 as taking after, where m is the flux linkage of stator circle winding per part as a delayed consequence of the static magnet. For persisting state conditions, expecting v and e domain unit twisted at repeat , the tantamount circuit transforms into the one showed up in Figure 12, where X= L, and V, I, E, and m are Phasor with rms amplitudes.
The tenacious state circuit condition can be formed as
$$V = E + (R + J\omega L)I \qquad (1)$$

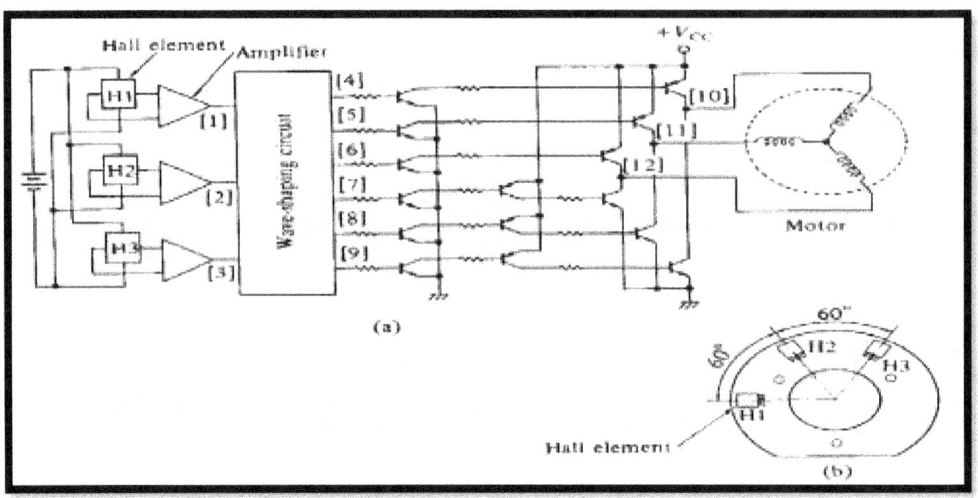

**Figure 10 sensible circuits for a 3-phase bipolar- driven PMBLDC motor, and arrangement of Hall elements**

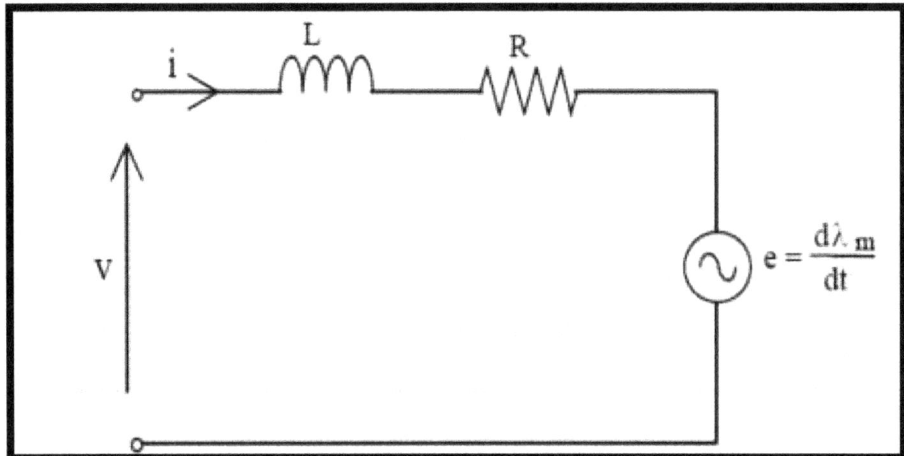

**Figure 11 Dynamic per part equivalent circuit of PMBLDC motors**

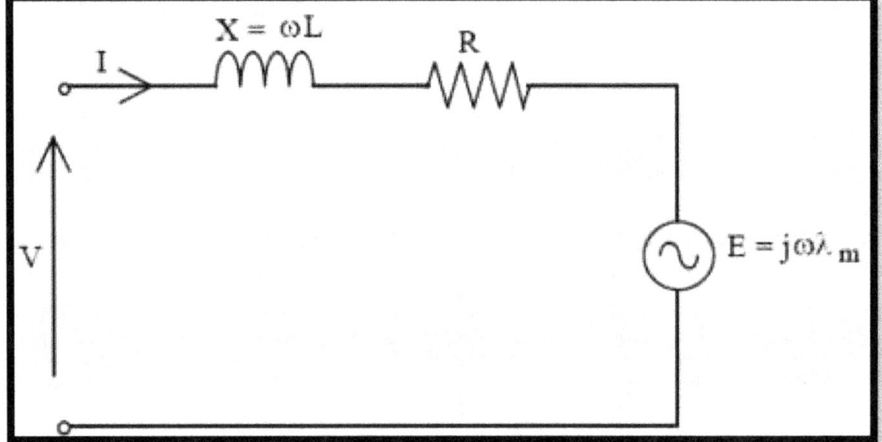

**Figure 12 Steady state per part equivalent circuit of brushless Direct current (DC) motors**

For most compelling mechanical power at a given rate, I and E are to specific gradation. This likewise offers maximum torque/ampere (minimum present/Nm). A brushless Direct current (DC) motor has position contribution from the rotor by method for Hall devices, ophthalmic strategies, [3] encoder and so forth. Accordingly the circuit will be dissected abuse extents of Electro Magnetic Field (E), terminal voltage (V), and supply current (I) as though it was a Direct current (DC) circuit. In any case, introductory note that once E and I zone unit to some degree, the engine mechanical force yield (before erosion, wind age, and then iron dilemmas) i.e. the electromagnetic harvest power is

$$P_{em}=m*E*I=m\omega * \lambda_m *I \qquad (2)$$

Where m is the collection of sections, |E|, |I|, and | m| remain the bounties of preachers E, I, then m, and the electromagnetic spinning remains

$$T_{em} = \frac{P_{em}}{\omega_r} = \frac{m\omega*\lambda_m*I}{\omega_r} \qquad (3)$$

Where $\omega_r$=2 $\pi$/P is the rapidity of blade in rad/sec and quantity of opposites is P formerly

$$T_{em} = \frac{mP}{2} * \lambda_m *I \qquad (4)$$

The genuine productivity of trough supremacy motivation stays as

$$T_{Load} = T_{em} - T_{Losses} \qquad (5)$$

Where $T_{Losses}$ is the entire twisting as a consequence of resistance, wind-age, and then firm fatalities plummeting the largeness (modulus).

$$T_{em} = \frac{mP}{2} \lambda_m I \qquad (6)$$

And in footings of blade speed persuaded Electro Magnetic Field is spoken by subsequent reckoning

$$E= \frac{P}{2}\lambda_m \omega_r \qquad (7)$$

**Performance of PM Brushless Direct current (DC) Motors:**

Speed-Torque (T~ω) bend Permanent arrogant ωL<<R and position observation protects V and E (and therefore I) in portion, the influence reckoning can be straight forward in algebraically caring by way of

$$V = E + RI \qquad (8)$$

The consistent T~ω curve is exposed in Diagram 13 for a continuous power. Competence is outlined.

$$\eta = \frac{P_{out}}{P_{in}} \qquad (9)$$

Where $P_{in} = mVI, P_{out} = T_{Load}\omega_r$

In terms of the power flow

$$P_{in} = P_{cu} + P_{fe} + P_{mech} + P_{out} \qquad (10)$$

The quantitative relation of output power and input power is Windage and friction. Losses also have important role to affect the machine performance.
Two examples of them area unit illustrated within the following are

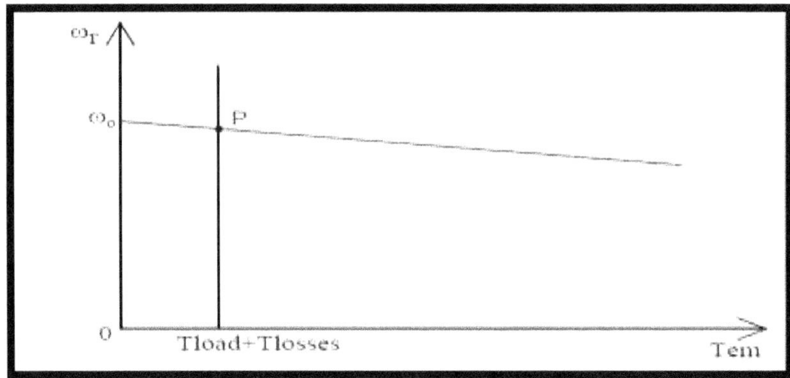


**Figure 13   T- $\omega$ arc of a brushless Direct current (DC) motorized with a continuous power source**

**Advantages and Disadvantages of motor:**

**Advantages PMBLDC Motor**
(i) There is no field twisting with the goal that field copper misfortune is disregarded.
(ii) Length of the engine is little as there is no mechanical Commutator, with the goal that size turns out to be little.
(iii) Better ventilation on account of armature obliged in the stator.
(iv)   Regenerative braking is conceivable.

**Disadvantages of PMBLDC Motor:**
(i) Motor field can't be controlled
(ii) It needs a force semi conductor swap circuit.
iii) Power rating is limited on account of the most extreme accessible size of perpetual magnets.
iv)  It needs a rotor position sensor.

**Purposes of PMBL Direct current (DC) motor.**
- Glass & Textile businesses.
- Power alternators
- Robotics and Computer applications
- Automotive applications

The PMBL Direct current (DC) engine is likewise called electronically commutated engine in light of the fact that the stage windings of PMBL Direct current (DC) engine is empowered by utilizing power semiconductor exchanging circuits. At this time, the force semiconductor exchanging circuits go about like a Commutator.

**Table 2: Compare PMBLDC motor & conventional Direct current (DC) motor**

| Features | PMBL Direct current (DC) motor | Conventional Direct current (DC) motor |
|---|---|---|
| Structure<br>Mechanical<br>Maintenance | Low maintenance<br>Field magnets on the rotor<br>The highest grade: Delta or star-connected 3-$\phi$ connection. | Maintenance is high<br>Field magnets on the stator<br>Ring connection |
| Commutation method | Electronic switching using power semi conductor devices i.e transistors, MOSFETS. | Mechanical contact between brushes and  Commutator |
| Winding connection | Normal Y-connected three phase winding with grounded neutral point or four-phase connection. The simplest:<br>Two-phase connection. | The simplest: Delta connection |
| Reversing method | | By a reverse of terminal voltage.<br>Automatically detected by brushes |
| Detecting method | Rearranging logic sequencer<br>Rotor position can be detected by using sensor for example,<br>Hall sensor; optical encoder. | |

## Reference:


1) Mehdi Ouada, M.S Meridjet , M Saad Saoud, Talbi N, "Increase potency of electrical phenomenon Pumping System primarily based BLDC Motor victimisation symbolic logic MPPT Control",WSEAS TRANSACTIONS.
2) Malik Sameeullah, Sunita Chandel, "style and Analysis of star electrical Rickshaw: A inexperienced Transport Model".2016 IEEE.
3) Durmus Uygun, Selim Solmaz, "Design and Dynamic Study of a six kW External Rotor static magnet Brushless DC Motor for electrical Drivetrains", 2015 IEEE fifth International Conference on Power Engineering, Energy and Electrical Drives POWSY.
4) Sanjana Ahmed, Ahmed Hosne Zenan, Mosaddequr Rahman, "A roadster Light-Weight star steam-powered Clean Car: Preliminary style and Economic Analysis.
5) Nishtha Shrivastava, Anil Brahmin, "Design of 3-Phase BLDC Motor for electrical Vehicle Application by victimisation Finite component Simulation", International Journal of rising Technology and Advanced Engineering, Volume 4, Issue 1, January 2014.

# CHAPTER – 11

# BUSINESS INNOVATIONS IN RETAILING

## BY
## Teena Mishra

**Abstract:**

Innovations in business models makes the world of retail business vuca. Innovations in the business models are increasingly building sustainable advantage in a market place which is explained by intense competition, unrelenting change and dynamic customer expectations. Firms like Apple with iTunes created new markets in the field of innovations. And some firms made changes in the existing markets for example, Priceline.com. A well-specified system of interdependent structures, activities and processes that assists a firm organizing logic for creating value for its customers and value appropriation (for itself and partners). A business model is all about to fit all activities together to create a value system.

**Keywords:** Innovations, Retailing, Demand etc.

**Introduction:**

Retailing is the process of selling merchandise and services to the customers. It involves the selling of small lots to a large number of customers by a business. For selling the products and services to the customers various step by step activities occurred. It is responsible for meeting the individual demands of the consumers with the manufactur. Retailing is one of the growing industries and struggling due to the changing demands of the market. Due to high market demand, competition, and global market, there is a need to restructure the retail organization. Retail stores are working continuously to attract and retain their customers. For this, they are providing valuable products to them. Selling is the old concept that focused to sell products. Today demands to give value to the customers. Customers are very smart and satisfying them is very difficult due to the highly competitive market. Marketing is a broad concept and selling is a part of it. To adopt marketing tactics there is a need for business innovations. Innovations are the prerequisite to satisfy market demand and to generate revenue for the organization. Due to globalization, increasing technology, changing environments, situations innovations are creating by the business organization. They are not only focusing on the external market but also on the internal market to create innovations. It is the innovations through which they can compete in the market and expand their market share. It helps to attract and retain customers for a long period.

**Innovation vs Invention:**

Innovations and inventions are closely related to each other. An invention is a new creation. Business innovation can produce an invention but the term is broader in scope. Innovations can include various concepts and practices in a new way. For example, the smartphone is an innovation and the telephone is an invention.

**Business Innovations:**

Business innovations are the process of introducing new concepts, ideas, workflow, methodologies products and services. It helps to improve the existing products, services or processes. It also involves in problem-solving or making new customers. The objective of business innovations is to create value for the organization. To create revenue opportunities or driving more revenue with the aid of channels and creating efficiencies to increase productivity or performance. Innovations lead to higher profits. The objective of the organization is to yield a competitive advantage. Retailer creates value for its customers and markets. Innovations in the retail sector is increasing for building sustainable advantage in a marketplace. In the current retail market, retailers grasp quickly the idea of innovative stores. According to Rickards 1985 et al. conventionally innovation is the two driving forces, technology push and market pull. In 1991 Crawford suggested that innovations normally comprised of both combinations. Newly retail concept is normally a new or different method of serving customer needs, the development of which is similar to research and development activity.

## Retail Innovations

The retail sector is growing speedily. There are various promotional activities in the retail store which attracts customers (fig. 1.1). In the present market, there is various way of innovations in the retail industry, it can be divided into the following classes:

- **Delivery**

Days are gone where you interact with customers and enjoy in the stores. Customers do not like long lines for the delivery in the store and save time. Various online stores like Amazon, Flipkart, myntra, etc. Shuti is a London-based fulfillment company that brings purchasers together with retailers and couriers. This was founded in 2008 and bought in 2013 by eBay. Doodle parcels is a service delivery that is located around train stations in the United Kingdom. This company started in the year 2014. Perch is an app that permits you to monitor your house from a smartphone, laptop, webcam or tablet.In-store creative ideas attract customers. It gives the opportunity to interact with the retailers. Aisle411 is an app through which customers can see a map that will represent the exact location of the product they want to purchase in a store. Yrstore is pronounced as 'your store', this is a pop-up store in London. It gives customers the ability to custom design and upload their designs. Klepierre Inspiration Corridor is a live digital shop that advises products pulled from live inventory. Iconeme created VMBeacon which permits mannequins to interact with the customers using a app. Zoovn helps cloud-based businesses which give personalize customers' shopping experiences. With online sales increasing exponentially and shoppers drastically reducing visits to stores, many retailers are trying to get even by employing cutting-edge technologies to their stores to attract more customers.

Retail innovations is focusing on change. Changes provide tangible value to the consumers because it provides something new or improvement in the existing field of services, technology or business systems. With the benefits offering to the consumers, it also provides benefits to the retailers. This may be in the form of increased sales, competitive advantage and business growth. Starbucks Mobile wallets permit people to pay for buying with a mobile device. Apple is one of the companies in the list of innovations. They introduced the IPod and consumers enjoyed music a lot. In recent years retail is concerned about what is next in retail and what is retail innovation? There are a digital transformation and innovative projects that are involved in the retail industry. Retailers face high competition, price pressure, a connected consumer with high expectations. It is an empirical fact that organizations that surpass at innovation are more profitable than the organizations that do not do. Boston Consulting Group asked thousands of senior executives to rank the organizations by their innovativeness. The top twenty organizations lead their industries in return to investors, profit margins and return on equity. Innovations is one of the finest ways to build market share. Also, market share is directly linked to the return on investment.

**Innovative retail trends are:**

a) **Social commerce:** According to the modern study 41% of customers responded that they were currently shopping online. Social media platform offers a variety of products to the shoppers. Social media apps or sites are increasing sales.

b) **Influencer marketing:** Influencer marketing used to all about selfies, heavily-edited product shots and carefully-constructed captions. There was a shift in the way brands and influencers in 2020.

c) **Online stores:** Online retailing and digital brands are increasing over the earlier few years.

d) **AR-powered money spending experiences:** Augmented reality (AR), artificial learning (AI), machine learning is the top technologies retail are seeking for consumers.

e) **Creative brand:** Amazon is one of the highest generated revenue which gives a new shopping experience to the consumers. In the marketplace, brands show creativity to consumers.

f) **Rising of Ethical and value-based brand:** Near about 71% of consumers prefer to purchase from brands that align with their values. According to Forrester shoppers evaluating products and brands are rising.

g) **Faster delivery:** Faster delivery service is one of the trends that attract customers in the retail market.

**Figure – 1: A retail store**

**Conclusion:**

There is a drastic change in retail organizations. There is the increasing demand of customers and competitive market which drives to create of innovations in the retail sector. There are various retail organizations like malls, department stores, online stores, specialty stores, hypermarkets etc. All are focusing to increase market share and sales of the business. Innovations become part of every business. There are various types of innovations in the retail sector like delivery procedures, display merchandising, shopping experiences, various types of brands, provide services and post-sales services. Due to many stores available in the market customers can purchase a product from anywhere but the retailer who provides innovative products and services are getting success in the long-term.


**References**

1) Reddy Vijaychandra (2014), Significance of Innovation in Business Process of Value Chain Science and Education Publishing, Journal of Behavioral Economics, Finance, Entrepreneurship and Accounting Vol. 2, No. 1, 18-25.
2) https://tinuiti.com/blog/ecommerce/retail-trends-emerging/
3) https://www.wifispark.com/blog/important-retail-store-innovation-ideas-for
4) https://study.com/academy/lesson/innovation-in-retail-definition-examples.html
5) https://www.i-scoop.eu/retail-transformation-commerce-retail-industry/retail-innovation-2019

# CHAPTER – 12

# USE OF OPTIMUM HYBRID SYSTEM FOR ECONOMIC ELECTRICITY SUPPLY

## BY

**Nagendra Singh, Mukesh Kumar Kumawat, Shiva Ram Krishna**

**Abstract:**

The goal of the proposed thesis is to obtaining optimum size of hybrid generating units has the minimum generation cost. In this study simulate different combination of energy resources and its results are compared to each other. Simulation model developed with the solar, wind diesel based hybrid system for fulfillment of load demand of industries by using of HOMER 2.81 version. Obtaining reliable and cost effective strength solution for the global expansion of telecommunication areas gives a completely difficult problem. Grid connection are may be available but in our simulation does not considered.

**Key words**: Hybrid system, renewable energy generation system, HOMER, Economic supply of Electricity.

## Background

Unremitting increase in power demand,  depletion of fossil fuels and environmental concerns forces  all stake holders of the power system to adopt alternative resources of energy, efficient conservation system and energy conservation  techniques. The installed capacity of the power plant is mainly depends on thermal power plants which are responsible for creating the pollution in the environment. On the other hand Solar, wind and other non-renewable energy sources are more economical, efficient and having less installation demands but less reliable. To address the issue of reliability, hybrid system comes into existence which provides power with more reliability and in the age of information technology and communication it can be used to fulfill the auxiliary power requirements at remote location. As telecommunication sector is the important sector where auxiliary power is required at its exchange offices, in current thesis solar, wind and diesel based hybrid system is considered for which the optimization is done with the help of HOMER software which is developed by the National Renewable Energy Laboratory, USA. Here telephone exchange office of deistic Bhopal is taken as the case system.

## Introduction

Locations distant form the urban areas need for energy efficient electric generating sources to overcome the problem of shortage of electricity. By this means required to plant some alternating system which is different of conventional system. Hybrid generation system is one of the best solutions for generation of electricity in rural region by proper using of nonconventional power resource like solar, wind and other available resources [1]. Power utilities in many nations around the world are turning away their concentration toward more energy- efficient and renewable electric power sources. The use of renewable energy sources in remote locations could help reduce the operating cost through the reduction in fuel utilization, also concentrating on enhancing the efficiency of system efficiency, and decreasing the noise and emissions. Hybrid energy system is a combination of various types of resources it may be renewable energy resources or usual resources in order to complete the load demand and increase the reliability of the system. Getting reliability and minimum effective cost of power solution for the worldwide expansion of many sectors such as telecommunication sectors, small scale production offices which are facing lots of problem due to short cutting of electricity [2]. Grids may be available or some cases remote area not available, their extension can be extremely costly in such type of commercial users. As the initial costs of conventional system are low where powering provided for these sites by diesel generator but these generators needed lots of maintenance cost as well as consume lots of fuel.

Renewable and alternative energy distributed generation (DG) sources, energy storage, and combined heat and power (CHP) are very promising technologies which can help reduce undesired emissions and fossil fuel dependence, and improve energy efficiency and reliability. While DG technologies are able to operate on their own, higher efficiency can be obtained by incorporating energy storage and CHP (when possible) as a hybrid system [3]. Constant speed of flow of wind is required for generation of wind electrical power in such remote locations. Hybrid system with interconnection of solar system, wind electrical system, storage battery for backup and diesel generator system is very reliable because the diesel generating system acts as a cushion to take care of changes in speed of wind and it always try to maintain the average power equal to the set point. Hybrid structure has capability to produce electricity of multistory building in rural areas. The utilization of wind turbines to produce electricity is tries by last 10 decades. Diesel engines have been a method of producing electricity since the 1945. However the field of engineering. Concerned with the coupling of wind power, solar power and diesel generators for development of stable generating unit system because system stability is becoming a crucial issue to the power company [4]. The intermittent nature of renewable energy generation sources, such as photovoltaic (PV) and wind power generation, has effects on the stability of the grid and availability of power. One way to increase the benefits of those technologies and mitigate their negative impacts is to use access and capacity-oriented energy storage. Access-oriented energy storage uses fast-acting energy storage technologies, such as a super capacitor or flywheel, to respond quickly to the rapid changes in generation and load [5]. Currently, some studies have focused on optimizing PV/wind/diesel hybrid energy systems so that the capacity of PV array, wind turbine, diesel generators, and storage battery are optimally selected [6]. The size and performance of such hybrid power-generating system strongly depend on meteorological variables, like radiation of sun energy, atmospheric temperature and wind speed; thus, in order to optimize the system, extensive studies related to meteorological variables have to be conducted [7]. Optimization works related to PV/wind/diesel hybrid energy systems can be found in the literature.

**Hybrid System**

Hybrid energy system is a combination of various renewable energy renovation systems along with conventional in order to fulfill the demand of different consumers with reliable operation. Fig. 1. shows the line diagram hybrid system has combine of different power generating systems and load[8].

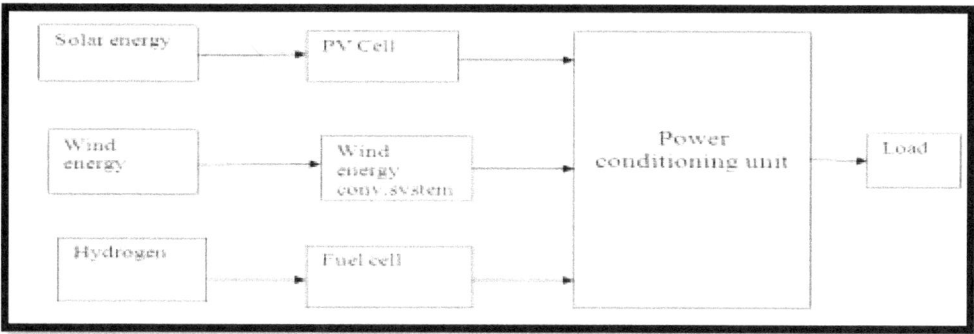


**Figure - 1 Line diagram of Hybrid power generation system**

## A) Photovoltaic System

It is a renewable resource of energy and in this method solar power directly converted into the electrical power means of using semiconductors is called the photovoltaic effect. In photovoltaic power generation system consisting of solar panels. Each solar panel composed of number of solar cells containing a photovoltaic material. Presently materials used for manufacturing of photovoltaic cell consisting the materials like polycrystalline with silicon, mono crystalline with silicon, amorphous silicon, cadmium telluride, and copper indium gallium[9]. The most excellent silicon photovoltaic component are available used commercially have about 18% efficiency. The efficiency of this pv module may rise over 25% within next 10-15 years. Solar energy radiant light and heat from the sun, is harnessed by using different methods like solar thermal heating method, solar photovoltaic method, solar thermal electricity generation method, by various architecture of solar panel[10]. Active and passive solar technologies are broadly used to capture the sun radiation and then solar energy converts and distribute. In the active solar techniques photovoltaic panels and solar thermal collectors are used to harness the energy. In passive solar techniques it is mounted on the top of the building or a place where radiation of sun collects easily. Materials used with favorable thermal mass or light dispersing properties, and designing spaces that naturally circulate air.

## B) Wind Energy System :

Wind power is the conversion of wind energy into a useful form of energy. Some of them such as using wind turbines to make electrical power, windmills used for converting wind energy into mechanical power, similarly wind water pumps are used for water pumping or drainage, or sails to propel ships[11]. Large wind farms where hundreds of wind turbines are using are interconnected with the electrical grids use for transmission of electrical power from one place to other place. For new constructions, onshore wind power supply is a cheap useful resource for generation of electricity, competitive with or in lots of locations inexpensive than fossil gasoline flora [12], small onshore wind farms provide electricity to isolated places. Utility agencies increasingly more buy surplus energy produced through small domestic wind turbines. Offshore wind is steadier and more potent than on land, and offshore farms have much less visible effect, however construction and maintenance fees are drastically higher.

## C) Power Conditioner:

It is also referred to as a line conditioner or power line conditioner, is a tool projected to enhance the pleasant of the strength this is introduced to electric load apparatus. At the same time as there is no reliable definition of a power conditioner, the time period most often refers to a tool that acts in single or greater approaches to deliver a voltage of the proper level and traits to allow load gadget to feature well[13].

## D) Fuel Cell:

It is a device that converts the chemical energy into the electrical energy by chemical reaction with oxygen or another oxidizing agent. Hydrogen is the maximum commonplace gasoline, but hydrocarbons consisting of herbal gas and alcohols like methanol are once in a while used. Gas cells are special from batteries in that they require a steady supply of gas and oxygen/air to maintain the chemical reaction; but, gas cells can produce electricity continually for as long as these inputs are supplied.

## Homer:

The HOMER is an optimization tool use to simulate different energy source for generation of electric power. It is an effective device for designing and studying hybrid power structures, which encompass numerous conventional mills structures, blended heat and strength, wind turbines, sun photovoltaic, storage batteries systems, hydro power generating device, biomass generating machine and lots of other inputs. HOMER facilitates decide how variable assets such as wind and sun may be optimally included into hybrid systems. HOMER determines the monetary feasibility of a hybrid power gadget optimizes the machine design and permits users to virtually recognize how hybrid renewable systems work. HOMER can serve utilities, telecoms, systems integrators, and many other forms of mission developers- to mitigate the monetary threat of their hybrid power projects [9].In [9], the HOMER software has been used to optimally size PV/wind/diesel hybrid energy systems by considering the weather profile of Malaysia. In this paper, a new optimization method, which considers the maximum availability and the minimum system capital cost, is developed for optimal sizing of a building-integrated PV/wind/diesel hybrid energy system.

## Needs of Hybrid System:

In 2002 power generated by thermal power plant is three quarter of the total generated power. If we see the rate of consumption of energy in current days than we have reserves of coal for about 200 years. Whereas stock for gases is approximately 40-60 years.  Since the development increased gradually, whereas natural  energy resources decreases and environmental problems increases day by day indicates us to develop some new power generating system, which overcome this type of problem. Hybrid power generating system is one of the best suited systems of power generation on today aspects because it is economical as well as environmental friendly [7,9,14].

## Hybrid System and its Importance

Hybrid technology has developed and upgraded in the resent years, the importance and benefits of renewable energy source are unchallenged. Hybrid system used in many houses of rural as well as urban areas. Since hybrid system is more economical than single renewable energy system hence many island installed hybrid system [15]. The main function of hybrid system including solar, wind and storage battery system is shown in fig.2.

**Fig.2 Schematic diagram of hybrid system**

In hybrid system wind power system and PV cells provide DC power. For the conversion of DC power obtained by solar and wind system a semiconductor-based device (power inverter) is used to convert the DC power in to AC power. This specific hybrid system shown in fig.2 has many benefits such as:-

- Solar and wind power obtained by nature so no need of fuel for the operation of wind and solar power so it is free of cost.
- Since solar and wind system does not induced any type toxic gages so do not pollute the environment.
- Solar power can be induced during the day and wind power can be obtained on day as well as night so the need of power can be fulfilled by combination of both systems.

**How Does a Hybrid System Work?**

A hybrid electric system that is the combine of renewable energy system likes wind and solar power plants have several advantages over single energy systems. Generally renewable energy systems (Solar & wind) are based on weather and geographical concisions of the country. If we talk about the Indian conditions, winds speeds are high in the summer when the sun shines brightest are also longest. In the winter session the wind speed is low and   sunlight is also available in low density. Because the peak operating times for wind and solar systems occur at different times of the day and year, hybrid systems are more likely to produce power when need it[16]. Many hybrid systems are operated alone generally it is called "off-grid" system, its means that this is not connected to electricity distribution system. For the times when the wind nor the solar system are not producing electrical power at that condition, most hybrid systems provide power through batteries or  used diesel engine generator. If the batteries run on low power, the diesel engine generator used to provide power and recharge the batteries.

**Proposed Methodology**

HOMER is a simulation tool developed by the U.S. National Renewable Energy Laboratory (NREL) to assist in the planning and design of renewable energy based on micro grids. It aims to optimize hybrid systems that consist of low-power renewable energy resources generation system and conventional energy resources generation system. Due to structural changes in supply and demand  of electric  energy very rapidly,  it is required to grown more  efficient electric power system. In this condition, the role of electric energy exchange is becoming critical. This work examines how the benefit from electric energy exchange can be optimized. It is also examine that how many factors affect the optimization of the electric power system.

**HOMER:**

The HOMER is defining as hybrid optimization model for electric renewable energy software. It is a powerful optimization tool for designing and analyzing hybrid power systems. Hybrid system may be containing a mix of conventional generators, combined heat and power, wind turbines, solar photo voltaic cells, storage batteries, hydropower, biomass and other inputs can be optimized by using Homer. HOMER helps to determine how variable resources such as wind and solar system can be integrated within hybrid systems and may be optimized. Design of grids can be evaluated by HOMER for both off-grid and grid-connected power systems for a variety of applications [17].

**How HOMER used to evaluate the Solution of the Problem?**

For obtain the best solution of the hybrid system by using Homer it is required to provide hybrid model with their inputs, cost of component connected with hybrid system, and availability of source. These available inputs are simulated HOMER for different system configurations, or combinations of components, and generates results that can view as a list of feasible configurations sorted by net present cost. Simulation results of any hybrid system display by HOMER in a large range of tables and graphs that help us to compare configurations in various aspects like system economical operation and technical advantages [18].

**Working of HOMER**

HOMER simulates the operation of a hybrid system in every step of operation by making energy balance calculations of every year. For every moment of operation, HOMER compares the electric and thermal demand in that time step to the generated energy, which is supply to the system at that time of operation, and calculates the flows of energy from each component of the system. For systems that include batteries or diesel engine generators, operation of diesel generators is decided by HOMER for each time step and whether to charge or discharge the storage batteries [19].HOMER performs these energy stability calculations for each hybrid system organization. It then determines whether a construction is possible, i.e., whether it can fulfil the electric demand under the conditions that specify in the system, and estimates the cost of installing and operating the system over the lifetime of the project. Cost calculations for any system for analysis of costs like as capital cost, replacement cost, operation and maintenance cost, fuel cost and interest on the system.

**Algorithm of HOMER**

- Step 1: Formulate a question that we need to answer from the HOMER.
- Step 2: Create a new HOMER file
- Step 3: Making the plan
- Step 4: Enter load details
- Step 5: Enter component details
- Step 6: Enter resource details
- Step 7: Ensure inputs and accurate errors
- Step 8: Observe optimization outcomes
- Step 9: Process the arrangement plan
- Step 10: Addition of variables sensitivity
- Step 11: Examine sensitivity investigation outcomes

**References**

1) Muralikrishna M and V. Lakshminarayana, "hybrid (solar and wind) energy systems for rural electrification", ARPN Journal of Engineering and Applied Sciences, VOL. 3, NO. 5, pp.50-59, October 2008.

2) Kashefi Kaviani, G. H. Riahy, and SH. M. Kouhsari, "Optimal design of a reliable hydrogen-based stand-alone wind/PV generating system, considering component outages," Renewable Energy, vol. 34, pp. 2380-2390, 2009.

3) Pragya Nema, R.K. Nema, SarojRangnekar, "PV-solar / wind hybrid energy system for GSM/CDMA type mobile telephony base station", International journal of energy and environment 2010.

4) Shafiullah, Amanullah M.T. Ooa, ABM Shawkat Ali b, Dennis Jarvis b, Peter Wolfs c, " Economic Analysis of Hybrid Renewable Model for Subtropical Climate", Int. J. of Thermal & Environmental Engineering, pp.23-30, 2010.

5) Prabodh Bajpai , Sowjan Kumar, "Sizing Optimization and Analysis of a Stand-alone WTG System Using Hybrid Energy Storage Technologies", AIP Journal 2011.

6) Hakimi, S. M. "Optimal sizing of reliable hybrid renewable energy system considered various load types", AIP Journal of Renewable and sustainable energy 2011.

7) Deepak Kumar Lal, BibhutiBhusan Dash, "Optimization of PV/Wind/Micro-Hydro/Diesel Hybrid Power System in HOMER for the Study Area", International Journal on Electrical Engineering and Informatics, Volume 3, Number 3, 2011.

8) Maherchandani, Chitranjan Agarwal, "Economic Feasibility of Hybrid Biomass/PV/Wind System for Remote Villages Using HOMER", International Journal of Advanced Research in Electrical, Electronics and Instrumentation Engineering Vol. 1, Issue 2, August 2012.

9) Noel N. Schulz, "Impact of Distributed Generations with Energy Storage Devices on the Electric Grid", IEEE SYSTEMS JOURNAL, VOL. 6, NO. 1, pp.108-116, MARCH 2012.

10) Saeed Jahdi Loi Lei Lai Daneil Nankoo, "Renewable Hybrids Grid-Connection Using Converter Interferences", International Journal of Sustainable Energy Development (IJSED), Volume 1, Issues 1/2, pp.51-58, March/June 2012.

11) Sandeep Puppala, M Ebraheem, " Non-Conventional Power Generation Using Solar And Wind With The Aid Of Hydro Power Generation," International Journal of Engineering Research and Applications (IJERA),Vol. 2, Issue 4, July-August 2012, pp.271-274.

12) Yandra Shivrath, P. Badari Narayana, "Modeling and Control Of Hybrid Photovoltaic wind Energy Conversion System," International Journal of Advances in Engineering & Technology, pp.192-202. May 2012.

13) Motin, Md. Forhad Zaman, M.R.I. Sheikh, "Energy Efficient Modeling of Solar Wind Hybrid Power System for a Tourist Island", international journal of advanced renewable energy research, Vol. 1, Issue.1, pp. 1- 7, 2012.

14) Satish Kumar Ramoji, B.Jagadish Kumar, "Optimal Economical sizing of a PV-Wind Hybrid Energy System using Genetic Algorithm and Teaching Learning Based Optimization," International Journal of Advanced Research in Electrical, Electronics and Instrumentation Engineering, Vol. 3, Issue 2, pp. 7353-7367, February 2014.

15) Vivek Kumar Soni and Ranjeeta Khare, "Optimal Sizing of HRES for Small Sized Institute Using HOMER", IEEE conference, pp.77-82, 2014.

16) Bogaraj, T., J. Kanakaraj, K. Mohan Kumar, "Optimal sizing and cost analysis of hybrid power system for a stand-alone application in Coimbatore region: a case study", archives of electrical engineering, vol. 64(1), pp. 139-155, 2015.

17) Rachit Srivastava and Vinod Kumar Giri, "Optimization of Hybrid Renewable Resources using HOMER", International Journal of Renewable Energy, Vol.6, No.1, Pp.158-163, 2016.

18) Miqdam T ChaichanP, Hussein A Kazem, Aedah M J Mahdy Pand and Ali A Al-Waeely, "Optimal Sizing of a Hybrid System of Renewable Energy for Lighting Street in Salalah-Oman using Homer software", International Journal of Scientific Engineering and Applied Science (IJSEAS) – Volume-2, Issue-5, May 2016.

19) Laith M. Halabi, Saad Mekhilef, Lanre Olatomiwa, James Hazelton, "Performance analysis of hybrid PV/diesel/battery system using HOMER: A case study Sabah, Malaysia", Energy Conversion and Management (Elsevier), 144 pp. 322–339, 2017.

# CHAPTER – 13

## THE CO-ORDINATION OF APPLIED MATHEMATICS ALONG SIDE ELECTRICAL ENGINEERING

## BY
## Kumar Avinash Chandra


**Abstract:**

The chapter of mine cites the ontogenesis of appositeness of the branch of Electrical Engineering as an Applied Mathematics (MA). There seem no foiling altercations seems obligatory for acclimatization betwixt the branch of physics, mathematics and of that electrical engineering (EE). Aforesaid systemization prevails in each EE and imperative colloquium of the paper to actualize the confabulation how and whereby the systemization be accomplished. The section of EE has potential within for to be linked and be individuate with the human demeanor. The recent advancement in Artificial Intelligenceis purely amalgamation of Advanced Applied Mathematics and electrical engineering which paved the walkway for the researchers, industries and scientists to work on the comprehensively newfangled division to supplant mechanical devices for human demeanor. The doctrine of EE can be confabulated as quadruplicate vantage points as in: discipline of intelligentsia under the scope of science and scientific philosophy, the wing of engineering having industrialized utilization factor and, communal structure of synergy span between contemporary world and millennium.

**Keywords:** Applied mathematics; Electrical Engineering; Artificial Intelligence;

**Acronyms:** Applied mathematics, MA; Electrical Engineering, EE; Artificial Intelligence, AI; Machine Learning, ML.


**Introduction:**

Basically, the root and fundamental logic for study of any branch of engineering is to inoculate the disciples to admire and cinch of the methodology for the elucidation of the conundrum that been earmarked as scientific approach, exhibited as organized progression dwelling research, generalization and application.The aforesaid methodology relies comprehensively upon the branch of science that concerns with the energy and object i.e. Physics and the subsidiary of science that designs the relation and perceptible approach to the laws of physics and precepts evaluated and illustrated i.e. Mathematics. The under graduate disciples of the engineering are therefore compulsorily taught mathematics and physics in their curriculum. The students are then qualified for fusion of the two terrains in blended approach which is root method for the any scientific methodology.The pioneering work in the field of the physics being the base of the curriculum in EE subjects enacts as the ground for the concepts and accord with the elemental law and the rapport administrating the electrostatics, phenomenon for magnetism and as well the d.c. circuitry allowing the flow of current through it. The interpretation of governing rule of motor and generators can be understood and be in accord only with the proper understanding of mechanics of physics and laws of motion stated in physics, which embodiment the consequent course work for the subjects in the EE curriculum. The proposition for light which explained in physicslike the other propositions as electrical conduction via gaseous state, atomic physics, wave, sound establishes the substratum for the illuminating engineering, and for communication and electronics, the sub part of EE and embodiment the consequent course work for the subjects in the EE curriculum.The EE subject course work enjoy the same adjuncts with the branches of mathematics in the similar fashion as EE subjects enjoys with the physics. The preceding subjectsfrom the domain of mathematics as in calculus, analytic geometry, Fourier series, empirical equations, partial and ordinary differential equations, harmonics, probability, matrices and determinants, complex numbers, elliptical integrations, line integrals are being taught in through the whole of first two years of engineering course work forms the base lining for the engineering course prevalent for all the branches of engineering. The adjunct of mathematicsand MA in engineeringcourse works enables the students to develop, acknowledge and to recognize the science of mathematics so as to attain the skills and tenacity of the science for the solution to problems.The course work of mathematicsand MA in the engineering curriculum though not in a great depth but, intention is here rather than to create master of the topic, to get the students the acquaint with the application to the complications in the practical world of the engineering notably in the arena of electrical engineering.

**Mathematics and Electrical Engineering**

The expansion of engineering along side of applied science is one and the same as the scope of mathematics in the field of engineering. Engineering being adjunct of scientific theories and the practical implantation of the same. The dominance of either facets dominance over other is beyond the scope of definition in the engineering arena. As in date today, particularly a person with scientific backdrop having significant extent can establish the self with of that section of professional activity which prevails and thus, portrays its indispensable nuance or context.

**Applied Mathematics and Electrical Engineering**

The discipline of engineering curriculum in EE is devised in such a mannerism that it can passed down to sway the locus, speed, acceleration and as well as direction of an object and is prevalent in industrial, combatant and in our day-to-day life as well. With the proper delineation howsoever, convince of EE can be exploited beyond an erratic system.Various aspects of the EE can be adjunct to the human behavioral. It can be designed in such a way so as it can think and act alike humans in a way it can be used to replicate human behavioral and at some level to replace the human process as well. Its a notion or perception which is intrinsic to the nature.Artificial intelligence, machine learning the new emerging topics in the field of engineering that is used to control and at some extent replacing the human effort at industrial and in our day to day life is one perfect examples of the applied mathematics conjecture in the engineering discipline particularly to the electrical field of engineering. Many companies are in race to today to design the AI and ML algorithm based on fuzzy logic, neural network i.e. completely MA induced into EE. Theoretical section of EE can be further studied into the four subsections as: philosophic section of science; scholarly curriculum of the science; a section of science with application related to industrial utilization; and the social conundrum of the contemporary world. We shall discuss the four sections in later portion of this article.

**Aspects of Mathematics in Electrical Engineering**

The aspects of engineering have changed drastically in recent few decades especially that can be when in regards to the EE. The phrase though, too divergent but holds its gravity as its consequences can not be abjured. The modern day's concept on linear system or circuit theories are not only limited to art of electrical only but requires application of mathematics. Intrinsic contributions made by famous mathematicians as Oliver Heaviside, Lord Rayleigh made it easy and simpler to solve the problems in electrical transmission and regeneration and reproduction of various signalsas well. The motivation from the same led to discovery of purely mathematician model for complex variables for the network theory, signal system and various other aspects of electrical engineering.

**Theoretical Electrical Engineering:**

Theoretical EE more often known as system theory which is a sub section of MA dealing with the machine design and diverse engineering structure so as to, they can excel in their performance when compared to prior options. Theoretical EE provides the requisite effort for the motion, sensors and various other essential components to conclude their assigned and expected work. Examining the intricacy of administrating the room temperature of a building for an illustration of aspects of theoretical EE. The above statement or intricacy can be considered as a classic issue of engineering that being familiar to us all. The furnace as a begetter of heat and thermometer, a device to measure the current temperature forms the essential part of the thermal system. The external system are considered to be taken as stagnant and irrelevant for the specified thermodynamic system. The control system which is basically the branch of the MA, is applied here to administer and maintain the room temperature at a desired value prespecified by the user or the system. The control system measures and track the record of the room temperature at regular interval of time and accordingly varies the thermal system with the fluctuation of the current room temperature. The thermostat control facets and compares the current and desired value of the thermostat setting, the preset desired value of the temperature and the control works accordingly. The furnace, heating source accordingly as per the signal receivedfrom the thermostat, works upon that basis. The control signal from the thermostat administers the furnace to alter the heating effect to intensify or soothe the furnace.

**Electrical Engineering as in Physical System**

The application of EE can be visualized in almost every facet of our day to day life practices. From our kitchen appliance to grooming kit, from needs of our daily commutation to comfort in the couch of our living room, EE plays its role. The mathematics lies behind the design of the ever machinery. The water heater in our bathroom or central air conditioner installed or the refrigerator in our kitchen, the dangling ceiling fan in our rooms the design aspects is purely based on the mathematical calculations. A slight error in the mathematical calculation in the design of the equipment can result in failure of the equipment or loss of efficiency of the designed equipment or the system. The microwave oven in our kitchen, all those equipment perform on precise principle led by MA behind their design. The main focus of the engineers of EE is own about administrating the external effects such as humidity, pressure, temperature, thickness, quality and other such variables of interest. Here, under the heading EE is represented the various arena where the utilization of electrical engineering can be precedented into various different facets of engineering as in space expedition, commutation in rail, road or airways, robotics, military and spy engineering, biotics etc.

**Electrical Engineering as in our Routine Activity**

The humans and the kinship with the utilization of EE is been propelled to a great extent in recent few years with the advancement in new technologies and scientific advancements. Researching Information theory and EE theory is encouraging way as suggested by Wiener.The recent advancements in the technologies has enabled the humans to be dependent more on machines that can act more like humans and some level they can replace human behavior. The automation system that since introduced has working and replaced humans with machine interface. The home automation system or digital personal assistant now a days is widely used is precisely based on this very principle. The most convenient feature of this being the adaptability of the system that can modify its functionality as in a way to order to achieve optimum and efficient performance level. Human beings or any living creature, for sure are the most convoluted and impeccable system capable fully for adaptation. Developing any mathematical model analogous to that needed to be adaptable and continuous learning and familiarized with the road map ahead.

**Electrical Engineering as in Industrial System**

Automation system introduced in the engineering was first gained its popularity from industrial utilization. Since the 18th century that started from Britain, the regular attempts been made to advancement in the field. As in now most of the industries throughout the world are automated and are working efficiently with minimal human effort. Robotics the most widely utilized and popular aspect of engineering is that controlling the industries now a days. The automobile sector, biomedicals or be any sector of engineering facets is one way or other is employs robotics in their system for enhancing their effectiveness and production rate. The branch of engineering, robotics purely based on fuzzy systems and MA, has his wings spread in various other sectors as well as in defense mechanism, supply chain or commutation. The advancement in EE and robotics is most likely to subtle the potential brunt upon the productivity and effectiveness of the system. The technical enhancements have helped in designing more mosaic and convoluted computer system and processors that are further more enhancing the capability and sophistication of the robotics, allowing them to act more like human as in thinking and logical capabilities, known as to *'Intelligent Systems'*.

**Summary**

Whenever, more scientific facets of engineering are needed to be introduced in a system, emphasis is on physics, MA and advanced mathematics dwindling the conventional methods of engineering in exercise. Today, in this world of 'face lifting' venture, advanced and applied mathematics has a crucial part in the scientific methods in adjunct with the physics. Unlike, few decades ago mathematics application was looked upon as extravagance in the pretext to scientific methods. Today, applied mathematics and its subsystems, fuzzy logics and more widely applied into various aspects of engineering precisely in context to electrical engineering.

**References**

1) Philips, R., Rohani Jahja Widodo and R.D. Harbor, "FeedbackControl System", in SistemKontrolLanjutan, 3rd Edition.
2) RohaniJahjha Widodo, "Automatic Controls for Reducing Energy Consumptions and Improving Energy Conservations", (CAFEO-10), 5-6 November, 1992.
3) Royce D. Harbor and Charles L. Philips, "Feedback Control System" Prentice Hall International, Inc, 2000.
4) Longhairs and short waves, Fortune, Newyork, vol. 32, no. 5, November 1945, pg 169.
5) Bishop R. H and R.C. Dorf, "Modern Control System", Ninth Edition, Prentice Hall, 2001.
6) Augstin, P and B.Z. Yuda, "Pengaturan Level Air BendunganMeggunakan SCADA", Prosiding Seminar Nasional Teknik SumberDaya Air 2010, ISBN 978-979-98539-9-8, 2010 pg 171-177.
7) Yuda, Z and I. Dede, "Kendali Level Air DenganMengunnan Parameter PID Controller", Procedding Seminar on Intelligent Technology and its Application (SITIA), volume 13, ISSN- 2252-8296, pg 555-565.

# CHAPTER – 14

# RAMIFICATIONS OF COVID-19 ON HIGHER EDUCATION AND IN JOB MARKET

**BY**
**Lalit Malik**

**Abstract:**

COVID-19 outbreak has badly affected the world economy by disrupting the premises over the globe whether it is schools, colleges, or universities by shaking the normal routines of productivity and growth of the masses. The impulsive stoppage of various organizations by not putting the juxtaposition as to preclude community transportation has substituted manual study e-learning. Students are now concentrating on applying various e-Learning tools and providing podiums for impressive engagement of students such as google meet, zoom, Microsoft team and so many. The pandemic has been manifested the pitfalls of the system of higher education and we have to prepare the faculties or professors for the digital era to adapt to the extremity of the need for making them familiar with all the resources which are being used to enhance the rapid growth of this swift atmosphere of higher education in the world. On the other hand even recruiters are using virtual technology to hire the right candidates and using AI and ML techniques to complete their recruitment process by efficiently using the digital techniques, various webinar to train their faculties and online session e.g: Conferences, seminars and workshops.

**Keywords:** COVID-19, higher education, work from home, virtual classes, E-Learning, Online Recruitment.

**Introduction:**

Covid-19 has triumphantly affected the planet. The hiring process has been changed up to large extent as according to Madeline Laureano founder of Aptitude research which is a renowned firm based on business hiring process study. We can complete our scheduling work through automation in a very short period, As per the report of the firm named hirevue famous for making online interview tools. Campuses are places where students live and study close to each other. Recently, the foundations of this unique education ecosystem mean different campuses around the world have been impacted significantly by the rapid spread of the coronavirus (Covid-19) outbreak, creating uncertainty regarding the implications for higher education. According to a UN report, around 160 crore children belonging to almost 200 countries were unable to go to schools and colleges. This happened for the first time in India. In India, 36 crore children were affected by the pandemic. According to the American study, when the students will return to school, their reading skills would be reduced by 30% approx., and in mathematics, students would fall behind for one long year.According to the HPE report of Britain, international university admissions declined by 80-100%. Universities like Harvard, Cambridge, etc. have to face a loss of around 1000 crores because of rare admissions of foreign students. According to the report of the world bank, the lockdown of 3 months and shutdown of schools have been a reason to put 47% of students under the category of learning poverty in a decade.According to another report, even after improvement in the current situation of the pandemic, 97 children would not be able to return to schools or colleges in our country.

**What do we get?**

What is the effect of a pandemic on the world's education system and new education policy especially in our country?

**UNICEF:** According to the report of the World Bank, new ways were found for online and offline classes to provide education to children. Teachers uploaded their lessons on youtube except that open exams were also the need of time and served as the most popular ones during the pandemic. Cambridge university decided to run an online session for 2020-21. Other than this Harvard University has freed 67 online courses for students from all our world. Our country got a new education policy. New education policy has been created in such a way that skills could be developed in every child. The government has decided to spend 6% of the GDP on this policy, but as of now, it is a big challenge to prepare teachers for the same. The use of technology is being increased in the hiring process by recruiters a day in and day out. According to the firm named aptitude research, last year Feb 2020, 58% of businesses/corporates were using software for their hiring process, and today this percentage has been increased to 77%. This software is giving the facility to submit their viewpoints through video conferencing or video calling as by the effect of covid-19. Every recruiter is not willing to join their staffs in their offices as they don't want to take risks of proximity due to pandemic, now recruiters are saving their time and hard work by using Artificial intelligence and Machine Learning based software through which they are now getting much more eligible and right candidates for the businesses as they are not biased to any special candidates who are not eligible.Software imbibing AI, ML will take the marks by solving puzzles, gaming, reasoning, and aptitude questions. AI and ML and almost vanished the chances of getting wrong decisions and reducing the biased atmosphere of the premises by putting more human values and take the right decisions for the right candidate. In Short, this would enhance the productivity of the companies by getting more sharp and expert candidates, who will sort much more problems in the context of productivity, business values, and society in a more efficient way.According to Gitanjali Rao, In the ever-changing world, in today's scenario 26 crore children and youngsters are getting the facility to go to school. Government has to think of this matter as very deep concern. We have to find the solution by providing the education online from home so that students could learn while sitting at their homes. But the problem is that in many countries still, internet facilities are not available, we have to work on it up to a large extent and no doubt, by the emergence of this breakthrough. Each & every individual could take the facility of getting their courses online without relocating to other places in the world.

**Problems:**

As we all know, still broadband/wifi connection installation is costly due to new 5G infrastructure or installation of fiber optics, this would be in the reach of upper-middle or rich classes not below that so labor class's children would face huge problems due to this. Every Govt/Ministry of IT and broadcasting have to make sure that internet facility would be another right which has to be given to this class so, in all fundamental rights, we should include internet facility right also as of now this is the need of time for every person e.g right to education for children.Nowadays, recruiters are hiring candidates through online gaming/puzzles, and they are measuring their cognitive, social, and emotional intelligence. Often this critical thing has been recognized that by using traditional methods of recruitment, Recruitments were less prone to respond to the follow-up messages of candidates, but now AI-based chatbots can give quick response without any human intervention. So the headache of human resources is now reducing as AI-based software can give the updates of every stage by confirming the candidates' engagement in a better way and companies are now feeling better about their brand name as well as established. Now Government is also highly concerned about to provide such a productive environment and introduce new guidelines for B.P.O and for the IT industry to take work from home or work from anywhere, companies are also showing interest to take all advantages to save their money and hard work. E.g: Bills, transportation costs, building rent, premise taxes, accessories, and other facilities that have been mandatory to provide to all their employees as a part of the job schedule/work environment. So after Covid-19. The government has decided to provide some relaxation in the rules of working at a fixed place e.g: office or premise even now employee are permanently allowed to work from home or work from anywhere and the government is planning to provide such environment so that employee can do work from anywhere, they can work and submit their work at the end of the day through emails, by using so many reliable system programs/software, they can communicate through these e.g: virtual meetings, pieces of training, video conferencing and audio and video tools which is helpful to provide such an environment.Covid-19 and global lockdown have necessarily indicated substantial interruption for the large no of students. Many undergraduates and other than that who had involved themselves for higher education in the various foreign universities have come back finally to their native place, and now they are encouraged to take their further course in an online mode.

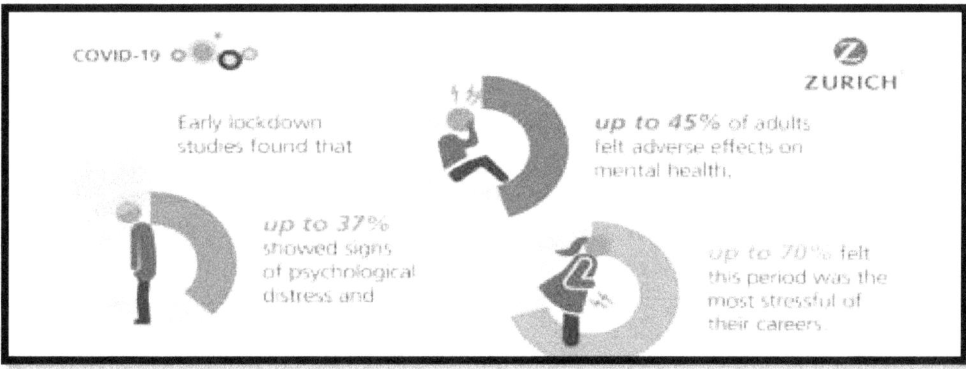


Now there's growing concern about the potential impact the current crisis might have on future demand, particularly from overseas students."Covid-19 is undoubtedly a compelling impact on this year as hiring in the corporates and admissions period for international students have been dismissed," says a spokesperson for Universities UK, which represents the higher education sector.So it's no dazzle that various colleges, universities, and businesses are restlessly waiting to see how the new registrations of students will be influenced by the present situation and future constraints.

**Responding to the uncertainties:**

According to various spokespersons in colleges and universities over the globe is restrained as they established the value: "Parents are progressively looking the outcomes through their wards which they have been devoted as an investment of education. Many colleges and universities entrenched their next bunch of new enrollments before the deadline for the coming sessions so that pandemics would not affect the process of intake for the next sessions and they have started the tour of their campuses through VR technology. These ceremonies will be celebrated throughout both sessions in a year. It is tough to envision the intensity of the impact until the current situation is not clear. Unfortunately, the number of inter-continental students will also face a lot of difficulties coming back to overseas countries for further education from their native places as they had returned to their hometowns due to the pandemic. Due to the second waves in the various countries, foreign students encounter a lot of constraints on a voyage.

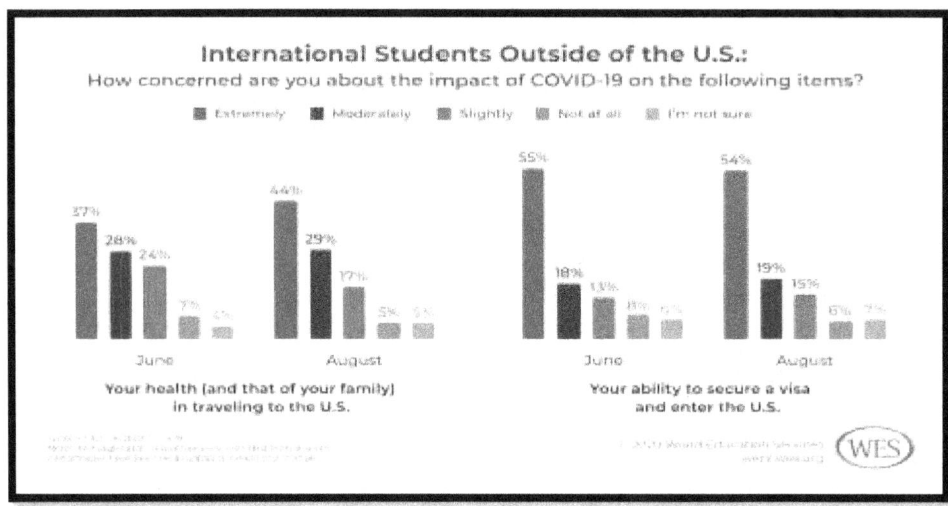


## Recession is the big concern:

Covid-19 is not just limited to a medical condition of an individual but it has also impacted the lives of students. Apart from that, the world has seen a serious downturn that reduced the demand for students in every field. According to the studies around 14% of the financially strong students, would only be able to return to their studies for the next financial year.Now people are making sure to continue their further studies from non-trendy universities so that they could stay closer to their family and their loved ones, even if they are unable to get a job. And due to this, there has been a lift in the number of students in such universities. Being so much affected by this recession, now families have cut down their consumption and their expenses. Their dreams of a fancy and comfortable lifestyle remained a dream. Moreover, the idea of sending their children overseas for education may not be fulfilled anymore.

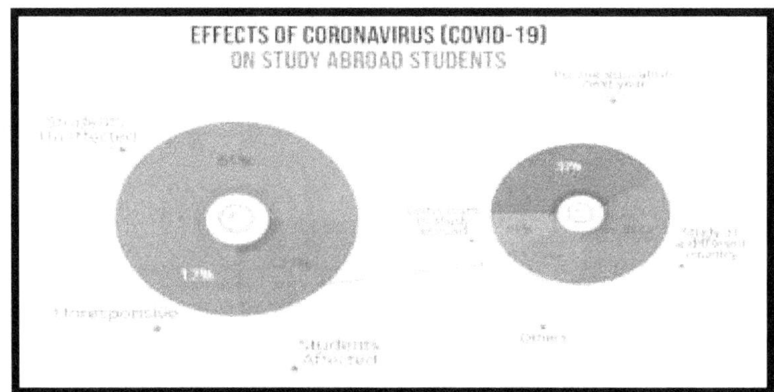


## Still an attractive place to study:

While the actual interest of the students for their future remains the same, the appeal for higher education from students all over the globe captivates them. Universities of the US and UK are considered to provide the best education to children all over the world. For certification at these universities, people invest their efforts till depth. According to my belief, we would come over this situation and will not sacrifice with the higher education of our children. Once the world proceeds to resume and the flights sustain, the standards of higher education at universities of the UK and US may assume to be perceived. Some parents of children, who are still studying, have unstable situations at their home, as there has been a disbalance created between their studies and the family life. Many parents used to visit university libraries so that they could find a quiet place to study distant from their homes. But with this pandemic situation of Covid, the libraries have been shut down. Those parents who want to continue their studies, have to wait for their children to sleep so that they could concentrate on their studies. Most of the time, these parents have to complete their academic work the whole night and rise from their bed early to feed other family members. On top of all these, it is a hardship for those who have to make their children attend school online and also make sure that the online material sent by the school is being completed by their children. Nowadays, without any surprise the students who are working from their home, for them IT has appeared as a burden. Even though the universities have provided a lot of study material to these parents, but still nothing had remained their own as they have to share their phones and laptops with their children so that they do not lack behind. Many parents' expenses have increased by the overuse of the printers at their home. Earlier the printer was used only for their work but now it is mostly being used for printing the online material sent by the school for their children. The cost of living has increased.

## Post pandemic Game changing opportunity

The stoppage of educational institutes is responsible for the positive change in society, now likewise work from home students would start the journey of learning from home. Covid pandemic has allowed all for adapting new techniques in curriculum. Now it is possible to study at Harvard, MIT, and Standford from their home town. It has been a game-changing opportunity for everyone. Now the classroom has been changed from offline to online and the traditional ways have been reconciled to edX, where high-quality online material is available. Merging online teaching with manual teaching is the new normal nowadays which is taking us in the direction of a higher quality of education.

## The era of virtual hiring persists after the covid-19 pandemic

Organizations and educational institutions are now using a hybrid model for their recruitments and hiring process. Now onwards they tend to hire the candidates online through virtual meetings and virtual interviews for the various remote jobs. According to that process candidates also upskilling themselves through various technologies like Virtual Reality, Artificial Intelligence, Internet of Things, Data Analytics, Machine learning, Deep learning, Blockchain, Cloud Computing, etc. on numerous platforms. According to jobwhite's research digital communication tools like Artificial intelligence programs outreaching as the day in and day out. Recruiters are using social media platforms for their recruitments and hiring process like Facebook, LinkedIn. This pandemic has changed the way of the hiring process and presents new innovative ideas or ways to recruit the right candidate. According to the report of www.staffingstreams.com, the survey has been done on 500 companies in which 90% of respondents said during this pandemic, undoubtedly we have changed the way of hiring. During a lockdown, 51% of staffing professional has been taken the interview through online mode and 42% has given remote offers to the candidates.

**How the Coronavirus Could Affect Your College Life and Plans**

"Breakout of Coronavirus has been widely spread on the education. The Chronicle of Higher Education on February 29, 2020, had reported that colleges and universities are thinking critically on this crucial issue and make planning that how they will react if the escalation of the virus extends and go on with large masses. They are taking into account the schedules of their academic years have been in dilemma, breaking off their sessions or term exams.Google became the first company in the world to announce the work from home opportunity for their employees during a pandemic, Twitter has also given the same opportunity to its employees according to their will. According to the latest report of job hiring outlook survey, 47% of the recruiters are working from home nowadays and from this 69% of people admit that they are more productive by adopting this system of working. Moreover, 60% of the job seekers and office workers would prefer to work in the same environment. It is cleared from the above statements that offices will remain at their places but by the upcoming trend of remote working the preference would be given to the hybrid model of working shortly.

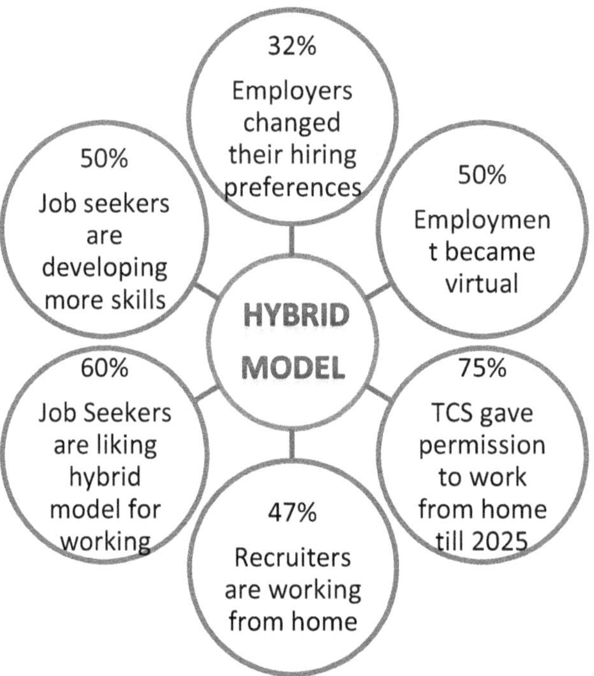


**Skill sets in demand:**

Nowadays work from home has become the reality. Digital-based jobs are likely to remain in remote mode in the years ahead. This is the reason that upskilling will be the most important factor in employability in the coming times. In a survey by naukri.com, about 50% of the job seekers said that they are not only focusing on their professional development through upskilling but also increasing the knowledge of their field. And also for preparing their resume they are taking the help of the professionals. It has been seen a hike in the registration mostly in online learning platform courses like machine learning and artificial intelligence. According to a technology platform namely, Great Learning 41% of learners are working professionals and 28% are highly graduates. This pandemic has made us learn that the skills that we have are different from the skills that are required by the industries.

**Employers will give preference to temporary employees instead of permanent:**

Remote hiring has increased three times as compared to before covid. According to the managing director of indeed.com, Sashi Kumar, administration of freshers (14%), tech-software (10%), customer servicing (8%), marketing (5%), and sales (4%) were different opportunities in this field. During this situation, the preferences of companies changed. Many research companies changed their preference to temporary and contractual employees instead of permanent employees.

**Remote hiring increased, prepared for a virtual interview:**

According to the job search sites, 1 out of 2 recruitment was through virtual interviews. Because of this, even the HR experts have made clear that the candidates have to make themselves comfortable for virtual interviews. And also they have to make sure about their body language, dressing sense, and also strong network range at their place.

**Increase in Online Education:**

The popularity of online courses is increasing rapidly all over the world. According to a report, students who have registered for online courses would increase by six times. Large and prestigious institutions are now offering online courses. Most students are interested in Computer Science, Data Science and Programming, etc. In India, not only educational institutes but also the government is promoting these courses.

In the last few years trend of online education has increased. Earlier only private institutes used to offer such online courses, but now universities all around the world have started allowing studying online by introducing different courses. Even some universities are offering the courses free of cost. According to a report within 3 months, around 200 high education institutes started 600 Massive Open Online Learning Course (MOOC) all around the world. Not only this in the last 6 years an enhancement has also been observed in this field, as 800 high education institutes offered more than 8 thousand MOOCs.

**Conclusion**

We can conclude from the above that Covid-19 has affected higher education drastically. Also, the global lockdown has interrupted the studies of the students in a huge way. In the starting phase of lockdown, many students were not able to afford electronic items for continuing their studies, but later by hook or by crook, they were forced to arrange it for their higher education as everything went online. Many undergraduates and other than that who had involved themselves for higher education in the various foreign universities have come back finally to their native place, and now they are encouraged to take their further course in an online mode. Not only studies but also recruitments, college placements, and even interviews started virtually.

**References**


1) https://covid19.who.int/
2) https://papers.ssrn.com/sol3/papers.cfm?abstract_id=3691541
3) https://www.highereducationdigest.com/impact-of-covid-19-on-higher-education/\
4) http://www.guninetwork.org/files/guni_impact_of_covid_19_pandemic_on_higher_educ ation_a_critical_review_india.pdf
5) https://www.researchgate.net/publication/342277024_Impact_of_Covid-19_on_higher_education_in_India
6) http://jgu.edu.in/blog/2020/06/29/impact-of-covid-19-on-higher-education-challenges-opportunities/
7) https://timesofindia.indiatimes.com/readersblog/lifekibaat/impact-of-covid-19-on-higher-education-in-india-24819/
8) https://www.collegedekho.com/articles/covid-19-impact-higher-education-india/
9) https://www.indiatoday.in/magazine/news-makers/story/20210111-school-of-hard-knocks-1755078-2021-01-03
10) https://www.nationalheraldindia.com/videos/covid-19-impact-six-million-children-out-of-school-in-india-2
11) https://www.weforum.org/agenda/2020/10/how-covid-19-deepens-the-digital-education-divide-in-india/
12) https://www.latestlaws.com/articles/impact-of-covid-19-on-education-system-in-india/
13) https://www.sciencedirect.com/science/article/pii/S1888429620300558
14) https://www.theleaflet.in/covid-19-impact-six-million-children-out-of-school-in-india/
15) https://www.coherentmarketinsights.com/blog/impact-of-covid-19-on-education-system-in-india-109

# FERRITE NANOPARTICLES FOR ADVANCED BIOMEDICAL APPLICATIONS IN DRUG DELIVERY: A REVIEW

## BY
## Smita Tolani

**Abstract:**

Magnetic Ferrite Nanoparticles have an advantage over conventional nanocarriers as they can be guided in the body using an external or internal magnetic field. These Magnetic nanoparticles create local hyperthermia heating up the carrier to trigger drug release in the sites. These particles can also been seen and tracked using Magnetic Resonance Imaging (MRI). This makes them attractive and unique in drug delivery systems in medicine. This review discusses the role of ferrite nanoparticles for advanced biomedical applications in Drug Delivery.

**Keywords:** Magnetic Ferrite Nanoparticles, Biomedical applications, Ligand exchange, Superparamagnetism, Nanoparticles, Drug Delivery.

## Introduction

Magnetite ($Fe_3O_4$) has biomedical applications for drug delivery and for treatment of common ailments since Greek time. With the advent of Nano-biotechnology, there is manufacturing and enhancement in the properties of ferrites due to nanotechnology. These advanced Magnetic Ferrite Nanoparticles find applications in modern clinical studies and biomedicine fields. [1-7] The growth in spinel and hexagonal ferrites in last few decades has been tremendous leading to their superparamagnetic behaviours, low coercivity, high magnetization and low melting points. Nowadays, Spinel Ferrites are of extensive use in the field of medicine due to their extensive applications ranging from biosensors, hyperthermia, humidity sensors, drug delivery systems etc.In conventional drug delivery systems, the drugs are either injected or swallowed in the form of pills. This leads to the drug being dispersed throughout the body to reach the affected organ for healing which also affects the healthy parts of the body adversely. Hence, targeted drug delivery should be an adopted approach with the help of nanotechnology is a way for reaching the drug delivery to the affected body parts rather than the healthy organs. As a result the affected tissues are being targeted to heal rather than the whole body absorbing the drug. Fig 1. Shows a typical drug delivery system.

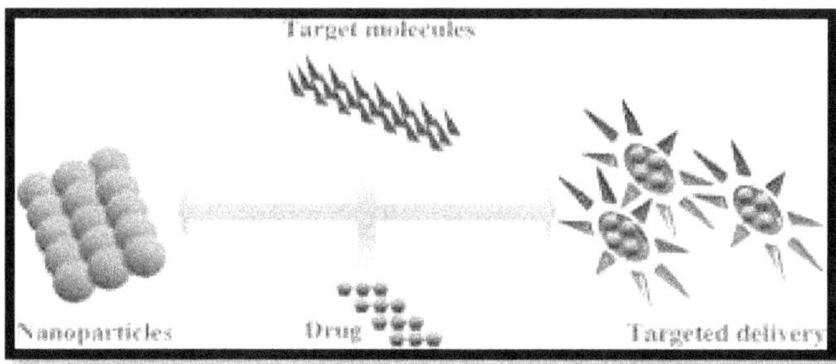


**Figure – 1: Drug Delivery System** [13]

There are many biomedical applications of magnetic nanoparticles which are highly advantageous because of their ability of better diffusion with tissues, easy ligand attachments and very less dipole to dipole interaction. The size [9], composition [10], shape [11] and defects [12] of the magnetic nanoparticles can be altered to critical diameter or below to turn it superparamagnetic.

**Applications in Drug Delivery:**

CFO nanoparticles capped by oleic acid of size nearly 6nm synthesized converted to citric acid (CA) was found to exhibit small values of coercivity and high dispersion in water. The saturation magnetization was observed to be moderate giving colloidal stability in water.  It was observed that CA- CFO Nanoparticles no cytotoxicity even after an incubation period which establishes the potential biomedical applications of CA-CFO nanoparticles. [14]  It has been observed that Magnetic Ferrite Nanoparticles have an advantage over conventional nanocarriers as they can be guided in the body using an external or internal magnetic field. These Magnetic nanoparticles create local hyperthermia heating up the carrier to trigger drug release in the sites. These particles can also been seen and tracked using Magnetic Resonance Imaging (MRI). This makes them attractive and unique in drug delivery systems in medicine. [8]

Magnetic Ferrite Nanoparticles can be used to design tiny nanorobots of different dimensions to be utilized for treatment and diagnosis by driving them magnetically in biological environment.[15-16] Magnetic Ferrite Nanoparticles can be employed for brain stimulation  by the method known as  Magneto-thermo-genetics based on AMF induced magnetothermal effect. [17, 18] It was reported by Manuchehrabadi et al. [19] that the heart valves and blood vessels of large animals can be successfully thawed by coating silicon dioxide onto IONPs with maximum preservation solution almost of 80 mL volume as shown in fig 2.

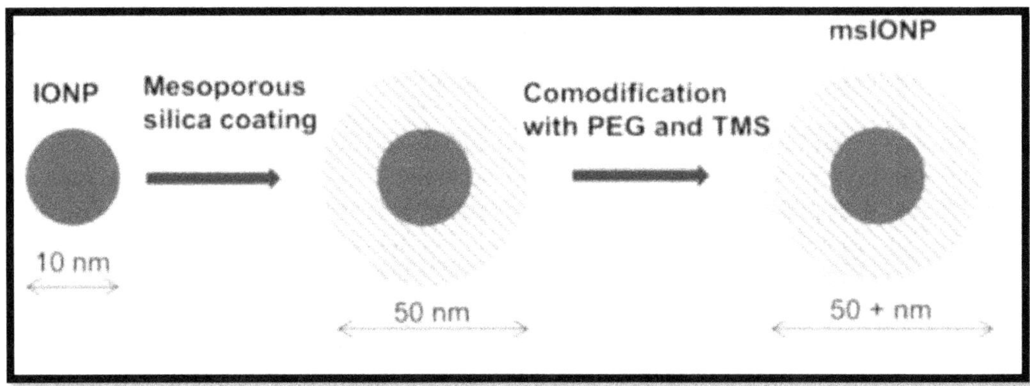


**Figure 2.  Synthesis of msIONPs [20]**

The tissues were heated uniformly melting them without formation of ice crystals. After melting of tissues, the nanoparticles were washed away to get pure workimg tissue. The tissue recovered at cell level due to this nanoheating approach is like a normal tissue indicating nanoheating doesn't damage the tissue. Thus, we can conclude that cryopreservation of human organs is possible with magnetic heating of ferrite nanoparticles. Ferrite nanoparticles coated with polyethylene glycol have been reported to have Photoluminescence in visible range around 430nm. The antimicrobial assay against *Escherichia coli* by drug loaded nanoparticles indicating their significant drug delivery potential. [21] It is investigated by Zimmermann et al. [22] lymphocytes containing magnetic nanoparticles can be controlled in the vascular systems and can be driven by magnetic field to the localized sites. It was further studied by Freeman and Geer [23] that these ferrite nanoparticles can pass throw narrow capillaries easily releasing drug at the target efficiently. A recent study by Mushtaq et al. [24] revealed that cobalt ferrite nanoparticles coated with hydrophilic polymers can be good magnetic nanocarriers. Superparamagnetic iron oxide nanoparticles (SPIONs) are highly compatible bio medically and can be tailored to various sizes and dimensions. These materials have superior ability to support induction heating as MRI agent. The localized tumour regions can be heated ultimately releasing drug and killing affected cells through thermal apoptosis [25]. Cobalt ferrite magnetic nanoparticles have biocompatibility with stable and non-toxic nature. These particles find application in anticancer drug carrier as these particles can generate heat under magnetic field as therapeutic agents in tumour environment. [26]

**Conclusion**

Ferrite Nanoparticles can be tailored to enhance their performance in drug delivery, biological activities and biomedical applications. The major challenge in use of ferrite nanoparticles driven by external magnetic field for targeted drug delivery is that the research is relying mostly on animals and there is apprehension in applying it in human beings. Also, there is scarcity of studies of these applications on human beings as subjects.

**References**


1) N. Lee, D. Yoo, D. Ling, M.H. Cho, T. Hyeon, J. Cheon, Iron oxide based nanoparticles for ultimodal imaging and magnetoresponsive therapy,Chem. Rev. 115 (2015) 10637e10689.
2) Y. Lu, Y. Xu, G. Zhang, D. Ling, M. Wang, Y. Zhou, Y. Wu, T. Wu, M.J. Hackett, B. Kim, H. hang, J. Kim, X. Hu, L. Dong, N. Lee, F. Li, J. He, L. Zhang, H. Wen, B. Yang, S. Choi, T. Hyeon, D. Zou, Iron oxide nanoclusters for T1 magnetic resonance imaging of non-human primates, Nat. Biomed. Eng. 1 (2017) 637e643.
3) J.H. Lee, J.T. Jang, J.S. Choi, S.H. Moon, S.H. Noh, J.W. Kim, J.G. Kim, I.S. Kim, K.I. Park, J. Cheon, Exchange-coupled magnetic nanoparticles for efficient heat induction, Nat. Nanotechnol. 6 (2011) 418e422.
4) J.H. Lee, Y.M. Huh, Y.W. Jun, J.W. Seo, J.T. Jang, H.T. Song, S. Kim, E.J. Cho, H.G. Yoon, J.S. Suh, J. Cheon, Artificially engineered magnetic nanoparticles for ultra-sensitive molecular imaging, Nat. Med. 13 (2007) 95e97.
5) J. Gao, H. Gu, B. Xu, Multifunctional magnetic nanoparticles: design, synthesis, and biomedical applications.
6) K. Fan, C. Cao, Y. Pan, D. Lu, D. Yang, J. Feng, L. Song, M. Liang, X. Yan, Magnetoferritin nanoparticles for targeting and visualizing tumour tissues, Nat. Nanotechnol. 7 (2012) 459e464.
7) O. Veiseh, J.W. Gunn, M. Zhang, Design and fabrication of magnetic nanoparticles for targeted drug delivery and imaging, Adv. Drug Deliv. Rev. 62 (2010) 284e304.
8) Noor Natheer Al-Rawi, Basma Azad Anwer , Natheer Hashim Al-Rawi, Asmaa Tahseen Uthman ,Iman Saad Ahmed, Magnetism in drug delivery: The marvels of iron oxides and substituted ferrites nanoparticles, Saudi Pharmaceutical Journal, (2020).
9) M. Artus, L. Ben Tahar, F. Herbst, L. Smiri, F. Villain, N. Yaacoub, J.-M. Grenèche, S. Ammar, and F. Fiévet, J. Phys: Condens. Matter, 23 (2011) 506001.
10) H. Yun, X. Liu, T. Paik, D. Palanisamy, J. Kim, W. D. Vogel, A. J. Viescas, J. Chen, G. C. Papaefthymiou, J. M. Kikkawa, M. G. Allen, and C. B. Murray, ACS Nano, 8 (2014) 12323.
11) Ò.` Iglesias and A. Labarta, J. Magn. Magn. Mater., 272–276 (2004), 685.
12) S. Singh, S. Munjal, and N. Khare, J. Magn. Magn. Mater., 386 (2015), 69.
13) Manjeet S. Dahiya, Vijay K. Tomer and S. Duhan, Metalferrite nanocomposites for targeted drug delivery, DOI: © 2018 Elsevier Inc.

14) Sandeep Munjal, Neeraj Khare, Chetan Nehate and Veena Koul, Water dispersible CoFe2O4 nanoparticles with improved colloidal stability for biomedical applications, Journal of Magnetism and Magnetic Materials, Volume 404, 15 April 2016, Pages 166-169.

15) G.Z. Lum, Z. Ye, X. Dong, H. Marvi, O. Erin, W. Hu, M. Sitti, Shape-programmable magnetic soft matter, P. Natl. Acad. Sci. USA 113 (2016) E6007eE6015.

16) J. Li, B. Avila, W. Gao, L. Zhang, J. Wang, Micronanorobots for biomedicine delivery, surgery, sensing, and detoxification, Sci. Robot. 2 (2017), eaam6431.

17) S. Nimpf, D.A. Keays, Is magnetogenetics the new optogenetics? EMBO J. 36 (2017) 1643e1646.

18) A. Tay, D. Di Carlo, Remote neural stimulation using magnetic nanoparticles, Curr. Med. Chem. 24 (2017) 537e548.

19) N. Manuchehrabadi, Z. Gao, J. Zhang, H. Ring, Q. Shao, F. Liu, M. McDermott, A. Fok, Y. Rabin, K. Brockbank, M. Garwood, C. Haynes, J. Bischof, Improved tissue cryopreservation using inductive heating of magnetic nanoparticles, Sci. Transl. Med. 9 (2017) 4586.

20) Y. Wang , Y. Miao , G. Li, M. Su, X. Chen H. Zhang, Y. Zhang, W. Jiao, Y. He, J. Yi , X. Liu , H. Fan , Engineering ferrite nanoparticles with enhanced magnetic response for advanced biomedical applications, Materials Today Advances 8 (2020) 100119.

21) Abhishek, S.J. Pawar, Structural, magnetic, and antimicrobial properties of zinc doped magnesium ferrite for drug delivery applications, 10.1016@j.ceramint.2019.10.243.

22) U. Zimmermann, J. Vienken, G. Pilwat, Development of drug carrier systems: electrical field induced effects in cell membranes, Bioelectrochem. Bioenerg. 7 (1980) 553574.

23) J.A. Freeman, J.C. Geer, Intestinal fat and iron transport, goblet cell mucus secretion, and cellular changes in protein deficiency observed with the electron microscope, Am. J. Dig. Dis. 10 (1965) 10051025.

24) M.W. Mushtaq, F. Kanwal, A. Batool, T. Jamil, M. Zia-ul-Haq, B. Ijaz, et al., Polymer-coated CoFe2O4 nanoassemblies as biocompatible magnetic nanocarriers for anticancer drug delivery, J. Mater. Sci. 52 (2017) 92829293.

25) K. Ulbrich, K. Hola, V. ˘ Subr, A. Bakandritsos, J. Tucek, R. Zboril, Targeted drug delivery with polymers and magnetic nanoparticles: covalent and noncovalent approaches, release control, and clinical studies, Chem. Rev. 116 (2016) 53385431.

26) Chaitali Dey, Arup Ghosh, Manisha Ahir, Ajay Ghosh, and Madhuri Mandal Goswami, Improvement of Anticancer Drug Release by Cobalt Ferrite Magnetic Nanoparticles through Combined pH and Temperature Responsive Technique.

# CHAPTER – 16

# CLOUD COMPUTING IN CURRENT TRENDS

## BY
## Kalpana Kushwaha

**Abstract:**

With technology swiftly changing the workforce strategy and business models, organizations are aggressively adopting cloud services, and are also looking forward to the recent trends in cloud computing that can help them leverage their investment in the long run.Cloud computing is booming and there are many trends to be discussed. Cloud computing has become one of the most defining trends in the past five years. Today, cloud computing is being used as a key agent for business transformation It had astonishing growth last year and is predicted to break its own record in the next few. These days it's almost impossible to find an organization that doesn't rely at least partially on cloud services. Whether its application software, operating systems, databases, web servers, IP addresses or virtual local area networks the cloud seems to offer it all. We at Hosting Tribunal took a look at a future that heavily utilizes the cloud at every step.

**Keyword:** Cloud Computing, Virtualization, Service-Oriented Architecture (SOA), Grid Computing, Utility Computing.

## Introduction:

Cloud Computing provides us means of accessing the applications as utilities over the Internet. It allows us to create, configure, and customize the applications online. It is the delivery of on-demand computing services from applications to storage and processing power.

## What is Cloud?

The term **Cloud** refers to a **Network** or **Internet** that describe a global network of server's .In other words, we can say that Cloud is something, which is present at remote location. Cloud can provide services over public and private networks, i.e., WAN, LAN or VPN.Applications such as e-mail, web conferencing, customer relationship management (CRM) execute on cloud.

## What is Cloud Computing?

Cloud Computing refers to **manipulating, configuring,** and **accessing** the hardware and software resources remotely. It offers online data storage, infrastructure, and application.

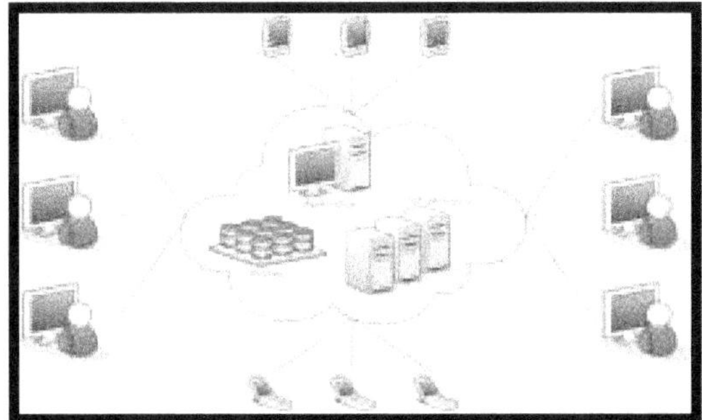

**Fig.1 Cloud Computing**

Cloud computing offers **platform independency,** as the software is not required to be installed locally on the PC. Hence, the Cloud Computing is making our business applications **mobile** and **collaborative.**

**Basic Concepts**

There are certain services and models working behind the scene making the cloud computing feasible and accessible to end users. Following are the working models for cloud computing:

- Deployment Models
- Service Models

**Deployment Models**

Deployment models define the type of access to the cloud, i.e., how the cloud is located? Cloud can have any of the four types of access: Public, Private, Hybrid, and Community.

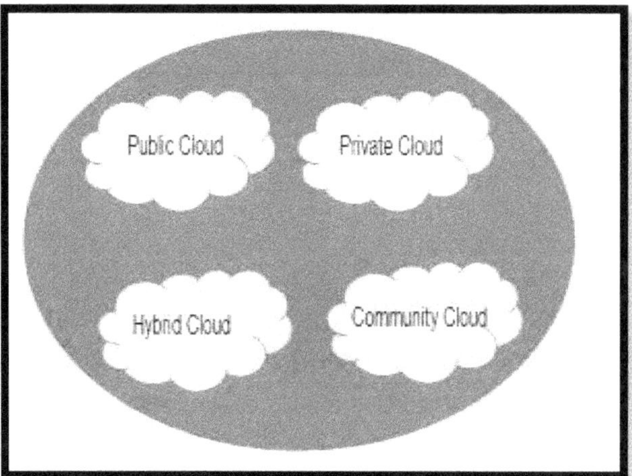


**Fig. 2 Type of Cloud Computing**

- **Public Cloud:** The public cloud allows systems and services to be easily accessible to the general public. Public cloud may be less secure because of its openness.

  **Example:** Amazon elastic compute cloud (EC2), IBM SmartCloud Enterprise, Microsoft, Google App Engine, Windows Azure Services Platform.

- **Private Cloud:** The private cloud allows systems and services to be accessible within an organization. It is more secured because of its private nature.

- **Community Cloud:** The community cloud allows systems and services to be accessible by a group of organizations.
  **Example:** Health Care community cloud

- **Hybrid Cloud:** The hybrid cloud is a mixture of public and private cloud, in which the critical activities are performed using private cloud while the non-critical activities are performed using public cloud.

  **Example:** Google Application Suite (Gmail, Google Apps, and Google Drive)

**Service Models**

Cloud computing is based on service models. These are categorized into three basic service models which are -

- **Infrastructure-as-a-Service (IaaS)** : IaaS provides access to fundamental resources such as physical machines, virtual machines, virtual storage, etc.

- **Platform-as-a-Service (PaaS)** : PaaS provides the runtime environment for applications, development and deployment tools, etc.

- **Software-as-a-Service (SaaS)** : SaaS model allows using software applications as a service to end-users.

The **Infrastructure-as-a-Service (IaaS)** is the most basic level of service. IaaS is also known as **Hardware as a Service (HaaS)**. Each of the service models inherit the security and management mechanism from the underlying model, as shown in the following diagram:

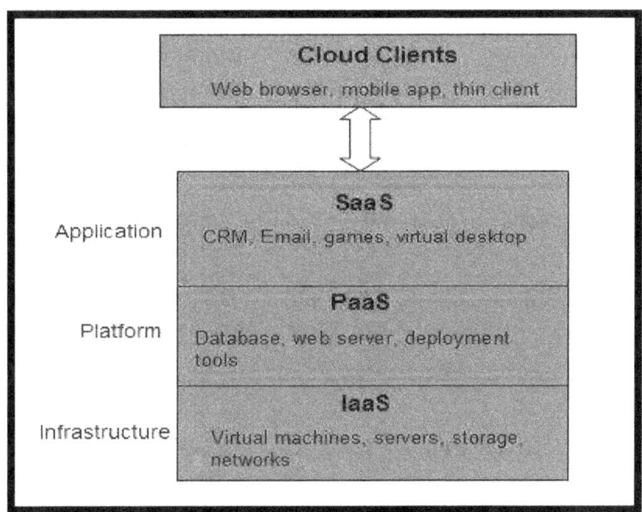


**Fig. 3 Model of Cloud Computing**

**Virtualization**: Virtualization means "formation of a virtual (moderately than actual) edition of something, like server, a desktop, a storage device, an operating system or network resources".Virtualization is a technique, which allows sharing single physical instance of an application or resource among multiple organizations or tenants (customers). It does this by assigning a logical name to a physical resource and providing a pointer to that physical resource when demanded.

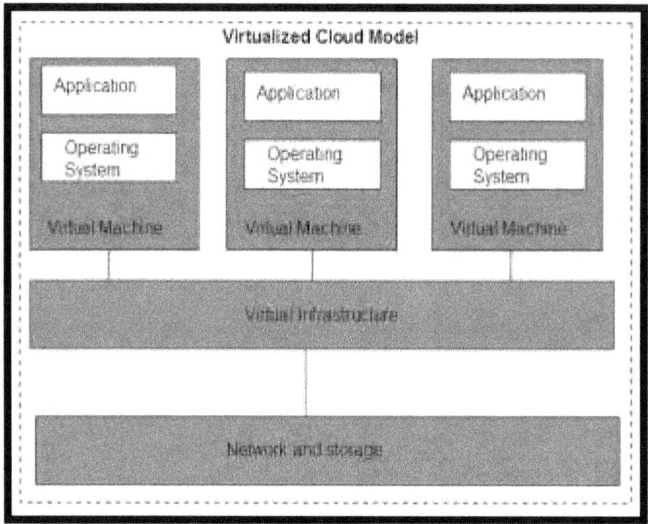


**Fig.4 Virtualized Cloud Model**

The **Multitenant** architecture offers virtual isolation among the multiple tenants. Here, A tenant is essentially a customer who purchases cloud computing resources. This could be an individual user, a group of users, or an entire department or company. Hence, the organizations can use and customize their application as though they each have their instances running.

**Service-Oriented Architecture (SOA)**

Service-Oriented Architecture helps to use applications as a service for other applications regardless the type of vendor, product or technology. Therefore, it is possible to exchange the data between applications of different vendors without additional programming or making changes to services.The cloud computing service oriented architecture elements are shown in the diagram below.

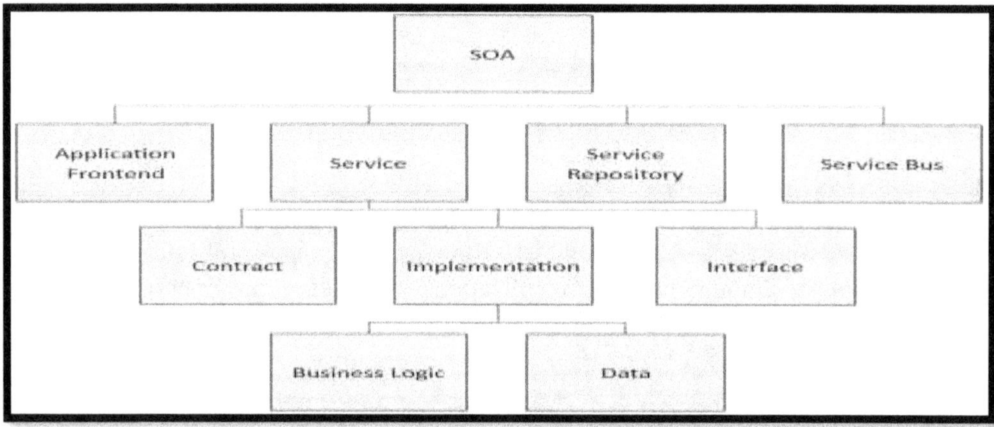

**Grid Computing:** Grid Computing refers to distributed computing, in which a group of computers from multiple locations are connected with each other to achieve a common objective. These computer resources are heterogeneous and geographically dispersed.Grid Computing breaks complex task into smaller pieces, which are distributed to CPUs that reside within the grid.

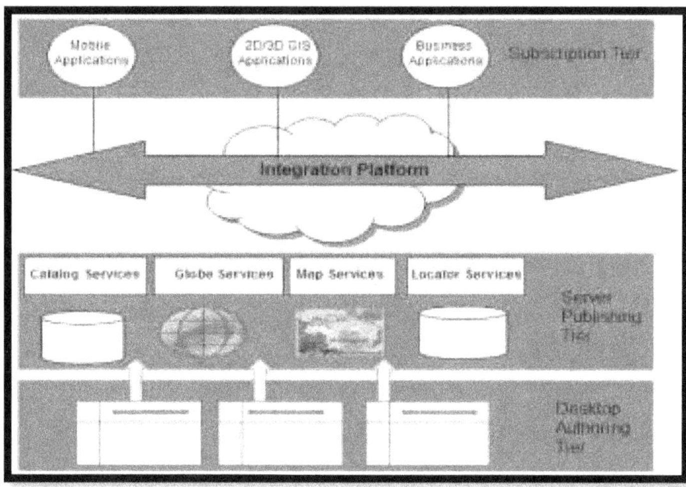


**Fig.5 Grid Computing**

**Utility Computing:** Utility computing is based on Pay-per-Use model. It offers computational resources on demand as a metered service. Cloud computing, grid computing, and managed IT services are based on the concept of utility computing.

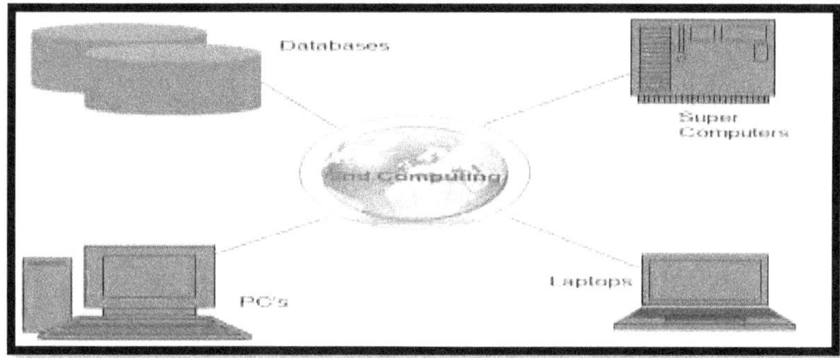


**Fig.6 Utility Computing**

**The Most Telling Cloud Computing Trends (Editor's Choice):**

- The global cloud computing market is forecast to go over $650 by 2025.
- Cloud initiatives are expected to account for **70% of all tech spending by 2020**.
- As much as 80% of organizations are predicted to migrate toward the cloud by 2025.
- In 2018, public cloud adoption grew to 92%.
- IaaS is expected to reach **$72.4 billion** worldwide by 2020.
- Serverless had a market share of 50% in 2018, making it the fastest growing extended cloud service.
- As many as **84% of enterprises run on a multi-cloud strategy.**

**Global Adoption Trends:**

- Dave Bartoletti from Forrester dubbed 2019 the year of global enterprise adoption of cloud. He and his colleague Lauren Nelson claim cloud computing will be the best way to turn rowdy ideas into functional software.
- 80% of organizations are predicted to migrate toward the cloud, hosting, and colocation services by 2025.
- 84% of enterprises run on a multi-cloud strategy.
- Serverless had 21% adoption in 2018, making it the fastest growing extended cloud service. This shows a 75% relative increase compared to 2017.

**Cloud Computing Revenue Is Rising**

With big growth comes big investment. It seems like cloud computing revenue is going to shoot through the roof in 2020.

- The global cloud computing market is forecast exceed $350 billion this year. This is a 18% rise since 2018 and the impressive  CAGR is bound to continue.
- According to research and predictions, cloud expenses are expected to amount to 70% of all tech spending by 2020.

**Public Cloud Usage Is Growing**

- Public cloud is a computing service that is offered by third-party providers for free or fee. It is available to anyone willing to use it. More and more enterprises are turning to the public cloud.

- Public cloud spend is growing 3 times faster than its private counterpart. The first marks a 24% growth, while the latter – just 8%.
- In 2018, public cloud adoption reached 92%. It was 89% the year before.
- 50% of enterprises spend more than $1.2 million a year for public cloud service, while another 13% spend the astonishing $12 million for the same amount of time.
- According to Bartoletti, now 60% of North American enterprises use public cloud platforms. Five years ago, this was at just 12%.
- 41% of enterprises are expected to rely on public cloud platforms by 2020.

**IaaS, PaaS, and SaaS Continue to Grow**

SaaS is already contributing to a big part of the quarterly revenues of software vendors. Usage of IaaS, PaaS, and SaaS is expected to increase dramatically in the following years.
- IaaS is expected to reach $72.4 billion worldwide by 2020.
- Research by KPMG shows PaaS investment grew to 56% in 2019. This is a 24% increase since 2016.
- In 2020, SaaS is predicted to grow with an 18% CAGR, according to a quote by Bain & Company.
- SaaS now contributes $20 billion to the quarterly revenues of software vendors. The number is expected to grow with 32% each year.

**Private and Hybrid Cloud growth**

Hybrid cloud strategies are preferred by companies. Hybrid cloud usage is expected to grow in the next years. Meanwhile, private cloud usage fell with 2% in 2019 and there's no growth predicted for the next year.

- In 2018, private cloud adoption grew to 75%. That's a 3% increase in absolute terms since 2017.
- Private cloud adoption fell to 72% in 2019, according to cloud computing trends.
- Hybrid strategy utilization grew to 58% in 2019. That's a 7% increase since 2018. In comparison, the usage of multiple public and private clouds has declined.
- Cloud technology trends show 28% of companies prefer hybrid cloud strategies. Public and private clouds are used equally by 17% of companies.
- By 2020, 22% of enterprise workloads will be handled by hybrid cloud platforms.
- 83% of enterprises will upload workload to the cloud by 2020 — 41% on public cloud platforms, 22% – on hybrid ones.

**Cloud Computing Companies Growth Trends for 2020**

In 2018, AWS marked significant growth. Azure usage also grew, especially among enterprises. Oracle, IBM, and Google Clouds were also adopted by many companies. In 2019, the AWS adoption fell by 1%, while the rest of the cloud computing services' adoption continues to grow.
- In 2018, <u>AWS was utilized</u> by 64% of cloud users. That number was at just 57% a year earlier.
- AWS was used by 68% of enterprises in 2018.
- Azure's cloud adoption rates reached 45% among users and 68% among enterprises in 2018.
- Oracle also saw some growth, as in 2018 it was servicing 10% of all enterprises.
- IBM cloud usage trends show its popularity among enterprises grew from 10% to 15% between 2017 and 2018.
- Cloud computing trends show the adoption of Google Cloud grew from 15% in 2017 to 19% in 2018.
- Azure adoption jumped to 52% in 2019.
- Among enterprises, Azure's usage reached 60% in 2019.
- AWS' adoption among enterprises fell down by 1% in 2019.
- VMware vSphere has a 50% adoption of the private cloud in 2019.
- Cloud computing growth is visible in IBM's cloud solution, which grew to 18%, Oracle's to 16%, and Alibaba to 4%.
- According to Forrester, cloud computing trends show the growth of the six big public cloud providers' (AWS, Azure, Google, IBM, Alibaba, and Oracle) will continue in 2020.

**Cloud Computing Security Trends**

Cyber security becomes and increasingly big spend for many organizations. Well-designed cloud infrastructure mitigates some vulnerabilities but the growing amount of users increase risks accordingly.
- Cloud computing market estimates more than half of organizations do not have a system for monitoring, managing or securing cloud applications.
- In 2020, 99% of the abused vulnerabilities will have already been known to security and IT professionals for at least a year.
- As more and more enterprises are starting to use the cloud, cybersecurity threats will increase.

**Cloud Computing Trends in IT**

- IDC claims that by 2020, cloud-based IT spending will reach 60% of all spending on IT infrastructure and 60-70% of all software, services and technology spending.
- 68% of enterprises consider optimizing and managing an important responsibility of central IT, while 62% place high importance on deciding and advising which apps to run on which platform. Finally, 59% consider setting policies for cloud usage to be vitally important.

**Conclusion:**

As it is clear to see, cloud computing isn't going anywhere soon. Global cloud computing trends show us that in 2019, public cloud adoption grew. IaaS, PaaS, and SaaS continue to grow as well. Private cloud use, on the other hand, declined a tad. Azure usage is also growing, while AWS' continues to be steady ahead without drastic changes. Cloud computing forecasts for 2020 show a further increase in cloud usage. Cloud initiatives will amount to 70% of all tech spending by 2020. More and more enterprises are adopting the cloud and for good reason. It is cheaper, easier to manage and an overall safer option, compared to the alternatives. As a result, cloud computing trends give plenty of reason for optimism for this industry's future. Obtaining cloud computing services can be viewed as a form of outsourcing, and as such it shares the essential risk profile of all outsourcing contracts concerning opportunistic behavior, shirking, poaching, and opportunistic renegotiation. Developing cloud computing is also an advanced technological development effort, and as such it shares all of the risks of large and uncertain development efforts and the essential risk profile of all development efforts where for a variety of reasons success cannot be ensured, including functionality, political, project, technical, and financial risks. Since E-Government services are almost by definition delivered online, rather than by visiting government service locations or through paper-based interaction, they would appear an obvious candidate for cloud-based delivery; consequently the risks of cloud-based delivery services are of critical interest to the safe execution of numerous E-Government missions. This paper focuses on understanding the risks, both through understanding standards and understanding contracting for cloud services. Standards for cloud computing may reduce many of the risks of opportunistic behavior on the part of vendors. Standards efforts cannot mitigate most of the development risks of cloud computing; no amount of legislation or standardization can make it possible for firms to do that which they could not have done, or that which is indeed algorithmically or computationally infeasible.

**Reference:**


1) E. K. Clemons and Y. Chen, "Making the Decision to Contract for Cloud Services: Managing the Risk of an Extreme Form of IT Outsourcing", *Proceedings of the 44th Hawaii International Conference on System Sciences*, 2011.
2) D. C. Wyld, "The Cloudy Future Of Government IT: Cloud Computing and the Public Sector around the World", *International Journal of Web & Semantic Technology (IJWesT)*, vol. 1, no. 1, January 2010.
3) Cloud Computing Tutorial Points, https://www.tutorialspoint.com/cloud_computing/index.htm

# CHAPTER - 17

# INTERNET OF THINGS IN GREEN TECHNOLOGY

## BY
## Vijaita Kashyap

## Abstract

Web of Things has many kind of effect in coordination and interfacing the physical devices to the Web with no human to human intercession or human to PC collaboration. It addresses the more extended term float and another most noteworthy rebellion spreading out inside the IT world. With the different orchestrate or advantages the people and things are related with anything and anyone from any place. It also focuses at how IoT can prompt a greener and cleaner climate through Green IoT. This paper gives a framework of IoT and Green IoT. It also features various developments and concerning of green IoT and how it can diminish imperativeness usage. This paper lights up the idea of Web of Things (IoT), its features, security issues, advancement allocation patterns.

**Index Terms:** Internet of Things (IoT), 5th Generation, Green IoT, Cloud Computing, Wireless sensor networks, Smart cities, Energy efficiency.

**Keywords:** Internet of Things (IoT), Green IoT, Revolution, Network, Environment.

## Introduction

The Web of Things (IoT) has been conceived to describe many advances and inquire about disciplines that make powerful worldwide network over the around the world physical objects. Empowering innovations like Radio-Frequency Distinguishing proof (RFID), sensor systems, biometrics, and nanotechnologies are presently getting to be exceptionally common, bringing the IoT into genuine usage tending to shifting applications, counting savvy lattice, e-health, and cleverly transportation. They anticipate an animating future that eagerly intercontinental our physical world using green structures. Green structures in IoT will improve in decrement of radiations and pollutions, abusing commonplace wellbeing and acknowledgment, and confining operational expenses and control use.

The Green Web of Things (G-IoT) is foreseen to introduce basic changes in our way of life and would offer help to grasp the vision of "green encompassing knowledge". After this, we'll be enveloped by a tremendous aggregate of devices, sensors, and "things," which further convey by means of 5G, can act "insightfully," and give greenback for customers in dealing with their tasks. These serious watchful things will moreover be setting careful and prepared to play out explicit cutoff points self-governingly, calling for unused conditions of green correspondence among individuals and things and between things themselves, where control usage is smoothed out and increased trade speed use. This improvement would be critical not so to speak to examiners, but rather also to associations and individuals the same. Thinking about these realities, the purpose of this remarkable issue was to focus on both speculative and execution points in green another time frameworks or frameworks that can be used in giving green structures through IoT enabling developments.

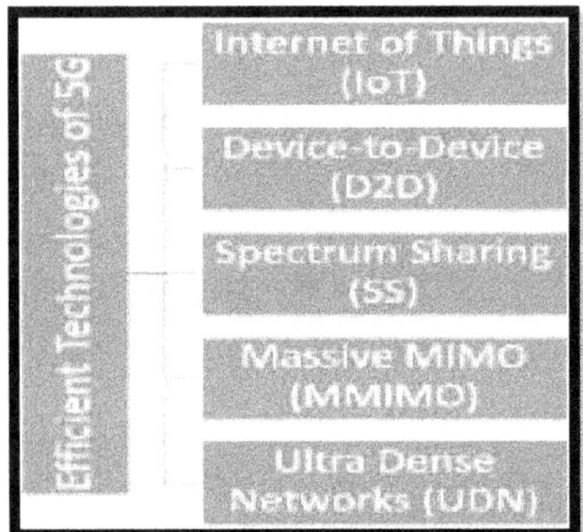


**Figure 1: Efficient Technologies of 5G**

These five capable developments need to allow the minimization of energy use to execute the carbon-di-oxide (CO2) transmissions for the coming 5G frameworks appeared in Figure 1. Primarily the motivation behind this paper is to offer a diagram of green IoT in arrangements of ideas, applications, advances, and difficulties. Portion II portrays the rudimentary ideas and requests of IoT. Portion III shows the existence pattern of green IoT. Portion IV tells about the ideal advances for green IoT. Portion V looks at of 5G in IoT. Portion VI presents the IoT for energizing urban areas. Portion VII presents difficulties and future researches headings of green IoT. Finally, Portion VIII concludes up the paper.

**Internet of Things:**

Web of Things: The Web of things (IoT) depicts the course of action of physical articles "things" that are embedded with sensors, programs, and different advancements for the explanation of interfacing and exchanging data with different devices and structures over the web. The Web of things has progressed because of the joining of various advances and constant investigations in different AI fields, item sensors, and embedded systems [1]. Conventional regions of embedded structures, distant sensor frameworks, control systems, computerization and many other things are added to engaging the Web of things. IoT advancement is generally inseparable from things identifying with the idea of the "sagacious domestic", checking machines and devices, (for example, illumination establishments, inside controllers, domestic security structures and cameras, and other domestic contraptions) that reinforce one or more normal natural frameworks, and can be controlled through devices related with that climate, for example, PDAs and sharp speakers. There are bunches of real concerns roughly dangers inside the acceleration of IoT, generally inside the scopes of security, and accordingly fabricating organizations and authoritative moves to address these worries have begun checking the improvement of overall principles. There are four basic parts in IoT innovation:

- Internet: At anytime, anywhere communication happens. It consists of cloud computing, dedicated web administrations, and IP for sharp objects.
- Hardware: Sensors, labels, actuators, and transceivers are the inserted communication equipment.
- Middleware: for keeping information at high capacity, computing, and set awareness.
- Presentation: to get it visualization and translation instruments for distinctive stages and applications.

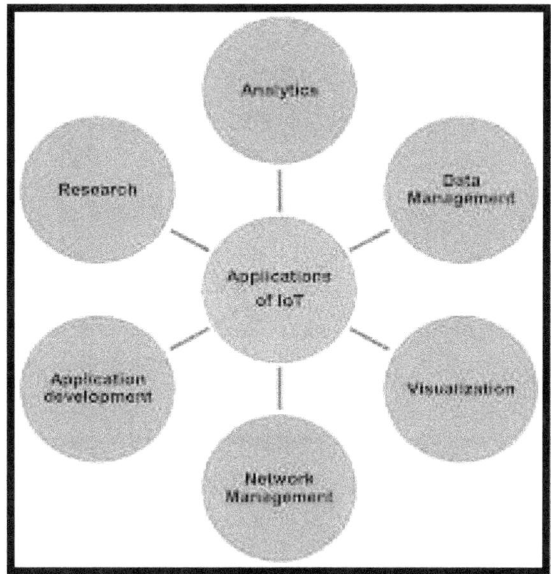


**Figure 2: Applications of IoT**

Figure 2 shows the unique applications of IoT such as information organization, expounding, visualization, heterogeneous organize administration, application progression, and purpose of investigation. Figure 3 seems excellent information realistic including reasonable urban areas and IoT applications extended by world. Clearly the verticals those are moving with the IoT and get it why it is the accompanying mechanical change. Regardless, the examination about the IoT is in its early stage and there are various difficulties that are needed to be tended, for example, the ground-breaking battery reinforcement, the modernization straightforwardness, data and setting mindfulness, wellbeing, and security concerns, diverse powerful things, and impedance free organization. The Web of Things (WoT) is a circumstance which isn't in a manner of speaking an arrange to trade data, yet interconnected with generous data and Cloud Computing to convey bits of knowledge, in setting up to have the option to know the practices, and without a doubt explain activities viable to the information caught by the exceptional items that are available around the growing more iridescent urban areas without requiring a human-to-human or human to PC connection. IoT climate configuration is appeared in Figure 5, where they have gotten data from the more savvy urban areas that are composed into Cloud Computing. They showed stream engages the collaboration among the cloud and the individuals, who are initially to be more actives (assumes). The cloud computing system is the centralization of the data of every sensor. Plus, it licenses them to associate and convey through the development of omnipresent organizes, and furthermore it handles the various issues of interconnections. The cloud is empowering the integration of huge information investigation to reach an understanding that permits the declaration of human flow designs. At long last, the human energetic design gives the instruments and criticism components to motivate the modification of the practices.

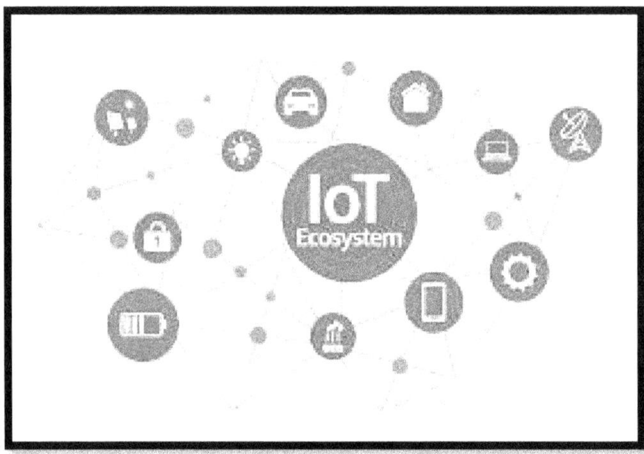

Figure 3: IoT Ecosystem

**GREEN IOT:**

Web of Things (WoT) could be a key enabler for numerous modernized applications, from marine checking to external space investigation. Be that as it may, complicated operations (such as gadget interconnection, information transmission, and benefit optimization) will devour considerable vitality in differentiating with the restricted vitality capacity of IoT gadgets. To move forward building supportability and eventually diminish systemic taken a toll, the vitality proficient (green) plan of IoT has gotten to be more unmistakable. In specific, with the nonstop infiltration of progressed data and communications (ICT) advances (such as VR/AR, UAVs, and automobiles), our savvy world is being encompassed by huge IoT information that needs energy-efficient caching, computing, organizing, and securing.

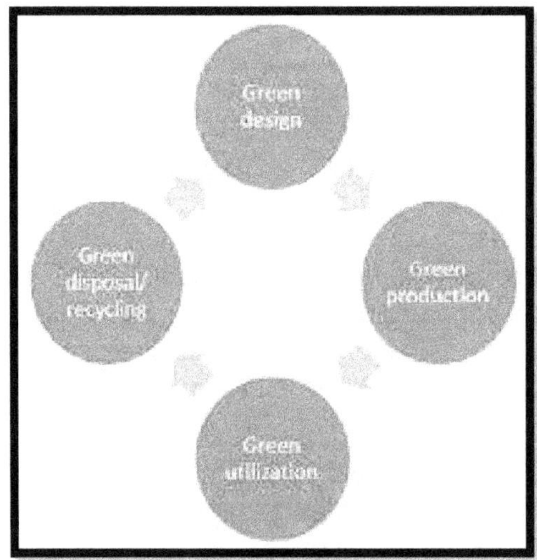


Figure 4: Life cycle of green IoT

**Technologies for Green IOT**

The Web of Things will demand an expansive stretch out of unused developments and capacities that various organizations haven't anyway aced, state, Scratch Jones, negative behavior pattern president and perceived agent at Gartner. "A repeating subject inside the IoT space is the energy of advances and associations and the brokers giving them. Architecting for this young and directing the open door it causes will be a key test for affiliations misusing the IoT. In various development zones, the requirement for capacities will also pose basic difficulties." The innovations and standards of IoT will have an awfully wide effect on organizations, influencing commerce methodology, hazard administration, and a wide run of specialized ranges such as an organize design.

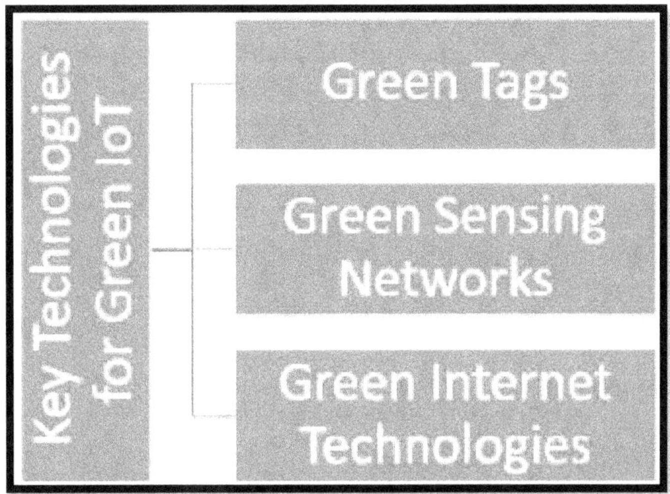


**Figure 5-Key technologies for green IoT**

**According to Jones, the top 10 emerging IoT technologies are:**
- IoT Security
- IoT Device (Thing) Management
- IoT Processors
- IoT Analytics
- IoT OS
- Low-Power, Short-Range IoT Networks
- Event Stream Processing
- IoT Standards and Ecosystems
- IoT Platforms

**Different techniques should be considered to achieve green WSN:**

- The sensor utilizes the energy for the necessary action and then sited into idle or sleep mode.
- Use of renewable energy for charging and utilization purposes. Instead of kinetic energy vibrations can also be used.
- For efficiency of energy the optimization techniques can be used.
- To diminish the data size and context-awareness algorithms and for that reason we need to reduce the storage space capability.
- The reduce the mobility power consumption we can use energy-efficient routing techniques.

**Applications**

a) Industrial Automation
b) Healthcare
c) Environment Monitoring
d) Residential Sector
e) People and Goods Transportation
f) Retail, Logistics, Supply Chain Management
g) Recycling

**WOT for Smart Cities**

**Smart city definition:**

Web of Things (WoT) is utilized by smart cities for various purposes like powers, meters to capture and analysis information and sensors. The smart cities basically use these 'Things" to progress the infrastructure, open utilities, administration, and more. Here it has been observed that how shrewd cities give a high quality and productive way of life for their inhabitants, and uses different strategies to reach these targets.

**Smart Architecture and Smart Infrastructure:**

Building chiefs all through the world are all the more routinely hoping to unite IoT contraptions and game plans into their systems in organize to decrease expenses and gain ground in the nature of their structures. A later report from Dain tree Systems found that almost 60% of building directors inside the U.S. are typical with the IoT, and 43% acknowledge the IoT would shape how they work their structures inside the accompanying a few quite a while. One zone with huge potential for progression is in lighting, as building chiefs may change to Driven bulbs in mastermind to save money and essentialness.

**Applications of IoT and Smart City Projects:**

The Europe is driving the world with their advancement level of shrewd city just like Amsterdam. The European Commission has distributed 365 million Euros for enabling its part nations to make wise urban areas. Furthermore, the undertakings have as of now begun to bear natural product. In 2011, Paris appeared an electric vehicle sharing system called Autolib and has since built up the 3,000 naval force of vehicles. The related vehicles can be finished GPS, and drivers can use the vehicle's dashboard to spare halting spaces ahead of time.

**The Future direction of the IoT and Smart Cities:**

The prospective of shrewd cities is about boundless, and the development of these cities ought to as it was quickening within the coming years. But this can be not the as it were a zone that the IoT will significantly alter within the close future.

**IOT Goes Green**

**Innovations in Sustainable Tech:**

At the point when we consider practically viable advancement, we will in general think around sun powered sheets, electric vehicles, and for sure low-tech ideas like a dormant sun-arranged arrangement. These are largely fundamental turns of events, however they're additionally or might be latent. Not in any manner like such a large amount of the advancement in our reality these days, these aren't things that get cannier through use. To push legitimacy advance, it's an ideal opportunity to go to the Web of Things (IoT). From successfully viable wearables to entire insightful urban communities, the IoT is adequately arranged to modify how we think around the climate, typical and manufactured. Keep your eyes on these three instruments making legitimacy more brilliant.

**Little Devices, Big Potential**

As a general public, we've come to revere wearables wellbeing trackers, definitely watches, and for sure wearable's used for rest. However, for such splendid little devices, they're incredibly imperativeness subordinate. Dismissal to connect your Fitbit and you won't have the option to check the time, never keenness degree your pulse. Presently, an advanced time of wearables is making a break from the charger with multi-source essentialness gathering development. These unused contraptions highlight handle not reasonable sun based, a straightforward game plan, yet to weight and temperature-delicate perovskites. A group of mineral, one kind of perovskite is used in sun-powered cells, however others can divert weight happening from development into power similarly. Since so various wearables are fixated on activity following, they're the finish setting for this energy-accommodating apparatus.

**Smarter Solar**

Sun-powered control might be a pillar of the legitimacy improvement, one of the essential models individuals think nearly when environmentalism and elective essentialness come up. Typically with extraordinary explanation – as an extensively recognized course of action, there are budgetary supports for sun-based board foundation, a collection of choices, and a notable comprehension of sun-powered control as a gadget, for sure in domestic settings. Children do science adventures including sun-powered control; it's sustainable essentialness 101. In the present time, regardless, we got the chance to start considering around sun situated in substantially more muddled manners as sun-powered gets the chance to be entwined with IoT. IoT is generally data and, out of nowhere so is sun-powered. This isn't reasonable disengaged imperativeness any longer. The present sun-based control structures are routinely attached to considerably more profound data systems that improve imperativeness yield, something as it was a possible feeling of IoT. This data by then allows the sheets to normally reposition themselves, moving dependent on the situation of the sun. The equivalent goes for wind turbines and different kinds of inexhaustible.

**The city as a Computer**

We will incorporate weight touchy cells to wearables and control up our sun powered loads up like never at some point as of late, however is this adequate to calm overall warming, pollution from entering, and other ecological concerns? On an individual level, however when a total city grasps efficient development facilitates with IoT – well, that is another story. In Los Angeles, for outline, a city known for its action and going with tainting, the entire city is adjusted for practicality. Over the city, sensors screen talk about and water quality and traffic. Different structures choose metropolitan walkability, dwelling issues, and that's only the tip of the iceberg, all with the purpose of extending green work inside the city. All joined, these systems can fundamentally decrease the city's carbon impression. Imagine in case all significant urban communities grasped this advancement – well, we may reasonable be going toward that path. Renewable technology, all alone, is profoundly significant. However, when coordinated with IoT, it turns out to be substantially more impressive. As we develop the connection between these devices, we position our general public to move back from more destructive fuel sources and saddle renewable at the following degree of proficiency.

**Challenges and Future Research Directions**

Even though there is an incredible study exertion to reach a green innovation, green IoT innovation is still in the initial stages. There is numerous deterrents and challenges matter that got to be tended to. Here are some of the key challenges:

- The combination of energy proficiency over IoT engineering to realize an suitable performance.
- For better environment we need green applications to play down.
- Constancy of green IoT with energy utilization models.
- Context-awareness with vitality dynamic IoT system.
- The gadgets and conventions both utilized to communicate must be energy productive with less control consumption.
- The trade-off among productive energetic range detecting and proficient range administration.
- Intricacy reduces of the green IoT organization.
- Proficient cloud management about control consumption.
- Proficient energy method for IoT such as wind, sun-powered, vibration, warm to create IoT promising.
- Encryption and control commands are for the security.

**Conclusion**

Here, the novelty approach for green IoT has been examined. The life cycle of green IoT is also been checked as well as the required advances to realize a system of green IoT. It inspired green IoT, challenges, and benefits. The part of IoT in 5G and savvy cities is also displayed. Furthermore, an investigation for future headings and also reviewed the challenges. Green innovation is a critical concept that each person ought to be well familiar with. Understanding the past of innovation in expansion to green innovation is significant to get it the potential future of green innovation. The coordinate comes about of our shopper way of life are regularly covered up from the open eye since it isn't a wonderful theme to think approximately, but it is imperative to urge the truth to empower arrangements to contamination, arranged out of date quality, and e-waste and sweatshop work. Since these things are frequently cleared beneath the mat, the open may not know much data almost these points until it is as well late to settle, with irreversible harm. Modular innovation offers an arrangement that would make both sides cheerful. Manufacturers save cash by specializing in certain parts, rather than being dependable for making entirety units. On the other side, the buyer gets the reserve funds passed on to them. Measured innovation offers customizable and indeed replaceable components that can effectively be supplanted. Although secluded innovation isn't a total arrangement since it still makes more e-waste, it may be a major step within the right heading. Measured innovation may be a venturing stone to other arrangements that can be indeed way better. For the case, innovation can be biodegradable after 5-10 a long time, depending on the appliance. One of the most prominent viewpoints of green innovation is that it empowers people to live their lives, but in a greener way that's not hurtful to the environment. Since green innovation covers an assortment of apparatuses, making it inside reach to be greener in ordinary life. Internet of Things (IoT) has altered our ecology system of information that has changed our life style a lot. And the improvement in green IoT make a big difference in cost and savings in the future.

## References


1) M. Elkhodr, S. Shahrestani and H. Cheung, "The Internet of Things: Vision & Challenges," 2013 IEEE Tencon, pp. 218–222, 2013.
2) Accenture Strategy, "SMARTer2030: ICT solutions for 21st century challenges," Global sustainability Initiative (GeSI), Brussels, Belgium, Technical Report, 2015.
3) Green Power for Mobile, "The Global Telecom Tower ESCO Market," Technical Report, 2015.
4) A. Fehske, G. Fettweis, J. Malmodin, and G. Biczok, "The global footprint of mobile communications: The ecological and economic perspective," IEEE Communication Magazine, vol. 49, no. 8, pp. 55 – 62, 2011.
5) IMT Vision-Framework and Overall Objectives of the Future Development of IMT for 2020 and Beyond, document Rec. ITU-R M.2083- 0,2015.
6) M. Albreem, "5G Wireless communication systems: vision and challenges," 2015 IEEE International Conference on Computer, Communication, and Control Technology, Malayia, 2015.
7) K. Ashton, "That Internet of Things" thing in the real world, things matter more than ideas," RFID Journal, 2009.
8) D. Brock, "The electronic product code (epc) a naming scheme for physical objects," Auto-ID Centre, White Paper, 2001.
9) International Telecommunication Union, "ITU internet report 2005: the internet of things," International Telecommunication Union, Workshop Report, November 2005.
10) Labellum World Smart Cities. [Online] Available: http://www.libelium.com/libelium-smart-world-infographic-smartcities-internet-of-things/ [accessed on: 23-9-2017].
11) M. Mowry, "A Survey of RFID in the medical industry with emphasis on applications to surgery and surgical devices," 2008.
12) T. Li, S. Wu, S. Chen, and M. Yang, "Generalized energy-efficient algorithms for the RFID estimation problem," IEEE ACM Transactions on Networking, vol. 20, no. 6, pp. 1978 - 1990, 2012.
13) V. Namboodiri and L. Gao, "Energy-aware tag anti-collision protocols for RFID systems," IEEE Transactions on Mobile Computing, vol. 9, no. 1, pp. 44 - 59, 2010.
14) F. Shaikh, S. Zeadally, E. Expositor, "Enabling Technologies for Green Internet of Things," IEEE Systems Journal, vol. 11, no. 2, pp.983 - 994, 2017.
15) M. Palattella, M. Dohler, A. Grieco, G. Rizzo, J. Torsner, T. Engel, and L. Ladid, "Internet of Things in the 5G Era: Enablers, Architecture, and Business Models," IEEE Journal on Selected Areas in Communications, vol. 34, no. 3, pp. 510 - 527, 2016.
16) Takruri, M., Attia, H.A., Awad, M.H.: Wireless charging in the context of sensor networks. Int J Appl Eng Res 11(12), 7736–7741 (2016)
17) Shafiee, N., Tewari, S., Calhoun, B., Shrivastava, A.: Infrastructure circuits for lifetime improvement of ultra-low-power IoT devices. IEEE Trans. Circuits Syst. I Reg Paper 64(9), 2598–2610 (2017)
18) San Murugesan, GR.: Harnessing Green IT: Principles and practices. Wiley Publishing (2012)

19) Rault, T., Bouabdallah, A., Challal, Y.: Energy efficiency in wireless sensor networks: a top-down survey. Comput. Newt. 67, 104–122 (2014)

20) Perera, C., Talagala, D.S., Liu, C.H., Estrella, J.C.: Energy-efficient location and activity-aware on-demand mobile distributed sensing platform for sensing as a service in IoT clouds. IEEE Trans. Comput. Soc. Syst. 2(4), 171–181 (2015)

21) Khodr, H., Kouzayha, N., Abdallah, M., Costantine, J., Dawy, Z.: Energy-efficient IoT sensor with RF wake-up and addressing capability. IEEE Sens. Lett. 1(6), 1–4 (2017)

22) Perles, A., Perez-Marin, E., Mercado, R., Segrelles, J.D., Blanquer, I., Zarzo, M., Garcia-Diego, F.J.: An energy-efficient internet of things (IoT) architecture for preventive conservation of cultural heritage. Future Gener. Comput. Syst. 81, 566–581 (2018)

23) Q. Meng and J. Jin, "The Terminal Design of the Energy Self-sufficiency Internet of Things," 2011 International Conference on Control, Automation and Systems Engineering (CASE), pp. 1-5, 2011.

24) Keysight Technologies, "Battery Life Challenges in IoT Wireless Sensors and the Implications for Test," Application Note, 2015.

25) S. Tozlu, M. Senel, W. Mao and A. Keshavarzian, "Wi-Fi Enabled Sensors for Internet of Things: A practical Approach," IEEE Communications Magazine, vol. 50, no. 6, pp. 134 - 143, 2012.

26) L. Roselli, N. Carvalho, F. Alimenti, P. Notte, G. Orecchini, M. Virili, C. Mariotti, R. Gongalves, and P. Pinho, "Smart Surfaces: Large Area Electronics Systems for Internet of Things Enabled by Energy Harvesting," Proceedings of the IEEE, vol. 102, no. 11, pp. 1723 - 1746, 2014.

27) J. Wu, I. Bisio, C. Gniady, E. Hossain, M. Valla, and H.Li, "Context aware Networking and Communications: Part 2," IEEE Communications Magazine, vol. 52, no. 8, pp. 64 - 65, 2014.

28) Z. Yan, X. Yu, and W. Ding, "Context-Aware Variable Cloud Computing," IEEE Access, vol. 5, pp. 2211 - 2227, 2017.

29) D. Martin, C. Lamsfu, and A. Alzua, "Automatic Context Data Life Cycle Management Framework," International Conference on Pervasive Computing and Applications, 2010.

30) Z. Yan, X. Yu, and W. Ding, "Context-Aware Verifiable Cloud Computing," IEEE Access, vol. 5, pp. 2211 - 2228, 2017.

31) M. Ali, S. Khan, and A. Zomaya, "Security and Dependability of CloudAssisted Internet of Things," IEEE Cloud Computing, vol. 3, no. 2, pp. 24 - 26, 2016.

32) N. Simoes and G. Souza, "A Low-Cost Automated Data Acquisition System for Urban Sites Temperature and Humidity Monitoring Based in Internet of Things," 2016 International Symposium on Instrumentation Systems, Circuits and Transducers, pp. 107 - 112, 2016.

33) D. Wu, L. Bao, and C. Liu, "Scalable Channel Allocation and Access Scheduling for Wireless Internet of Things," IEEE Sensors Journal, vol. 13, no. 10, pp. 3596 - 3694, 2013.

34) Y. Han, Y. Chen, B. Wang, and K. Liu, "Enabling Heterogeneous Connectivity in Internet of Things: A Time-Reversal Approach," IEEE Internet of Things Journal, vol. 3, no. 6, pp. 1036 - 1047, 2016.

35) S. Murugesan, "Harnessing green IT: Principles and practices," IEEE IT Prof., vol. 10, no. 1, pp. 24-33, 2008.

36) W. Ejaz, A. Anpalagan, M. Imran, M. Jo, M. Naeem, S. Qaisar and W. Wang, "Internet of Things (IoT) in 5G Wireless Communications," IEEE Access, vol. 4, pp. 10310 - 10314, 2016.

37) P. Rysavy, "IoT & 5G: Wait or Move" Cahnnel Partners, 2016.

38) A. Ijaz, L. Zhang, M. Grau, A. Mohamed, S. Vural, A. Quddus, M. Imran, C. Foh and R. Tafazolli, "Enabling Massive IoT in 5G and Beyond Systems: PHY Radio Frame Design Considerations," IEEE Access, vol. 4, pp. 3322 - 3339, 2016.

39) P. Ramaswamy, "IoT Smart Parking Systems for Reducing Green House Gas Emission," 2016 International Conference on Recent Trends in Information Technology, 2016.

40) S. Fang, L Xu, Y. Zhu, J. Ahati, H. Pei, J. Yan and Z. Liu, "An Integrated System for Regional Environmental Monitoring and Management Based on Internet of Things," IEEE Transaction on Industrial Informatics, vol. 10, no. 2, pp. 1596 - 1605, 2014.

41) S. Mahalank, K. Malagund, and R. Banakar, "Device to Device Interaction Analysis in IoT based Smart Traffic Management System, An Experimental Approach," 2016 Symposium on Colossal Data Analysis and Networking, 2016.

42) G. Shyam, S. Manvi, and P. Bharti, "Smart Waste Management Using Internet of Things (IoT)," 2nd International Conference on Computing and Communications Technologies, 2017.

43) M. Palattella, M. Dohler, A. Grieco, G. Rizzo, J. Torsner, T. Engel and L. Ladid, "Internet of Things in the 5G Era, Enablers, Architecture, and Business Models," IEEE Journal on Selected Areas in Communications, vol. 34, no. 3, pp. 510 - 527, 2016.

44) P. Sores, J. Santana, L. Sanchez, J. Lanza and L. Munoz, "Practical Lessons From the Deployment and Management of a Smart City Internet-of-Things Infrastructure: The SmartSantander Testbed Case," IEEE Access, vol. 5, pp. 14309 - 14322, 2017.

45) M. Marjani, F. Nasiruddin, A. Gani, A. Karim, I. Hashem and A. Siddiqa, "Big IoT Data Analytics: Architecture, Opportunities, and Open Research Challenges," IEEE Access, vol. 5, pp. 5247 - 5261, 2017.

46) B. Ahlgren, M. Hidell and E. Ngai, "Internet of Things for Smart Cities: Interoperability and Open Data," IEEE Internet Computing, vol. 20, no. 6, pp. 52 - 56, 2016.

47) J. Zhou, T. Leppnen, E. Harjula, C. Yu, H. Jin and L. T. Yang, "Cloud Things: a Common Architecture for Integrating the Internet of Things with Cloud Computing," Proceedings of the 2013 IEEE 17th International Conference on Computer Supported Cooperative Work in Design, pp. 651-657, 2013.

48) B. Montgomery, "Future Shock: IoT Benefits Beyond Traffic and Lighting Energy Optimization," IEEE Consumer Electronics Magazine, vol. 4, no. 4, pp. 98 - 100, 2015.

49) I. Ganchev, Z. Ji and M. ODroma, "A Generic IoT Architecture for Smart Cities," Irish Signals & Systems Conference 2014 and 2014 China-Ireland International Conference on Information Technologies, Ireland, 2014.

50) Chkirbene, Z., Gouissem, A., Hadjidj, R., Foufou, S., Hamila, R.: Efficient techniques for energy saving in data centre networks. Comput. Common. 129, 111–124 (2018)

51) Pardew, C.A., Bellaredj, M.L.F., Davis, A.K., Swaminathan, M., Kohl, P., Fuji, T., Nakazawa, S.: Design and characterization of inductors for self-powered IoT edge devices. IEEE Trans. Compony. Package. Manuf. Technol. 8(7), 1263–1271 (2018)

52) Popli, S., Jha, R.K., Jain, S.: A survey on energy efficient narrowband internet of things (NBIoT): architecture, application, and challenges. IEEE Access 7, 16739–16776 (2018)

53) Vieeralingaam, G., Ramanathan, R.: Parametric study of RF energy harvesting in SWIPT enabled wireless networks under downlink scenario. Procedia Comput. Sci. 143, 835–842 (2018)

54) Sharad, S., Sivakumar, P.B., Anantha Narayanan, V.: A novel IoT-based energy management system for large scale data centers. In Proceedings of the 2015 ACM 6th International Conference on Future Energy System pp. 313–318 (2015).

# CHAPTER - 18

# EXPANSION OF CROSS-CULTURAL COMMUNICATION SKILLS IN ENGINEERING STUDENTS

**BY**
**Shweta Rathore**

**Abstract**

It is additionally necessary for an engineering specialist to have great cross-cultural communication skills to guarantee effective business co-activity with worldwide accomplices, which is of outrageous significance in any field of expert action of a specific engineering specialist because of the worldwide propensities in the present business. the understudies for procurement of the language and cross-cultural language abilities during the time spent examinations just as in extra-educational program exercises, by methods for focusing on the major social peculiarities of countries which show themselves in totally various styles of the executives, method of creating designing items and oversight of designing cycles in business, just as broad mentality towards accomplishment of business objectives. Engineers have generally centered on hard-expertise information procurement, however the inexorably multicultural work practices of expert designers presently request better delicate aptitude capability, for example, unknown dialect capacity, correspondence certainty, and cross-cultural experience. Studentsand staff within a university engineering department were reviewed to distinguish how cross-cultural language utilize possibly affected scholastic and communication execution. The outcomes show that engineering faculties might be focusing on subject substance to the detriment of encouraging the advancement of delicate aptitudes.

**Keywords:** cross-cultural, communication, aptitudes.

**Introduction:**

Cross-cultural communication is the investigation of how people from contrasting foundations impart across societies. As should be obvious, the definition is direct, however figuring out how to actualize cross-cultural communication into your vocation isn't as high contrast. Cross-cultural communication is the means by which individuals having a place with various societies speak with one another, there will undoubtedly be conflicts between various societies. One strategy to lessen these conflicts is organizing variety while employing. At the point when individuals from contrasting societies run after a shared objective, the danger of hostile misconceptions decline and the nature of work increments. Culture is a perspective and living whereby one gets a bunch of mentalities, qualities, standards and convictions that are instructed and fortified by different individuals in the gathering. This arrangement of fundamental suspicions and answers for the issues of the world is a mutual framework that is given from age to age to guarantee endurance. A culture comprises of unwritten and composed standards and laws that control how an individual connects with the rest of the world. Individuals from a culture can be recognized by the way that they share some similitude. They might be joined by religion, by geology, by race or identity. Our social comprehension of the world and everything in it eventually influences our style of communication as we fire getting methods of one's way of life at around a similar time we begin figuring out how to impart. Culture impacts the words we express and our conduct.

**Reflect on your own culture**

The first and most generally failed to remember step in turning out to be socially mindful is to reflect on your own culture. To find out about others, you should initially think about yourself. Play out a self-assessment and consider the way of life with which you recognize, what parts of that specific culture relate to you, and what style of communication you have adopted. Reflecting upon your own way of life will assist you with distinguishing contrasts between others. At the point when encircled by similar individuals, it's anything but difficult to fail to remember that what you do and how you act are not the widespread standard. That is the reason seeing yourself basically will improve your social mindfulness. After reflecting, it's time you accumulate all the data you can on new societies. This takes loads of time and won't occur incidentally. Spotlight first on societies with which you communicate or focus through promoting. That way, you can start executing your freshly discovered mindfulness into your advertising procedure.

Here are social credits that you can consider while exploring:

- Dress
- Greetings
- Language(s) spoken
- Body language
- Eye contact
- Gestures
- Work ethic and standards
- Attitudes toward drugs
- Gender jobs
- Personal space
- Food and engaging conventions
- Attitudes toward rules and authority
- Family life


As recently referenced, don't over-sum up and consistently relate. It's OK in the event that you don't have the foggiest idea about each part, everything being equal that would be difficult to learn in a lifetime. It is important that you are deliberately putting forth an attempt to expand your mindfulness and fuel your vocation with this information.

**Understanding Cultural Diversity:**

Given diverse social settings, this brings new communication difficulties to the working environment. In any event, when representatives situated in various areas or workplaces communicate in a similar language (for example, correspondences between English-speakers in the U.S. what's more, English-speakers in the UK), there are some social contrasts that should be considered with an end goal to streamline correspondences between the two gatherings. In such cases, a viable communication technique starts with the agreement that the sender of the message and the recipient of the message are from various societies and foundations. Obviously, this presents a specific measure of vulnerability, making interchanges considerably more intricate. Without getting into societies and sub-societies, it is maybe generally significant for individuals to understand that a fundamental comprehension of social variety is the way to viable cross-cultural communications. Without fundamentally considering singular societies and dialects in detail, we should all figure out how to all the more likely speak with people and gatherings whose first language, or language of decision, doesn't coordinate our own.

**Developing Awareness of Individual Cultures:**

However, learning the fundamentals about culture and in any event something about the language of correspondence in various nations is significant. This is vital in any event, for the essential degree of understanding needed to participate in suitable welcome and actual contact, which can be a precarious territory between socially. For example, kissing a business partner isn't viewed as a proper business practice in the U.S., yet in Paris, one kiss on each cheek is a satisfactory welcome. Furthermore, the confident handshake that is broadly acknowledged in the U.S. isn't perceived in all different societies.

**LarayBarna's Sources of Miscommunication in Cross Cultural Exchanges**

**i) Assumption of similarities:** This refers to our tendency to think how we behave and act is the universally accepted rule of behavior. When someone differs, we have a negative view of them.

**ii) Language Differences:** Problems occur when there is an inability to understand what the other is saying because different languages are being spoken. Talking the same language itself can sometimes lead to discrepancies as some words have different meanings in various contexts, countries or cultures.

**iii) Nonverbal Misinterpretation**: The way we dress, the way we express ourselves through our body language, eye contact and gestures also communicates something. A simple gesture like nodding the head is considered to be YES in certain cultures and NO in others.

**iv) Preconceptions and Stereotypes**: Stereotypes involves putting people into pre-defined slots based on our image of how we think they are or should be. It may consist of a set of characteristics that we assume that all members of a group share. This may be true or may be false. But stereotypes may lead to wrongful expectations and notions. A preconceived opinion of another can lead to bias and discrimination.

**v) Tendency to evaluate:** Humans tend to make sense of the behavior and communication of others by analyzing them from one's own cultural point of view without taking into consideration why the other person is behaving or communicating a certain way.

**vi) High anxiety:** Sometimes being confronted with a different cultural perspective will create an anxious state in an individual who does not know how to act or behave and what is considered to be appropriate (For example: A Japanese man and an American having a business meeting where both are unsure of the other's cultural norms).To decrease the above boundaries to cross cultural communication, one can require the push to build up one's listening abilities. This will guarantee that we begin hearing the genuine significance of what is being said as opposed to comprehension at face esteem. Getting mindful of our discernments towards others will guarantee that we make moves to not prejudge an individual or generalization them. By tolerating individuals and their disparities and recognizing that we don't know all that will make us open up to individuals and their disparities bringing about us utilizing relevant data for better agreement. Looking for criticism and facing challenges to open up channels of communication and being liable for our emotions and activities will go far in guaranteeing that miscommunication is relieved.

**Conclusion:**

Cross-cultural communication skills are brimming with centrality for an English student and these days, numerous researchers have perceived that a decent cross-cultural communication aptitude is the way in to an effective talk. For those of us who are local English-speakers, it is blessed that English is by all accounts the language that individuals use in the event that they need to contact the amplest conceivable crowd. Nonetheless, in any event, for local English speakers, cross-cultural communication can be an issue: simply witness the shared incomprehension that can now and then emerge between individuals from various English-talking nations.

**References**

1) Barna, LaRay M, Stumbling Blocks in Intercultural Communication in Bennett, M. Basic Concepts of Intercultural Communication, 1998.
2) Communication Theory. (2017). Cross Cultural Communication. [online] Available at: https://www.communicationtheory.org/cross-cultural-communication/ [Accessed 8 May 2018].
3) Deloitte Consulting &Bersin, 2014. Global Human Capital Trends 2014: Engaging the 21st-century workforce, s.l.: Deloitte University Press.
4) Hurn B.J., Tomalin B. (2013) what is Cross-Cultural Communication? In: Cross-Cultural Communication. Palgrave Macmillan, London
5) Toegel, G. (2016). 3 Situations Where Cross-Cultural Communication Breaks Down. [Blog] Harvard Business .

# CHAPTER - 19

# IMPACT OF INTERDISCIPLINARY APPROACH IN HIGHER EDUCATION SYSTEM POST COVID

**BY**
**Anuradha Mishra & Amrita Soni**

**Abstract:**

The spread of pandemic Covid-19 has drastically interrupted each part of human existence including instruction. It has made a remarkable test on education. In numerous instructive foundations around the globe, grounds are shut and educating learning has moved on the web. Internationalization has eased back down extensively. In India, around 32 crore students halted to move schools/universities and all instructive exercises finished. Not withstanding of every one of these difficulties, the Higher Education Institutions (HEIs) have responded decidedly and figured out how to guarantee the coherence of instructing learning, exploration and administration to the general public with certain apparatuses and procedures during the pandemic. This article features on significant effects of Covid-19 on HEIs in India. A few estimates taken by HEIs and instructive specialists of India to offer compatible instructive types of assistance during the emergency are examined. Because of Covid-19 pandemic, numerous new methods of learning, new viewpoints, new patterns are arisen and the equivalent may proceed as we proceed to another tomorrow. In this way, a portion of the post Covid-19 patterns which may permit envisioning better approaches for instructing learning of advanced education in India are delineated. Some productive proposals are likewise highlighted do instructive exercises during the pandemic Circumstance.

**Keywords:** Higher Education, Covid-19, Impact, Education, Post Covid-19, India.

**Introduction:**

In any person's life, education plays a critical role. Education is considered as passport of the future for which a person has to prepare it today. Every country in the world requires a governing body to prepare its people for better future. In India, Higher Education plays that major role. It ensures that proper education is provided to every individual of this nation keeping up with all the challenges. COVID-19 situation brought a challenge for the education system of the country. It was necessary to keep up with the situation. Along with this, Higher education system also made some necessary changes in the educational system of the nation by making it inter-disciplinary.

**Higher Education System in India**

Higher Education System in India is governed by University Grants Commission (UGC), a statutory body made by Government of India under Ministry of Human Resource Development (MHRD) now Ministry of Education under UGC Act 1956. It provides standards, norms, rules and regulations for all the higher educational institutions in India. It also provides recognition to Universities in India and disbursement of funds to colleges and Universities.

**Interdisciplinary Approach**

The term "Interdisciplinary approach" is commonly used in the area of education or science. It relates to the combination in are of one or two or more subjects in academic disciplines.

Generally, it is used in one operation to encourage awareness of different subjects. It enables a person at a specific time to gain insights into different disciplines and how to integrate them to accomplish new innovative aspects.

**Definition of COVID-19**

COVID-19 is the name assigned to the disease caused by the novel coronavirus SARS-CoV2 by the World Health Organization (WHO).'SARS' refers to 'Severe Acute Respiratory Syndrome', 'CO' stands for Corona, 'VI' for Virus, and 'D' for disease. It is also related to some type of common cold.

**Symptoms of COVID-19**

Symptoms of COVID-19 can include cold, fever and shortness of breath. In serious cases, infection can cause pneumonia or flu or influenza. More rarely, the disease can be fatal.

**How Does COVID-19 spreads?**

COVID can be spread through droplets from an infected person coughs, sneezes or by talking. It can be also spread through touching any contaminated surface. The virus can live up to 8-9 hours on any surface

**Occurrence of COVID-19**

COVID-19 is a serious pandemic issue which has been facing by the world since November,2019. The first COVID-19 case was discovered in China's Wuhan area. As China is connected with many countries through trade basis, impact of Corona Virus was seen increasing in other countries too. The disease is so severe that reportedly 1.67 million people lost their lives worldwide.

**COVID-19 in India**

In India, the first case was reportedly found in January 2020, Kerala. The first death reported in India was observed on March, 2020. Due to the severity of the virus, Janta Curfew was announced by prime Minister for 21 days on March 22, 2020. It was the first time in the history of Independent India that lockdown was observed. Cases were increasing at a rapid speed so government kept on extending lockdown till 30th June, 2020. All the International, state and district borders were secured and all the modes of transportation by land, air and water were cancelled. All institutions were closed due to the outbreak of COVID. According to a report of UNESCO, published in June 2020, 67% of the total student population were affected due to this pandemic. Around 1.2 billion of student population were affected due to COVID. In India, around 32 crore students were affected by nationwide lockdown and various restrictions imposed by Government. According to Ministry of Human Resource Development (MHRD), now Ministry of Education (MOE), Around 993 universities, 39931 colleges and 10725 standalone institutions were closed down. All the campuses were closed-down, teaching students were moved at online level.

**Ministry of Education's Policy on Interdisciplinary Approach**

On 27th July 2020, Ministry of Education announced New Education Policy 2020 (NEP 2020). In the policy many changes were announced regarding Education Policy. But the highlight of the Policy was interdisciplinary holistic approach available for students with ease of entry and exit option in multiple disciplines. Ministry of Education announced that by the year 2030, every district of India will have a multidisciplinary college. Every standalone technical, agriculture, legal, health-science institutions in these or related fields will become inter-disciplinary.

**Factors that can impact learning**

Although educational system is severely affected due to this pandemic, Higher Education's response towards education was quite positive. Government made many arrangements for the students, so that their education doesn't get interrupted due to this pandemic. Indian Government also made arrangements for the students who were studying in other countries. All educational bodies including schools, colleges, universities, coaching institutes were closed due to outbreak of COVID-19. Due to this lockdown all the educational activities like school and college examinations were postponed. All entrance test dates were rescheduled several times. Administrative activities including admission procedure were hindered. As physical teaching was not possible, all educational institutions governed by Higher Education shifted to online mode. Teachers started teaching through various online applications like Google Meet, Hangouts, Skype, and Zoom. Students were encouraged to study through online mode.

a) **Online Education:**
Due to COVID-19 pandemic, all the educational institutions in India were closed down and online teaching was promoted amongst students, so that there is no loss of their studies. As a result of the outbreak of COVID-19, the use of online applications has increased rapidly. Meetings, webinars, programmes of educational institutions are conducted on online platform. This has made every individual more aware about the usage of technological platforms. Along with this, students are able to attend online lectures from the comfort of their home without being much worried about Corona Virus.But in rural areas, students were not able to attend online classes due to lack of internet facility. In addition, many students were not able to afford the internet packages provided by their respective service provider which acted as a barrier in their learning process.

b) **Efficiency:**
COVID-19 has impacted online education at a rapid speed. It has opened many technological platforms for students. Online education helps faculties to provide PDFs, presentation, notes to their students which is beneficial in their learning process.
But this process has made task of faculties tedious too. Along with this, as all the study material is available by faculties, students are not learning or exploring new knowledge on their own. In such case, inter-disciplinary education will become promising.

c) **Technological Barriers:**
One of the key factors for online education is internet connectivity. Students and faculties may both face connectivity issues due to weak network issues. In rural areas and small towns, internet connectivity is still a problem. This issue can impact both teaching as well as learning phase.

d) **Less Interactive Sessions:**
Sometimes students learn better in the presence of their peers. Due to COVID-19 situation, all students are isolated in their homes. Students are less interactive in their online classes in comparison to physical classes.

e) **Extra-Curricular Activities:**
   In this era of pandemic, gatherings of students in cultural or sports activities is impossible. Due to this, students are not able to learn teamwork, stage presentation and many other things which they used to learn from extra-curricular activities.

f) **Health of students and faculties:**
   Classes has been shifted to online platforms and students and teachers are working on either laptops or smartphones. This has made parents concerned about their child's health. As continuous usage of such gadgets can have negative effects.

**Advantages of Inter-disciplinary education**

   **To students:**

a) **Availability of Multiple options:**
   Inter-disciplinary Education will provide accessibility of various options available to students for learning and developing at same time. It will provide exposure to students on variety of thoughts, perspectives, concepts and different subjects.
   <u>For example:</u> Science student can also learn about history.

b) **Benefits in their interests:**
   The inter-disciplinary approach will help students to identify their interests and guide them to develop themselves in specialised areas. During the lockdown due to COVID-19, from college activities many new talents of students came in front. The inter-disciplinary approach will provide new direction to hidden talents or interests of students and guide them in proper manner.
   <u>For example:</u> A student of science may also feel that he has some significant interest in history too.

c) **Critical Thinking:**
   The inter-disciplinary approach will help students to analyse situations and problems and form their concepts in various subject areas.

d) **Online Courses:**
   Due to COVID-19 pandemic, many colleges and universities have started various inter-disciplined courses for students. Many students can attend these classes from anywhere in the world just with the help of internet connectivity and gain knowledge about various disciplines.

e) **Acquiring New Knowledge:**
   Inter-disciplinary approach will help students to acquire new knowledge about various subjects. As a result of COVID-19, it has been observed that many issues like economics, social science, science, culture and many more are related. This approach will help students to think from every perspective and analyse situation accordingly.

f) **Research & Development:**
   COVID-19 period made everyone aware that various disciplines are inter-related and with the new education policy Universities are encouraging students to conduct research on various societal topics which can be beneficial in aftermath of pandemic period.
   <u>For example:</u> Research scholars can study about impact of digital payments on elderly people due to COVID-19 outbreak.

g) **Expert Knowledge:**
By studying interdisciplinary subjects, students can also get knowledge from experts of their field which will be beneficial for them in developing career opportunities.
<u>For example:</u> Students of Science can interact with experts of management background to learn about leadership qualities.Similarly, management students can gain some technical knowledge too.

h) **Interactive Sessions:**
Students will be able to interact with other fellow classmates of various disciplines which will help them in gaining new knowledge and enhance their communication skills and due to COVID situation, students from every corner of the world can interact with each other. <u>For example:</u> Student of Commerce stream can interact with management discipline student and can gain knowledge about teamwork and managerial skills.

i) **Preparing students for new job opportunities:**

Inter-disciplinary education will help students to learn variety of aspects like team-building, leadership, techno-friendly, presentation and many more which will help them to prepare for new job opportunities.
<u>For example:</u> Commerce students can also learn about digital marketing which might help them in future for gaining job opportunity.

**To Teachers/Faculties:**

a) **Strong Mentorship:**
Faculties and teachers will gain by building a strong mentorship for students. They will be able to guide them in a proper way. It will also be beneficial for faculties to understand student's needs in a better way and develop their thought process.

b) **Career grooming:**
By teaching inter-disciplinary subjects, faculties will be able to master variety of subjects which will be beneficial in terms of their career. Faculties can also become expert in their subjects and can give webinars, lectures or seminars.

c) **Individual Growth:**
Not only just career growth, inter-disciplinary subjects will also be helpful in their individual growth as a personality.

## Challenges

Despite all the arrangements but due to sudden changes in the educational system and severe pandemic situation, there will be many challenges faced by students and teachers. They are:

**For students:**

a) **Distraction:**
Students may get distracted from the various topics they are learning. Concentration is the key for students while learning inter-disciplinary subjects.

b) **Affordability:**
Due to COVID-19 pandemic, many people have lost their jobs which makes difficult for the parents of students to pay fees of their courses on time. Fees of inter-disciplinary courses decided by the University or Colleges should be low so that without any hesitation and difficulties students can get enrolled in these subjects.

c) **Fieldwork and Practical exposure:**
Some of the disciplines like sports, archaeology require fieldwork for students to understand better. Due to COVID-19, it might be a problem for students to understand their discipline in a better way.

Along with that disciplines like science & technology require laboratories which may become a problem for students as due to COVID-19 guidelines, all educational institutions have to conduct online classes.

**For Faculties or Teachers:**

a) **Knowledge of various disciplines:**
Before imparting knowledge to students, faculties will be required to study other disciplines too for linking subjects with each other.

b) **Unique classroom experience:**
Faculties have to provide different classroom as well as practical experience to students but due to COVID-19 guidelines, it might be not possible for them.

c) **Teacher Learning:**
For the successful implementation of inter-disciplinary courses, teacher-training is very much essential. Due to COVID-19 situation, all the classes are shifted on online mode, so teachers are required to have basic knowledge of technology. But in many cases, specially in rural India, teachers don't have proper resources to impart online education.

d) **Social Distancing Teaching may continue:**
As the Covid-19 situation prevails, it might be very difficult for educational institutions to get re-open. Even if does, learning through social distancing will continue which might become obstacles for educational institutions which have poor infrastructure quality.

## Conclusion

COVID-19 is a serious situation which is facing by whole world. As there is no confirmed report that how long this situation may continue, it is for the betterment of students that online education should be provided. Ministry of Education should provide more clear rules and regulations regarding inter-disciplinary education, so that those changes can be quickly and easily implemented. Along with this, technological barriers faced by students and faculties should be resolved so that there is no hurdle in education.

## References


1) Pravat Kumar Jena (2020), Impact of Covid-19 on Higher Education in India,
   a. URL: https://www.researchgate.net/publication/342277024
2) Shazia Rashid and Sunishtha Singh Yadav (2020), Impact of Covid-19 Pandemic on Higher Education and Research
   a. URL: https:// journals.sagepub.com/doi/abs/10.1177/0973703020946700
3) Research and higher Education in the time of Covid
   a. URL: https://www.thelancet.com/journals/lancet/article/PIIS0140-6736(20)31818-3
4) https://timesofindia.indiatimes.com/home/education/news/multidisciplinary-focus-of-nep-2020-transforming-the-indian-higher-education-system/articleshow/77501207.cms
5) https://indianexpress.com/article/explained/reading-new-education-policy-india-schools-colleges-6531603/
6) https://www.hindustantimes.com/education/nep-2020-implementation-of-new-education-policy-in-our-education-system/story-bw4OiekFCamI7NPoNkgAoJ.html

7) https://pib.gov.in/PressReleaseIframePage.aspx?PRID=1654058

8) https://elearningindustry.com/advantages-and-disadvantages-online-learning

9) http://onlinelearningsuccess.org/advantages-and-disadvantages-of-online-and-classroom-learning/

10) https://www.indiaeducation.net/online-education/articles/advantages-and-disadvantages-of-distance-learning.html

## CHAPTER - 20

## CHALLENGES OF TAKING UP AN INTERDISCIPLINARY RESEARCH PROBLEM STATEMENT IN INDIA

**BY**
**Mary Annie Sujitha J**

**Abstract:**

Research as such is an interesting and challenging task, but when encountered with an interdisciplinary problem statement, especially in India, it becomes way more complicated than it should, in the first place! Paper works, protocols, 'through proper channel', ethical committee clearance, lab availability, permission slips, petty politics, and what not! The challenges of taking up an Interdisciplinary Research Problem Statement go on and on especially in India. Let's dive into this chapter to understand the issue at hand in detail and let's walk through practical and feasible solutions as well.

**Keywords**: Interdisciplinary Research, Research Trends, Research Problem Statement, Research Panel, Research Committee, Research Scholars, Researchers, R&D.

**Introduction**

In the present-day scenario, it is almost impossible to research a very specific problem statement pertained to a single domain. The technological advancements and developments have enabled researchers and scientists to breakthrough barriers whatsoever! But this kind of mind-blowing research has been only possible where interdisciplinary research practices were encouraged, for instance in developed countries like the United States of America. But, as far as the research trends of the Indian research culture is concerned, interdisciplinary research is viewed as something that is not legit and this is the status update as of December 2020! Though the Government indirectly encourages interdisciplinary research, the top management people of colleges and universities are still skeptical about the whole idea of interdisciplinary research. Thereby the list of challenges of taking up an Interdisciplinary Research Problem Statement in India is a pretty lengthy list indeed!

**Case Study:**

Ms. Anjali, who completed her undergraduate and postgraduate in the electronics engineering domain drafted her research proposal and was all excited to present it before her research panel in India. Her main problem statement revolved around 'Cyberpsychology'. Having a special affinity towards psychology though pursuing engineering, Ms. Anjali wanted to research cyberpsychology since she had been eyeing the increasing cybercrime rate. She wanted to figure out a way to bring down the cybercrime rate through her research. Being an engineer, she understood the nuances of digital communications and technology well, and thereby she was focused to work on the problem that focused on cyberpsychology.

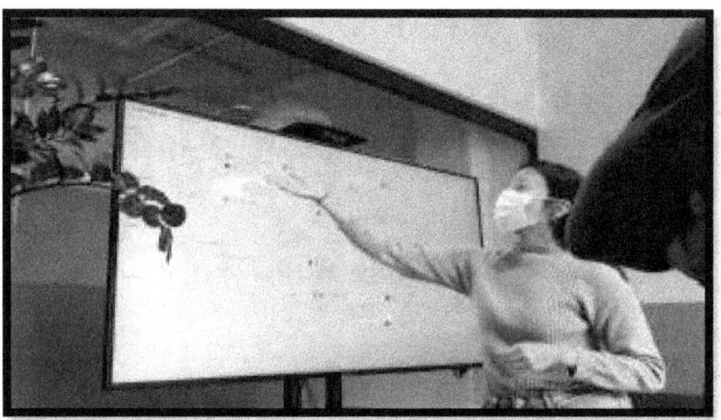

On the day of her research proposal presentation, Ms. Anjali was all excited. She started off with her presentation and the panel members gave a mixed response. They neither rejected her proposal, nor accepted it. The research panel tried to advise her on changing the problem statement more inclined towards her roots (Electronics Engineering), but Ms. Anjali was persistent in carrying out this particular research problem statement. She was then redirected to the Vice-Chancellor for the final decision. The Vice-Chancellor of the university was briefed about the scenario and he discussed with Ms. Anjali about traditional research trends and practices. He tried to convince her to change her problem statement even though Ms. Anjali clearly stated why she particularly chose this interdisciplinary research problem statement. He stressed on the fact that the particular problem statement did not fall under her roots (Electronics Engineering) and that dealing with a multidisciplinary problem statement is not advisable. Upon hearing this, Ms. Anjali tried her best to convince the Vice-Chancellor. But since the Vice-Chancellor took a final decision that she can't proceed with the interdisciplinary research problem statement, Ms. Anjali also took her stand and said that she doesn't want to pursue her research in that particular university. She also stated that she will definitely try to go abroad and pursue her research revolving around the same problem statement.

**Case Study Analysis:**

The above case study depicts a very sensitive but important issue to be addressed at this point. Ms. Anjali seems to be a person with a broad vision. She, being a young and energetic youth takes up a multidisciplinary research problem statement to address the societal issues and bring about a solution for it. But, the elders, be it at the management level or the scientific research panel, fail to encourage Ms. Anjali to take up the multidisciplinary research problem statement. This happens to be the case in many researchers' lives too. If proper teaching is not given to the academic supervisors and higher officials at this point, then the scope of research will not be fruitful in the years to come. And this is a serious threat especially in a developing country like India.

**Cyberpsychology - A Multidisciplinary Domain:**

Cyberpsychology is the study of the impact of technology especially digital media and computers on human psychology. Cyberpsychology is a budding domain that started to gain the attention of researchers from the 1990s but early works from the 1980s can also be seen. Cyberpsychology gained traction since digital communications paced up and evolved. The human-computer interaction (HCI) changed human behavior in due course of time and that is why the importance of cyberpsychology started to increase day by day.

Cyberpsychology can be viewed as an integrated result of clubbing the following broad domains:

1. Clinical Psychology
2. Neuroscience
3. Computer Science
4. Electronics & Communication
5. Law
6. Police Services (Cyber Crime Branch)
7. Medicine (Psychiatry)

Clinical Psychology is the most primary expertise that is required when it comes to cyberpsychology. This is due to the fact that from a clinical psychologist's point of view, certain psychological aspects can be understood easily. And it doesn't stop there, a person who knows about the brain activities will be able to give the medical insights required to carry out the research scientifically and thereby a Neuroscientist's expertise is required as well. Now, since the cyber world is a virtual world, coding expertise is a must, and also knowledge about computers, in general, comes in handy. Digital media is accessed from various electronic gadgets. Thereby electronics and communication expertise is also required. The answer to the question, 'what next' will be answered by the law. That is the reason why knowledge of the law is needed. When dealing with cybercrimes, police service and expertise is again a mandatory aspect. And finally, a psychiatrist's help is required to clarify from a psychiatric medicine point of view. This is how all the seven domains get involved when it comes to cyberpsychology.In today's scenario, the impact of technology on the mental health of the people is pretty adverse. This affects both the personal life and the professional life of the population and this in turn impacts society. That is why cyberpsychology research is important and that means, multidisciplinary research methodology has to be fine-tuned, approved and executed. Cyberpsychology is not the 'only' example that involves multiple disciplines, but there are more domains (especially budding ones) that need the support of other disciplines as well. When a research problem statement is framed especially around this kind of domain, it requires multidisciplinary research methodologies to be followed, and there arise huge complications to carry out such research in the first place. It is high time to change how multidisciplinary research problem statements are viewed especially in India

**Challenges faced by Researchers who take up Multidisciplinary Research Problem Statements**

The price to be paid for the complicated response to multidisciplinary research is that researchers, who have dreams to carry out quality research by taking up a multidisciplinary problem statement, tend to lose their valuable time and energy in the process of justifying the relevance of their problem statement in the first place. Even if they justify, the next steps that follow become a nightmare for them. The following are some of the issues faced by researchers who take up multidisciplinary research problem statements:

- The multidisciplinary research protocols are not predefined and thereby there is a chaos when it comes to the rules.
- Different subject matter experts' help is required.
- Availability of labs of different departments becomes an issue.
- While publishing a research article, all the names of the people who helped in some way or the other expect their names to be included in the author list which causes an issue while publishing the research articles.
- 'Through proper channels' - becomes an issue.
- University internal petty politics - ego clashes.
- The time duration of the research work may exceed the deadline and thereby the stipend and scholarship tends to get cancelled.
- Lack of open-mind thinking of the present supervisors.

The list actually goes on, but the most prominent and practical issues are stated above. The challenges stated above are an additional list of challenges to the actual research challenges that arises while carrying out the research itself. From a researcher's point of view, the actual research challenges can be dealt with but the above-mentioned challenges are a mental burden that will not only deteriorate the quality of the research but induce psychological abuse aftermath in the researchers. In the present day scenario, so many new domains are coming into the picture and to research and explore these new evolving domains, it is essential to have a broad perspective to face new challenges that arise with it. And if that kind of perspective is not developed at this juncture, it is going to be very difficult in the days to come.

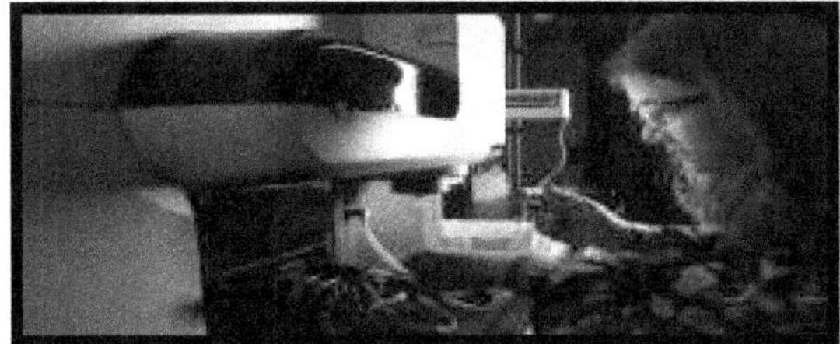

**Suggestions/Solutions:**

People living in India have a predefined notion on very many things in general and that is based on conventional and traditional beliefs and methods. Though the 'Digital India' movement and 'Make in India' movements are being nurtured and are being paid special attention, it is essential to do things the right way or at least try to do it in a way that will yield fruitful results in the near future. The following suggestions/solutions can be considered in the longer run:

- Special protocols need to be framed for multidisciplinary research.
- Special funds and grants need to be allocated to multidisciplinary research.
- Paper works and other formalities need to be minimized.
- All the universities and colleges and R&D of industries as well needs to be open to experiment new research methods upon getting approval from MHRD, UGC and other concerned research bodies such as DST, DBT, ISRO, DRDO, CSIR, ICMR, ICAR, BARC, TIFR, NRDC, NIF, NIBMG, etc.
- Researchers need to be told about the importance of thinking beyond just publishing research articles, i.e., go to the next level of foreseeing how their research can be

materialized and can be developed into new products or services that will benefit the society.

- The Vice-Chancellors and top management persons of colleges and universities need not be an aged person always. Young academicians/researchers with inclination towards administration need to be considered as well.
- Behavioral Analysts and Psychologists need to be appointed in universities and R&D departments to address unwanted petty/internal politics and psychological abuse in the workplace.
- The authorship policies in research papers need to be revised and given weightage according to the contribution of each researcher.
- There are more suggestions; however the above-mentioned suggestions if taken seriously will    definitely yield fruitful results in the near future.

## Conclusion:

Gone are those days when just the traditional and conventional research practices used to fetch fruitful results. As humankind has witnessed evolution generations after generations, it is important to embrace the change in research trends and practices as well. Change is the only constant and it is important to accept and welcome change as it is the chief trait of 'Survival of the Fittest'. Today's R&D scenario presents us enough challenges already and therefore it is important to do the best to minimize the challenges that are faced by researchers who take up multidisciplinary research problem statements. This chapter talked about the challenges taking into account one specific new research domain - cyberpsychology, but there are many more domains that need special attention as well. The suggestions and solutions mentioned in this chapter will definitely yield fruitful results provided, it is adapted and executed with the intention to facilitate quality research and help the researchers' community. Take some time, open your mind and think, you will understand.

## References:


1. https://arki.group/en/publications/cyberpsychology-evolution-of-the-notion-and-current-state/
2. https://www.rcsi.com/dublin/news-and-events/news/news-article/2014/10/father-of-cyberpsychology-to-discuss-online-experiences-of-the-next-generation
3. https://press.rebus.community/idsconnect/chapter/the-benefits-and-challenges-of-interdisciplinarity/
4. https://scholarworks.wmich.edu/cgi/viewcontent.cgi?article=1002&context=ijad
5. https://esrc.ukri.org/files/research/research-and-impact-evaluation/esrc-interdisciplinary-research-report/

## CHAPTER - 21

## IMPACT OF COVID-19 ON HIGHER EDUCATION IN INDIA

### BY
### Jagrati Patidar & Amrita Soni

**Abstract:**

The spread of pandemic Covid-19 has drastically interrupted each part of human existence including instruction. It has made a remarkable test on education. In numerous instructive foundations around the globe, grounds are shut and educating learning has moved on the web. Internationalization has eased back down extensively. In India, around 32 crore students halted to move schools/universities and all instructive exercises finished. Notwithstanding of every one of these difficulties, the Higher Education Institutions (HEIs) have responded decidedly and figured out how to guarantee the coherence of instructing learning, exploration and administration to the general public with certain apparatuses and procedures during the pandemic. This article features on significant effects of Covid-19 on HEIs in India. A few estimates taken by HEIs and instructive specialists of India to offer compatible instructive types of assistance during the emergency are examined. Because of Covid-19 pandemic, numerous new methods of learning, new viewpoints, new patterns are arisen and the equivalent may proceed as we proceed to another tomorrow. In this way, a portion of the post Covid-19 patterns which may permit envisioning better approaches for instructing learning of advanced education in India are delineated. Some productive proposals are likewise highlighted do instructive exercises during the pandemic Circumstance.

**Keywords:** Higher Education, Covid-19, Impact, Education, Post Covid-19, India.



**Introduction:**

As the world turns out to be progressively interconnected, so do the dangers we face. The COVID-19 pandemic has not halted at public fringes. It has influenced individuals paying little mind to identity, level of training, pay or sexual orientation. Yet, the equivalent has not been valid for its outcomes, which have hit the most weak hardest. On March 11, 2020 World Health Organization (WHO) pronounced Covid-19 as a pandemic. Coronavirus has influenced more than 4.5 million people groups around the world (WHO). In India, the principal influenced instance of Covid-19 was recognized on 30 January 2020 in the area of Kerala and the influenced had a movement history from Wuhan, China (Wikipedia). In India, the principal demise was accounted for on March 12, 2020 and the country noticed Janta Curfew for a day on March 22, 2020. India again noticed 14 hours Janta Curfew on March 24 to battle the Coronavirus pandemic and evaluate the nation's capacity to battle the infection. At that point, the first period of lockdown was declared by the Prime Minister on March 25, 2020 for 21 days. Observing the impacts of the infection, Indian Government has been broadening the lockdown time frame in various stages and the lockdown 5.0 was announced on April 30 which is viable from first June to 30th June 2020. In all the periods of lockdown beginning from lockdown1.0 to lockdown 5.0, the instructive organizations all through the country have never got any unwinding to begin their instructive exercises. Hence, pandemic Covid-19 affected altogether on the schooling area. As per the UNESCO report, Covid-19 has influenced almost 68% of complete world's understudy populace according to the information taken during first seven day stretch of June 2020. Flare-up of Covid-19 has affected about 1.2 billion understudies and young people across the globe by school and college terminations. A few different nations have likewise actualized restricted terminations affecting huge number of extra students. In India, in excess of 32 crores of understudies have been impressive by the different limitations and the cross country lockdown for Covid-19 (Wikipedia). Most Governments around the globe have incidentally shut instructive establishments trying to control the spread of the pandemic Covid-19. This overall conclusion has affected radically the world's understudy populace. Governments around the globe are putting forth attempts to reduce the prompt effect of conclusion of instructive organizations especially for more powerless and impeded networks and attempting to encourage the progression of schooling for all utilizing diverse advanced methods of learning. As per an overview report of the Ministry of Human Resource Development (MHRD), Government of India, directed on advanced education it was seen that there are 993 universities, 39931 Colleges and 10725 independent organizations recorded on their entry, which add to schooling (DNS Kumar, 2020). Despite the fact that the nation has been adjusting to the new-age learning, yet there still lies a snag in making whole progress as just 45 crore individuals of our absolute populace of the nation approach the web/e-learning. Individuals living in country territories are still a lot of denied of the advances and along these lines hampering the reason for online training. The Covid-19 pandemic trained the whole society on how need is the mother of innovation by permitting instructive establishments to receive web based learning and present a virtual learning society. The pandemic has been guiding the instruction area forward with mechanical development and progressions. The pandemic has essentially disturbed the advanced education area. Countless Indian understudies who are joined up with numerous Universities abroad, particularly in most noticeably terrible influenced nations are presently leaving those nations and if the circumstance endures, over the long haul, there will be a delicate decrease in the interest for worldwide advanced education moreover.

**Quotation on Education - "The stem of Education are bitter, but the fruit is sweet."**

**Position of higher Education within education cooperation Areas (Excluding Non- formal Education)**

| (Educational Institutions) | (Educational levels) | (Main Functions) |
| --- | --- | --- |
| •Graduate School University (Undergraduate)Junior college/ Polytechnic Technical Training School Broadcast University Online University Virtual University | •Higher Education | •Education Research Contributions to Society |
| • Higher school(General/ vocational Education) Junior High School | •Secondary Education | •Education |
| • Elementary school | •Primary Education | •Education |
| •Kindergarten Nursery School | •Pre-School Education | •Education care |

**Impact on Higher Education-**

Pandemic Covid-19 has seriously influenced the absolute instructive arrangement of India just as the globe.

a) Blended effect on Academic exploration and Professional Advancement: Covid-19 has both negative and positive effects on examination. On the off chance that we take the negative side, it has made outlandish for specialists to travel and cooperate with others broadly and globally. Some joint exploration work or undertaking work are made confounded to finish. Some logical lab testing/research work couldn't be led. On the off chance that we take a gander at the positive side, academicians got a lot of time to improve their hypothetical exploration work. Academicians got to know mechanical techniques and improved their examination. Online classes and e-gatherings became typical techniques for dividing mastery between understudies and academicians around the world with comparable issues. They could get a lot of time to focus on expert advancement by doing investigate and to improve information by sharing thoughts through online classes and e-gatherings. They upgraded their specialized expertise and could get the extension for distributing articles in diaries, distributing books in this extra time.

b) Seriously influenced the instructive evaluation framework: Most of the outside assessments have been delayed and practically all the inside appraisals have been dropped. The dropping of evaluations has negative effect on understudies' learning. Numerous foundations have been dealing with the inner evaluations through online mode utilizing diverse computerized apparatuses however the delay of the outside appraisals, directly affects the instructive and word related eventual fate of understudies' life. This vulnerability has made tension among understudies as they are stuck in a similar evaluation/class without advancement. Also, numerous understudies who had seemed last/load up assessments would endure a great deal as when they get their declarations, it very well may be past the point of no return for them to apply for the approaching scholarly year in different nations because of lockdown.

c) Decreased business openings: Many passageway tests work enlistments got dropped which made negative contact with an incredible test in the life of an understudy of advanced education. The Indians who have been managing their responsibilities abroad got vexed of their occupation withdrawal moreover. In India, there is no enlistment in Govt. area and new alumni are in weight of dreading withdrawal of propositions for employment from corporate areas on account of the pandemic circumstance. Numerous understudies may lose their positions from India and abroad. The pass out understudies may not land their position outside India because of different limitations brought about by Covid-19. Every one of these realities infer towards increment of joblessness rate because of this pandemic. With increment of joblessness circumstance, the interest for schooling may bit by bit diminish as individual's battle for food as opposed to training (Pravat, 2020b).

**Higher Education:**

a) MPhil courses to be ended under the new policy. All courses at under Graduation (UG), Post-Graduation (PG), and Ph.D level to be interdisciplinary.

b) New design: another vision and engineering for advanced education has been visualized with huge, well-resourced, lively multidisciplinary establishments. The current 800 universities and 40,000 colleges will be united into around 15,000 astounding institutions.

## Teacher Education:

Teacher preparation projects will be thorough and will occur in dynamic, multidisciplinary advanced education foundations. The 4-year coordinated stage-explicit, subject-explicit Bachelor of Education offered at multidisciplinary foundations would be the transcendent method of turning into an educator. Unsatisfactory and dysfunctional teacher education institutes will be shut down.

## Professional Education:

a) All professional education will be an indispensable piece of the advanced education framework. Independent specialized colleges, wellbeing science colleges, legitimate and farming colleges, or establishments in these or different fields, will be discontinued.

| Life cycle stage | Corresponding Education level | School / College Grade | Duration (years) |
|---|---|---|---|
| Pre-primary School level | Foundation education stage | KG (3 Years), Grade 1 & 2 | 5 years |
| Primary school level | Preparatory education stage | Grade 3,4 & 5 | 3 years |
| High School level | Middle School education stage | Grade 6,7 & 8 | 3 years |
| Pre-university level | Secondary education stage (adolescents) | Grade 9,10,11,12 | 4 years |
| College level | Under-graduation education stage | Grade 13,14,15 & 16 | 4 years |
| University level | Post-graduation education stage | Grade 17,18 | 1 to 3 years |
| Doctoral level | Research leading to Ph.D stage | Grade 19-22 | 3 to 4 years |
| Post-Doctoral level | Independent research stage | Grade 22-25 | 2 to 3 years |
| Life-long learning | Updating the Knowledge & skills lifeline. | — | Lifelong |

## Arising approaches of India for Higher Education during Covid-19:

Numerous difficulties are made by Covid-19. The HEIs have reacted decidedly and embraced different procedures to confront the emergency during the pandemic. The Government of India has likewise taken number of preventive measures to forestall spread of pandemic Covid-19. The MHRD and University Grants Commission (UGC) have made a few courses of action by dining of numerous virtual stages with online storehouses, digital books and other web based instructing/learning materials, instructive channels through Direct to Home TV, Radios for understudies to proceed with their learning. During lockdown, understudies are utilizing well known online media devices like WhatsApp, Zoom, and Google meet, Telegram, You tube live, Facebook live and so on for internet showing learning framework. ICT activity of MHRD (e-Broucher-https://mhrd.gov.in/ictinitiatives) is additionally a novel stage which consolidates all International Journal of Advanced Education and Research www.alleducationjournal.com 79 computerized assets for online training (Pravat, 2020a). UGC has delivered Guidelines on Examinations and Academic schedule considering COVID-l9 pandemic and ensuing lockdown on 29th April, 2020 (UGC notice). All terminal assessments have been delayed and moved to

July 2020 and recommended beginning of classes from August 2020. UGC has additionally arranged total schedule for the scholarly meeting 2020-2021with new dates keeping taking into account the lockdown. A portion of the computerized activities of UGC and MHRD for advanced education during COVID-19 are pointed as beneath:

a) e-GyanKosh (http://egyankosh.ac.in/) is a National Digital Repository to store and share the computerized learning assets which is created by the Open and Distance Learning Institutions of India. Things in eGyanKosh are secured by copyright, with all rights saved by Indira Gandhi National Open University (IGNOU).

b) Shodhganga (https://shodhganga.inflibnet.ac.in/) is a stage for research understudies to store their Ph.D. proposals and make it accessible to the whole insightful network in open access. The vault can catch, record, store, spread and protect Electronic Theses and Dissertations presented by the scientists.

c) Gyandarshan (http://www.ignouonline.ac.in/gyandarshan/) is a webbased TV channel committed to instructive and formative requirements for Open and Distance Learner. An electronic TV channel gave to instructive and formative requirements of the general public.

d) Gyandhara (http://ignouonline.ac.in/Gyandhara/) is a web sound directing help offered by IGNOU. It is a web radio where understudies can tune in to the live conversations by the instructors and specialists on the top story and interface with them through phone, email (gyandhara@ignou.ac.in) and through visit mode.

e) e-Adhyayan (digital books) is a stage that gives 700+ digital books to the Post-Graduate courses. All the digital books are gotten from e-PG Pathshala courses. It additionally encourages play-rundown of video content.

f) e-Pathya (Offline Access) is one the verticals of e-PG Pathshala which is programming driven course/content bundle that encourages understudies seeking after advanced education (PG level) in distance learning just as grounds learning mode. It likewise encourages disconnected admittance.

g) Public Digital Library of India (NDLI) (https://ndl.iitkgp.ac.in/) is a vault of e-content on different orders for a wide range of clients like understudies (of all levels), educators, specialists, bookkeepers, library clients, experts, in an unexpected way abled clients what not other long lasting students. It is being created at Indian Establishment of Technology Kharagpur. It is intended to assist understudies with planning for entrance and serious assessments, to empower individuals to learn and get ready from best practices from everywhere the world and to encourage specialists to perform between connected investigations from different sources. It is a virtual vault of learning assets with a solitary window search office. It is likewise accessible to access through versatile applications.

**Post Covid-19 Trends of Higher Education-**

Change is unavoidable which has been constrained upon the general public because of Covid-19. The open doors made by the pandemic Covid-19 will lead towards a superior tomorrow. Tomorrow will be another morning which will completely be in our own hands. New innovations will absolutely challenge the conventional standards, for example, homeroom addresses, methods of learning and methods of appraisal. The new patterns will permit the schooling area to envision better approaches for instructing learning and a few patterns might be pointed as beneath.

a) May support customized picking up: Learning may not be limited to classes or to a particular limits. Worldwide Journal of Advanced Education and Research www.alleducationjournal.com Students may be the real understudy with one teacher driving numerous understudy in the new age. The learning modules might be adjusted to suit distinctive learning styles and the taking in substance may come from various sources to meet the students' desires and needs. Understudies may seek after their learning in the new worldview according to their decision.

b) Understudy Attendance may back off: Many guardians might be hesitant to send back their youngsters to schools/universities out of nowhere after the finish of lockdown. Some helpless family guardians who have lost their business during the pandemic will be unable to bear the cost of the use to send their youngsters to establishments. This may prompt home schooling for an additional couple of months.

c) Learning with social removing may proceed. All will keep up social separating and dodge warm handshake, embrace, individual welcome, and closeness for quite a while. Imperceptible limitations may imperative the fun and delight of grounds life. Sports, Gyms, competitions might be in low stuff for a more drawn out period coming about less proactive tasks of understudies

d) Interest for Open and Distance Learning (ODL) and web based learning may develop. Coronavirus has constrained the human culture to keep up social separating. It has made more difficulties to keep instructing learning by keeping up social removing. To address these difficulties there is more interest for ODL and online methods of schooling and a similar pattern may proceed in future too.

e) Public and International understudy portability for higher investigation might be diminished: Student wellbeing and prosperity issues are significant integral components for understudies and their folks for development to global foundations for higher examination. New methods of social removing will proceed for a long while and may influence nearby eye to eye instructing learning. The vast majority of the guardians will want to discover functional choices closer to their home and may limit for less development inside the nation because of the pandemic. The worldwide schooling has additionally been influenced by the emergency. Numerous global colleges have been shut and are conveying all instructive exercises on the web. Numerous worldwide meetings in advanced education have been dropped or transformed into a progression of online classes. Thus, the public and worldwide understudy development might be lessened.

f) Encouraging learning may run with innovation. An ever increasing number of understudies will rely upon innovation and computerized answers for showing learning, amusement and associating themselves with the rest of the world. Understudies will utilize web innovation to discuss for all intents and purposes with their educators and individual students through E-mail, WhatsApp, and Videoconference, Instant message, online class or some other instrument.

## Conclusions:

This study has illustrated different effects of Covid-19 on advanced education in India. The new pandemic made an open door for change in instructive methodologies and presentation of virtual training in all degrees of schooling. As we have no idea how long the pandemic situation will continue, a progressive move towards the on the web/virtual schooling is the interest of the current emergency. UGC and MHRD have eaten numerous virtual stages with online safes, digital books and other internet instructing/learning materials. Mix of the customary innovations (radio, TV, landline telephones) with portable/web advances to a solitary stage with all stores would improve better openness and adaptability to schooling. This would incorporate upgrading the organization stage to engage it to meet the important volume of instructive requests of understudies. All specialist organizations require to be activated to give legitimate admittance to the instructive assistance stages to the burdened gatherings of populace too. Virtual training is the most favored method of instruction during this season of emergency because of the flare-up of Covid-19. The post Covid-19 instruction is by all accounts training with generally acknowledged on the web/virtual schooling which may maybe be an equal arrangement of training. This paper has not covered any factual examination on effect of Covid-19 on advanced education anyway further inside and out investigation with measurable exploration may likewise be embraced.

**References:**


1) WHO. WHO Coronavirus Disease (COVID-19) Dashboard. Retrieved on June 3, 2020. From https://covid19.who.int/
2) Pravat Ku Jena. Impact of Pandemic COVID-19 on Education in India. Purakala. 2020b; 31(46):142-149.
3) MHRD notice (20 March, 2020). COVID-19 Stay Safe: Digital Initiatives. Retrieved on May 25, 2020. From https://www.mohfw.gov.in/pdf/Covid19.pdf
4) MHRD online. Online Learning Resources of MHRD. Retrieved on June 6, 2020 from https://mhrd.gov.in/sites/upload_files/mhrd/files/upload_document/Write_up_online_lear ning_resources.pdf
5) UGC notice (29 April, 2020). UGC Guidelines on Examinations and Academic Calendar in view of COVID-19 Pandemic Retrieved on June 5, 2020. from https://www.ugc.ac.in/pdfnews/5369929_Letterregarding-        UGC-Guidelines-on Examinations-and- Academic-Calendar.pdf
6) UNESCO. COVID-19 Educational Disruption and Response. Retrieved on June 3, 2020 from https://en.unesco.org/covid19/educationresponse
7) DNS Kumar (29 April 2020). Impact of COVID-19 on Higher Education. Retrieved on May 25, 2020 from https://www.highereducationdigest.com/impact-ofcovid- 19-on-higher-education/
8) Sandhya Ramesh. What it means for COVID to never go away and become endemic- like HIV, malaria, measles, 2020.

# CHAPTER - 22

# IMPLEMENTATION OF MACHINE LEARNING IN BIOINFORMATICS

## BY
## Garima Bhatt

**Abstract:**

Machine learning is the adaptive process that produces computers make strides from encounter, by illustration, and by analogy. So It may be a discipline of techniques that gives, in one shape or another, brilliantly data preparing capabilities for taking care of genuine life. Bioinformatics is one of the application of Machine Learning. Bioinformatics is the intrigue science of deciphering organic information utilizing data innovation and computer science. Machine learning (ML) centers on programmed learning from information set. Machine learning incorporates the learning speed, the ensure of joining, and how the information can be learned incrementally. We ordinarily allude to methods like Manufactured Neural Systems (ANNs), Genetic calculations (GAs), and Fluffy frameworks together with crossover strategies counting a combination of a few of these strategies.One of the major issues is to classify the typical qualities and the invalid qualities which are contaminated by a few kind of maladies. In genomic investigate, classifying DNA arrangements into existing categories is utilized to memorize the capacities of a modern protein. So, it is critical to distinguish those qualities and classify them. In arrange to recognize the contaminated qualities and the ordinary qualities with the utilize of classification strategies here we utilize the machine learning methods. This paper gives a survey on the components of quality grouping classification utilizing Machine Learning strategies, which incorporates a brief detail on bioinformatics, writing overview and key issues in DNA Sequencing utilizing Machine Learning.

**Keywords:** Machine learning (ML), Neural Systems (ANNs), Genetic calculations (GAs).

## Introduction

Machine learning is absolutely related with computational insights, it not as it were centers on diverse prediction-making utilizing measurements but too ties to scientific optimization which assist conveys method, hypothesis and application space within the person field.Machine learning has numerous characteristics, one is utilized to diminish false-positive rates, and it has the capacity of computing machine in arrange to extend the execution based on past data.Bioinformatics is additionally one of another application of Machine Learning. Too, it can be seen in numerous investigate that Machine Learning instruments play a crucial part within the field of Bioinformatics.

## Machine Learning in Bioinformatics:

Machine learning, a subfield of computer science including the development of calculations that learn how to form predictions based on information, includes a number of developing applications within the field of bioinformatics. Bioinformatics bargains with computational and numerical approaches for understanding and handling natural data. Prior to the development of machine learning calculations, bioinformatics calculations had to be expressly modified by hand which, for issues such as protein structure forecast, demonstrates amazingly difficult. Machine learning procedures such as profound learning empower the calculation to form utilize of programmed include learning which suggests that based on the dataset alone, the calculation can learn how to combine different highlights of the input information into a more theoretical set of highlights from which to conduct assist learning.This multi-layered approach to learning designs within the input data allows such frameworks to create very complex forecasts when prepared on expansive datasets. In later a long time, the estimate and number of available organic datasets have skyrocketed, empowering bioinformatics analysts to form utilize of these machine learning frameworks.Machine learning has been connected to six biological domains: genomics, proteomics, microarrays, systems biology, and text mining.

## Genomics

Genomics includes the think about of the genome, the total DNA grouping, of life forms. Whereas genomic arrangement information has generally been meager due to the specialized trouble in sequencing a chunk of DNA, the number of accessible arrangements is developing exponentially. Be that as it may, whereas crude information is getting to be progressively accessible and open, the natural translation of this information is happening at a much slower pace. In this manner, there's an expanding require for the advancement of machine learning frameworks that can consequently decide the area of protein-encoding genes inside a given DNA sequence. This is often a issue in computational science known as quality expectation. Gene prediction is commonly performed through a combination of what are known as outward and natural searches. For the outward look, the input DNA grouping is run through a huge database of groupings whose qualities have been already found and their areas clarified. A number of the sequence's qualities can be recognized by deciding which strings of bases inside the arrangement are homologous to known quality arrangements. In any case, given the impediment in estimate of the database of known and explained quality arrangements, not all the qualities in a given input grouping can be distinguished through homology alone. Subsequently, an natural look is required where a quality forecast program endeavors to distinguish the remaining qualities from the DNA grouping alone. Machine learning has moreover been utilized for the issue of numerous grouping arrangement which includes adjusting numerous DNA or amino corrosive arrangements in arrange to decide districts of likeness that may demonstrate a shared developmental history. It can be utilized to distinguish and visualize genome improvements.

## Proteomics

Proteins, strings of amino acids, pick up much of their work from protein collapsing in which they adjust into a three-dimensional structure. This structure is composed of a number of layers of collapsing, counting the essential structure (i.e. the level string of amino acids), the auxiliary structure (alpha helices and beta sheets), the tertiary structure, and the quartenary structure. Protein auxiliary structure expectation could be a primary center of this subfield as the assist protein folding (tertiary and quartenary structures) are decided based on the auxiliary structure. Fathoming the genuine structure of a protein is a fantastically costly and time-intensive prepare, assisting the require for frameworks that can precisely anticipate the structure of a protein by analyzing the amino corrosive grouping directly. Earlier to machine learning, analysts required to conduct this forecast physically. This trend started in 1951 when Pauling and Corey discharged their work on anticipating the hydrogen bond arrangements of a protein from a polypeptide chain. Nowadays, through the utilize of programmed include learning, the most excellent machine learning methods are able to attain an precision of 82-84%. The current state-of-the-art in auxiliary structure forecast employments a framework called DeepCNF which depends on the machine learning demonstrate of manufactured neural systems to attain an exactness of around 84% when entrusted to classify the amino acids of a protein grouping into one of three auxiliary classes (helix, sheet, or coil). The hypothetical restrain for three-state protein auxiliary structure is 88–90%.

**Microarrays**

Microarrays, a sort of lab-on-a-chip, are utilized for naturally collecting information around expansive sums of organic fabric. Machine learning can help within the examination of this information, and it has been connected to expression design distinguishing proof, classification, and hereditary organize acceptance. This innovation is particularly valuable for observing the expression of qualities inside a genome, supporting in diagnosing distinctive sorts of cancer based on which qualities are expressed. One of the most issues in this field is recognizing which qualities are communicated based on the collected data. In expansion, due to the gigantic number of qualities on which information is collected by the microarray, there's a huge sum of insignificant information to the assignment of communicated quality recognizable proof, assist complicating this issue. Machine learning presents a potential arrangement to this issue as different classification strategies can be utilized to perform this distinguishing proof. The foremost commonly utilized strategies are outspread premise work systems, profound learning, Bayesian classification, choice trees, and irregular woodland.

**Systems Biology**

Systems biology focuses on the study of the emergent behaviors from complex interactions of simple biological components in a system. Such components can include molecules such as DNA, RNA, proteins, and metabolites. Machine learning has been utilized to help within the demonstrating of these complex intuitive in organic frameworks in spaces such as hereditary systems, flag transduction systems, and metabolic pathways. Probabilistic graphical models, a machine learning procedure for deciding the structure between distinctive variables, are one of the foremost commonly utilized strategies for modeling hereditary networks. In expansion, machine learning has been connected to frameworks science problems such as recognizing translation figure official locales employing a strategy known as Markov chain optimization. Genetic algorithms, machine learning procedures which are based on the normal handle of advancement, have been utilized to demonstrate hereditary systems and administrative structures. Other frameworks science applications of machine learning incorporate the assignment of protein work expectation, tall throughput microarray information investigation, examination of genome-wide affiliation considers to way better get it markers of infection, protein work expectation.

**Text Mining**

The increase in accessible organic distributions driven to the issue of the increment in trouble in looking through and compiling all the important accessible data on a given point over all sources. This errand is known as Information extraction. Usually vital for natural information collection which can at that point in turn be bolstered into machine learning calculations to produce unused natural knowledge. Machine learning can be utilized for this information extraction errand utilizing methods such as characteristic dialect preparing to extricate the valuable data from human-generated reports in a database. Content Nailing, an elective approach to machine learning, competent of extricating highlights from clinical account notes was presented in 2017.This technique has been connected to the look for novel medicate targets, as this assignment requires the examination of data put away in organic databases and journals. Annotations of proteins in protein databases frequently don't reflect the total known set of information of each protein, so extra data must be extricated from biomedical writing. Machine learning has been connected to programmed comment of the work of qualities and proteins, assurance of the subcellular localization of a protein, examination of DNA-expression clusters, large-scale protein interaction examination, and atom interaction analysis.

**Challenges of Machine Learning in Bioinformatics**

Bioinformatics deals with computational and numerical approaches to get it and handle natural information. It incorporates the following:

a. Cataloging of biological information
b. Exploration of biological data
c. Analysis of DNA sequences
d. Genomes (genomics) and protein (proteomics), elucidating evolutionary relations between sets of sequences (phylogenetic trees)
e. Gene expression examination (mainly microarray information examination - tests that permit quantitative testing of numerous qualities at the same time, to explain useful hereditary systems)
f. Multiple sequence alignment (MSA) - a method of comparing protein, DNA and RNA sequences

Machine learning that permits algorithms to memorize from cases, from involvement and through similarity can be utilized all through the range of bioinformatic applications. Machine learning procedures such as Markov models, back vector machines (SVM) and neural systems are effectively utilized for the examination of organic information. Many approaches to machine learning are utilized in bioinformatics. Well-known classical machine learning calculations (e.g. bolster vector machine [SVM], irregular timberland, covered up Markov models, Bayesian systems, and Gaussian systems) are utilized basically in genomics, proteomics and systemic science. Profound learning, which is broadly utilized in picture handling, discourse and characteristic dialect handling is additionally appropriate in bioinformatics and it can be said that in bioinformatics it is the foremost well known counterfeit insights approach. Profound neural systems and repetitive neural systems are basically utilized in anticipating protein structure, protein classification and examination of quality expression direction, whereas convolutional neural systems, basically utilized for picture investigation, are utilized in bioinformatics to analyze quality control.

**Conclusion**

Nowadays, one of the most challenging issues in computational science is to convert the gigantic volume of information, given by recently created innovations, into information. Machine learning has ended up an vital apparatus to carry out this change. The incorporation of machine learning has given bioinformatics the specified boost to quicken the improvement included within the field of bioinformatics.The article can serve as a portal to a few of the most representative works within the field and as an quick categorization and classification of the machine learning strategies in bioinformatics. In conclusion, the Machine Learning field is an energizing and quickly advancing space particularly in life sciences, as information volumeshere will outpace those of conventional Huge Information disciplines, like space science or retail.

**References**


1) Angermueller, C., H. J. Lee, W. Reik, and O. Stegle, "DeepCpG: accurate prediction of single-cell DNA methylation states using deep learning," Genome Biol., vol. 18, no. 1, Dec. 2017.
2) Mitchell TM. Machine Learning 1997McGraw-Hill.
3) Durbin R, Eddy SR, Krogh A, et al. Biological Sequence Analysis: Probabilistic Models of Proteins and Nucleic Acids 1998Cambridge University Press.

4) Ananiadou S, McNaught J. Text Mining for Biology and Biomedicine January 2006Artech House Publishers.

5) GaryB Fogel David W Corne Evolutionary Computation in Bioinformatics2002 Morgan Kaufmann

6)  Agatonovic-Kustrin, S., Beresford, R. (2000). Basic concepts of artificial neural network (ANN) modeling and its application in pharmaceutical research.

7) Barton, G.J. and Sternberg, M.J.E. (1987) A strategy for the rapid multiple alignment of protein sequences: Confidence levels from tertiary structure comparisons.

8) Benedetti, G. and Morosetti, S. (1995) A genetic algorithm to search for optimal and suboptimal RNA secondary structures.

9) Benson, D.A., Karsch-Mizrachi, I., Lipman, D.J., Ostell, J. and Rapp, B.A., Wheeler DL (2002) GenBank.

10) Boegl, K., Adlassnig, K.P., Hayashi, Y., Rothenfluh, T.E. and Leitich, H. (2004) Knowledge acquisition in the fuzzy knowledge representation framework of a medical consultation system.

11) Bohr, H., Bohr, J., Brunak, S., Cotteril, R.M., Fredholm, H., Lautrup, B. and Peterson, S.B. (1990) A novel approach to prediction of the 3-dimensional structures of protein backbones by neural networks.

12) Brown, M.P.S., Grundy, W, N., et al. (2000) Knowledge-based analysis of microarray gene expression data by using support vector machines.

13) Brusic, V., Rudy, G., Honeyman, M., Hammer, J. and Harrison, L. (1998a) Prediction of MHC class-II binding peptides using an evolutionary algorithm and artificial neural network.

14) Brusic, V., Van Endert, P., Zeleznikow, J., Daniel, S., Hammer, J. and Petrovsky, N. (1998b) A Neural Network Model Approach to the Study of Human TAP Transporter.

15) Brusic, V. and Zeleznikow, J. (1999) Knowledge discovery and data mining in biological databases.

16) Chellapilla, K. and Fogel, G.B. (1999) Multiple sequence alignment using evolutionary programming.

17) Chen, J-H., Le, S-Y. and Maizel, J.V. (2000) Prediction of common secondary structures of RNAs: a genetic algorithm approach.

18) Coley, D.A. (1999) An introduction to genetic algorithms for scientists and engineers.

# CHAPTER – 23

## COVID-19: IMPACT OF BANKING SECTOR

## BY
## Poonam Sharma & Neha Mathur

**Abstract:**

In today's era, as everyone knows that to defeat a pandemic like covid-19, the Indian government announced complete lockout in the country from 24 march 2020 and was then extended to 3 may 2020 by the Indian government. The Indian government needs to lockout so that the lives of the people of the country can be saved. This is going to severely affect various sectors of our country. Banking is the backbone of the Indian economy. This article is an attempt to assess the causal impact of an pandemic like covid-19 on banks due to lockdown. As a result, all commercial organizations, educational institutions and public and private sector offices have been closed. The article has indicated a very serious impact of the lockdown on banks in the event of moving beyond July 2020.

**Key words:** COVID-19, Indian Economy, Indian Banks, NPA, Lockdown

**Introduction:**

**Covid-19:** COVID-19 affects different people in different ways. Most infected people will develop mild to moderate illness and recover without hospitalization.

**Most common symptoms:**

- Fever
- Dry cough
- Tiredness

**Less common symptoms:**

- Aches and pains
- Sore throat
- Diarrhoea
- Conjunctivitis
- Headache
- Loss of taste or smell
- A rash on skin, or dis colouration of fingers or toes.

**Problem Statement**

The rapid spread of epidemics such as covid-19 has led to a steep decline in key indices, indicating a significant impact on its impact and GDP growth.The first news of the outbreak of novel corona virus came from Wuhan city of China on 31 December 2019. This corona virus is a new virus that has not yet been identified in humans. The literature indicates that the corona virus is a very large family of viruses. Its spreading speed is very fast . This corona virus can cause anything from the common cold to the more severe autism syndrome. To prevent this from spreading across the country, the Indian government announced a lockout on 24 march 2020.

Extended to 3 may 2020. Many actions taken by many governments around the world, WHO praised the timely action by Indian Prime Minister Narendra Modi and many people as a lockdown, because of the cure of the disease or in the absence of vaccine to prevent the virus from spreading was the best option. By the way , various institutions like IMF and World Bank,Central Banks economists, fund managers and consulting firms from different countries have expressed their fears about the devastating effect of lockdown in GDP world especially in general and emerging economics like India.On 14 April, the IMF released its global growth projections. It was revealed that the great depression was likely to occur after the great depression in the 1930s, which could be better than global financial organizations.

**Indian Banking Sector: A Backdrop:**

A Bank is an institution that has the primary function of depositing and lending money to needy individuals, businesses and governments. Banks around the world are considered trustworthy. When a person deposits money in a Bank, it does not mean to the Banks what the amount is. The person knows that the money is safe with the Bank. The Bank provides many facilities to customers such as providing loans, debit cards and credit cards measures to generate demand and ease the liquidity by ensuring public sector banks lend further to NBFCs, introducing partial credit. Guarantee scheme, organizing loan mela etc. prominent position in India's economy and contribute to employment in India. Unfortunately of Banks has deteriorated. The condition of Public Sector Banks has deteriorated. Facilities. Indian Banking industry which is almost 200years old. Since the beginning of the reforms in 1991, it has been expanded and modernized (KPMG 2017) as certain that the Banking sector is poised to become the fifth largest banking industry in the world in the year 2020 and will be the third largest by 2025. There are currently 34 Banks in India, out of which 12 are Public sector Banks. 14 Banks were nationalized in 1969 and 6 Banks were nationalized in 1980. The Reserve Bank of India announced in August 2019 that banks can have an exposure of up to 20 per cent of their Tier 1 capital to a single NBFC. This limit was 15 per cent earlier. This helped boost credit flow as bank funding to NBFCs grew by 30 per cent year on year. The Government has taken a series of measures to generate demand and ease the liquidity by ensuring public sector banks lend further to NBFCs, introducing partial credit guarantee scheme, organizing loan mela etc.

**Non -Performing Assets:**

A non- performing assets is an assets that is used by financial institutions for loans and advances on which the principal amount is outstanding and on which no interest is paid for a period of time. Loans are become to non-performing assets when they are outstanding for 90 days or more. The loan is outstanding when principal or interest payments are late or missed.

**Ten decisions taken by RBI to counter the corona virus impact on economy**

The Reserve Bank of India asked all lending institutions to allow three month moratorium on EMI payments in order to infuse liquidity into the system amid novel corona virus crisis. RBI governor Shaktikanta Das in a press conference said these are extraordinary circumstances, and unprecedented measures are required to support the sagging economy as all the economic activities have come to a halt.

a) **Repo Rate** - RBI announced that it was cutting the Repo rate by 75 bps, or 0.75% to 4.4. The Repo rate was earlier 5.15; last being cut in October 2019.

b)  **Reverse Repo**- The regulator also announced that it would cut the reverse repo rate by 90 bps, or 0.90%. on a daily average , banks had been parking Rs 3 lakh crore with the RBI. The current reverse repo rate was 4 %.

c)  **Loan Moratorium** - In a massive relief for the middle class, the RBI Governor also announced that lenders could give a moratorium of 3 months on term loans, outstanding as on 1 march, 2020. This is applicable to all commercial banks including regional, rural, small finance, co-op bank, all India financial institutions and NBFCs including housing finance and microfinance.

d)  **CRR**- The RBI also announced that the cash reserve ratio would be reduced by 100 bps, or 1%, to 3%. This would be applicable from March 23, and would inject Rs.137, 000crore.

e)  **LTRO** -The RBI will also undertake long term Repo operations; allowing further liquidity with the banks. The banks however are specified that this liquidity will be deployed in commercial papers, investment grade corporate bonds and non -convertible debentures.

f)  **Ease of working Capital financing**- Lenders were allowed lending to recalculate drawing power by reducing margins and / or by reassessing the working capital cycle for the borrowers. The RBI also specified that such a move would not result in asset classification downgrade.

g)  **Working capital interest** -A three month interest moratorium shall also be permitted to all lending institutions.

h)  **Deferment capital interest**- The net stable funding ratio, which reduces funding risk by requiring banks to fund their activities with sufficiently stable sources of funding was postponed to October 1, 2020. The NSFR was earlier supposed to be implemented by April 1, 2020.

i)  **MSF**- Marginal standing facility has also been increased to 3 % of SLR, available till June 30, 2020. This measure should provide comfort to the banking system by allowing it to avail an additional 137000 crore of liquidity under the LAF window in times of stress at the reduced said the RBI.

j)  **Fresh Liquidity** - The impact of all the announcements today shall inject almost 3.2% of GDP, the Governor said in his brief today. The RBI also added that since February 2020 it had injected Rs 2.8 lakh crore of liquidity, equivalent to 1.4 percent of GDP.

**Research Methodology:**

As stated earlier, the purpose of this chapter is to assess the impact of covid-19 in India's banking sector. In order to achieve this objective , some conclusions have been drawn from the existing literature available on various sites of the internet as highlights of interviews with renowned economics and fund managers, economic and financial advisors and senior officials of economic bodies, chambers of commerce and industry. At present, there is no factual data on the impact of Covid -19 on various sectors of the economy including banks and only a rough estimate is available only about the number of positive cases. The use of statistical tools was not possible due to the unavailability of quantitative data. Therefore a descriptive article has been prepared with the help of online views of experts regarding the impact of ongoing epidemic.The COVID-19 situation will not only accelerate the adoption of technology, but will renew focus on the following four key areas of banking:

**Embracing Neo Technologies:**

 In the post -epidemic and economic crisis, emerging technologies will play a key role in speeding up transactions and reducing costs for banks. The Indian banking sector has already realized the role of technology in achieving access and scale. These technologies will play a key role in the digital transformation of banks and financial institutions and re-imagine the digital delivery of services.

**Channels of Digitization:**

According to the world 2017 global search report , India is the world's second largest non-populous household with 190 million adults without accessing a bank account by going to bank branches to use digital channels, preference banks will enable their customers to negotiate multiple automated and digital channels to present this column channel mix. Banks will consider such important factors as demographic, internet access, lat mile, connectivity, customer banking, behaviour patterns, etc. To effectively adopted by Indian banking consumers.

**Security, Privacy and Customer Trust:**

 According to the RBI for the financial year 2017, India's banking sector saw an increase in Cyber fraud and a loss of 13 points 7 million dollars. With the increasing use of cashless and digital economy, it will be mandatory for banks to implement secure structures and systems. Banks to identify both internal and external weaknesses.

**Policy and Compliance:**

Focus should be on digital payments and infrastructure especially in rural India. India is already on its path to introduce the personal data protection bill on the lines of GDPR in the EU.

**Other Impact:**

a) An epidemic like corona is likely to result in a major shift in savings and risk to households. This increase can increase the flow of savings in bank deposits among the instruments of savings, which are always considered safe.

b) An epidemic like corona may increase the demand for loans from banks, slowing down secured lending like personal loans or credit cards.

**Conclusion:**

The impact of the corona like epidemic on banks in India has left some banks to struggle due to deposits, as loans are protected by deposits. The condition of private banks may force customers to lend less, which may lead to poor liquidity. The RBI has given a 3 month grace period to all banks due to corona which has brought some relief from the rules governing bad credit recognition, but banks NPA have increased. It is well known to the bankers that since the implementation of the lockdown by the government of India on 25 March, 2020 RBI has taken a lot of steps in doing business in the banking sector. RBI has also relaxed the deadline for bad credit rules due to corona and barred borrowers from paying dividends for the year ended 31 march 2019. The situation of Banks has deteriorated due to the lockdown. But now after withdrawing the lockdown it will take longer to return to normally.

**Suggestions:**

- The RBI should now focus on the financial system and its context to maintain liquidity in the event of Covid-19.
- After the withdrawal of the lockdown, there should be a facility to provide loans to keep all small and medium enterprises on track.
- Government of India should reduce the uncertainty in the economy and financial stress.
- Both the money market and the capital market must be operated properly.
- The government should make the economy strong enough to avoid the coming crises.

**References**


1) Wu, D. D., & Olson, D. L. (2020). The effect of COVID-19 on the banking sector. In Pandemic Risk Management in Operations and Finance (pp. 89-99). Springer, Cham.
2) Demirguc-Kunt, A., Pedraza, A., & Ruiz-Ortega, C. (2020). Banking sector performance during the covid-19 crisis.
3) Andersen, A. L., Hansen, E. T., Johannesen, N., & Sheridan, A. (2020). Consumer responses to the COVID-19 crisis: Evidence from bank account transaction data. Available at SSRN 3609814.
4) Singh, J., & Bodla, B. S. (2020). Covid-19 pandemic and lockdown impact on India's banking sector: a systemic literature review. COVID-19 pandemic: a global challenge, 21-32.
5) Ozili, P. K., & Arun, T. (2020). Spillover of COVID-19: impact on the Global Economy. Available at SSRN 3562570.
6) Ari, A., Chen, S., & Ratnovski, L. (2020). COVID-19 and non-performing loans: lessons from past crises. Available at SSRN 3632272.
7) Dr. Chanduji P.Thakur.(2020)A Study on Impact of Covid-19 on Banking Sector:An Indian Perspective;Indian Journal of Reserach,9(6)92-93.
8) Dr.Singh.Bodla. (2020) Covid-19 Pandemic and Lockdown Impact on India's Banking Sector: A Systematic Literature Review, 21-32.
9) Dev, S. M., & Sengupta, R. (2020). Covid-19: Impact on the Indian economy. Indira Gandhi Institute of Development Research, Mumbai April.
10) Ramasamy, D. (2020). Impact Analysis in Banking, Insurance and Financial services industry due to COVID-19 Pandemic. Pramana Research Journal, 10(8).

# CHAPTER – 24

# INTERDISCIPLINARY RESEARCH AND INNOVATION IN PHARMACEUTICAL SCIENCES

**Manu Singhai & Surbhi Rani**

## Abstract

It is generally hoped and believed that interdisciplinary research will stimulate the kinds of radical innovations that are needed to solve some of the major problems facing society. Indeed, previous forms of incremental development, that have come out of discrete knowledge domains, now seem to have proved themselves insufficient in the face of the complex social and environmental challenges that we currently face. If we consider that researchers and professors are increasingly demanded productivity, then a strategy to maximize their research results is desirable. In an educational environment such as a University/Institute/College, at some point research shall become part of learning activities. Research offers an opportunity for investigators to explore unanswered questions, highlight best practices, and engage in collaboration. Pharmacists who engage in collaborative research improve their chances of publication through increased access to high-impact research opportunities as compared with pharmacists with individual or single department research efforts. The pharmacy team efforts in interdisciplinary research can take the form of clinical questions being answered among groups within a single pharmacotherapy practice area (eg, ambulatory care, cardiology, infectious diseases, and family medicine). Pharmacists should play a key role in initiating and conducting research at an academic or community medical center. Individuals interested in initiating research who do not have experience should seek out a mentor and/or additional avenues for training to assist them in refining their research skills.

**Keywords:** Interdisciplinary Research, Collaborative Research, Interinstitutional Pharmaceutical R&D, Innovation, Development, Pharmaceutical Sciences.

## Introduction

Is science becoming more interdisciplinary? According to Porter and Rafols [1], the answer is yes. If we consider that researchers and professors are increasingly demanded productivity, then a strategy to maximize their research results is desirable. In an educational environment such as a University/Institute/College, at some point research shall become part of learning activities. Because of the growth in the field of interdisciplinary research, a natural question arises: should interdisciplinary research begin in undergraduate years? In a correspondence to Nature [2], Tong states that: Making the transition to postgraduate research from undergraduate modules is not easy and is not necessarily successful at present. Earlier engagement with interdisciplinary research methodologies and results is likely to reveal fresh horizons to the next generation of scientists. Wilson exposed the interdisciplinary research and publication opportunities in information systems and healthcare. Differently from the cited frameworks or research methods [3], this work proposes a general methodology for interdisciplinary research to increase productivity in a University context that may be combined with them, and it suggests a natural way to incorporate the interdisciplinary research in educational activities [4].It is generally hoped and believed that interdisciplinary research will stimulate the kinds of radical innovations that are needed to solve some of the major problems facing society. Indeed, previous forms of incremental development, that have come out of discrete knowledge domains, now seem to have proved themselves insufficient in the face of the complex social and environmental challenges that we currently face. There is a constant struggle to connect the foundational sciences to the clinical or applied sciences within the various areas of health science education [5]. Accordingly, interdisciplinary approaches to knowledge production and innovation have grown in importance. They are now perceived as being fundamental to the future research landscape. So, it is this potential of interdisciplinary research, to deliver game-changing solutions, through radical innovations, that seems to have generated such a widespread, and considerable, investment of faith in its potential [5]. Research offers an opportunity for investigators to explore unanswered questions, highlight best practices, and engage in collaboration. Research can engage health care professionals to identify treatments or procedures to enhance patient care, quality of life, and outcomes. Research may also include experiences in a unique practice site or teaching methodology of trainees, staff, or patients. Ultimately, the goal of the research is to improve individual patient care via the dissemination of knowledge through publications. Publications can range from abstracts and oral presentations to articles that highlight best practices and areas for improvement [6]. For more than a decade, analysts of the pharmaceutical industry have argued that the conventional blockbuster model of drug discovery and development is unsustainable, despite many years of investment in new life science technologies [7]. For interdisciplinary research, the approach to innovation in this work must be considered in the context of a real problem. The proposed approach has three phases, which are represented in Figure 1. Given a real problem, in the first phase, two or more fields shall be considered to be applied in its solution. After choosing the fields to approach the problem, in phase two, the researcher or group of researchers shall try to elaborate a new fundamental or methodology based on their knowledge of the select fields. If somehow the combination of two or more concepts of different fields generates a new fundamental concept to the problem or a new methodology to approach it, then its application to the real problem is phase three, which is an innovation that may produce a new technology [6].

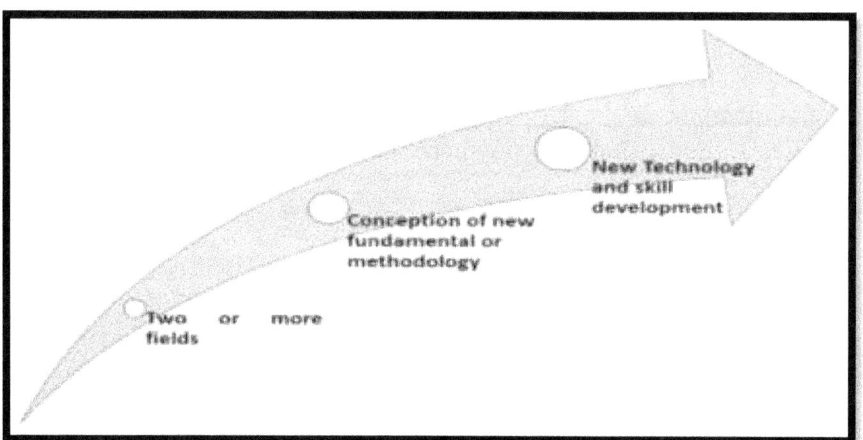


**Figure 1- Approach to innovation in interdisciplinary research**

**Collaborative research**

Collaborative research can be broadly categorized as intra- or interinstitutional. As the name simply, intra-institutional research takes place within a single institution whereas interinstitutional research involves multiple institutions. This example could illustrate pharmacy-driven research if the project was led by the pharmacy with medicine providing expertise on a single aspect. The pharmaceutical industry is continuing to face several innovation challenges – low productivity, patent expiry, rising costs of R&D, a high attrition rate of compounds in Phase 2, high regulatory hurdles, increasing concern about adverse side effects, and so on. But a major challenge that is often ignored is what we call the 'problem of maturity' [7].Pharmacists who engage in collaborative research improve their chances of publication through increased access to high-impact research opportunities as compared with pharmacists with individual or single department research efforts. Similarly, pharmacist integration into interprofessional research teams is highly desirable to achieve desired outcomes. To engage in effective research, successful mentors must be identified to provide a foundation for trainees to learn and implement fruitful investigations in their practice. Additional emphasis should be placed on the importance of interprofessional research groups early in training to enhance collaboration and publication opportunities [8].Resident-based research effectiveness will be evaluated based on the integration of the pharmacist into collaborative research and the achievement of organizational goals. We will identify organizational collaborative research resources and highlight examples of best practices. Through this exercise, we will create a blueprint for success criteria that are needed for multidisciplinary research collaboration [6].

Collaboration may also extend to practitioners in other disciplines, including nurses, hospital administrators, microbiologists, or statisticians. Additionally, there can be collaborations within the pharmacy department itself. For example, a seasoned clinical specialist may look to junior practitioners, staff pharmacists, technicians, or trainees for assistance with data collection on a large project. This is practitioner-driven research, but there is also trainee-driven research. For instance, a student, resident, or fellow may develop a research question and then seek the expertise and mentorship of a veteran researcher to accomplish his or her goals. Examples of inter-institutional collaborative research include a researcher from a private company working with the research group of an academic faculty member or a postgraduate resident traveling to an outside institution several times over a year to learn a new research technique. Another example of inter-institutional collaboration is the application of a research study protocol between multiple and geographically diverse hospitals [6].

**Focus on the pharmacist practitioner for collaborative research**

- Pharmacists at an academic or community medical center or within a health system (that may include retail) take the lead.
- Create the team: inter-pharmacy collaboration, intra-pharmacy collaboration, a committee for research, and individuals.
- Recruit mentors to aid in the research process.
- Introduce a research agenda for the team to foster ideas.
- Delineate the roles of physicians, nurses, and other health care professionals as necessary stakeholders.
- Become familiar with the best practices of pharmacy and other disciplines.
- Utilize information technology (IT) colleagues to advance data procurement.
- Seek out pharmacy trainees to improve efficiencies.
- Understand and become an expert on the research process (IRB, HIPPA requirements, your IT support team).
- Be attentive to barriers to multidisciplinary research.

An integrated curricular model can facilitate the building of connections between the foundational and clinical sciences by presenting multi-disciplinary material within a cohesive framework in a single course [9]. Although content is delivered together by both clinicians and scientists in an integrated curricular model, examples of integration in therapeutic decision-making must be presented to student pharmacists. The pharmacist's educational training in pharmacokinetic and pharmacodynamic principles, as well as expert knowledge on drug formulation and dispensing, places them in the best position to monitor drug safety and to create individual pharmacotherapy regimes [10].

## Interdisciplinary research and innovation

**Accelerating progress in pharmaceutical R&D:** The power of interdisciplinary knowledge With pharmaceutical companies facing rising pressure to expand their pipelines and accelerate their discovery cycle, forward-thinking organizations are recognizing the vast potential of working across disciplines to drive innovation. Indeed, many of the most promising developments, such as novel drug delivery mechanisms and new therapeutic classes, are now focused on the intersections of scientific fields historically seen as disparate [11].However, that traditional view of pharmaceutical research, biology, and chemistry as well-separated scientific disciplines has generated domain and information siloes that hinder innovation. This perception is part of the fabric of the scientific world, underlying how degrees are defined, how departments are organized, and how knowledge is communicated. However, approaching these disciplines as separate or "in the competition" limits the scope of pharmaceutical innovation.

## The promise of interdisciplinary innovation in pharmaceutical R&D

Combining expertise from different fields is allowing scientists to deliver ground-breaking new therapeutic approaches for age-old healthcare challenges. For instance, interdisciplinary research has recently yielded an ingenious strategy to deliver insulin orally [12]. Since insulin is a peptide hormone, it is vulnerable to digestion and so is traditionally given by injection [13]. However, as injections are inconvenient and can be unpleasant, scientists have long been searching for alternative dosing strategies. Using cross-disciplinary work, it could soon be possible to take a pea-sized pill that can mechanically inject insulin into the tissues of the stomach lining, allowing patients to finally escape the hassle of subcutaneous injections. This remarkable innovation does not stem from a single field, but rather combines biology, chemistry, physics, and bio-engineering all in one.Another fascinating example is a digital pill that tracks when patients have taken their medication [14]. A tiny sensor in the pill, when activated by stomach fluid, sends a timestamped signal via a wearable patch to a mobile app. This novel technology was originally developed to address compliance issues with schizophrenia medication – it's not unusual for patients suffering from this condition to depart from prescribed dosing, and doctors often struggle to get a full picture of medicine-taking patterns from patient consultations. With this revolutionary new technology, doctors can now access a full record of each patient's treatment history while increasing compliance. Such examples illustrate the tremendous power and potential of overcoming the disconnect between traditionally separate scientific areas to improve patient outcomes. In reality, making significant progress in the evolving landscape of pharmaceutical R&D depends on an understanding of both biology and chemistry. It relies on an appreciation of the impact of fundamental physical, chemical, and biological properties on the way drugs interact with the body. Indeed, integrating knowledge across multiple fields is becoming ever more important as therapies become more sophisticated [15]. For example, the most challenging aspect in the development of biologic therapies is often mastering the formulation chemistry. Ultimately, we require a deep and cross-disciplinary knowledge of the fundamental properties of these innovative therapies to unlock their full potential.

## How to bridge the disciplinary divide

Breaking down the barriers to multidisciplinary research is no simple task. To more fully capitalize on interdisciplinary innovation opportunities, we must focus on the barriers that are embedded in the foundational aspects of our organizations, culture, and approaches that hinder collaboration. While this is a complex undertaking, here are several specific suggestions to help tear down these siloes [16].

## The Need for 'SMART REGULATION'

The key challenge for ensuring that necessary structural change in the sector is manageable, is the construction of smarter regulatory approaches that are more responsive to the opportunities emerging from the life sciences and do not simply support the status quo of multinational dominance [17]. At present, the lengthy, expensive and demanding nature of the drug regulatory system is sustaining the unchallengeable supremacy of the Big Pharma companies. The high costs and long delays of taking a product through the cumbersome regulatory system ensures that only the largest companies are able to operate throughout the innovation life cycle [7]. For novel technologies or products that may disrupt conventional Big Pharma strategy, such as stem cells, it is difficult to identify a route to market for the smaller companies that are at the forefront of developing the science [18]. Regulatory systems can, over time, become dysfunctional and out of step with changes in the science and technology that they regulate. Furthermore, as regulatory systems evolve, they can become so complex that any change or addition to one set of regulations can have unpredictable consequences for other parts of the system and the companies affected by them. As a starting point for further discussion in this area, we draw a number of lessons for better regulation of the life sciences.

First, since regulatory initiatives can have a transformative impact on innovation (both positive and negative, but also unpredictable), sensitivity towards the impact of regulation on particular industry sectors and innovation strategies is crucial when designing or redesigning regulatory systems for novel therapies that have no established route to market [19].

Second, because regulatory change in one policy area can have unexpected consequences for other policy areas, or even entire innovation sectors, it is vital that regulators are made aware of potentially useful but vulnerable products and processes under development, and their location within broader innovation networks [20].

Third, smart regulatory systems will always strive to enable positive changes in innovation strategies and adequately discriminate among products on the basis of socially and economically relevant criteria, as this will be more effective and efficient than an indiscriminate strategy that simply tries to constrain undesirable behaviour. An enabling criterion will positively affect the speed of the regulation's influence. The appropriateness of its product, or process discrimination will determine its effectiveness in guiding product development in desirable directions [7].
*Finally,* the development of path-breaking regulation for path-breaking technology should always be a last resort. When considering which regulatory option is most appropriate for a new, innovative technology, a good default rule would be to invoke the regulatory system in operation for the industry sector for which the innovation is path-dependent, rather than path-breaking [7].

## Interpharmacy Collaboration

The pharmacy team efforts in interdisciplinary research can take the form of clinical questions being answered among groups within a single pharmacotherapy practice area (eg, ambulatory care, cardiology, infectious diseases, and family medicine). There are excellent examples of collaborative research that is individually led with pharmacists as key Stakeholders University of Iowa, University of Illinois at Chicago and University of Rhode Island. Other areas of practice investigators include transplant, critical care, pediatrics, and the behavioral sciences [21].


**Committee for Research**

Academic medical centers have the infrastructure that supports pharmacy-led research. Duke University Hospital, for example, has a Pharmacy Research Committee that serves as a scientific advisory committee designed to enhance pharmacy staff, residents, and student knowledge [21]. This committee oversees and guides research activities and helps to identify extradepartmental research support resources. Other academic institutions have pharmacist-led committees that provide oversight, although some of these may be more college-based than hospital-based [22].

**Research Process**

Identification and development of research questions is one of the most crucial steps in the research process, and it sets the direction for the rest of the research project. Clinicians should spend considerable effort in identifying and refining areas where further knowledge is necessary. When identifying areas of knowledge deficit, pharmacists should consider topics of conflicting clinical practice or suboptimal outcomes. In refining a research question, it is important to appreciate what previous investigations have demonstrated in order to identify knowledge gaps and logical subsequent questions generated from previous research [23]. In the Initiation phase the determination of the project goals are performed, deliverables and process outputs, or let us say to choose the real problem to solve, and to understand what its solution is, it shall be useful to identify two or more fields for an interdisciplinary approach, in order to document its constraints and assumptions, to define strategy, to identify performance criteria, to determine resource requirements, to define the budget and to produce a formal documentation. It is worth to highlight that in some real problems it may be a requirement to have an interdisciplinary approach. The Planning phase consists of refining the project and to do that a more profound study of the problem and the chosen fields may be performed. These studies shall promote a new fundamental or methodology. Therefore, in the *executing phase*, an educational material may be prepared and applied in a classroom for an approach, even if new concepts are not generated. Clearly, if they are developed a new technology may be developed and used [21].

If in the Planning phase controls are established then educational, technology, economics and social parameters are defined and available for measurement, allowing the Control phase to be performed. Finally, depending on the results of the measured parameters papers may be written, at that would be the closing phase.

**Conclusion:**

It is conceivable that the pharmaceutical multinationals will continue to survive in their present form and pursue the same strategies of small molecule blockbuster innovation, which will involve further waves of largescale mergers and acquisitions, and the subsequent disruption of asset-stripping and R&D rationalisations. Graduate programs have evolved beyond the traditional programs of pharmaceutics, pharmacology, and medicinal chemistry to include interdisciplinary programs that are increasingly aligned with departments or schools of medicine and engineering. With the advent of niche areas and more translational/interdisciplinary areas, pharmacy schools may need to redefine or expand disciplines to cover areas that are now relevant to the pharmaceutical sciences. Although time is often cited as a barrier to research and publication, intrainstitutional and interinstitutional collaborative efforts can enhance research productivity. Creating a research culture at an institution is essential in promoting research activities. Pharmacists should play a key role in initiating and conducting research at an academic or community medical center. Individuals interested in initiating research who do not have experience should seek out a mentor and/or additional avenues for training to assist them in refining their research skills. Exposing trainees to collaborative research can serve as a platform for engaging them in collaborative research throughout their career.

## References


1) Porter A, Rafols I. Is science becoming more interdisciplinary? Measuring and mapping six research fields over time. Scientometrics. 2009 Dec 1;81(3):719-45.
2) Tong VC. Let interdisciplinary research begin in undergraduate years. Nature. 2010;463(7278):157-.
3) King G, Currie M, Smith L, Servais M, McDougall J. A framework of operating models for interdisciplinary research programs in clinical service organizations. Evaluation and program planning. 2008 May 1;31(2):160-73.
4) Wilson EV, Lankton NK. Interdisciplinary research and publication opportunities in information systems and health care. The Communications of the Association for Information Systems. 2004 Sep 17;14(1):51.
5) Brown B. Interdisciplinary research. European Review. 2018 Oct;26(S2): S21-9.
6) Badowski M, Mazur JE, Lam SW, Miyares M, Schulz L, Michienzi S. Engaging in collaborative research: focus on the pharmacy practitioner. Hospital pharmacy. 2017 Jan;52(1):33-43.
7) Mittra J, Tait J, Wield D. The future of pharmaceutical innovation: new challenges and opportunities. Innov Pharm Technol March. 2011; 2011:32-4.
8) Vaidean GD, Vansai SS, Moore RJ, Feldman S. Student scientific inquiry in the core doctor of pharmacy curriculum: critical issues in designing and implementing a student research program. INNOVATIONS in pharmacy. 2013 Jan 1;4(4).
9) Willett NJ, Boninger ML, Miller LJ, Alvarez L, Aoyama T, Bedoni M, Brix KA, Chisari C, Christ G, Dearth CL, Dyson-Hudson TA. Taking the next steps in regenerative rehabilitation: Establishment of a new interdisciplinary field. Archives of Physical Medicine and Rehabilitation. 2020 Feb 5.
10) Brown KP, Raccor BS, Hilgers RH, Breivogel CS. Interdisciplinary pharmaceutical sciences activity within a pharmacy practice skills course. Currents in Pharmacy Teaching and Learning. 2019 Mar 1;11(3):270-6.
11) Crouthamel M. *The Rise of Patient Centricity in the Pharmaceutical Industry* (Doctoral dissertation, Temple University. Libraries).
12) Khan HA. Education, science and technology in developing countries: Some thoughts and recollections. Commission on Science and Technology for Sustainable Development in the South; 2004 Nov.
13) Wong CY, Martinez J, Dass CR. Oral delivery of insulin for treatment of diabetes: status quo, challenges and opportunities. Journal of Pharmacy and Pharmacology. 2016 Sep;68(9):1093-108.
14) Elenko E, Underwood L, Zohar D. Defining digital medicine. Nature biotechnology. 2015 May;33(5):456-61.
15) Hornyak GL, Moore JJ, Tibbals HF, Dutta J. Fundamentals of nanotechnology. CRC press; 2018 Dec 14.

16) Nowotny H, McBee D, Leahey E, Downey GJ, Feinstein NW, Kleinman DL, Peterson S, Fukuda C, Smith-Doerr L, Croissant J, Vardi I. Investigating interdisciplinary collaboration: theory and practice across disciplines. Rutgers University Press; 2016 Nov 25.

17) Wirtz BW, Weyerer JC, Geyer C. Artificial intelligence and the public sector—applications and challenges. International Journal of Public Administration. 2019 May 19;42(7):596-615.

18) Petrova E. Innovation in the pharmaceutical industry: The process of drug discovery and development. InInnovation and marketing in the pharmaceutical industry 2014 (pp. 19-81). Springer, New York, NY.

19) Ashford NA. An innovation-based strategy for a sustainable environment. InInnovation-oriented environmental regulation 2000 (pp. 67-107). Physica, Heidelberg.

20) Paraskevopoulou E. Non-technological regulatory effects: Implications for innovation and innovation policy. Research Policy. 2012 Jul 1;41(6):1058-71.

# CHAPTER – 25

# INTRODUCTION TO BIOINFORMATICS IN BIOLOGICAL SYSTEM AND DATABASE

## BY
## Juhi Namdev

## Abstract

The new technologies and advancements in the recent years has marked a potential and promoted in well knowing of the genetic basis of phenotypes and genotypes. Genomics changed the paradigm of biological queries in the full genome wide scale prevailing and explosion of data and giving many possibilities for the future. Therefore, the huge amount of information that has been generated. Challenges can be overcome for storage and processing of biological information and studies. Computational biology or Bioinformatics have sought to overcome the rising challenges, the chapter presents introduction and overview of Bioinformatics and its application in the analysis of biological data emerging methodologies and tools. We will discuss the main principles of bioinformatics types of biological information and data bases.

**Keywords:** Databases, Genomics, biological, information, computation, phenotype.

## Introduction

The revolution in the present field of science concern with new technologies and advancements which has been provided a huge amount of data and information. The information available in the public data bases where and still are a challenge for professionals from different areas however, it is still challenging. The most challenging thing is to make sense of the enormous amount of structural sequences and data that have been generated at multiple levels of living systems in Bioinformatics development of the tools is necessary however, statistical and computational. They are capable of assisting in understanding the mechanism of underlying biological questions according to the study. The era of Life Science emerges, why the development of Sciences such as bioinformatics which is an integrated interface of molecular biological system although recently Bioinformatics and genomics has been highly evolved and promoted the impact on the available knowledge. The chapter aims to present introduction and overview of the Sciences and principles of bioinformatics therefore, biogical system database information sequence analysis and Molecular modeling genomic analysis and new technologies.

## Bioinformatics

Bioinformatics has been originated a decade before DNA Sequencing became feasible in the history moments, it is highlighted for its development in the structure of DNA by Watson and Crick in 1953. Where, the accumulation of data and knowledge of Biochemistry and structure of protein with the studies of Pauling, coren, and Ramchandra in 1960. The development of large-scale capillary DNA sequences and making of dye deoxynucleotides with fluorescence in 90s has followed by obtaining a large amount of data however for next generation Sequencing technologies are listed to complete genomics is growing as well as for volume of data it becomes necessary to utilize computers in research area to understand the genetic variations and evolutionary functional mechanism underlying the genetic makeup and advanced techniques.

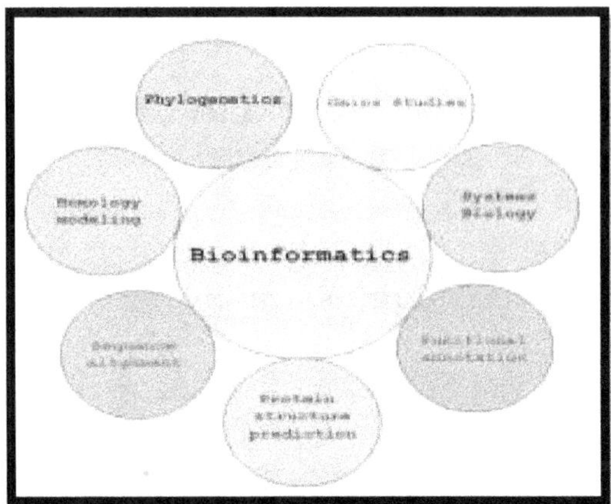


**Fig.1: Bioinformatics applications**

A computational view is represented to highlight the goals of bioinformatics:

a) To organize the data in such a way that researchers can accept the information and create new entries.
b) To enable tools and sources to help in data analysis.
c) To utilize tools to analyze the data and interpret it significantly.

**Organization of Information**

As the large volume of data has been generated its organization and storage have been became necessary. Therefore, data bases were created which constitutes a used number of biological information stored and processed to allow interdisciplinary or scientific community access at increasing the amount of data has been accompanied by the increase in Biological database, dissemination and makeup updating all have been carried out by nucleic acid Sequencing and transformation. The information sources used by Bioinformatics can be classified as raw DNA sequence, protein sequence, macromolecular structure, genome Sequencing. Public databases store huge amount of information they are classified into primary and secondary database is the primary database composed of experimental data which is published without careful analysis related to previous publication. Therefore, secondary database there is a compliation and interpretation of data called contained curation process. Primary databases gene bank at National Centre for Biotechnology information NCBI, DNA database of Japan DDBJ, and European Molecular biological laboratory EMBL, these databases are member of national nuclear right sequence database collaboration INSDC and share information among each other the deposit information daily basis. Secondary databases we can point protein information resources protein data Bank, structural classification of proteins to and these data bases are acccurated and presented the information related to protein they describe aspects of their structure, function and classification.

**Databases**
1. Protein sequence (primary)
- SWISS-PROT
- PIR-International
2. Protein sequence (composite)
- OWL

- NRDB
3. Protein sequence (secondary)
- PROSITE
- PRINTS
- Pfam
4. Macromolecular structures
- Protein Data Bank (PDB)
- Nucleic Acids Database (NDB)
- HIV Protease Database
- ReLiBase
- PDBsum
- CATH
- SCOP
- FSSP
5. Nucleotide sequences
- GenBank
- EMBL
- DDBJ
6. Genome sequences
- Entrez genomes
- GeneCensus
- COGs
7. Integrated databases
- InterPro
- Sequence retrieval system (SRS)
- Entrez

## Analysis of Biological Sequences

The essential widely used biological sequence comparison alignment has been processed by the increase in the availability of data generated by NGS Technologies the process consists of the following two or more tight sequence by comparing DNA and RNA or amino acid peptide or protein by seeking a series of individual characters or patterns that are arranged in the sequence of the model. However, we compare the sequences, there are applications for the procedure, that allow information for the evaluationary relationship between individual, organism and genes production, functions, structures and among others however alignment technique are necessary for wall genome analysis where comparison between different genomes or from the sample species allow to identify variation in the sequence of models and associated with specific phenotypes.

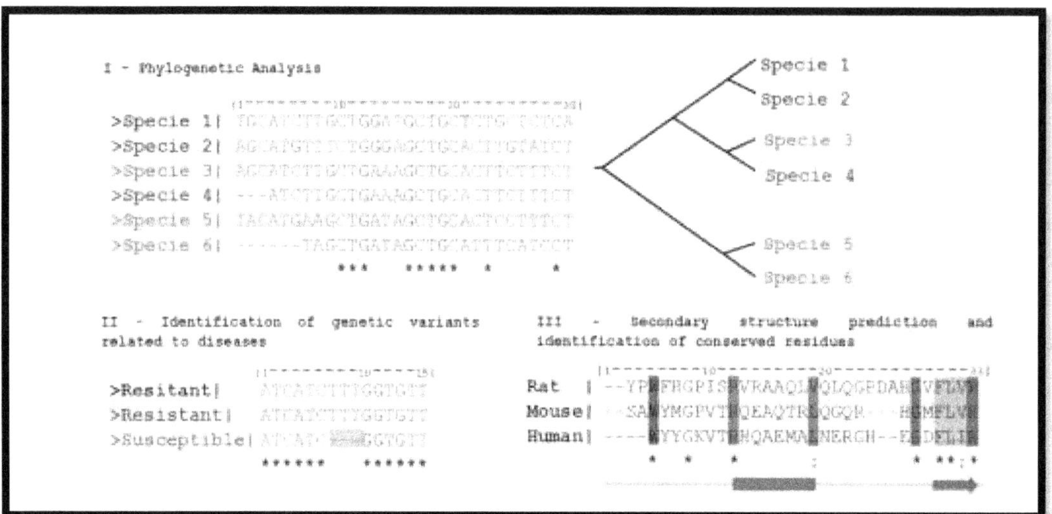

**Fig. 2: Sequence alignment with its applications.**

The alignment of structure stands out as a important bioinformatic tool which involved in the comparison of structures refers to the analysis of similarities or differences between two or more structures. Alignment refers for the determination of amino acid that would be equivalent between such structures and the sequence of alignment is arranged in row and characters in columns. It is as to the algorithm which is used to search the best match sequences in the model inserting gaps which represent one or more pneumatized in events. Therefore, for same sequence and alignments are possible. Alignment can be categorized by type according to the number of sequence that are compared which can be simple or multiple. The simple alignment specially depicts the similarity relationship between the two sequences while the multiple sequences consider a value greater than the three sequences.

**The Key Concepts**

- Algorithm: A logical sequence of instructions for execute of a task.
- Gaps: Regions which were identified by "-" that represent indel.
- Indels: Insertions or character of deletions.
- Matches: The corresponding specific areas between two different sequences.
- Mismatches: The regions with non-identical characters in other or different sequences.
- Gap penalty (GP): Parameter which is needed to assign a score for a gap.
- Identity: The percentage of similar characters between the two sequences.
- Similarity: The degree of resemblance between the sequences based on the identity.
- Homology: The evolutionary hypothesis between the two sequences that can be derived

The extent of alignment these can be classified as Global or local as the algorithm used it may be classified as optimal for heuristic system. Although, they are representing an optimal result presents, the best alignment for a given duration of analysis.Proteins are the alignments of structures and also an important bioinformatics tool. Therefore, the comparison of structures refers to the analysis of similarities and differences between two or more structures. alignments refers to the determination of the amino acid that are equivalent between such structures Although trivial, sequence similarity analysis is the complex sense the algorithm used to calculate a cost to the alignment of such sequences which is used to minimize The differences and to obtain the best possible results.

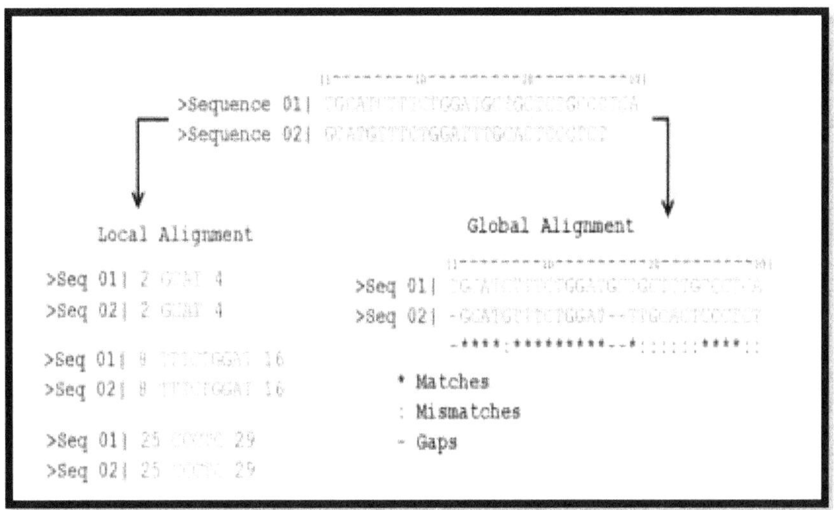

**Fig.3: Global and local alignment of amino acid sequences.**

The sequence alignment is in row arrangement and the characters in columns. It depends upon the algorithm which is used to search the best match for the sequences. Therefore, while inserting the gaps represents one or more nucleotide with Indel events and for the same sequence "n" alignments are possible. Scoring system, in which matches are positively and mismatches are negatively punctuated as created the most widely created substitution matrices are belonging to point accepted mutation (PAM). The alignment are categorized by according to the number of sequences that are compared with simple or multiple sequences. They are classified as a global and the local system. Although not representing an optimal Result, that represents the best alignment for a given period of analysis.

**Simple Alignment**

In simple alignment, the dynamic programming of algorithms, Dot Matrix analysis or K-tuple methods are utilized. The programming method is based on the Bellman's optimality principal that states that the solution to Complex problem if resolved by its various sub-problems in this methodology, then it can be applied to produce global and local alignment through Needleman wunsch and smith waterman algorithms respectively. A scoring scheme is required for Matches and mismatches for the amino acids and nucleotides and value for gap ("-") the algorithm can be calculated the optimum alignment between the sequences. The Dot Matrix approach is simple and efficient in the detection of Indels and repetitions. An identity matrix is possibly a graphic visual life for the regions of similarities. Therefore, in this method, the sequences are arrange one vertical and other horizontal the regions with the same characters are signal representing the corresponding matches the diagonal line represent regions of similarities while the other points represent random correspondence multiple alignments.

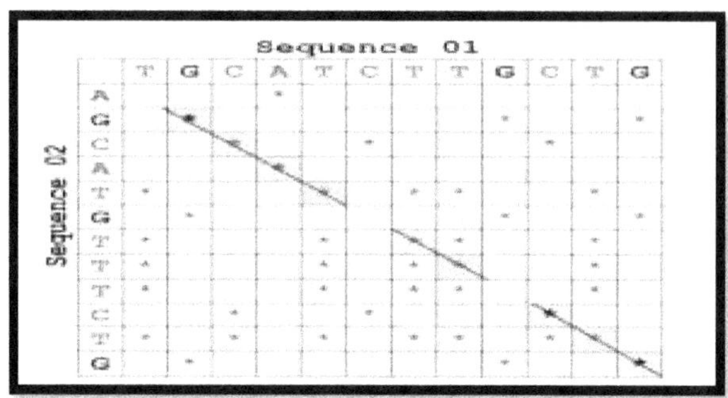


**Fig.4: Dot matrix method of two DNA sequences.**

## Multiple Alignment

Similar to simple elements the dynamic programming method is usually utilized in global alignment, each possible pair performed is punctuated through a weight sum of pair with addition of similarity in the values. Although, alternative methods were developed to push the calculations among which, where highlighted for progressive integrative methods or Markov models.

## BLAST

BLAST is a specific local alignment algorithm derived from smith-waterman algorithm which represents a maximum alignment scores of two sequences in addition to dynamic programming which arises from the algorithm mentioned above blast method is based on the k-tuple method to identify the sequences in the databases. BLAST is fast and reliable method, used for identification from the query sequence, which is compared to the database which is utilized. Blast is divided into four stages:

   a)  The compiling of word list k-tuples.
   b)  The searching for correspondence in the databases.
   c)  The extending alignment from the identified words.
   d)  The assembling of the paste alignments according to high scored segment pairs.

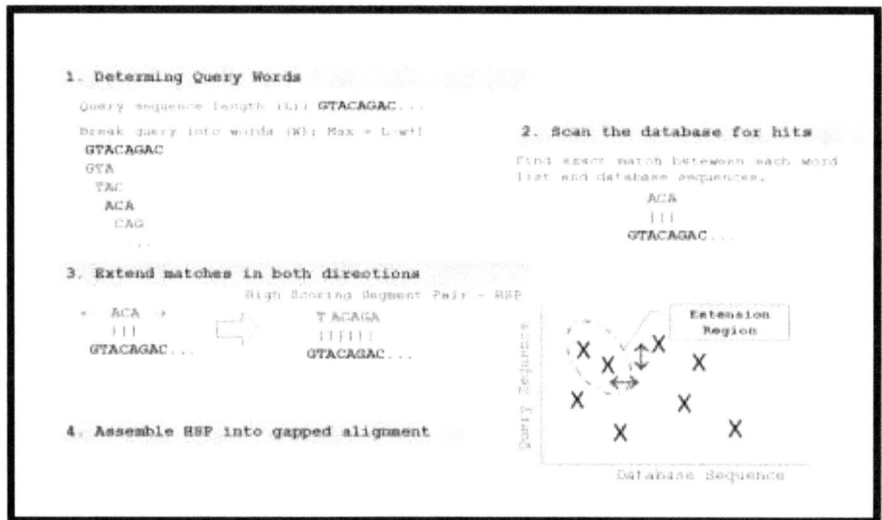


**Fig. 5: Process of BLAST operation.**

## Molecular Modeling

Molecular modeling refers to the modeling of -D structures of protein from the structure of another homologus protein. Structure has been already determined, it is based on the evolutionary sequences which share the same folding pattern of tertiary structures. The determination of 3-D structure helps in understanding the functions and interaction of protein as well as functional units for the identification of the target therapeutics.Methodologies suchas, X- ray diffraction, crystallography, nuclear Magnetic resonance (NMR), are applied in the determination of the structure but due to limitations to its use, therefore experimental methods are implemented such as, ab initio modeling, this type of modeling uses for physical and chemical principles to calculate the confirmation and it shows accurate results.

The process consists of five major steps:
   a) Reference
   b) Identifications
   c) Selection of templates
   d) Alignment construction
   e) Model validation

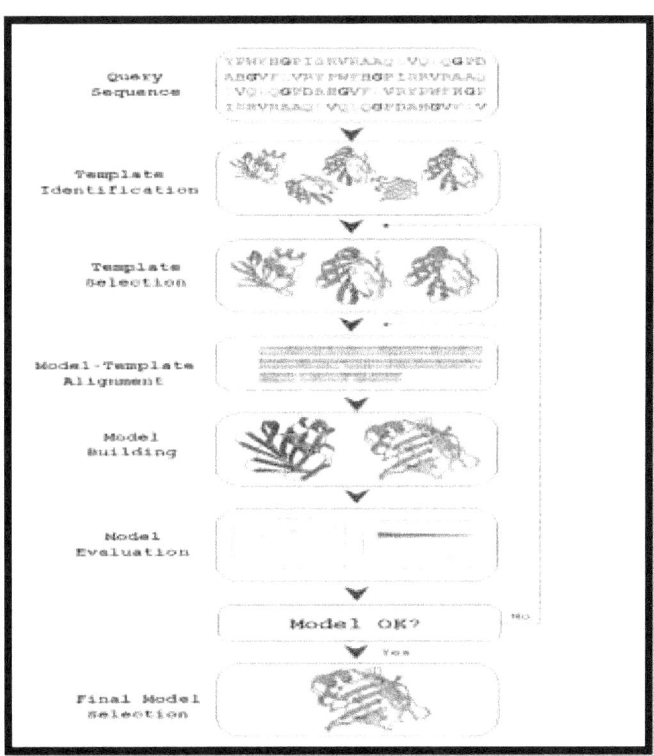


**Fig. 6: Stages of 3-D structures by comparative modeling**

The initial step is for identifying amino acid sequences of protein, whose structure has been previously resolved and similar to the targeted sequence. The comparison can be performed by using the blast method for references with higher indexes and identification should be chosen while the selection of templates, it is necessary to choose one or more structures considering the criteria such a, it should belong to the same family and also performs the same functions. As templates structure is confirmed, the Global alignment between the target and templates sequences is carried out. The identity is greater than 50%, the final model depends on the quality of the alignment. The alignment modeling constructed by using the following methods, rigid body assembly, corresponding segment, aud spatial constraint.Software such as MODELLER and SWISS MODEL should be utilized for the construction of model. The alignment functions as an input file utilized for modeling, that the results in a set of atomic which coordinates for "n" 3-D models for the targeted protein contains the atoms of the major and side chain of amino acid residue. The software calculates several chemical and special parameters which were added to force the field to tend calculations in the certian directions.The validation of model consists in the verification of possible errors related to the method utilized, evaluation of quality by factors such as bonding length, the planetary of peptide.

Bonds, ring planarity and torsion angles in the chains, chirality, steric hindrance and energy function are necessary.

## Biological Systems

The identification of genetic variation give several approach in genomics underlying the quantitative characteristics and determine the phenotype. However, organism is a complex system where many factors such as development, growth and response to the environment directly influence the function of the body.

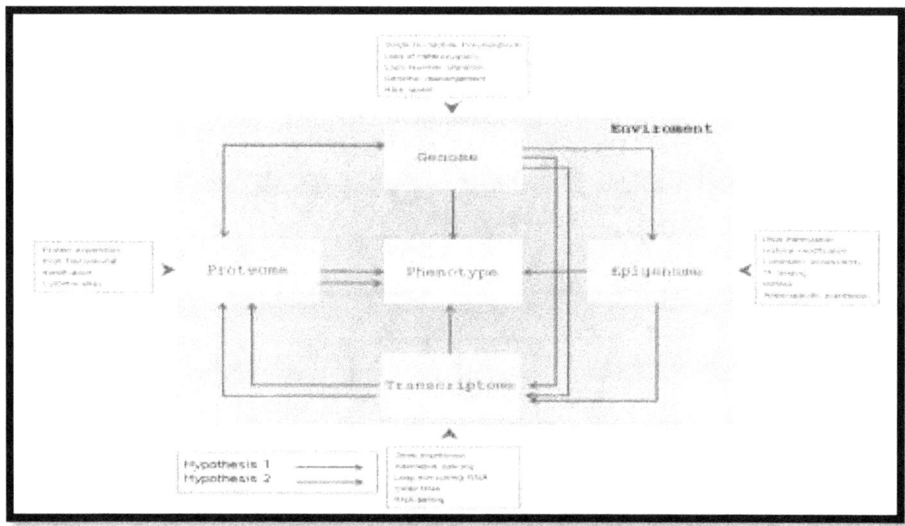


**Fig. 7: Hypothesis of the origin of a complex trait in a systems biological view.**

Biological system represents a holistic approach to the complexity of the living system in which the whole is greater than the sum of its par. It is a multidisciplinary science to develop new forms in technologies to explore the new dimensions for the documentation of data and to generate new hypothesis and discoveries, creating a cycle of innovations and creativities. The system approach at the economic level which makes it possible to reach complete and informative theories about phenotype and genotype associated with issues which are compared to a single data analysis in identification of genes and proteins it is not enough to understand the complexity of the system. The system can be derived from understanding the four key properties:
   a)  Structure
   b)  Dynamics
   c)  Method Of Control
   d)  Design Of Method

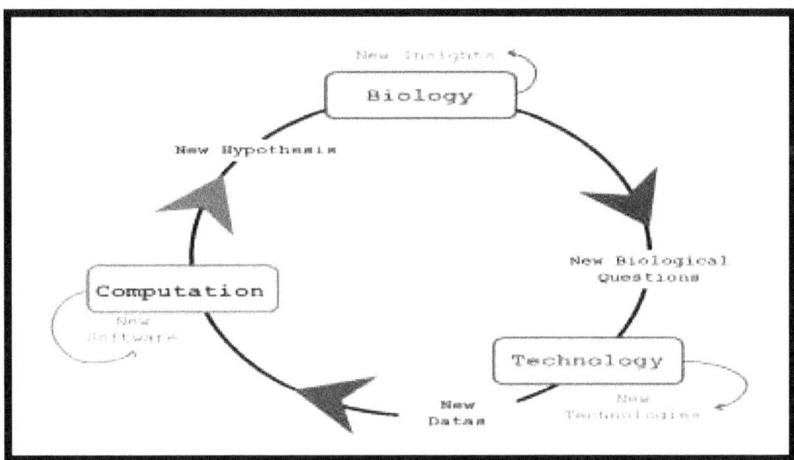


**Fig. 8: Biological system as a multidisciplinary science**

The available data when combines it can compensate the missing or unreliable information so the many evidences which same targeting will be less respectable to false possibilities a particular biological model is only possible if the level of regulations are different such as genetic genomics or proteomics. Then, they are considered in the analysis. Therefore, data integration emerge to the link of ability to generate large amount of data and to understand the Biology for making key genomic factor and interaction that explain biological functioning.

## Data Integration

Differential expression studies have been adopted widely as a method of Investigation of the function of genes on the Global scale in this method the genes are treated individually without considering the interactions between them however, the living functions exhibit a complex behavior which result from a set of genes interacting with each other. It is divided into two methods, first is multistage analysis where two different scales are utilized at same time to construct the models considering the hierarchy or linear mode. Other is multi-dimensional analysis where data sets are combined simultaneously for the determination of complex models. Therefore, the method depends on two primary molecular hypothesis. The standard model is that change in DNA which is responsible to cause changes in the gene expression and in protein or phenotype. Other hypothesis to which indicates that molecular variation at multiple levels are used to contribute to the determination of phenotype. Several studies have been take place to investigate the method of functioning of genes on the global platform for biological activities which exhibit a complex behavior, which result as a set of genes interacting with each other. The integrated biological systems approaches to using gene network for core expression which is used widely to understand genetic makeup or architecture of complex phenotype. The different levels of information can be integrated with the network such as the body which is made up of multiple network like molecular, cellular, organs, that are added and communicate at multiple scales among the multiple approaches. They are utilized for the identification for biological network which are used of genetic co-expression and networking at multistage analysis method. It is assume that genes are connected to strength in quantified by correlation of the compound between them it is possible to detect group of highly or co-expressed genes that shares common function for  inner metabolic pathway and the connectivity of genes describes the importance of the  network gene are highly associated with biological activity and heavily regulated processes.

**Conclusion**

The advancement and capabilities of data generation analysis and interpretation of the results has pointed to a promising future however, that the wide progress in all area of Sciences that highlighted the emergence in new analytical techniques and strategies it is the beginning of new discoveries hypotheses and generating a feedback mechanism. The analysis of biological sequences where Bioinformatics now give a used variety of information in wide range of subject areas including structural Biology, gene expression, studies genomics in this chapter we provide an introduction and overview of current state of field of bioinformatics. Bioinformatics has not only provided the greater and depth to the life science investigation but also added in dimension of breadth as well which are able to examine in the mutual biological systems in detailed and also able to compare them related to uncover common principles that can apply across many systems highlighted by unusual features that are unique to some techniques.

**References**


1) Altelaar AFM, Munoz J and Heck AJR (2013). Next-generation proteomics: towards an integrative view of proteome dynamics. Nat. Rev. Genet. 14: 35-48.
2) Altmann A, Weber P, Bader D, Preuss M, et al. (2012). A beginners guide to SNP calling from high-throughput DNA-sequencing data. Hum. Genet. 131: 1541-1554.
3) Chaisson MJP, Wilson RK and Eichler EE (2015). Genetic variation and the de novo assembly of human genomes. Nat. Rev. Genet. 16: 627-640.
4) Daugelaite J, O' Driscoll A and Sleator RD (2013). An overview of multiple sequence alignments and cloud computing in bioinformatics. Int. Sch. Res. Not. e615630.
5) Hawkins RD, Hon GC and Ren B (2010). Next-generation genomics: an integrative approach. Nat. Rev. Genet. 11: 476-486 10.
6) Hong S, Chen X, Jin L and Xiong M (2013). Canonical correlation analysis for RNA-seq co-expression networks. Nucleic Acids Res. 41-95.
7) Hunt LT (1984). Margaret Oakley Dayhoff 1925-1983. Bull. Math. Biol. 46: 467-472.
8) Jensen ON (2006). Interpreting the protein language using proteomics. Nat. Rev. Mol. Cell Biol. 7: 391-403.
9) Junqueira DM, Braun RL and Verli H (2014). Alinhamentos. In: Bioinformática da biologia à flexibilidade molecular (Verli H, ed.). SBBq, São Paulo, 38-61.
10) Kogelman LJA, Cirera S, Zhernakova DV, Fredholm M, et al. (2014). Identification of co-expression gene networks, regulatory genes and pathways for obesity based on adipose tissue RNA Sequencing in a porcine model. BMC Med. Genomics 7: 57.
11) Luscombe NM, Greenbaum D and Gerstein M (2001). What is bioinformatics? A proposed definition and overview of the field. Methods Inf. Med. 40: 346-358 10.1053/j.ro.2009.03.010. Madhusudhan MS, Marti-Renom MA and Eswar N (2005). Comparative protein structure modeling. In: The proteomics protocols handbook (Walker, J.M., ed.). Human Press, New Jersey, 831-860.
12) Manohar P and Shailendra S (2012). Protein sequence alignment: A review. World Appl. Program. 2: 141-145.
13) Marioni JC, Mason CE, Mane SM, Stephens M, et al. (2008). RNA-seq: an assessment of technical reproducibility and comparison with gene expression arrays. Genome Res. 18: 1509-1517.
14) Fitch WM. Distinguishing homologousfrom analogous proteins. Syst Zool 1970;19:99-110.
15) Tatusov RL, Koonin EV, Lipman DJ. A genomic perspective on protein families.Science 1997;278(5338):631-7.

# CHAPTER – 26

# CORONA VIRUS: COVID-19 MEDICATION

## BY
## ROSHAN KUMAR

## Abstract

Crown infections are a group of interrelated infections in well-developed beings and flying beings, malady. In primates, Crown infections cause parcel diseases that can span from metastases mellow to deadly. A variety of instances of light ailments are included the typical cold, while other deadly kinds can trigger Air state, MERS, and COVID-19. However, it must be vaccinations or antiviral medicines for human prevention or treatment diseases of the coronary infection. That's because it can, prevention normally forest prevention activities will work to prevent metastasis infections. This latest infection with the crown. Towards the episode's conclusion enhanced access to COVID-19 in-house RT-PCR by the World Health Organization agreements. China South is integrated into the most recent areas of the sponsored network Spain, France, United Kingdom, Canada, Australia, India, Korea, Japan, Iran and Italy Pakistan, Asia and then about 185 countries worldwide. All over the spot. Various states in the Republic of India summoned absolutely these pandemic circumstances Different provisions of the 1897 Act on the control of infectious diseases.

**Keywords:** Respiratory illness, MERS, COVI-19, Epidemic etc.

## Introduction

Coronaviridae family contains Crown infections with the taxon Orthocoronavirinae, demanded Nidovirales and Riboviral domain. [1, 2] Infections with a single stranded RNA positive sense, and a spiraling equality nuculocapsid are bundled. The ordination size varies from around 26-32 kilobases of Crown Infections. One of the largest of the RNA viruses,[3] it includes club-formed trademark spikes danger from its surface generating an image connotative to the sun in negatron micrograms. This is the name of a hopped-up crown.[4] A further respiratory tract infection that Original recognized in the metropolis of Hubei, province, severe respiratory disease was induced, by China. In evolving numbers, the infection is currently spreading individually Other than 100 states, ninety-four of them are still outstanding In China, weigh. Crown infections test a large cluster of infections square simple dimensions of humans and other animals, for example. So normally any one of us tends to see new infections of the (novel) crown not recently delineated in humans. There are multiple tests different kinds of infections with human crowns and those that normally occur make mellow parcel ailments in the upper respiratory region. The initial thought of this infection was out of a supply that has tangled citizens, however, we seem to have Square measurement that watches infection from one person to the next. Until then it is nebulosis, but this infection effectively spreads among humans. But this interpretation of COVID-19 triggers this infection depends on what we predict about crown infections all of which are bushed. This infection typically occurs from person to person. Like conventional cold, this square measurement, made sometimes by personal hacks or wheezes, is unfolded by beads. One can be exposed to anyone who is drained after shut touch (inside six feet). People square measure, after having signs, thought to be most contagious. There have been claims that if someone with neighboring asymptomatic effects gets drained, this is not the first method to disperse the infection throughout the grid. China, the Asian country, Japan, Iran, Italy, Spain, France, UK,

USA, Canada, Australia, India, Pakistan, East Pakistan and then more than 185 countries worldwide are among the most recently established sponsored zones of the network. The COVID-19 infection is effectively and economically spreading in an extremely network, wherever it is imagined that, with each infected individual, a few people will likely become ill at the risk of not being guaranteed with simple measures such as hand smoothness. A image of 1 tainted person has been presented. A few of these square measure nevertheless unusual things. That infection is known to be more serious than an occasional flu. However, many infection diseases, for example rubella or pox, are particularly infectious.

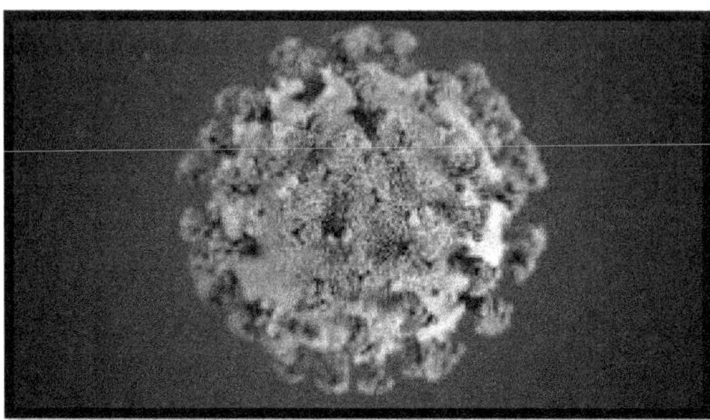

**Figure 1: Structure and Shape of Corona-Virus**

Crown infections area unit Monumental organic phenomenon spherical particles with bulbous projections on the surface [5]. Approximately 100,200 nm (.12 μm) are the conventional distance across the infection particles. The gap over the envelope is ~80 nm (0.08 μm), as well as ~20 nm (0.02 μm) in the spikes field. A simple attempt by AN to treat negatrón-thick shells is present in the envelope of the infectious agent in micrographs of negatron [6,7]. The envelope of the infectious agent has a bilayer of fluids in either layer (M), envelope (E) and spike (S) anchored to the specific protein area area unit (HE). The nucleo capsid, framed with various macromolecule duplicates of the nucleocapsid (N), is inside the envelope and is the unit of area guaranteed to be a positive-sense single-abandoned polymer ordination in an extremely persistent globule in the form of a string conformation [9].

**Treatment of COVID-19**

In order to differentiate relevant Latin scientific papers over the course of the quarter of 2020 a written survey was done via PubMed. SARS-CoV-2, SARS-coV, MERSCoV, and COVID-19 combined, in combination with care and medication, search words include a coronavirus, an exceptionally intense metabolic disease of coronavirus.[10] The researchers have included case studies, case arrangements and survey papers as a result of the absence of the RCT. The designers reviewed the titles openly and modified the integration works. Other related papers have been distinguished from the recorded reference survey. The ClinicalTrials.gov search term for corona virus was distinguishing from dynamic clinical preliminaries by using ClinicalTrials.gov as the medical search term for corona virus infection and, subsequently, a registry of studies on new respiratory corona virus disorders within the Chinese Routine Register. After the official recipient, the molecule of infection uses cell receptors and endosomes in cells. TMPRSS2 facilitates the cell passage by means of S macromolecule, the bunch sort a pair of transmembrane amina alkanoic acid proteinase3. Once in a cell, the infective polyprotein agent incorporates square measure that complicates the ciffer of replicase-transcriptase. At that point, the infection coordinated polymer by means of the RNA enzyme. Square of specific proteins tests music community that helps infectants to get together and arrive at them. [11, 12] These stages of the cycle of infectious agents tend to be focussing on the therapy (Figure 2)

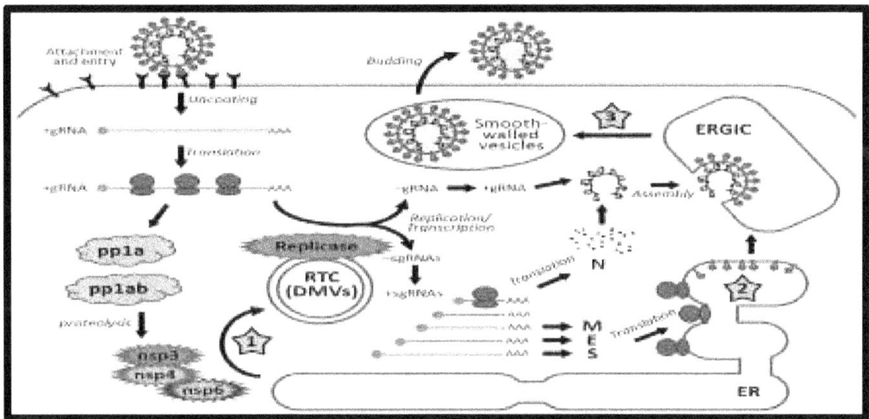

**Figure 2: Viral Life Cycle and Drug Tar**

The promising drug targeting includes non-functional protectins (e.g., proteinase close to 3-chymotrypsin, papainlike proteinase and polymer-subordinated RNA polymerase) (nCoVs). The infective material portion and the impersuadable guidance pathways provide additional drug targets. Table 1 [13, 14] their activity mechanism and major pharmacological limits of the selection of the suggested medicines or associated COVID-19 therapies.

**Plaquenil and chloroquine**

Plaquenil and chloroquine have a long history of countering and treating protozoa and consequently treating long-running inflammations with the essential autoimmune disorder (SLE) and creaky joint inflammation (RA). Antimalarial medicines and plaquenil tend to be widely distributed through the cells by reducing host receptor glycosylation, chemical action, and endosomal fermentation. These specialists also have immunomodulatory effects by dropping protein output and reducing the movement of the autophagus and the lysosomal in cells [15, 16]. SARS-CoV-2 in vitro is suppressed by antimalarial drug with a semimaximally viable fixation (EC50) in the low-micromolar cycle. In the after-6 hours of development (hydroxychloroquine: EC50=half-dozen.14 chlorosin: EC50=203.90μM) Plaquenil is in vitro with the sub-CE50 for comparison to SARS-CoV-2 and chloroquine (hydroxychloroquine: EC50=half-dozen.14 chlorosin: EC50) [21]. Extreme Acute Air Syndrome (MERS) Care. A Chinese newsletter was successful in treating the progression of a total of one hundred COVID-19 cases concerning enhanced radiological observations, the increase of the freedom of the infectious agent and the decrease in the progression of malady. [18] However, for peer review and prevention the preliminary clinical structure and tests have not yet been implemented or circulated. A current existing foreign non-RDI study involving 36 patients (20 in Plaquenil selection and 16 in the benchmark statistical techniques) has shown an improved leeway of virology with hydroxyl chloroquine, 200 mg in oral contrast and a typical robust thinking in the patient's management. Day half a dozen virological leeway for the Plaquenil and for the management meetings was determined from cavum-based on the individual basis of seventyth (14/20) compared to 12.5 per cent (2/16) (P = 001). The researchers also did not mask the option of Plaquenil azithromycin in half a dozen patients which had a number of mainly free infectious agents (6/6, 100%) contrasting and monotherapy with Hydroxyl chloroqine (8/14, 57%).[19] Despite the findings of this study, there were several crucial issues, such as tactile sizes (only 20 of them in the mediation arm and easy ones).Treatment resulting from basic disease or medical prejudice; the burden of infectious agent of variable size between monotherapy with plaquenil and mixing therapy; no clinical or security findings reported. These limitations and questions about cardiotoxicity interfering with mixing therapy do not improve the receipt of this technique until further examination is carried out. Another planned research into 30 patients in China in Plaquenil irregular, 400 mg, five-day, additionally plain care patients (stable thinking, interferon, and totally different antivirals) or common thinking alone During 1:1 the findings of virology were not differentiated. On day 7, virological leeway was comparative, with 86.7% vs 93.3% clearing, moreover, of treatment and regular reflection for Plaquenil {to customary|easy} (p>.05).[20] On day 7, virological leeway was comparative, with 86.7% vs. 93.3% of care collections.

Additionally customary for anti-inflammatory clearance please take care of the collection and standard thought gathering, on a separate basis (P > 05). Some RCTs of every antimalaria and anti-inflammatory work are located in the field. Treatment with COVID-19. Health care employees' antimalarial bar inquiries (NCT04303507) and postexposure bar anti-inflammatory if high-risk Dosage of COVID19 antimalarial has been included and enormous are400mg orally daily18However, aphysiological doses are included in the region organized or reported (NCT04308668). The pharmacokinetic show survey mainly focused urged the optimal dose routine for The stacking portion of 400 mg may be anti-inflammatory in COVID-19 treatment twice a day one day and two hundred mg twice daily. Oddly, optional 600 mg full portion day by day is provided for wellbeing and hooked up. Whipple's clinical experience. Required to specify further review area unit COVID-19's perfect section. A relatively antimalarial and anti-inflammatory region ample presence in SLE and enteric disease has all been demonstrated. Since this could happen, the 2 specialists will cause uncommon and real adverse effects (< 10 percent), including QTc extension; hypoglycemia; neuropsychiatric effects; and retinopathy [22, 23]. The subsequent source of these medicines in light-weight capacity for substantially ill patients and people who draw from the QT span Azithromycin and fluoroquinolones, for example, are recommended. No extraordinary antagonism Antimalarial impacts shall be taken into account at the proposed COVID-19 sections and words. Using the In a physiological condition, antimalarial and anti-inflammatory are generally thought-proof. A No newborns displayed some simple visual toxicity to 12 reviews or 588 patients who were appropriate to the antipalmarial or anti-inflammatory disease during physiology (P >05). [20] Virological leeway was comparable at day 7, with 86.7% compared to 93.3%.

The assisted oral combination specialization for HIV, which has been shown to in vitro inhibition against other novel coronaviruses, indicates that 3-cha-trypsin-like proteolytic enzymes are obstructing lopinavir and ritonavir.[25] Lopinavir/ritonavir, an America Food and Drug Administration (FDA), does not provide any in-vitro info on SARS-coV-2. Considered pushed out of the report, the largest part of the study was a detective audit of lopinavir/ritonavir in the treatment of extreme acute respiratory syndrome and of MERS. SARS clinical studies lead to lower mortality and the rates of insertion but its analysis, observational existence foreshadows final results. The temporal order of the first pinnacle replication of infectious agents.

**Lopinavir/Ritonavir and different Antiretrovirals**

The fact that delayed origin of lopinavir/ritonavir care has no effect on clinical results is evident at a lightweight level (beginning 7-10 days). For the first half of cases reporting and limited analysis the early reporting on lopinavir/ritonavir for the COVID-19 area unit care considers that the period to be considerably reduced from facet to organisation's effect has been at the center of 13 days (interquartile run [International QR],[26], without any inter-band variations. Moreover, no major contrasts were found with independence for infectious agents or 28day mortality rates (19.2% versus 25.0%; −5.8% of total differentiation [95% CI −17.3% to 5.7%]). While lopinavir/ritonavir was largely inadequate to treat COVID-19, a subgroup analysis did not discover a shorter risk of clinical improvement for patients within twelve days of obtaining care from The World Heath Organization (HR, receiving the immediate treatment impact of lopinavir/ritonavir). Therapy. the most widely used and considered dosing regimen of lopinavir/ritonavir The treatment of COVID-19 is 400mg/100mg twice daily up to 14 days. Notable drugs reassure communications and possible antagonistic drugs Cautious audit of prescriptions and interpretation (summarized in Table 1), Area unit needed if the drug is used. Lopinavir/ritonavir antagonistic results Include, for instance, channel misery and therefore disease (up to 28%), Hepatotolerance (2 percent -10 percent). [29] These unfriendly effects can also occur in COVID-19 patients. be aggravated by light-weight mixing or infectious agent contamination the reality is that approximately 200 to half hours of patients have elevated transaminase levels COVID-19 introduction. Some 1/2 lopinavir/ritonavir patients reported a recent RCT Unfavorable effect of the related degree and 14% of patients discontinued treatment Antagonistic results thanks to the channel. Transaminitis caused by drugs is especially important because Thanks to COVID-19 it will worsen liver injury. Aminoalcanic acid substantially Transferase increases in an exceptionally few {measure} measure of the associate degree of rejection COVID-19 preliminary investigative proof that induced lopinavir/ritonavir The capacity of patients to urge certain different drugs may be decreased by hepatotoxicity. Various SARS-CoV-2 has been distinguishing by catalyst screening of the associated degree tiretrovirals, proteolytic enzyme inhibitors and inhibitors of integrase strand movement Operation. Darunavir's activity against SARS-CoV-2 was demonstrated by in vitro cell models. InCOVID-19 with such medicines, there are no human clinical info, butan RCT darunavir/cobicistat is foot in China.

**Diagnosis**

The stunningly touchy COVID-19-RdRp/Hel test can also help to improve the laborative pronostics of COVID-19[29]. It can clarify the time dynamics that the new corona virus (SARS-CoV-2) of 2019 can take to spread anti corona virus and suggest the potential quest of protein for COVID-19. In combination with immune globulin, IgM and immune gamma globulin response, the host body response to severe acute metabolic process Corona virus a pair (SARS-CoV-2) syndrome is not examined using AN ELISA-based recombinant nuclear-capside macromolecule test[30] to assess the mist diagnosis charge of RAI for corona virus I The CT aspects are the same as the CT aspects of different viruses in order to get people acquainted with viable CT patterns.[31] Proper molecular diagnostic assessments are necessary if corona virus unwelcome analysis is to be verified in 2019 (COVID 19). Once again, the IDSA (Infectious Diseases Society of America) sought to expand AN evidence-based diagnostic gospel to help physicians, medicinal researchers, the sufferer and political decision makers make a couple of macromolecule magnification tests with superior use of extreme acute metabolic syndrome corona virus [32].

**Table 1: Mechanism dose, drug target, toxicities and contraindication of drug used in COVID-19**

| Drug | Target | Dose | Toxicities | Contraindication |
|---|---|---|---|---|
| Chloroquine | Blockade of viral entry by Inhibiting glycosylation of host receptors, proteolytic-processing, and endosomal acidification. Additional immunomodulatory effects through inhibition of cytokine production, autophagy, and lysosomal activity in host cells | 500 mg by mouth every 12-24 h × 5-10 days. Available as:250-mg tablets (salt); 500-mg tablets (salt); 500-mg tablets of chloroquine phosphate (salt) 300mg | Abdominal, cramps, anorexia, diarrhea, nausea, vomiting. Cardiovascular effects (including QTc prolongation), hematologic effects (including hemolysis with G6PD deficiency, use if benefit outweighs risks), hypoglycemia, retinal toxicity, neuropsychiatric and central nervous system effects, idiosyncratic adverse drug reactions. | Hypersensitivity to chloroquine, 4-aminoquinoline compounds, or any component of formulation. Presence of retinal or visual field changes of any etiology (unless benefit outweighs risk) |

| Hydroxychlo roquine sulfate | Hydroxychloroquine shares the same mechanism of action as chloroquine | 400 mg by mouth every 12 h × 1 d, then 200 mg by mouth every 12 h × 4 d; alternative dosing: 400 mg by mouth daily × 5 d or 200mg by mouth 3 times/d for 10 days | Adverse drug reactions similar to chloroquine but less common | Known hypersensitivity To hydroxychloroquine, 4aminoquinoline derivative, or any component of the formulation |
|---|---|---|---|---|
| Lopinavir/rit onavir | 3CL protease | 400mg/100 mg by mouth every 12 h for up to 14 d. Available as: lopinavir/ritonavir, 200mg/50-mg | gastrointestinal intolerance, nausea, vomiting, diarrhea, Pancreatitis, hepatotoxicity, cardiac conduction abnormalities | Hypersensitivity to lopinavir/ritonavir or any of its ingredients, including ritonavir. Co-administration with drugs highly dependent |

## Prevention and Control

Techniques and methods are the same for prevention and management at three levels: broad, case-related, and normal world level. Officially blanketed by COVID 19 into class B criminal disease administration and allow for Class A infectious disorder to be prevention and management steps, the national health committee in the People's Republic of China has released on 20 Gregorian calendar in the year 2020 a No.1 announcement queue [10]. The National Commission of Health notes on 22 January 2020 that country-wide recommendations for the hemorrhage and manipulation, for science institutions, of COVID-19 are issued.[34] The NCH issued protocols for the quick impairment and efficient management of the epidemic on the twenty eight Gregorian calendar month 2020

This includes a case-by-case isolation, identification and monitoring of contacts, environment-friendly medical services, and the use of personal defensive equipment [36], mobile precautions and entirely different defensive measures and is envisaged and intended to prevent them. Prevention and control (PPC) steps to reduce the danger of promotion of contaminated people accommodate: use of facial tissue masks; tissue overlay and tissue sneezing, which are then safely withdrawn (or, when tissues are not provided, using a bended elbow to cowl cough or sneeze). During this document, fitness workers were assisting in using aerosol-generating methods for the use of particulate breathers such as those commissioned N95 or FFP2 and in the use of scientific masks while treating suspected and well-tried cases. In accordance with this guideline, people with metabolic process signs are advised to use science masks, all fascinating following contamination obstacle tips, both in the fitness and in the home care environment. A character, except for metabolism, is not required to place signs and symptoms once publicly on clinical masks in conformity with this guideline. Right use and disposal of masks will remain relevant for a distance from the risk of widespread transmission. [38] The Chinese agency has revealed a gospel to expand knowledge and management of COVID-19 among ordinary populations as well as articles listed in the quest journals. The key message in the tenet discusses triggers, the manner in which face masks can be picked and put, relevant washing habits, the preventive action at various locations (for example at home, on public transport and in the public domain). The booting theory suggests approaches for taking fear among the well-known population in addition to scientific knowledge on approaches to managing the COVID-19 eruption [39].

## Treatment

Passive protein administration via transfusion of convalescent plasma may additionally offer the only non permanent methodology for conferring on the spot immunity to inclined people. There square measure severa examples during which convalescent plasma has been used effectively as postexposure prevention and/or remedy of infectious diseases, along with completely different outbreaks of coronaviruses (e.g., SARS-1, geographical area metabolic process syndrome [MERS]). Convalescent plasma is employed within the COVID-19 pandemic, restricted info from China endorse medical profit, that embody tomography resolution, discount in microorganism masses, and elevated survival.[40] In respect to respiratory illness, the sketch sees these phases as detection, assessment, treatment, escalation, and recovery, and throughout the analysis section it emphasises the wish to actively notice, test, isolate, and trot out cases our gift day strategy to covid-19. in contrast to for respiratory illness, no immunogen or antiviral marketers square measure accessible for covid-19, and therefore the mainstay of remedy is confirmative care, in excessive dependency gadgets if necessary, for the foremost seriously sick sufferers [41]. Antimalarial drug and Plaquenil are determined to be atmosphere friendly on SARS-CoV-2, and same to be atmosphere friendly in Chinese COV-19 patients. We have a tendency to think about the impact of Plaquenil on metabolic process microorganism tons of. 600mg of Plaquenil a day and their microorganism load in cavity swabs was once examined day after day in a very clinic putting. [42] Antimalarial drug is acknowledged to dam virus contamination by method of growing endosomial hydrogen ion concentration and by method of meddling with the glycosylation of cell receptor of SARS-CoV. The authors to boot speculated on the chance that the recognized immunomodulant impact of the drug might to boot embellish the antiviral impact in vivo. [43] Tocilizumab (TCZ), an antibody con (IL-6), emerged as AN alternative remedy for COVID-19 sufferers with an opportunity of protein storms recently. Within the current study, we have a tendency to aim to speak regarding the medical care response of TCZ remedy in COVID-19 contaminated sufferers. [44] Comorbidities and multi-organ accidents within the medical care of COVID-19. [45] A run|phase II|clinical trial|clinical test} clinical trial of remdesivir was once meted out through the University of NE center, and a clinical test medical trial accustomed be meted out via the China-Japan relationship Hospital.The outcomes of those scientific trials are going to be written in Apr 2020. Remdesivir raised pulmonic perform, shrunken respiratory organ microorganism masses, and ameliorated extreme respiratory organ pathology. In distinction, prophylactic LPV/RTV-IFNb only barely shrunken microorganism tons of and did not have a bearing on completely different illness parameters, and therapeutic LPV/RTV-IFNb accelerated pulmonic perform, but failed to decrease virus replication or extreme respiratory organ pathology.[46] If clinical information verify the organic results, antimalarial drug and Plaquenil may additionally be employed in prevention as properly as healing remedy for people uncovered to SARS CoV-2. [47] Overall, there's no special cause to estimate that sufferers with COVID19 contamination can advantage from corticosteroids, and such treatment is also harmful. [48] Organism antibodies will only apprehend one substance epitope that limits the utilization of MAb114 and REGN-EB3 within the remedy of COVID19. However, the development of COVID19-specific antibodies needs an extended time. It's not convenient to use organism antibodies for brand new pathogens to medical exercise in a very short time [49].

**Conculsion**

The COVID-19 pandemic speaks to the simplest worldwide general well-being emergency of this age and, possibly, since the pandemic contagious disease outburst of 1918. The speed and volume of clinical preliminaries propelled to explore potential treatments for COVID-19 feature each the necessity and talent to make nice proof even within the center of a pestilence. No treatments are indicated compelling to this point.

## Reference

1) De Groot RJ, Baker SC, Baric R, EnjuanesL, Gorbalenya AE, Holmes KV, PerlmanS, Poon L, Rottier PJ, Talbot PJ, Woo PC, Ziebuhr J. "Family Coronaviridae". InKing AM, Lefkowitz E, Adams MJ, Carstens EB, International Committee on Taxonomy of Viruses, International Union of Microbiological Societies. Virology Division (eds.). Ninth Report of the International Committee on Taxonomy of Viruses. Oxford: Elsevier, 2011; 806–28.

2) Woo Patrick C. Y.; Huang, Yi; Lau, Susanna K. P.; Yuen, Kwok- Yung. "Corona virus Genomics and Bioinformatics Analysis". Viruses, 2010; 2(8): 1804–1820.

3) Almeida JD, Berry DM, Cunningham CH, Hamre D, Hofstad MS, Mallucci L, McIntosh K, Tyrrell DA. "Virology: Corona viruses". Nature, 1968; 220(5168): 650.

4) Goldsmith CS, Tatti KM, Ksiazek TG, Rollin PE, Comer JA, Lee WW. "Ultrastructural characterization of SARS corona virus". Emerging Infectious Diseases, 2004; 10(2): 320–26.

5) Neuman BW, Adair BD, Yoshioka C,Quispe JD, Orca G, Kuhn P. "Supramolecular architecture of severe acute respiratory syndrome corona virus revealed by electron cryomicroscopy". Journal of Virology, 2006; 80(16): 7918–28.

6) Fehr AR, Perlman S. Maier HJ, Bickerton E, Britton P. "Corona viruses: an overview of their replication and pathogenesis". Methods in Molecular Biology. Springer, 2015; 1282: 1–23.

7) Lai MM, Cavanagh D. "The molecular biology of coronaviruses". Advances in Virus Research, 1997; 48: 1–100.

8) Chang CK, Hou MH, Chang CF, Hsiao CD, Huang TH. "The SARS coronavirus nucleocapsid protein forms and functions". Antiviral Research, 2014; 103: 39–50.

9) Chinese Clinical Trials. http://www/chictr.org/enindex.aspx. Accessed March 31, 2020.

10) Chen Y, Liu Q, Guo D. Emerging coronaviruses: genome structure, replication, and pathogenesis. J Med Virol, 2020; 92(4): 418-423.

11) Fung TS, Liu DX. Coronavirus infection, ER stress, apoptosis and innate immunity. Front Microbiol, 2014; 5: 296.

12) Savarino A, Boelaert JR, Cassone A, Majori G, Cauda R. Effects of chloroquine on viral infections: an old drug against today's diseases? Lancet Infect Dis., 2003; 3(11): 722-727.

13) Al-Bari MAA. Targeting endosomal acidification by chloroquine analogs as a promising strategy for the treatment of emerging viral diseases. Pharmacol Res Perspect, 2017; 5(1): e00293.

14) Zhou D, Dai SM, Tong Q. COVID-19: a recommendation to examine the effect of hydroxychloroquine in preventing infection and progression. [published online March 20, 2020]. J Antimicrob Chemother. 2020.

15) Devaux CA, Rolain JM, Colson P, Raoult D. New insights on the antiviral effects of chloroquine against coronavirus: what to expect for COVID-19? Int J Antimicrob Agents. Published online March 11, 2020.

16) Yao X, Ye F, ZhangM, et al. In vitro antiviral activity and projection of optimized dosing design of hydroxychloroquine for the treatment of severe acute respiratory syndrome coronavirus 2(SARS-CoV-2). Clin Infect Dis. Published online March 9, 2020.

17) Gao J, Tian Z, Yang X. Breakthrough: chloroquine phosphate has shown apparent efficacy in treatment of COVID-19 associated pneumonia in clinical studies. Biosci Trends, 2020; 14(1): 72-73.

18) Gautret P, Lagier JC, Parola P, et al. Hydroxychloroquine and azithromycin as a treatment of COVID-19: results of an open-label non-randomized clinical trial. Int J Antimicrob Agents. Published online March 20, 2020.

19) Chen J, Liu D, Liu L, et al. A pilot study of hydroxychloroquine in treatment of patients with common coronavirus disease-19 (COVID-19). J Zhejiang Univ (Med Sci). Published online March 6, 2020.

20) Gao J, Tian Z, Yang X. Breakthrough: chloroquine phosphate has shown apparent efficacy in treatment of COVID-19 associated pneumonia in clinical studies. Biosci Trends, 2020; 14(1): 72-73.

21) Kalil AC. Treating COVID-19—off-label drug use, compassionate use, and randomized clinical trials during pandemics. JAMA. Published March 24, 2020.

22) Osadchy A, Ratnapalan T, Koren G. Ocular toxicity in children exposed in utero to antimalarial drugs: review of the literature. J Rheumatol.

23) Chu CM, Cheng VC, Hung IF, et al; HKU/UCH SARS Study Group. Role of lopinavir/ritonavir in the treatment of SARS: initial virological and clinical findings. Thorax, 2004; 59(3): 252-256.

24) de Wilde AH, Jochmans D, Posthuma CC, et al. Screening of an FDA-approved compound library identifies four small-molecule inhibitors of Middle East respiratory syndrome coronavirus replication in cell culture. Antimicrob Agents Chemother, 2014; 58(8): 4875-4884.

25) Gautret P, Lagier JC, Parola P, et al. Hydroxychloroquine and azithromycin as a treatment of COVID-19: results of an open-label non-randomized clinical trial. Int J Antimicrob Agents. Published online March 20, 2020.

26) Tang, Y.W., Schmitz, J.E., Persing, D.H. and Stratton, C.W., 2020. Laboratory diagnosis of COVID-19: current issues and challenges. Journal of clinical microbiology, 58.

27) Chan, J.F.W., Yip, C.C.Y., To, K.K.W., Tang, T.H.C., Wong, S.C.Y., Leung, K.H., Fung, A.Y.F., Ng, A.C.K., Zou, Z., Tsoi, H.W. and Choi, G.K.Y., 2020. Improved molecular diagnosis of COVID-19 by the novel, highly sensitive and specific COVID-19-RdRp/Hel real-time reverse transcription-PCR assay validated in vitro and with clinical specimens. Journal of Clinical Microbiology, 58.

28) Guo, L., Ren, L., Yang, S., Xiao, M., Chang, D., Yang, F., Dela Cruz, C.S., Wang, Y., Wu, C., Xiao, Y. and Zhang, L., 2020. Profiling early humoral response to diagnose novel coronavirus disease (COVID-19). Clinical Infectious Diseases.

29) Li, Y. and Xia, L., 2020. Coronavirus disease 2019 (COVID-19): role of chest CT in diagnosis and management. American Journal of Roentgenology, 214(6): 1280-1286. 32. Hanson, K.E., Caliendo, A.M., Arias, C.A., Englund, J.A., Lee, M.J., Loeb, M., Patel, R., El Alayli, A., Kalot, M.A., Falck-Ytter, Y. and Lavergne, V., 2020. Infectious Diseases Society of America guidelines on the diagnosis of COVID-19. Clinical Infectious Diseases.

30) National Health Commission of People's Republic of China. Pneumonia infected with novel coronavirus is included in the management of legal infectious diseases. 2020.

31) Gautret P, Lagier JC, Parola P, et al. Hydroxychloroquine and azithromycin as a treatment of COVID-19: results of an open-label non-randomized clinical trial. Int J Antimicrob Agents. Published online March 20, 2020.

32) Chu CM, Cheng VC, Hung IF, et al; HKU/UCH SARS Study Group. Role of lopinavir/ritonavir in the treatment of SARS: initial virological and clinical findings. Thorax, 2004; 59(3): 252-256.

33) Tang, Y.W., Schmitz, J.E., Persing, D.H. and Stratton, C.W., 2020. Laboratory diagnosis of COVID-19: current issues and challenges. Journal of clinical microbiology, 58.

34) National Health Commission of People's Republic of China. Notice on printing and distributing the technical guide for prevention and control of novel coronavirus infection in medical institutions (First Edition). 2020.

35) National Health Commission of People's Republic of China. Notice on printing and distributing the work plan for prevention and control of pneumonia caused by novel coronavirus infection in the near future. 2020.

36) Wei, Q. and Ren, Z., 2020. Disinfection measures for pneumonia foci infected by novel coronavirus in 2019. Chin J Disinfect, 37: 59-62.

37) CDC. 2019 Novel coronavirus, Wuhan, China. 2020. 38. WHO. Advice on the use of masks in the community, during home care and in health care settings in the context of the novel coronavirus 2019-nCoV outbreak (Interim guidance). 2020. WHO/nCov/IPC_Masks/2020. Accessed 3 Feb 2020.

38) National Health Commission of People's Republic of China. Guidelines for public protection against novel coronavirus infection. 2020.

39) Bloch, E.M., Shoham, S., Casadevall, A., Sachais, B.S., Shaz, B., Winters, J.L., van Buskirk, C., Grossman, B.J., Joyner, M., Henderson, J.P. and Pekosz, A., 2020. Deployment of convalescent plasma for the prevention and treatment of COVID-19. The Journal of clinical investigation, 130(6): 2757-2765.

40) Watkins, J., 2020. Preventing a covid-19 pandemic. 42. Gautret, P., Lagier, J.C., Parola, P., Meddeb, L., Mailhe, M., Doudier, B., Courjon, J., Giordanengo, V., Vieira, V.E., Dupont, H.T. and Honoré, S., 2020. Hydroxychloroquine and azithromycin as a treatment of COVID-19: results of an open-label non-randomized clinical trial. International journal of antimicrobial agents, p.105949.

41) Wang, M., Cao, R., Zhang, L., Yang, X., Liu, J., Xu, M., Shi, Z., Hu, Z., Zhong, W. and Xiao, G., 2020. Remdesivir and chloroquine effectively inhibit the recently emerged novel coronavirus (2019-nCoV) in vitro. Cell research, 30(3): 269-271.

42) Luo, P., Liu, Y., Qiu, L., Liu, X., Liu, D. and Li, J., 2020. Tocilizumab treatment in COVID-19: A single center experience. Journal of medical virology, 92(7): 814-818.

43) Wang, T., Du, Z., Zhu, F., Cao, Z., An, Y., Gao, Y. and Jiang, B., 2020. Comorbidities and multi-organ injuries in the treatment of COVID-19. The Lancet, 395(10228): e52.

44) Sheahan, T.P., Sims, A.C., Leist, S.R., Schäfer, A., Won, J., Brown, A.J., Montgomery, S.A., Hogg, A., Babusis, D., Clarke, M.O. and Spahn, J.E., 2020. Comparative therapeutic efficacy of remdesivir and combination lopinavir, ritonavir, and interferon beta against MERS-CoV. Nature communications, 11(1): 1-14.

45) Colson, P., Rolain, J.M. and Raoult, D., 2020. Chloroquine for the 2019 novel coronavirus SARS-CoV-2. International journal of antimicrobial agents, 55(3): 1059

46) Russell, C.D., Millar, J.E. and Baillie, J.K., 2020. Clinical evidence does not support corticosteroid treatment for 2019-nCoV lung injury. The Lancet, 395(10223): 473-475.

47) Mair-Jenkins, J., Saavedra-Campos, M., Baillie, J.K., Cleary, P., Khaw, F.M., Lim, W.S., Makki, S., Rooney, K.D., Convalescent Plasma Study Group, Nguyen-Van-Tam, J.S. and Beck, C.R., 2015. The effectiveness of convalescent plasma and hyperimmune immunoglobulin for the treatment of severe acute respiratory infections of viral etiology: a systematic review and exploratory meta-analysis. The Journal of infectious diseases, 211(1): 80-90

# CHAPTER – 27

# CLOUD COMPUTING: THE EMERGENCE OF A NEW VIRTUAL ERA
## BY

## Ria Kikani

**Abstract:**

Cloud computing is the most widely used technology in today's world. Not only the present but even the future lies in Cloud computing. As globalisation is growing with interconnectivity, the term cloud computing generally refers the data centres available to end number of users across the Internet without needing a direct management interaction by the user. Apart from having the on-demand services, pay-as-you-go model and other unexpected operating expenses it also has the most well-built and designed architecture of computation. Starting from the introduction and history of cloud computing, architecture of cloud computing, cloud characteristics, cloud service models, cloud deployment models, cloud computing platforms, cloud security, issues & challenges of cloud computing are described in this chapter.

**Keywords:** Computation, Cloud computing, Model, Service, Security, Architecture.

## Introduction

The term cloud has been used from a long time in the industry as an abstraction of network. However, with time it became the icon of computer networks. Cloud computing is the hottest and in demand topic in not just the IT sector but the entire industry. Cloud computing is the delivery of computing services such as servers, storage etc. However, the companies that offers such computing services are profoundly called as cloud providers. In other words, it means storing and accessing data over the internet instead of the computer's hard drive. The storing of data and running programs from the computer's hard drive is called local storage and computing. Although we do not realise but we use cloud computing in almost every industry and day to day life. Today, almost a lot of organizations right from tiny start-ups to large scale industries are embracing cloud computing. There are end number of uses of this technology. It provides a resource sharing platform to its users. However, the resources can be dynamically reconfigured or scaled as per user's requirement. So, in simple words cloud simply means enormous structures, limitless entities and recurring inter-links of particles. Similarly, cloud computing can also be depicted as enormous computing power, limitless data/resource storage and recurring inter-links of advancing technologies.

## I.    The growth of cloud computing over the years

The first idea of cloud computing dated back to 1950s. The five main technologies that played an important role are distributed systems, virtualization. Web 2.0, service orientation and utility computing. Let us have an introductory understanding of each phase.

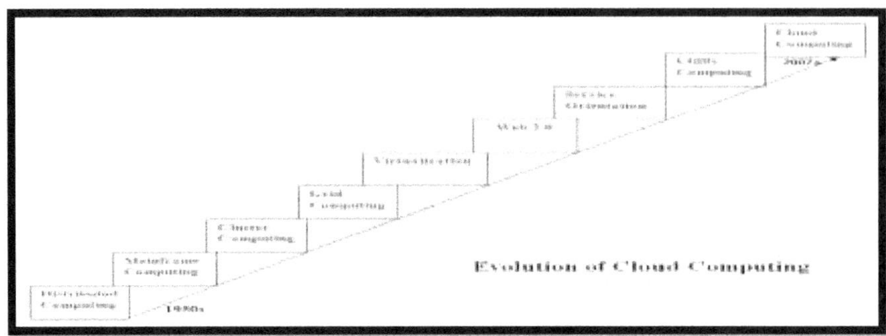


**Figure 1. Evolution of cloud computing**

### Distributed Systems

The distributed system depicts as a single operation to the users but is a structure of various individualistic and self- sustaining systems. It has features such as concurrency, scalability and non- dependence in failures. However, the issue with the system was that they need to be present or available at the same geological location. Hence this drawback resulted into three different types of computing.

### Mainframe Computing:

Mainframes came into the picture in 1951. It is considered as a dependable computing machine. It focuses on dealing large data sets and input-output operations. The biggest advantage is they have at the most no downtime and high fault tolerance. However, its expensiveness brought cluster computing as an alternative.

### Cluster Computing:

As the name suggests, it is connected to one another by a strong network of high bandwidth. Large datasets were also computable and new nodes could also be attached to expand the cluster. The expenditure issue was now solved to a great extent but the geological pitfall still remained and hence grid computing was now the new answer to all such drawbacks.

### Grid Computing

The concept of grid computing falls back to 1990s. As the word Grid suggests, different system networks were placed at different geological location and were connected to each other using the internet. As each network comprises of different networks, the grid consisted diverse nodes. However, the new problem aroused as distance increased and also it had low availability of high bandwidth connectivity.

### Virtualization:

It was introduced nearly four decades back. Virtualization is also referred as a virtual layer over the hardware machine which allows multiple instances to run simultaneously. Hardware virtualization is the widely used type of virtualization.

### Web 2.0:

Web 2.0 acts as an interface using which the services can interact with users or clients. It makes reciprocated and zestful web pages. No doubt, social media is the biggest example of Web 2.0.

*Service Orientation:*

The most viable features are its low- cost and flexibility. Two main and significant concepts introduced were Quality of Service (QoS) and Software as a Service (SAAS).

*Utility Computing:*

It has the service for storage, infrastructure and other requirements which are billed on pay-as-you-go basis. Finally, after this the Cloud computing service was introduced


## Challenges faced before cloud

Before cloud computing, it was costly to build and manage software. For all the infrastructure the users own, he/she needed a team of experts to handle all the resources. This drawback didn't let the business to expand their own software. Apart from cost, there was no feature of scalability available and that led to a downtime to integrate update resources. There were issues of security as well. Afterall security is of utmost importance for any user. These are just a few insights of the challenges faced. There were definitely more than we can even count.

## Factors contributing to the growth of cloud computing

- The applications are delivered quickly within a short time. The cloud makes hardware resources available and helps in configuring as per user requirement.
- The developers have many options of different programming languages using which they can build their applications.
- The developer can also add or delete resources to any particular application to handle load.
- The cloud provides a 'pay-as-you-go' utility for billing methods.


## Characteristics of cloud

- Data protection is an essential characteristic of cloud computing as data security is the main asset to any business or organization.
- The next most important characteristic of cloud computing is on-demand self -service. A person can monitor, provision and manage the resources as per requirement.
- Rapid elasticity is the term used as the resources can be scaled in and out i.e. horizontally or vertically as per user requirement.
- The computing services have a broad network access that are provided and managed over standard networks and diverse devices.
- Resource pooling is a feature that pools hardware resources and abstracts it so multiple users can have an access to it.
- The user can access the cloud from anywhere with a facility of internet connection and a cloud account. Such a feature is known as ubiquitous access.
- The user has to pay only what he/she uses. This feature is known as measured service as it helps to monitor the resources.
- A few examples of cloud resources are servers, networks, database, storage, security, runtime, platform etc.

**Cloud Services**

*Infrastructure as a Service (IaaS):*  We are already aware that cloud provides the users with a pay-as you-go utility for networking, storage, servers and even other computing resources. The organizations us their own platforms and applications which are built on top of a secure, scalable and a standardized infrastructure where the virtualization is performed by the hypervisor. The hypervisor controls and provisions access. There are many key features of IaaS. The essential use of IaaS is that the organizations instead of purchasing the hardware just pays for the IaaS which ultimately reduces the cost expenditure. It saves the cost of buying and maintaining which is further scalable depending on storage needs. It enables virtualization of administrative tasks which frees up the time for other employees to do work.

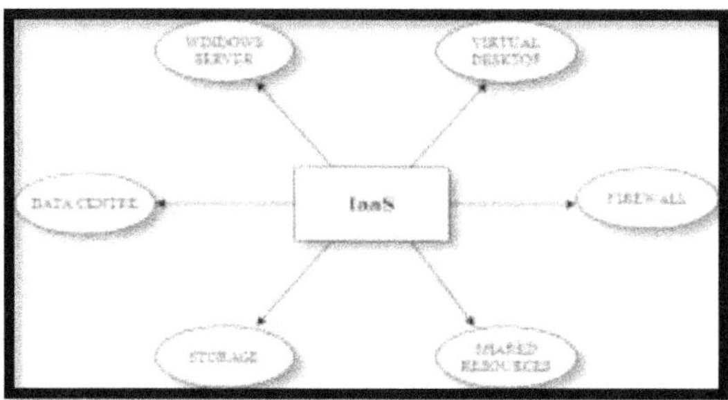

**Figure 2. Features of infrastructure as a service**

*Platform as a Service (PaaS):* The cloud provider can access a cloud-based development environment in which any cloud user can build and deliver applications with the services provided. The cloud user can build and deliver applications with the services provided. The cloud user can build tools to develop, test or customize the applications. It also has the feature of automatic scaling and provides a built-in application monitoring. The best example over here is that it sends notifications to the application owner when his/her application crashes or goes to sleep. It also has a platform which can host applications. The cloud provider manages the security, operating system, server software and backups. The user faces a zero downtime while updating or redeploying the application.

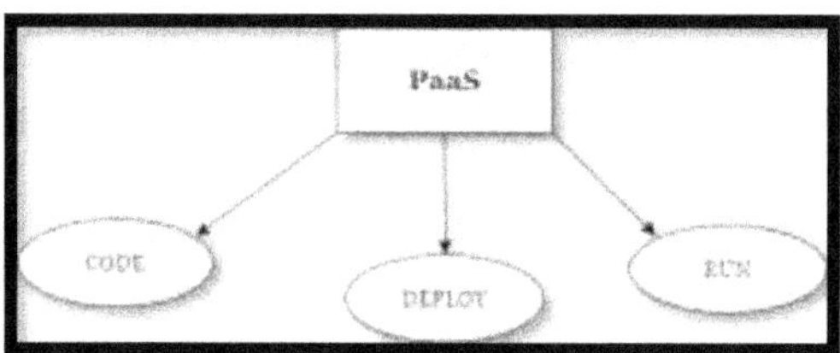

**Figure 3. Features of platform as a service**

*Software as a Service (SaaS):* The cloud provider delivers applications and software through the internet that are ready to be consumed. The users can store and analyse data to collaborate on projects. The applications reside on a remote cloud network which is accessed through web or an API. The SaaS provides its users with software and applications on a subscription model. The main benefit is that the SaaS providers manage, install and upgrade so that the users do not have to look into this at all. The data is totally secure in cloud and the resources can also be scaled as per user requirement.

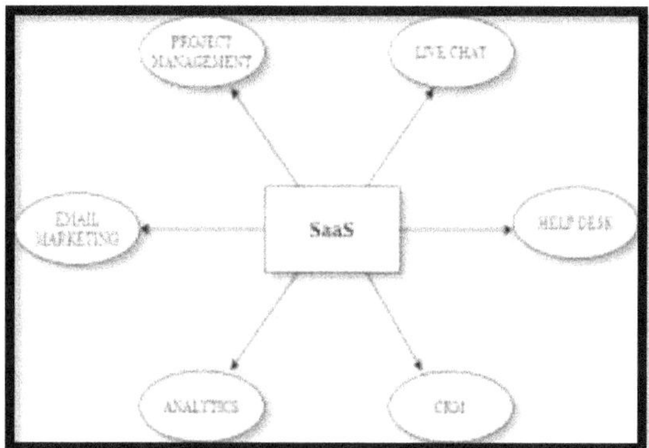

**Figure 4. Features of Software as a service**

## Cloud deployment models

Today almost many businesses rely on a complex network of IT applications and services. Each user has his/her own requirements and necessity for security, cost and availability. However, over the past few years many enterprises have adopted cloud to improve their output efficiency to accelerate scalable computing resources. There are four different models for deployment as per the firm's requirement.

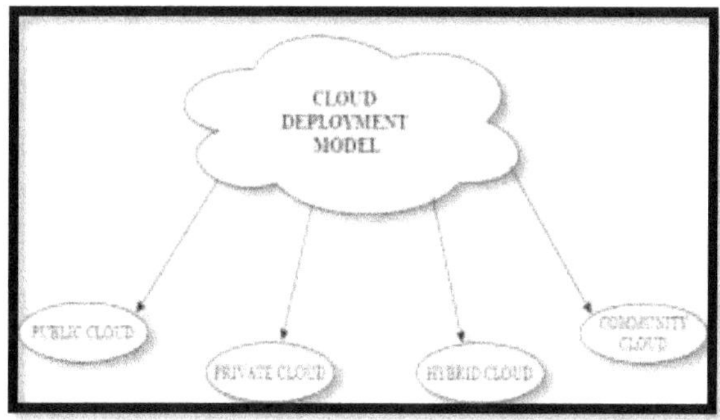

**Figure 5. Types of cloud deployment model**

### *Public Cloud:*

The public cloud is owned and operated by cloud providers who offer rapid access over the public network. The services in public cloud are pay-as-you-go and it offers speed and agility for faster deployment. It is more preferable if an enterprise wants to avoid large capital expenses. It enables scalable and flexible IaaS for storage and compute services. It also has a powerful PaaS and gives access to SaaS from CRM to data analytics. A few public cloud providers are IBM, AWS, Microsoft Azure, Google etc.

### *Private Cloud*

The private cloud is beneficial if the firm needs the most control over the data. This is the best choice as it is operated solely for a single organization. It is hosted in the data centre. As this cloud is purchased by the enterprise, it also has an expenditure cost. It gives the control of how data is stored and shared to one another. This offers to be a best option if cloud security is the major concern for the enterprise. Apart from cloud security it also provides with an on-demand availability along with reliable and supportive workloads. It facilitates high automated management of resource pooling and provides self-service interface which enables the IT staff to provision, allocate and deliver IT resources.

### *Hybrid Cloud:*

A hybrid cloud is an amalgamation of private cloud foundation and public cloud services. It allows the data to be shared between public and private cloud. Most companies with private cloud evolve to manage workloads across data centres, private clouds and public clouds which ultimately creates hybrid cloud. The hybrid cloud lets the companies to keep critical data with the traditional on-premises data centre or the private cloud and takes advantage of public cloud resources like SaaS and IaaS for elastic virtual resources.

### *Multi-Cloud*

As each firm has its own type of different workloads and requirements, many enterprises use multiple clouds to have a wide range of services. This usage of services from different cloud providers results into multicloud. It is more flexible over price, servers and geographic locations. It provides customized pricing and reduces latency. A multicloud can be integrated with a private cloud to support applications. In short, this approach gives the best of both private cloud and public cloud.

### Cloud Providers

### *Amazon Web Services (AWS):*

Amazon Web Services is a cloud computing platform which provides services such as database storage, content delivery and other essential functions and services to enhance the working of an enterprise. Due to its features like scalability, flexibility etc many firms are moving towards AWS. The have a pay-as-you-go utility and doesn't charge anything from the user. It also gives free promotional credits on registering for AWS account it is one of the leading cloud service providers among all. Using the internet, the users can access highly durable storage such as Amazon S3, and Amazon EBS. It also has a high-performance database such as Amazon Redshift and Amazon Dynamo DB.

### *Microsoft Azure:*

Microsoft Azure is a cloud computing service which is used for building testing and deploying the application. It is both a private and a public cloud. It uses virtualization which differentiates the coupling with the help of an abstraction layer known as a hypervisor. There are numerous amounts of virtual machines available and each virtual machine can run many operating systems.

### *Google Cloud Platform:*

Google cloud platform is one of the leading Cloud Computing services offered by google after AWS. The Google cloud platform is basically used for Google search and YouTube. The data stored in Google Cloud is secure and can be accessed easily. It offers varieties of services from infrastructure as a service to platform as a service. Google cloud also provides a strong stability.

### *IBM:*

This cloud organization can deploy and access its resources such as storage networking and compute power with the help of internet. There are several tools which help the customer to draw on deep industry expertise. The speed and agility of the cloud fulfils the requirement of the customer and make them feel satisfied

**Emerging trends in cloud computing**

*Artificial Intelligence Platform*

Artificial Intelligence is the digital future of the world that would result into making the virtual world more intelligent. The amalgamation of cloud computing and artificial intelligence results into "The Intelligent Cloud". It has high efficiency and speed which ultimately reduces human workload.

*Serverless Computing*

The serverless computing architecture is event driven. As soon as the user requests, a state is prompted. It serves the application and then it is destroyed. This computing is also referred to as Function as a Service (FaaS). The only requirement is to set an API gateway.

*Edge Computing*

It transfers the computing services towards the network. It lowers the entanglement of interconnected systems and helps in analysing data. It enables autonomous decisions and is a strategic building block of the smart world.

**Real world examples of cloud computing**

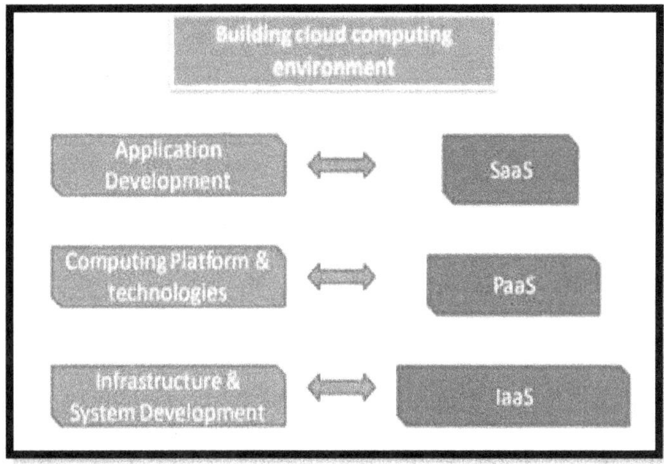


- *Dropbox, Gmail and Facebook:*
  The Dropbox lets the users to manage and use files on any device through its website and also provides 1TB of free storage. On the other hand, Gmail has an unlimited storage on the cloud. Facebook has the messenger app which allows the Facebook user to exchange data.

- *Cloud Computing in Education sector:*
  An e-learning software called SlideRocket is launched where the students can build and manage their presentations and submit it to the specific person. They can even have web conference over the cloud.

- ***Cloud Computing in Healthcare Sector***
  The major example here is the Dell's Secure Healthcare cloud. It lets the administrators exchange information and lets large data sets to be exchanged instantly lowering down the cost and boosting its efficiency.

## Challenges faced in cloud computing

- It has network connection dependencies.
- There are limited features for storage and accessibility.
- Usually when a company allocates the data over the cloud, it loses its control as they trust another party to take care of the data. This results into security issues of the sensitive data over the cloud.
- Lastly, there are technical issues and faults that may result into downtime and can be a challenge to the users.

## Unfolding career opportunities in cloud computing

In today's world, cloud computing is the most rapidly growing and in-demand career field. Almost 85% of the companies are using cloud for some or the other reason and making great strides in their business profits. We need to understand that cloud computing is the future and shall rule the world for years to come. To make an unbeatable career in cloud computing, there are many domains such as:

- Cloud Developer
- Cloud Security Engineer
- SysOps Administrator
- Cloud Architect and so on.

## Future of cloud computing

Everything is aligned to cloud in one way or the other except the data kept in remote storage for safer and security reasons. Cloud has end number of distinct features which makes its future brighter in the industry. Let us have an insight into the future aspects of cloud technology.

- ***Cloud -based tracking:*** Tracking requires the data from Global Positioning System also known as GPS. Using cloud and location tracking, we can locate almost everything that we can think of right from lost luggage, mobile phones, cars, shipment orders etc.
- ***Cloud-based adjustments:*** Devices which are required to be read by users such as electric meters and parking meters can now directly generate a report.
- ***Cloud-based smart devices:*** Cloud can be used to communicate the devices with the users so that the users can co-ordinate the activities as per requirement.

## Conclusion

In this chapter we discussed the various aspects of cloud computing with a view to have an overall understanding of the subject, which would ultimately enable us to develop a working cloud-based application. Conclusively, on the basis of all above mentioned aspects and research, I present my perception on this fantabulous emerging technology of Cloud Computing that working on computer was once a dream, so was having optimized Mobile phones and so was having fully-fledged developed technologies like Artificial Intelligence and all these happened. Therefore, I dream for the best possible evolution of cloud in such a way that, one day long after even if you and me are no longer active in this field but Cloud shall expand prominently. Just like the clouds in the sky, this Cloud will propagate and eventually the Cloud technology will be even more handy, beneficiary and utilitarian, that as the droplets of rainy cloud showers on one and all present on land and rejuvenates them; this Cloud will bestow even more on the era with its droplets in the form of updating technologies, unending resources and inevitable assistance. And that dream can be achieved by simply getting into it.

**Refrences**


1) On technical security issues in cloud computing: Meiko Jensen, Jorg S & Nils G – 2009 IEEE
2) Garrison, G., Kim, S., Wakefield, R.L.: Success Factors for Deploying Cloud Computing. Commun. ACM. 55, 62–68 (2012)
3) Yang, H., Tate, M.: A Descriptive Literature Review and Classification of Cloud Computing Research. Commun. Assoc. Inf. Syst. 31 (2012).
4) Shyam Patidar; Dheeraj Rane; Pritesh Jain "A Survey Paper on Cloud Computing" in proceeding of Second International Conference on Advanced Computing & Communication Technologies, 2012.
5) Yashpalsinh Jadeja; Kirit Modi, "Cloud Computing - Concepts, Architecture and Challenges" in Proceeding of International Conference on Computing, Electronics and Electrical Technologies [ICCEET], 2012.
6) Qi Zhang, Lu Cheng and Raouf Boutaba, "Cloud computing: state-of-the-art and research challenges".

# CHAPTER – 28

# BIOMASS A POTENTIAL ENERGY RESOURCE

## BY
## Akshata Mandloi


**Abstract**

Biomass energy is a significant part of renewable energy. Development and effective utilization of biomass energy can have positive impacts on solving environmental and energy related issues. Biomass being the renewable energy source, can be of major significance as the focus of national energy policy and strategy has been primarily on renewable resources and their conservation. Biomass, a renewable energy source, has the highest potential to contribute to the energy requirement of modern society for both developing and industrialized countries over the globe. The major sources of biomass energy aquatic plants and algae, wood and wood wastes, waste from food processing industries, agricultural crops and their by products, animal wastes and municipal waste. Biomass, as one potential source of renewable energy and the conversion of plant material into useable form of energy, mainly fuel for an internal combustion engine or as electricity, can be achieved using numerous routes, each having their own merits and demerits. In the recent times, the prime focus of research has been on environment friendly and sustainable energy from biomass for the replacement of conventional fossil fuels. The current studies have been focusing on investigation of global potential as well as utilization of biomass energy and how it contributes to the sustainable energy development. At one hand increased production of biomass for energy generation has the potential to counterbalance the substantial use of fossil fuels, whereas on the other hand it also has the potential to decrease food security, threaten conservation areas, and pollute water resources. The total effect of biomass energy production on climate depends on the crop, it can be either warming or cooling. It also depends on the reflectance of solar radiation between the preexisting vegetation and biomass crop, the technology used for converting biomass into useable energy, and the difference in carbon stocks. In this review, potential of biomass resource, its significance and various aspects of biomass energy has been discussed.

**Keywords:** Biomass, Renewable Energy Source, Sustainable.


**Introduction**

In recent years, there has been an alarming depletion of conventional fossil fuels, which has led to an increased utilization of renewable energy source. An increase in demand of renewable energy sources has contributed in increasing popularity of utilization of bio-energy or biomass energy [1]. Biomass energy can be a viable alternative in the near future and also a more sustainable source of energy supply. Biomass-energy has been the center of attraction due to the following facts: (1) It helps in restoration of barren or degraded lands by increasing water retention, biodiversity and soil fertility. Biomass-energy play a robust role in the supply of energy to many developing countries, (2) It has served as a major factor in reducing the poverty in developing countries, (3) being environment friendly, it is $CO_2$ (carbon-dioxide) neutral and also acts as carbon sinks, (4) it meets the energy requirements readily, with cheap conversion devices, and (5) the energy derived can be delivered in all forms according to the requirement of people ( heat and electricity, liquid and gaseous fuel) [1]. Biomass energy is on of the major source of energy in numerous regions and countries like Africa, Bhutan, East Sahelian Africa, Nepal and Asia. In these countries, the major use of bio-energy is firewood for heating and cooking [2]. In the global energy system, the future of biomass energy depends on the complex coordinated working of four main factors [3]. First, being the conversion technology and the possibility of using new microbe and plant varieties as well as novel conversion processes of biomass-to-fuel for escalating the produce of usable energy from each unit of available water and land. Second comes the inherent productive capacity of the ocean and land ecosystems that can be utilized for bio energy production. The third is the substitutional uses for the water and land resources that are applicant sites for bio energy yield. Fourth is the ex-situ association of bio-energy technologies for invasive species and for extent of water and air pollution. The factors must be efficiently combined to reduce the societal and ecosystem costs of bio energy yielding and to increase the advantages [3,4,5,6]. In this chapter, we briefly review a backdrop on biomass resources and it's potential for generation of energy, current scenario of various biomass conversion technologies, utilization of biomass-based energy, economics related to biofuels and significance of bio-energy for protection of environment.

**Biomass resources**

Biomass energy can be defined as any heat energy source which are extracted from biological non-fossil materials. Biomass energy can be derived from land and freshwater and even from oceans. Biomass energy widely ranges from sugarcane to methane collected from landfills or from firewood to ethanol which is produced from corn [7]. Potential future energy sources such as electricity generation from photosynthetic cells or hydrogen from engineered microbes could also be categorized as biomass energy, however these have a separate series of challenges than those for present biomass energy, which are obtained from terrestrial plants [8]. Essential sources for biomass energy are aquatic plants, algae, wood and wood wastes, waste from food processing, agricultural crop and their waste by products, animal wastes and MSW [9]. The size of wood waste as a resource depends on the amount of harvested wood for paper, pulp and lumber. Just like crop, fuel wood can also be grown as plantations. Rapidly growing species like eucalyptus, poplar or willow can be harvested in every few years. Poplar coppices, with short-rotation, can be grown in the rotation of three-seven years, makes it possible to extract 10-13 tons of dry matter per hectare per annum on good or average quality soil [10]. Forest product industries producing waste wood such as board ends, bark, sawdust etc. are largely used for the production of energy. In several cases, these industries, has now become one of the net exporters of generated electricity, the generation of electricity occurs by combustion wastes. Biomass materials such as agricultural residues that are basically byproducts of agriculture. These agricultural byproducts include rice husks, cotton stalks, jute sticks, rice and wheat straw, jowar and maize cobs, coconut shells, etc. [11]. A variety of biomass can be grown for the huge purpose of energy production. Crops that are involved in the production of energy are: seaweed (kelp), sugar cane, elephant grass, sugar beets and many others. There are two major determining factors which shows whether a crop can be utilized for energy use [12,16]. Energy crops that are most suitable have a high yield of dry material per unit are of land. A high yield lowers the cost of energy production and land requirements from biomass [17].

> ***Potential of biomass resource –***
> To ensure the future supply of fuels and meet the related requirements biomass has the largest potential and hence can be considered as the best alternative. According to scientific studies, on total terrestrial surface, the potential of energy produced by biomass (bio energy) is about 3500 EJ/year. Biomass yield and the related potential varies from one country to another it even differs from medium yields in temperate to high-level yielding in tropic and sub- tropic countries. However, enough water supply in the top soil and root zone, temperature higher

than 5°C can help in favorable growing conditions and ensure efficient photosynthesis. C-4 plants, have the most efficient photosynthesis, such as sorghum, sugarcanes and corn (maize) can help in attaining high biomass yield[13]. In the current scenario, prime focus of researchers is on replacing conventional fossil fuel with environment friendly and sustainable energy biomass [14,15].

**Biomass conversion technologies**

One potential source of renewable energy is biomass. Generally, fuel for an IC (internal combustion) or electricity by conversion of plant matter into suitable form of energy can be achieved through various routes, each having its own merits and demerits [17]. Conversion routes of biomass can be categorized as thermo-chemical, biochemical, and chemical. Study of thermo-chemical conversion processes are primarily done using lignocellulosic material (wood sludge), peat and coal as feedstock [18]. Thermal conversion of biomass has several benefits as it leads to useful products along with contributing in solving pollution issues arising from biomass collection [19]. The products obtained by thermo-chemical processes are differentiated into tar components and a carbon rich solid residue, volatile fraction consisting of gases, vapours [20]. Pyrolysis, direct liquification and gasification are the processes comprised by thermal degradation. The most efficient process for biomass conversion is pyrolysis as it produces energy fuels with fuel-to-feed ratios. Pyrolysis is one of the most efficient method which can compete and eventually replace non-renewable fossil fuel resources [25]. Thermal degradation of biomass with incomplete combustion, that is, with very limited quantity of oxidizing agent or in absence of oxygen is known as the pyrolysis conversion process [26]. Furthermore, for applications, the reaction products are classified into three different groups: permanent gases, bio-oil or tar (a pyrolytic liquid), or simply into char and volatiles [27]. For power generation in turbine and engine gas and liquid products are used [28]. Fuel, chemicals and other "bio-based" products are the various applications of the resulting bio-oil [29]. Fast pyrolysis of biomass produces bio-oil which is a renewable liquid with a lower heating value. High percentage of alkylated compounds (especially methyl derivatives) is one of the major characteristic of bio-oils. Another important advantage of biomass pyrolysis for production of liquid is the decoupling nature of the plant [28]. Biomass pyrolysis oils are chemically very complex, highly oxygenated, corrosive, viscous and relatively unstable, these chemical and physical properties are one of the major drawbacks in the utilization of biomass pyrolysis oils for fuel applications [31].Another widely recognized thermo-chemical routes is gasification as its end products can find efficient application by home users or industries, specifically in decentralized production of energy coupled with fuel cell, micro turbine/gas, boiler and turbine/engine [22]. Small quantities of ash and char and high production of gaseous products are the result of thermal treatment of gasification of biomass [23]. To provide heat for the endothermic pyrolysis reaction gasification generally involves combustion as well as pyrolysis [24]. A well-known technology, gasification, is classified on the basis of gasifying agent – $O_2$-enriched air, air, airsteam, steam, steam-oxygen, etc. [32]. Another advantage of gasification process is that gives the opportunity to convert renewable biomass feedstocks into synthesis gases or clean fuel gases. Hydrogen and carbon monoxide are the major constituents of synthetic gas or bio-syngas [33].

The production of liquid fuels and fermentation or anaerobic digestion which eventually result in production of biogas occurs through alcoholic fermentation that completes biological conversion of biomass [34]. For anaerobic digestion, marine crops, manure and high moisture herbaceous plants (vegetables, cotton, sugarcane, corn and sugar beet) are most suitable.

**Energy derived from biomass**

The oldest form of energy used by humans is biomass, in the form of wood. As per the ancient times utilization of biomass has been through direct combustion, and this process is still widely used in many parts of the world. As bio-energy can be modernized globally that is, it has the potential to be produced and used cost competitively and efficiently in more convenient forms of electricity, gases, or liquids [27]. In developed countries, future utilization of the main biomass processes are expected to be direct combustion of wastes and residues for generation of electricity [30]. Ethanol and biodiesel (known as biofuels) are produced from biomass through thermo-chemical or biochemical processes [35].

➢ *Steam and electric power*

The chain for production of bio-electricity begins with biomass fuel cultivation, or its collection from other operations as wastes or residues. Generally, essential cost and logistical components for production of bio-electricity are storage of fuel, its transport and pre-treatment.Bagasse, forest and other agricultural residues are predominant feedstocks for the generation of bio-electricity. All organic materials have the potential to get converted into useful energy forms, but the modern bio-electricity systems have another major advantage that is it can deal with a wide rang of materials rich in lignocellulose. Bio-electricity is produced in the 'ready for commercial use' form by combustion of biomass, its advanced gasification and pyrolysis technologies [31]. The latest generation of biomass energy conversion processes is biomass gasification, its application improves efficiency, reduces bio-electricity general investment costs by utilizing gas turbine technology [32]. In power gas turbines, biomass can be used as primary and secondary energy source. As secondary energy source, biomass is utilized in making of fuel, which is further used to fire a gas turbine A useful thermal energy and simultaneous production of electricity from one single source is known as cogeneration. Secondary energy source can also be used to produce a fuel from biomass as another alternative. Biomass is converted into biogas (a combustible gas) by gasifiers. Mixture of $CO_2$ (carbon di-oxide) and $CH_4$ (methane) along with small quantity of $H_2S$ (sulfuric acid) forms biogas. Biogas is usually burnt in internal combustion engines for production of electricity which may also include recovery of heat for combined power and heat production [1].

➢ *Ethanol*

An oxygenated renewable bio-based resource which also has the potential to reduce the emissions of particulate in compression – ignite engines is ethanol (ethyl alcohol) [36,37]. Production of ethanol can be done using various raw materials, these raw materials are categorized into three different categories of agricultural raw materials – (a) simple sugar, (b) starch, and (c) lignocellulose. Cellulose, hemicelluloses, lignin extracts and other compounds are the components of lignocellulosic biomass. Cellulose feedstocks like corn stalks, MSW, rice straw, switchgrass, sugarcane bagasse, and pulpwood can produce ethanol. To exhaust emission of GHG (greenhouse gas) and reduce use of petroleum can be efficiently done by using ethanol-blended fuel [38]. A major disadvantage of using ethanol to gasoline causes an increase in the content of oxygen of the fuel, reducing the exhaust emission and improving the combustion of gasoline, generally attribute to combustion in motor vehicles, like unburned hydrocarbons and carbon monoxide [39].

> ### *Biodiesel*

Biodiesel or FAME (fatty acid methyl esters) is a robust alternative to the largely used petroleum derived diesel fuel as it can be generated by domestic natural sources like soyabeans, recycled cooking oil, rapeseeds, and coconuts which thus reduces our dependence on exhausting petroleum fuels from foreign sources [39]. Production of biodiesel is a very technological and modern area; its high relevance is because of the increase in environmental advantage and in petrol prices [40]. Fuels for diesel engines can be replaced by vegetable oils, but as they have higher viscosity in comparison to usual diesel fuel and also require engine modifications. To use vegetable oils in place of diesel fuels, viscosity must be reduced and this can be done in the following ways – a) pyrolysis or thermal cracking, b) blending (diluting with hydrocarbons), c) emulsification and the most common way to produce biodiesel d) alcoholysis (transesterification) [1].

**Significance of bio-energy in protection of environment**

The use of fossil fuels over the globe is one of the largest anthropogenic emissions of carbon-dioxide which has been one of the major reasons behind climate change and global warming [33]. Increased renewable energy production and enhanced energy efficiency will reduce $CO_2$ emissions, but renewable energy and energy efficiency cannot potentially reduce $CO_2$ emissions over the globe. One of the key alternatives to substitute fossil fuels and reduce emissions of GHG is bio-energy. Using and producing biofuels for transportation can offer replacements for fossil fuels that can effectively provide solution to various environmental issues. Combustion of fossil fuels for generation of electricity largely contributes to GHG emissions. For electricity production, using biomass also reduces emission of $CO_2$ [1]. Thus, bio-energy plays a robust role in protecting the environment.

**Conclusion**

To ensure fuel supply in future which meets the needs, a potentially best option can be biomass. One practical way, for utilization of biomass in developing countries can be the modernization of related technologies which lead to better production and conversion of biomass. Considering the large amount of terrestrial plant growth, diverting a small fraction of entire plant growth can efficiently fulfill the energy needs globally. However, for the potential production of biomass energy without negative food security or climate impact lies mainly in utilization of abandoned agricultural lands. Direct combustion of wastes and residues for generation of electricity, biodiesel as liquid fuels, combined power and heat production from energy crops and ethanol is expected to be the future of utilization of biomass processes in developed countries.

**Reference:**


1) Demirbas, M. F., Balat, M., & Balat, H. (2009). Potential contribution of biomass to the sustainable energy development. *Energy Conversion and Management, 50*(7), 1746-1760.
2) Field, C. B., Campbell, J. E., & Lobell, D. B. (2008). Biomass energy: the scale of the potential resource. *Trends in ecology & evolution, 23*(2), 65-72.
3) Beringer, T. I. M., Lucht, W., & Schaphoff, S. (2011). Bioenergy production potential of global biomass plantations under environmental and agricultural constraints. *Gcb Bioenergy, 3*(4), 299-312.
4) Balat, M. (2011). Production of bioethanol from lignocellulosic materials via the biochemical pathway: a review. *Energy conversion and management, 52*(2), 858-875.

5) Jahirul, M. I., Rasul, M. G., Chowdhury, A. A., & Ashwath, N. (2012). Biofuels production through biomass pyrolysis—a technological review. *Energies*, *5*(12), 4952-5001.

6) Balat, M., & Balat, H. (2010). Progress in biodiesel processing. *Applied energy*, *87*(6), 1815-1835.

7) Mussatto, S. I., Dragone, G., Guimarães, P. M., Silva, J. P. A., Carneiro, L. M., Roberto, I. C., ... & Teixeira, J. A. (2010). Technological trends, global market, and challenges of bio-ethanol production. *Biotechnology advances*, *28*(6), 817-830.

8) Vassilev, S. V., Baxter, D., Andersen, L. K., & Vassileva, C. G. (2013). An overview of the composition and application of biomass ash. Part 1. Phase–mineral and chemical composition and classification. *Fuel*, *105*, 40-76.

9) Abbasi, T., & Abbasi, S. A. (2010). Biomass energy and the environmental impacts associated with its production and utilization. *Renewable and sustainable energy reviews*, *14*(3), 919-937.

10) Sharma, A., Pareek, V., & Zhang, D. (2015). Biomass pyrolysis—A review of modelling, process parameters and catalytic studies. *Renewable and Sustainable Energy Reviews*, *50*, 1081-1096.

11) Srirangan, K., Akawi, L., Moo-Young, M., & Chou, C. P. (2012). Towards sustainable production of clean energy carriers from biomass resources. *Applied energy*, *100*, 172-186.

12) Lin, Y., & Tanaka, S. (2006). Ethanol fermentation from biomass resources: current state and prospects. *Applied microbiology and biotechnology*, *69*(6), 627-642.

13) Long, H., Li, X., Wang, H., & Jia, J. (2013). Biomass resources and their bioenergy potential estimation: A review. *Renewable and Sustainable Energy Reviews*, *26*, 344-352.

14) Sánchez, J., Curt, M. D., Robert, N., & Fernández, J. (2019). Biomass resources. In *The Role of Bioenergy in the Bioeconomy* (pp. 25-111). Academic Press.

15) Li, Y., Zhou, L. W., & Wang, R. Z. (2017). Urban biomass and methods of estimating municipal biomass resources. *Renewable and Sustainable Energy Reviews*, *80*, 1017-1030.

16) Henry, R. J. (2010). Evaluation of plant biomass resources available for replacement of fossil oil. *Plant biotechnology journal*, *8*(3), 288-293.

17) Demirbaş, A. (2004). Ethanol from cellulosic biomass resources. *International journal of green energy*, *1*(1), 79-87.

18) Ravindranath, N. H., Somashekar, H. I., Nagaraja, M. S., Sudha, P., Sangeetha, G., Bhattacharya, S. C., & Salam, P. A. (2005). Assessment of sustainable non-plantation biomass resources potential for energy in India. *Biomass and Bioenergy*, *29*(3), 178-190.

19) Watkins, D., Nuruddin, M., Hosur, M., Tcherbi-Narteh, A., & Jeelani, S. (2015). Extraction and characterization of lignin from different biomass resources. *Journal of Materials Research and Technology*, *4*(1), 26-32.

20) Lauri, P., Havlík, P., Kindermann, G., Forsell, N., Böttcher, H., & Obersteiner, M. (2014). Woody biomass energy potential in 2050. *Energy Policy*, *66*, 19-31.

21) Mushrif, S. H., Vasudevan, V., Krishnamurthy, C. B., & Venkatesh, B. (2015). Multiscale molecular modeling can be an effective tool to aid the development of biomass conversion technology: A perspective. *Chemical Engineering Science*, *121*, 217-235.

22) Chadwick, D. T., McDonnell, K. P., Brennan, L. P., Fagan, C. C., & Everard, C. D. (2014). Evaluation of infrared techniques for the assessment of biomass and biofuel quality parameters and conversion technology processes: A review. *Renewable and Sustainable Energy Reviews*, *30*, 672-681.

23) McKendry, P. (2002). Energy production from biomass (part 2): conversion technologies. *Bioresource technology*, *83*(1), 47-54.

24) Uzoejinwa, B. B., He, X., Wang, S., Abomohra, A. E. F., Hu, Y., & Wang, Q. (2018). Co-pyrolysis of biomass and waste plastics as a thermochemical conversion technology for high-grade biofuel production: Recent progress and future directions elsewhere worldwide. *Energy conversion and management, 163*, 468-492.

25) Faaij, A. (2006). Modern biomass conversion technologies. *Mitigation and adaptation strategies for global change, 11*(2), 343-375.

26) Chhiti, Y., & Kemiha, M. (2013). Thermal conversion of biomass, pyrolysis and gasification. *International Journal of Engineering and Science (IJES), 2*(3), 75-85.

27) Vimmerstedt, L. J., Bush, B. W., Hsu, D. D., Inman, D., & Peterson, S. O. (2015). Maturation of biomass-to-biofuels conversion technology pathways for rapid expansion of biofuels production: a system dynamics perspective. *Biofuels, Bioproducts and Biorefining, 9*(2), 158-176.

28) McKendry, P. (2002). Energy production from biomass (part 1): overview of biomass. *Bioresource technology, 83*(1), 37-46.

29) Hood, E. E. (2011). *Plant biomass conversion* (Vol. 376). P. Nelson, & R. Powell (Eds.). Chichester: Wiley-Blackwell.

30) Adams, P., Bridgwater, T., Lea-Langton, A., Ross, A., & Watson, I. (2018). Biomass conversion technologies. In *Greenhouse Gas Balances of Bioenergy Systems* (pp. 107-139). Academic Press.

31) Pardo-Planas, O., Atiyeh, H. K., Phillips, J. R., Aichele, C. P., & Mohammad, S. (2017). Process simulation of ethanol production from biomass gasification and syngas fermentation. *Bioresource technology, 245*, 925-932.

32) Molino, A., Chianese, S., & Musmarra, D. (2016). Biomass gasification technology: The state of the art overview. *Journal of Energy Chemistry, 25*(1), 10-25.

33) Sansaniwal, S. K., Rosen, M. A., & Tyagi, S. K. (2017). Global challenges in the sustainable development of biomass gasification: An overview. *Renewable and Sustainable Energy Reviews, 80*, 23-43.

34) Mielenz, J. R. (2001). Ethanol production from biomass: technology and commercialization status. *Current opinion in microbiology, 4*(3), 324-329.

35) Digman, B., Joo, H. S., & Kim, D. S. (2009). Recent progress in gasification/pyrolysis technologies for biomass conversion to energy. *Environmental Progress & Sustainable Energy: An Official Publication of the American Institute of Chemical Engineers, 28*(1), 47-51.

36) Lan, W., Chen, G., Zhu, X., Wang, X., & Xu, B. (2015). Progress in techniques of biomass conversion into syngas. *Journal of the Energy Institute, 88*(2), 151-156.

37) Küçük, M. M., & Demirbaş, A. (1997). Biomass conversion processes. *Energy Conversion and Management, 38*(2), 151-165.

38) Chum, H. L., & Overend, R. P. (2001). Biomass and renewable fuels. *Fuel processing technology, 71*(1-3), 187-195.

39) Chen, Z., Wang, M., Jiang, E., Wang, D., Zhang, K., Ren, Y., & Jiang, Y. (2018). Pyrolysis of torrefied biomass. *Trends in biotechnology, 36*(12), 1287-1298.

40) Ren, J., Liu, Y. L., Zhao, X. Y., & Cao, J. P. (2020). Biomass thermochemical conversion: A review on tar elimination from biomass catalytic gasification. *Journal of the Energy Institute, 93*(3), 1083-1098.

# CHAPTER - 29

# GEOGRAPHIC DIFFERENCES IN COVID-19 CASES, DEATHS AND INCIDENCE INDIA

## BY
## Nivedita Kumari

## Abstract

As an ongoing pandemic, diseases caused by severe acute respiratory syndrome Coronavirus –2, also called COVID -19 is a contagious respiratory and vascular disease. SARS COv-2, known as coronavirus or COVID -19 has shaped a public health emergency in international concern affecting the all over the world and also including the territories around them. Several situation and condition were understood and noted during including the notation of cases of coronavirus all over the world. On mid December 2019, the very first case of coronavirus was noted in China in the city Wuhan, then from the next enquiry the cases became to multiply. Then in End January 2020, the first case of coronavirus seen in India. Then it was seen that this case is transmitted from the Indian student from Kerala who returned from Wuhan University, China.The data driven analysis will necessarily provide deep insights into the study of early risks assessments for 50 immensely affected countries. The History of COVID 19 was not new, through the reference of several studies and publications, it was noted that around 800 BCE, this pre-named coevolution with bat and avian species. Coronaviruses (CoV) are a large family of viruses that cause illness ranging from the common cold to more severe diseases. A novel coronavirus (n-CoV) is a new strain that has not been previously identified in humans. The new virus was subsequently named the "COVID-19 virus". Here is in this chapter we will study about the overall geographical location of India related to COVID – 19 cases in India during different time count and study.

**Keywords:** Covid-19 cases in India, Case causality report, Case Recuperation Rate; Period Predominance Rate; Geographical variety.

## Introduction:

Extreme intense respiratory disorder is the main cause of novel coronavirus. This transmission-based virus is breaking out by Wuhan, a city in China. Several studies and publications cited that the main centric point of this novel coronavirus from Wuhan is the Wuhan wet market. This was during mid of December 2019, when Coronavirus cases started to identified and then multiplied through transmission on a scale. Firstly, noted that its symptoms of this coronavirus are as same as normal seasonal cough and fever symptoms. But after this change to some other symptoms, some of them are chest pain, issues in breathing. From there testing, Now coming to geographical location study of India, As the first case of coronavirus was seen in January 2020 in India as mentioned above by a student who lifted from Wuhan university. China, as mentioned earlier. This first case of COVID – 19 was detected on last week of December 2019, and on 30th January 2020, the first case was raised in India. Then it started to multiply the cases day by day. Before considering the main case study and stats graph. Let us understand the testing measurement and data stats of the COVID – 19 in India from the first case detected till the present date.

a) **Testing and data stats outcomes:**

Testing – Emergency medical response unit is the New Delhi's ministry that is the policy making team in Union health Ministry's war room. The central surveillanceunit (IDSP) and experts from national centre of disease control (NDC) and apart of these experts are as part of policy decisions to decide how coronavirus should be handled to control in country. National institute of Virology (NIV), Pune has verified 15 labs for corona virus check-up all across. Early March was the time when more labs were being trained to test for COVID -19 check-ups. And on March 13, if we see data all over the world then, 52 labs have the capabilities for virus testing. Isolation process played a vital role in development of drugs, vaccines and rapid diagnosis kits in the country. After some more research and study of genetic behaviour of the virus. Then National institute of Virology (NIV) has shared two SARS CoV-2 sequences through Global science initiative and primary source that provide open-access to genomic data of influenzas virus, also have responsibility of COVID -19 virus. Previously, Global science initiative and primary source (GISAID) encoded through establishment in 2008, as an alternative to share viruses notes like avian influenzas through the medium of conventional domestic public-domain archives. For virus testing in India, about 6,50,000 testing kits were sent by China, but when these kits showed low accuracy in results when used for testing, hence decision was taken to discontinue the use of these kits for testing. Then finally in May, National institute of virology introduced another antibody test kit ELISA for rapid testing which has the capability for testing 90 sample at a single time of testing, the time run for these 90 samples is about 2.5 Hours.

b) **Initial testing:**

The initial stage of testing has only a few labs were processed and prepared initially for testing samples, then these started to collect samples only from those who have travel history for only selected 12 countries. These listed 12 countries were designated as dangerous or say high risk, and also tested those who come in contact with anyone tested positive among the people who were returned from these 12 destinations. After all these arrangementsthe ministry of health said that only ten percent of test capacity had been used percent per day till 15 March which it claimed that the number of tests which was done at that time duration is the enough tests. After several testing and other studies some unspecified result is being arranged, and said that community transmission may be undetected undergo without the testing process.

c) **Community transmission testing process:**

Dated on 15th March 2020, the process of community transmission testing was started, as an arrangement 65 laboratories of Indian council of medical research (ICMR) and Department of health research, (DHR-ICMR), started a process to test randomly. As this process show a good result as, total 500 random test were done. In which no positive result is being found in them. Initially, the labs tested samples only from those with a travel history to 12 countries designated as high-risk, or those who had come in contact with anyone testing positive for the coronavirus, or showing symptoms as per the government guidelines.On 20 March, the government decided to also include all pneumonia cases, regardless of travel or contact history after the country saw a sharp increase in the number of cases. The first and second confirmatory tests for the virus has been made free by the government.On 9 April, ICMR further revised the testing strategy and allowed testing of the people showing symptoms for a week in the hotspot areas of the country, regardless of travel history or local contact to a patient.

**Further process of research and treatment**

In Rajasthan, after several research and some studies, several combinations were tested over the conditional studies, then finally the combination is Anti-swine flu, anti-HIV drug, anti – malaria successfully. As per company president Adar Poonawalla, a vaccine for COVID-19 will be delivered within a year. However, it may not be effective on 20 to 30% people.wo other companies are also trying to develop a vaccine: Zydus Cadila, which is replicating viral vector and developing a DNA plasmid vaccine,In mid-July, Zydus Cadila too had followed with human trials of its vaccine named *ZyCoV-D*. In early August, SII's got approval from DCGI for trial phases II & III.SII has also joined GAVI in a partnership with Bill & Melinda Gates Foundation to produce 100 million doses of vaccine for developing countries.In September, India's science minister Dr. Harsh Vardhan announced that the first vaccine for use will be available by first quarter of 2021.30 million health workers directly dealing with COVID patients, especially doctors and other medical personnel are supposed to be first to receive the vaccine.

**Conclusion:**

India witnessed an outbreak of the coronavirus, otherwise known as COVID-19, or SARS-CoV-2 in late January 2020 when three Indian students travelled to the southern state of Kerala from Wuhan in China - the epicentre of the outbreak. All three tested positive for COVID-19, confirming a local contagion. At the same time, several other cases were detected in other parts of the country, most of which were linked to people with a travel history to affected countries. Infections increased rapidly since March, with a significant growth in testing.The state of Kerala was commended for acting speedily in containing further spread of the virus. Thousands were consistently being placed in home or institutional quarantine, monitored for symptoms and infections. However, India had one of the lowest testing rates for the virus compared to other countries, despite ramping up over recent months.

The Modi-led government announced a nation-wide lockdown in the end of March. This continued into May, when districts were divided into zones depending on the level of infections. With the responsibility lying mainly with state governments, red zones saw intensified checking and pool testing.

Relaxations on lockdown measures varied depending on the status of zonal infections. An increase in daily cases and a rising death count put India ahead with the fastest infection rate worldwide in August 2020. The government, however, claimed that recoveries were significantly higher than the number of active cases. The south-western state of Maharashtra reported the most cases across the country.

The vast population affected by the government's four hours' notice- lockdown caused widespread panic and chaos, especially for migrant workers in the informal sector. Nearly two months in, the economic impact of the virus and preventive measures were devastating, urgently requiring the economy to reopen.

**References**

1) Sheikh, Knvul; Rabin, Roni Caryn (10 March 2020). "The Coronavirus: What Scientists Have Learned So Far". *The New York Times*. Retrieved 24 March 2020.
2) Harshit Sabbarwal (3 September 2020). "India's Covid-19 tests per day highest in the world, says health ministry". *Hindustan Times*. New Delhi. Retrieved 19 October 2020.
3) "COVID-19: Andhra govt closes Tirupati Tirumala temple to visitors till March 31". Thenewsminute.com. 19 March 2020. Retrieved 19 March 2020.
4) "Rameswaram Ramanathaswami Temple to remain closed till March 31". Business Standard India. 21 March 2020.
5) "COVID-19: Mecca Masjid management asks people not to come for prayers". Telangana today. 27 March 2020. Retrieved 27 March 2020.
6) Sharad, Arpita. "Followers catch up on church service streaming live on various platforms". The Times of India. Retrieved 30 March 2020.
7) SOP on preventive measures to contain spread of COVID-19 in religious places/places of worship (PDF) (Report). Ministry of Health and Family Welfare. 4 June 2020. Retrieved 6 June 2020.
8) "Virus hits Indian sports". The Economic Times. Press Trust of India. 6 March 2020. Retrieved 7 March 2020.
9) "Punjab to ban public transport from March 21". The Indian Express. Retrieved 19 March 2020.
10) "Govt bans public transport in Srinagar to prevent spread of Coronavirus". Greater Kashmir. 19 March 2020. Retrieved 19 March 2020.
11) Slater, Joanna; Masih, Niha (28 March 2020). "In India, the world's biggest lockdown has forced migrants to walk hundreds of miles home". The Washington Post. Retrieved 13 May 2020.
12) Borbon, Christian (28 March 2020). "Indian migrants forced to walk home amid COVID-19 lockdown". Gulf News. Retrieved 13 May 2020.
13) Ara, Ismat (29 March 2020). "'No Work, No Money': Thousands Stranded on Anand Vihar Bus Stand". The Wire.
14) Team, N. L. "NL Interview: BarkhaDutt on covering migrant crisis, the media economy, and falling out with promoters". Newslaundry. Retrieved 21 October 2020.
15) Jha, Somesh (29 March 2020). "Fighting Covid-19: After the long walk, jobless migrants head home by bus". Business Standard India.
16) Pandey, Devesh K. (29 March 2020). "Coronavirus | Migrant workers to be stopped, quarantined at borders, says Centre". The Hindu. ISSN 0971-751X. Retrieved 2 May2020.
17) "Punjab to ban public transport from March 21". The Indian Express. Retrieved 19 March 2020.
18) "Govt bans public transport in Srinagar to prevent spread of Coronavirus". Greater Kashmir. 19 March 2020. Retrieved 19 March 2020.
19) Slater, Joanna; Masih, Niha (28 March 2020). "In India, the world's biggest lockdown has forced migrants to walk hundreds of miles home". The Washington Post. Retrieved 13 May 2020.
20) Borbon, Christian (28 March 2020). "Indian migrants forced to walk home amid COVID-19 lockdown". Gulf News. Retrieved 13 May 2020.
21) Ara, Ismat (29 March 2020). "'No Work, No Money': Thousands Stranded on Anand Vihar Bus Stand". The Wire.
22) Team, N. L. "NL Interview: BarkhaDutt on covering migrant crisis, the media economy, and falling out with promoters". Newslaundry. Retrieved 21 October 2020.

23) Jha, Somesh (29 March 2020). "Fighting Covid-19: After the long walk, jobless migrants head home by bus". Business Standard India.
24) Pandey, Devesh K. (29 March 2020). "Coronavirus | Migrant workers to be stopped, quarantined at borders, says Centre". The Hindu. ISSN 0971-751X. Retrieved 2 May2020.

# CHAPTER - 30

# GREEN INFORMATION SYSTEMS FOR A SUSTAINABLE FUTURE

## BY
## Palak Chandak & Parul Hardikar

**Abstract**

Accordingly to the facts, in the past information technology was mostly seen as a contributor to environmental degradation, recent studies suggest that information systems (IS) can indeed enable sustainable processes, products and services. Specifically, information systems are expected to create an impact on an individual's belief about environmental sustainability, enable more sustainable work practices through remote work and virtualization, or improve the efficiency of the resources. In this manner, notions such as energy informatics or green business process management have emerged. Thus the IS discipline is challenged to explore the potential of information systems to contribute to the betterment of the natural environment by enabling more sustainable work practices at individual , organizational and societal levels.

**Keywords:** Green Technology, Sustainability, Energy, Innovation, Environmental Objectives, Business intelligence.

**Introduction:**

The field of Information Systems (IS) studies the design, development, implementation, use and impact of Information Systems', which are defined as "integrated and cooperating sets of people, processes, software, and information technologies to support individually, organizationally, or societal goals". Green Technology describes the use of technology and science to create products that are more environmentally friendly. It specifically refers to products or services that improve operational performance while reducing costs, energy consumption, waste or negative effects on the environment. While technology has become increasingly popular in the modern age, elements of these business practices have been in use since the Industrial Revolution.Green Information Systems (GIS) is basically defined as the development of information systems that provide the digital infrastructure for sustainable business processes. <u>For Example</u>: Dynamically route of vehicles to avoid traffic and minimize energy consumption. Green Information Systems innovation plays a vital role in corporate sustainability, especially for the organizations in emerging economies that face both economic and environmental pressures, Moreover to support Sustainable Development, employees need to work together on tasks using all kinds of GIS functions like online collaboration and electronic workflow. Most researchers examine GIS implementation at either the organizational or individual level, but few have studied from the technology-enabled collaboration point of view. Green Information Systems is described as the use of Information Systems to achieve environmental objectives. Computers, computing and Information Systems in general consume extremely large amount of resources, the energy to power them as well as the problems that arise in the disposing of obsolete hardware so green computing is important for all classes of systems, ranging from handheld systems to large-scale data centers. Sustainability is the ability to produce enough energy for the world to support its biological systems. Using the power of technology to process large amount of information, decision making algorithms allocate resources based on the real-time information. Applications are widespread. Smart girds implement renewable resources and storage capabilities to control the expenditure of energy.

- **Green Technology**
  Refers to the application of knowledge for practical purposes. The field of "green technology" encompasses a continuously evolving group of methods and materials, from techniques for generating energy to non-toxic cleaning products. The present expectation is that this field will bring innovation and changes in daily life of similar magnitude to the "information technology" explosion over the last two decades.

- **Sustainability**
  It describes about the needs of society in ways that can continue indefinitely into the future without damaging or depleting natural resources. In short, meeting present needs without compromising the ability of future generations to meet their own needs.

- **Energy**
  The most emerging and urgent issue for green technology, this includes the development of alternative fuels, new means of generating energy and energy efficiency.

- **Innovation**
  Developing alternatives to technologies whether fossil fuel or chemical intensive agriculture that have been demonstrated to damage health and the environment.

- **Environmental Objectives**
  GIS refer to initiatives, policies, rules, guidelines, and programs that directly or indirectly address environmental sustainability so as to achieve environmental objectives.

- **Business intelligence**
  It is the foundation for a green information system network that supports an organization's ability to manage, communicate and develop its intangible assets sustainably. As interactions with other developed countries intensifies, so does the need to share information and knowledge. These intangible assets serve as a new commodity for business intelligence.

- **Green Computing**
  It refers to the environmentally responsible use of computers and related resources. Such practices include the implementation of energy-efficient central processing units (CPUs), servers and peripherals as well as reduced resource consumption and proper disposal of electronic waste (e-waste).

- **PowerManagement**
  It is a feature included in many electrical appliances, like copiers, computers, monitors and printers, that turns off the power or switches the system to a standby mode when inactive. Power management features can save individuals and organizations substantial energy costs over time. Modern laptops and PCs have integrated power management control panels that allow a user to fine tune how quickly a screen turns off.

- **Virtualization**

  Virtualizationmeans creation of a virtual (rather than actual) version of something, such as an operating system, a server, a storage device or network resources. Implementing server virtualization, for instance, using VMware or open source competitor Xen, drastically reduces the number of servers required in an enterprise. That translates directly into reduced energy consumption, less maintenance and a smaller data center footprint.

## USES

There has been a rising concern and various researches in the different ways that green information systems have an impact on the sustainability as we use various energy resources from nature like wind, water, sunlight, etc, different types of transportation, the ways of building and manufacturing for the current society. In Information Technologies, using Green Technology reduce energy consumption and save the environment. Some of these well-known IT applications include: the smart electric car which tend to have great fuel efficiency; use of solar panels; smartphones; computers, tablets and other gadgets that use less battery power; implementation of cloud computing. So, different uses of the Green Information Systems are:

- Modern and advanced wind turbines are being generated by transforming the traditional turbines with various forms of sensors and controllers embedded in it which enable the turbines to operate efficiently at various wind speeds and even in the poor weather conditions.
- Concept of Smart Grid Technology is being developed. It is an automated and widely distributed energy delivery network which allocates more energy in a very efficient and effective manner.
- Various high-tech smart buildings use designed sensors to adjust the surroundings from a distance such as temperature controls which enables the smart system to make the adjustments by sensing the heat and light. Depending on the heat sensed, it can decide whether to switch on the air conditioner or not.
- Smart meters allow users to make changes to the use of energy at various times which helps to reduce the carbon emissions, create less air pollution. Smart meters also help to create a smart energy system which can better match supply and needs with the current demands, and integrate other alternative renewable energy sources such as wind, solar.

## Impact

Information Systems have changed societal behaviours in the last few decades. Today for many Information System researchers the role and contribution of Information Systems has become a matter of great concern. IS communities all around the world have started looking at the contribution IT can play in making and minimizing environmental impacts. Nowadays Information Technology is focusing on lessening the direct environmental impacts by making IT equipment more and more energy efficient. Consequently, these efforts can positively reduce IT costs so there is a strong incentive for organizations tom adopt them and evidences from surveys also shows that Information Systems organizations are responding to these incentives by adopting green practices. Many businesses have learned that implementing green IT solutions not only help in satisfying the meeting shareholder expectations but also help in improving their organizations' corporate image. And hence they are focused on implementing green business models. By adopting these effects they have a positive effect on the environment. Moreover they save money with the efficientuse of technology. While reduction in cost is the largest impact of implementing green Information Systems practices in an organizations, environmental stewardship follows closely behind. With all these positive impacts many companies are now adopting the mindset of introducing green Information Systems as it is the right thing to do so.

Green Technologies that are improving organization are Radio-frequency identification (RFID) has transformed transportation and logistics by increasing the success rate of companies as well as growingnew sources of profits through information-based means. Information Systems facilitates the companies to capture, monitor, utilize and standardize data that improves power efficiency. Apart from that companies are reducing energy and increasing supply chain efficiency by decreasing printed items and having them available online.

**Effects**

While environmentally friendly living in a positive ideal, there are several possible effects of Green Processed and technology such as high implementing costs, lack of information, no alternative process technology, uncertainty about performance and so on. Looking at the more dynamic view of green Information Systems, researchers have framed the impacts as primary, secondary and tertiary. Waste – Manufacturing technology creates large amounts of wastes, and used computers as well as electronics get thrown out when they break or become outdated.

- Primary Effects – These are direct impacts from the hardware during the life of the product which includes its production, use and disposal of computer equipment.
- Secondary Effects – These are the effects of ICTs i.e. Information and Communication Technologies and their environmental impact on various developments.
- Tertiary Effects – These are longer term effects which occur when widespread use of ICTs leads to drastic changes in lifestyles and economic structures. It can be seen specifically some of the cases, such as the growth of home-based businesses built on e-commerce platforms.

So, these transformative effects are limited but by comparing the use of internet and automobiles it is clear that the widespread use of automobiles which also led to fast food chains, suburbanization and other lifestyle and economic changeswere not evident until decades after the introduction whereas the widespread adoption of the Internet was clearly seenin only a decade or less in many countries.

**Motivation**

According to the current scenario, the recent studies have shown the rise in the dependence on the electronic data which is leading to the rapid growth in the size and the number of various data centres. The main reason is the use of Internet communications and media. Green computing benefits the environment by improving energy efficiency, decreasing the emission of greenhouse gases, and it is also encouraging the concept of reuse and recycling. Recent studies show how the various systems of production and consumption work together to interact with the environment. In order to find the solution of the problem related to the current environmental issues keeping future needs in mind, we should know how consumption and production go hand in hand. Most of the organizations and companies focus only on the production process and manufacturing procedures. Various departments use different forms of information, sharing and data acquirement to produce 60 percent of U.S. economic production and also the employment. The various businesses in these certain departments have great importance financially and for societal tasks such as education facilities, health care facilities, public utilities, entertainment, banking and finance, transportation, and even the trade between retailers and wholesalers.

All of these gulp energy and resources which ultimately influence the atmosphere. Companies who have just-in-time can increase the types of transportation, therefore leading to an increase in pollution as well as use of energy. Other than utilities and transportation, these services are not generally linked with environmental impacts. Thus, represent an unexploited resource for improving the environment. All of these service companies are very well positioned in order to control their suppliers, as well as their consumers, for a complete change. There are various benefits of using green technology in business workplaces as it does not affect the environment and is eco-friendly.

- One of the basic ways of going green in the business workplace is reducing the overall energy consumption. Certain Small changes such as replacing the lights and by using LED bulbs can save some money as well as the energy, insulating the workplace building to smart windows that may offer shade when ultraviolet rays level increase. So many more such significant changes could greatly reduce spending.Moving to a green web host is also a benefit as many companies have a web hosting industry as well which has an emission problem. These emissions have become so harmful that it eclipses the airline industry because data centres for websites consume an incredible amount of power. Green Web Host websites reduces the carbon footprint as they carefully calculate the amount of energy, they use every year to host websites and according to the consumption they purchase 3 times that amount in wind energy. This consumption equates to more electricity from the grid forcing power plants to produce more energy.

- Implementing Cloud-based business services, Green business methods could help the particular organization from recovering even through the most devastating disasters. Improved disaster recovery is one of the most promising aspects. Since important documents, payrolls, customer information and other confidential details all are saved online allowing one to immediately get back to work after a catastrophe.

- It also provides certain environmental solutions for some problems like disposal and recycling of waste products. It effectively changes the toxic waste production in such a way that it doesn't harm our environment. Green technology has no adverse effect on our planet and it uses sustainable production of energy. It uses various innovative methods in order to create the number of environmentally friendly products.

**Conclusion**

This concept of Green information technology has many benefits and doesn't have any adverse impact on our environment therefore, awareness is very crucial. Related courses and programs at an undergraduate, and graduate level are still in very early stage. Currently very few text books are available on this topic so online references, videos and other available material can be used for teaching purpose to impart knowledge to the generation. Information Systems bridge the gap between countries, organizations, and societies, and it enhances their operations through its platform for collaboration. Green Information Systems is successfully giving rise to the principles, aim of sustainability by providing the alternatives to save energy for the future needs and use current energy efficiently and effectively. Adopting these innovative methods, we can secure the future ahead. In other words, going green can save million dollars as we can see it is clearly a very motivating factor for the technical companies. To conclude we can simply say that this technology exits and we can learn and gain as much possible knowledge and help to achieve the principles of sustainability again global warming.

## References

1) https://www.slideserve.com/wind/green-information-systems-concepts-and-principles-powerpoint-ppt-presentation
2) https://www.tandfonline.com/doi/full/10.1080/02681102.2017.1315358
3) https://aisel.aisnet.org/bise/vol4/iss1/8/
4) https://greentechbox.com/why-green/the-main-features-and-benefits-of-green-technology.html
5) http://green-it2009.blogspot.com/2009/04/conclusion.html